D1212517

YALE STUDIES IN POLITICAL SCIENCE, 21

Peasant Communism in Southern Ita

by Sidney G. Tarrow

New Haven and London | Yale University Press

1967

To my mother

For my father

Preface

My book is what is sometimes unflatteringly called a "case study." This may be defined as a study that either describes a case at hand from less than one theoretical perspective or that approaches more than one theoretical objective with little regard for cases. I hope this book falls in the latter category, for it has pretensions to theoretical usefulness in the widely divergent fields of political development and comparative communism, and it uses its locale— southern Italy—as a demonstration area rather than a refuge.

Any such venture requires a series of apologies, not least of all to an area of Europe that has too often been invaded by smug Northerners in search of underdeveloped game. If southern Italy emerges from this study as a mere battleground on which hostile historical forces clash, its uniqueness trod underfoot by scholarly passion for uniformities and its backwardness silhouetted by invidious comparison to more fortunate places, all that is entirely the author's fault and intention. It may be said in self-defense that I myself maintain an image of the *Mezzogiorno* as ostentatiously memorable and unique.

Second, I wish to apologize to scholars in the fields of political development and comparative communism for presuming to contribute to both fields with a modest study about a curious corner of Europe. The simple axiom that organized Marxism cannot be understood apart from the pattern of political development in the society in which it is found is in itself banal: inasmuch as it implies that there are national varieties of communism it is unexceptionable, but trivial; if it is interpreted to mean that levels of economic development determine party strategy, it is more interesting but incorrect. What I have tried to show in this study is that both the level of development *and* party strategy are independent factors that interact to produce observably different patterns of party structure and political behavior. It follows that there are not, as is often supposed, merely two ideal types of Marxist movements—those in backward and advanced societies—but four, since Leninist and non-Leninist strategies each interact differently with backward and advanced settings. Hence the relationship between the study of political development and the analysis of comparative communist movements is far more complex than might be supposed.

The value of Italian Communism for both fields is that it presents us with the same national strategy in two radically different political settings—North and South. Hence the crucial importance of explaining, early in the book, just how southern and northern Italy differ and precisely what Italian Communism's national strategy is all about. For these two lengthy excursions I must also apologize. The eventual discussion of communism in southern Italy would not be theoretically meaningful had all this ground been left uncovered.

It is with respect to the later sections of the book that methodological apologies must be made, for even the casual reader will note a great promiscuity of approaches and techniques. Much of the data is qualitative and impressionistic—such as the chapters on ideology and the peasant movement—and the quantitative data are open to criticism of their source (the membership and organizational data are from party documents) or their scope (the voting statistics are provincial rather than local). These are important considerations, but it should be remarked that these data are employed not only to measure geographical variations in a phenomenon that is otherwise constant, but also to link these variations to specific regional characteristics. It is in the latter respect that the variety of approaches is an advantage (while in the former it may be a disadvantage), because the link between social structure and political parties only emerges clearly when it is present in the party's electorate, membership, organization, and leadership and in its ideology and behavior.

A final cavil should be made in connection with the last chapters of the study. The reader may discover toward the end of the book a certain irony in its title. What began in 1945 as an ideology of peasant liberation in a backward society became an ideology of backwardness in contact with that society, and the peasant movement that emerged was pulled in opposite directions by its harsh milieu and the national strategy of the party that directed it. It is in precisely this contradiction that the irony of the title, *Peasant*

Communism in Southern Italy, will be found. But irony is necessary only to underscore the dilemma of a "modernized" Marxism in a backward setting; it may adapt to structures that are not modern but traditional, not revolutionary but regressive. It is in this finding, if nowhere else, that the study's general relevance to the problem of Marxist movements in developing societies may be found.

My interest in the improbable bifurcation of northern and southern Italy dates from my association in Florence with John Clarke Adams of Syracuse University, whose romantic attachment to Italy I wholly share. I began to study Italy's internal contradictions at the Istituto Gramsci in Rome, where its director, Franco Ferri, alerted me to the contradictions within his political party in southern Italy. It was his gracious introductions to his comrades that enabled me to study there at first hand. These introductions were a hunting license to pry, and I fear I brought a rifle when my passport called for a popgun. It is to Dr. Ferri's credit as a scholar that his understanding of my goal did not deter him from facilitating my research.

An American scholar with a burning interest in your party's problems is not a comfortable person for politicians to have around, and this is why I am so grateful to Communist leaders like Emilio Sereni, Giorgio Napoletano, and many others, who represent Italy's most gifted and devoted political elite. They made me see that my real interest lay, not in the trivia of party organization, but in the dialectical problem of party development in a changing society. That my conclusions perhaps differ from their own only increases the debt I owe to them and many of their comrades throughout Italy.

A group of friends and colleagues in Italy added a dispassionate note to what might otherwise have been a more emotional study. Giovanni Enrico Marciani and Salvatore Cafiero at the SVIMEZ provided much advice and technical information; Gianfranco Poggi, then of the University of Florence and now of Edinburgh University, helped with the research design and the interview schedule; Gloria Ammassari helped lift the trapdoor of Christian Democratic politics for what enlightenment we could find below. Guglielmo Negri and Virgil Zimmerman provided me with office space at the Centro di Ricerche Amministrative in Rome.

At the University of California at Berkeley, my most important debt is to David E. Apter, who knows little about southern Italy but much about politics. His supreme virtue as a dissertation supervisor was his ability to see a major finding through a forest of data and then point it out to its author. I also wish to thank Heinz Eulau of Stanford University, who stubbornly tried to show me that there is no substitute for empirical verification in social science research.

The manuscript was read and commented upon at various stages by Shlomo Avineri, Donald Blackmer, Giuseppe Di Palma, A. F. K. Organski, Alan Stern, Richard Webster, and Dwight Waldo. Hayward Alker provided useful technical advice on the presentation of the electoral data. I also wish to thank Donald Blackmer, Joseph Lopreato and the Istituto Carlo Cattaneo of Bologna for allowing me to refer to their as yet unpublished studies. Roger Masters would read none of the manuscript, but to him I am indebted for the free flow of his opinions. I also wish to thank Ernst Haas of the University of California at Berkeley; it was his unique devotion to good scholarship that allowed this book to be written in the first place.

I was aided at various times by a Ford Foundation research training fellowship, a grant from the Department of Political Science at Berkeley and an award from the Concilium on International studies of Yale University. I also wish to thank Ann Doherty of the Institute of International Education, who aided my year in Rome immeasurably.

By far my greatest debt is to my teacher, friend, and colleague Joseph LaPalombara, who some may have seen as the Cavour of Italian political science but who, for me, is a combination of Mazzini and Garibaldi. He has taught me so much about Italy that I now presume to tell him where he errs. Remaining my friend in the face of such provocation speaks of a more generous soul than I had yet suspected. I thank him deeply.

I do not want to thank my wife for anything. I would, however, like to thank Susan Rosemary Fellows, who helped with the interviews, mailed the questionnaire, calculated the electoral statistics, and edited the entire manuscript. It is I, moreover, who have gotten the very best deserts, and only she can know how glad I am. Gail Mau typed the manuscript and constructed the index, and Marian Neal Ash, as managing editor of the Yale University Press, managed and edited with great statesmanship.

I do not hope to spread responsibility among all these people, but they represent, for me, such an array of intelligence, friendship, and imagination that I feel this invocation may well protect me from them when they read this book.

S. G. T.

New Haven, Conn.
May 1967

Contents

Preface   vii
List of Tables, Maps, Figures   xiv
1. Introduction   3
2. The Economic Setting   12
3. The Social Structure   40
4. The Political System   71
5. The Italian Communist Party: History and Theory   96
6. The Italian Communist Party: Structure and Behav-
     ior   130
7. The Communist Vote: North and South   162
8. The Party Structure: North and South   198
9. The Party Leadership: North and South   226
10. The Ideology of Backwardness   247
11. The Mobilization of the Peasants   272
12. The New Structure of Power   300
13. The Demobilization of the Peasants   343
Bibliography   369
Index   380

List of Tables, Maps, Figures

TABLES

2.1 Occupational Distribution of the Population by Region and Sector   28

2.2 Industrial Employment in Southern Italy by Section, 1951   29

2.3 Distribution of Personnel in Industry by Position, 1951   30

2.4 Southern Italy: Agricultural Zones, 1950   32

2.5 Southern Italy: Agricultural Zones and Tenure, 1950   34

3.1 Population Evolution in Continental Southern Italy   42

3.2 Natural Population Increase by Region   42

3.3 Size of Population Centers by Region, 1951 and 1961   43

3.4 University Enrollment by Region and Major Field, 1963   62

3.5 Secondary School Enrollment by Region and Institution, 1958–59   63

3.6 Preference for Private or Public Employment by Region   66

4.1 Understanding of Local Issues by Region   76

4.2 Attention to Electoral Campaign by Region   77

4.3 Preferred Methods of Influencing Government by Region   80

5.1 General Elections to the Chamber of Deputies   108

6.1 Social Groups and Political Parties: Estimated Votes   132

6.2 Occupational Classes: Percentage Preferring Various Parties   134

6.3 Occupational Classes: Percentage Supporting PCI, by Socioeconomic Status   136

6.4 Occupational Classes: Percentage Supporting PCI by Age Group   138

6.5 Social Composition of PCI Membership, 1948–62   140

6.6 Paternal Occupation of Italian Legislators, 1946–58, by Party   144

6.7   Social Class of Italian Legislators on Entering Politics, 1946–58, by Party   145

6.8   Educational Level of Italian Legislators, 1946–58, by Party   145

6.9   Age of First Party Registration and First Party Office of Italian Legislators, 1948–58, by Party   147

6.10 Positions Held by Italian Legislators in Party Bureaucracy, 1946–58, by Party   148

6.11 Party Professionalism Among Italian Legislators, 1946–58, by Party   148

6.12 Changes in PCI Organizational Structure, 1954–63   152

6.13 Attitude Profiles of PCI Supporters by Occupation and Sex   159

7.1   Number of Eligible Voters and Percentage Who Voted in Selected Elections, 1870–1948, by Province and Region   166

7.2   Comparison of Party Votes in 1921 and 1946, by Region   172

7.3   Percentage of Vote for Republic or Monarchy in the Referendum of 1946 by Region and Size of Commune   174

7.4   Chamber of Deputies Elections, 1946–63, by Party and Region   175

7.5   Consistency of Communist Vote in 1963, by Province and Region   180

7.6   Distribution of Communist Party Vote in Provinces, Provincial Capitals, and Medium-Sized Cities in the 1963 Elections, by Region   189

7.7   Relation of Communist Provincial Vote to Urbanization in the 1963 Elections, by Region   191

7.8   Communist Party Vote in the Marsica by Commune, 1963 Election   193

7.9   Index of Preference Voting for the PCI by Electoral College   195

7.10 Provincial Elections, 1960: Variation in Communist Voting Patterns from Last National Election, by Region   196

7.11 Causes of Voting Shifts in Southern Italian Villages

        Showing Large Shifts between the Elections of 1948
        and 1953   197
8.1   Evolution of PCI Membership by Region, 1950–63   200
8.2   Geographic Profile of PCI Party Membership, 1963   201
8.3   Social Composition of the PCI by Region, 1963   206
8.4   Social Composition by Province of the PCI in Puglia,
        1954   207
8.5   Geographic Distribution in the PCI of Women and
        Youth, 1962–63   210
8.6   Organizational Structure of the PCI by Region, 1962   215
8.7   CGIL Membership by Region, 1948 and 1962   219
8.8   Number of Cooperatives in the *Lega dei Cooperativi*
        by Region, 1950–62   223
9.1   Regional Components of PCI National Leadership,
        1946–63   228
9.2   Route of Party Recruitment of PCI Provincial Secre-
        taries by Region   228
9.3   Social Status by Family Origin of PCI National Leaders
        by Region   231
9.4   Size of Commune of Origin of PCI National Leaders
        by Region   232
9.5   Professional Distribution of PCI Federal Committee
        Members by Region, 1954   235
9.6   Party Membership of Family Members of PCI National
        Leaders by Region   236
9.7   Salaried Personnel in PCI Provincial Federations by
        Region   237
9.8   Perceptions of Party Centralism of PCI Provincial Sec-
        retaries by Region   240
9.9   Individual Role Perceptions of PCI Provincial Secre-
        taries by Region   242
9.10 Attitudes of PCI Provincial Secretaries Toward Party
        Goals in the South by Region   244
11.1 Distribution of Agricultural Land By Size and Method
        of Cultivation, 1948–49   292
11.2 Incidence of Expropriated Land on National Agricul-
        tural Property by Class of Hectarage above 50
        Hectares   294

12.1   Ratio of Voters to Members in the Christian Demo-
        cratic Party by Region   318
12.2   Members and Sections in the Christian Democratic
        Party by Region   319
12.3   Factional Strength of the Christian Democratic Party
        by Region, 1959   320
12.4   CGIL and CISL Union Membership for Selected Years
        by Region   337

MAPS

1. The Topography of Italy   19
2. Communist Vote by Province, 1946   178
3. Communist Vote by Province, 1963   179

FIGURES

1a. Size of Communist and Catholic Vote, Northern Italy,
    by Province   182
1b. Size of Communist and Catholic Vote, Southern Italy,
    by Province   182
2a. Size of Communist and Far Right Vote, Northern Italy,
    by Province   184
2b. Size of Communist and Far Right Vote, Southern Italy,
    by Province   184
3a. Size of Communist and Socialist Vote, Northern Italy,
    by Province   186
3b. Size of Communist and Socialist Vote, Southern Italy,
    by Province   186
4a. Communist Vote in Provinces and Provincial Capitals,
    Northern Italy   188
4b. Communist Vote in Provinces and Provincial Capitals,
    Southern Italy   188
5a. Communist Voters and Members, Northern Italy, by
    Province   203
5b. Communist Voters and Members, Southern Italy, by
    Province   203

PEASANT COMMUNISM IN SOUTHERN ITALY

1. Introduction

Southern Italy—the *Mezzogiorno* to Italians—has fascinated foreigners and frustrated its natives for centuries. It is difficult to find anything like it in Western Europe or anywhere else in the political world. But although the region has inspired poetry, drama, opera, fiction, and much polemic, it has encouraged little serious analysis. Most political analysis emerging from the Mezzogiorno has fastened upon its peculiar patterns of social and political disorganization. Antonio Gramsci called it "a great social disaggregation." [1] Edward Banfield, with his concept of amoral familism, expands Gramsci's idea into a general principle of social organization.[2] Yet few writers have explored in any depth the impact the phenomenon of disorganization has had upon political structures or political movements. The first part of the present study will delineate the social, cultural, and political patterns that characterize the South of Italy.

The second part of the study will focus upon an unusual political movement—the Italian Communist Party—in Southern Italy. It too is an enigma, even in a country that has spawned various fascist, terrorist, and anarcho-syndicalist movements. In its relations with Moscow, the Italian Communist Party (PCI) has caused consternation in East and West. Its domestic programs have been castigated by left and right alike in Italian politics. United States diplomats spend much time guessing about its intentions. The party's growing electoral success in the face of a general prosperity has baffled its enemies, while its policy contradictions have alienated its friends.

In the Mezzogiorno, this Marxist party takes on contours that distinguish it both from conventional images of communism and

1. Antonio Gramsci, *Antologia degli Scritti* Carlo Salinari e Mario Spinella, eds. (2 vols. Roma, 1963) *I*, 74.

2. Edward Banfield, *The Moral Basis of a Backward Society* (Glencoe, 1958).

from its parent party in the North of Italy. Western political scientists have been content to characterize communist parties as either ideologically rigid and organizationally flexible or ideologically flexible and organizationally rigid. In reality, things are somewhat more complex. A bitter former Communist calls the party in the South "a collection of some of the most reactionary elements in the Mezzogiorno." And yet the Communist Party in southern Italy has more than doubled its vote since 1946. It has mobilized thousands of peasants for the violent assault upon the big landed estates. It has earned the hatred of such diverse bastions of southern Italian society as the Mafia and the Roman Catholic Church. Finally, its presence has helped convince the Italian state to begin a massive program of economic development in the region. In fact, it begins to appear that many of the old obstacles to political integration between North and South have become weaker mainly as a result of the presence in both North and South of this militant left-wing party.

These observations alone suggest that the PCI in southern Italy plays a role that is powerful, contradictory, and somewhat exotic; a role that conventional theories of Western political scientists are unable to account for. I will analyze that role in regard to the structure of the vote, the membership, organization, leadership, and ideology of the party, and the curious romance with the peasantry that resulted in the dramatic occupation of the land in 1950.

If there is a poetic tension in the study, it lies in the reciprocal links between the society of southern Italy and the role of the PCI in that setting. In each of the dimensions noted above, the party is virtually unique in Western European politics. Ironically, the social patterns Gramsci called *disgregazione sociale* survive to haunt the party he created, and stubbornly impinge upon its role in southern Italy.

In a certain sense, political parties are dependent variables of their environments. As David Apter writes, "They depend upon the degree of modernization in a society for their number and diversity; they require a constitutional framework or political regime congenial to their functioning . . . ; and they depend upon the groupings in the society for their membership." [3]

3. David E. Apter, *The Politics of Modernization* (Chicago, 1965), p. 182.

But if the structure of political parties is strongly influenced by their settings, their strategy depends upon the ideological choices of party leaders. The importance of Lenin in the development of Marxist theory was that he pointed out the role of "consciousness" in overcoming the "spontaneity" of the masses.[4] In analyzing the character of the PCI in southern Italy, we therefore need to distinguish between those aspects of party role influenced by the social and political setting and those aspects where the ideological choices of party leaders are more important. The problem is really a dialectical one; to what extent can a party transcend its environment through leadership, ideology, or organization, and to what extent is it dependent upon its setting?

Dialectical, too, is another focus of analysis: the impact of the PCI upon social life and politics in southern Italy. With a large portion of the popular vote and an organization in every province, the PCI inevitably affects its setting deeply. To what extent can we relate the very real changes in economic development, political structure, and political dialogue in the South of Italy since 1945 to the role of the Communist Party in the region?

At the risk of neglecting the historical and incidental interests of the study, its analytical concerns may be distilled into three groups: first, the general dimensions of the social, cultural, and political life of southern Italy; second, the effect of this setting upon the role of a modern political party, the PCI; and, third, the impact of the party upon the society's social and political configuration.

SOUTHERN ITALY AS A DEVELOPING SOCIETY

Ten years ago, political scientists, equipped with models derived from Western experience, began examining non-Western societies. They soon learned that many of their models were deceptive. The skeptical attitude that resulted has been carried back to the study of Western politics, where it now begins to appear that much of this theoretical equipment is insecure even on its home ground. As anthropological studies like those of Edward Banfield, Julian Pitt-Rivers, and Lawrence Wylie have shown, political roles and political attitudes in many parts of Western Europe may be quite

4. Lenin, *What Is to Be Done?* (New York, 1929), p. 52.

similar to politics in some developing areas of, for example, Asia and Africa.[5]

Nowhere is this more evident than in southern Italy, where modern political institutions are weak or inept, where cultural values are startlingly traditional, and where civic virtues are notoriously backward. As Banfield writes:

> No one will further the interest of the group or community except as it is to his private advantage to do so . . . only officials will concern themselves with public affairs . . . there will be few checks upon officials . . . organizations (i.e. deliberately concerted action) will be very difficult to achieve and maintain.[6]

Moreover, for many years southern Italy has been regarded as a developing society, one that was somehow "different." The statesmen of southern Italian politics—men like Benedetto Croce, Gaetano Salvemini, and Francesco Nitti—premised their political thinking on the underdevelopment of the Mezzogiorno. And in 1950 the Italian government recognized this too, with the establishment of the Cassa per il Mezzogiorno, the Fund for the Development of Southern Italy.

As the early chapters of this study will reveal, southern Italy is "different" from the North along almost every significant dimension. Yet it would be a mistake to characterize it simply as a "traditonal" society. The intriguing characteristic of southern Italy is that traditional social roles and relationships have long been dying, while the roles and relationships associated with modern industrial society have been slow to develop.[7] In other words, southern Italy is best understood, as her early statesmen recognized, as some kind of developing society.

But the path of development is not unilinear, and the social and political patterns of southern Italy are not identical with those of all other developing societies. For a start, the presence of *northern*

5. Banfield, *The Moral Basis of a Backward Society;* Julian Pitt-Rivers, *People of the Sierra* (Chicago, 1961); Lawrence Wylie, *Village in the Vaucluse* (Cambridge, Mass., 1957).

6. Banfield, *The Moral Basis of a Backward Society*, pp. 85–89.

7. On the roles and relationships associated with modern industrial society, see Apter, pp. 56–62.

Italy in the same nation-state prevents this from being so. Southern Italy is a fragmented developing society: one in which the social structure has lost the functional coherence of its traditional antecedents, and in which strategic social roles are poorly integrated.

Moreover, southern Italy is a developing society with a "twist." First, in the growth of its major social groupings, and in the formation of dominant values, it differs perceptibly from prevalent patterns in Western Europe. Second, the pattern of its inclusion in an Italian national state worked to retain some traditional social relationships that the same process of development had destroyed elsewhere. Third, because of its juxtaposition with the political institutions of the North, unusual political role patterns and attitudes have been produced.

The political patterns of the Mezzogiorno will be the major focus of analysis. But here, again, we find elements that are atypical of Western European politics as commonly understood. Some of these elements are: diffuse and personalized political organizations that *inhibit* the effective aggregation of interests, leaving political conflict suffused in the society; political socialization patterns that combine great political consciousness with much political cynicism; and the absence of effective state monopoly over the use of violence.

These characteristics of southern Italian politics emerge only through a scheme of analysis free of many conventional assumptions about Western politics. The failure to apply such a scheme mars Banfield's otherwise excellent study of southern Italy, especially in regard to the problem of political organization. Failing to find the familiar Western panoply of organized groups in southern Italy, Banfield assumes that the region suffers from political and organizational incapacity. He asks, "Why is there no political 'machine' in Montegrano, or even any stable or effective party organization? . . . What accounts for the political incapacity of the village?" [8]

Banfield is ignoring a basic factor in politics: similar tasks may be performed by a variety of structures in different political systems. Political capacity in southern Italy is *highly* developed, de-

8. Banfield, pp. 30–31.

spite the weakness of Western-style institutions or organizations, and has a pattern of political forms of its own. These political forms, which I have called *clientelismo,* or the "clientele system," are typical of certain types of developing societies.

An important factor related to the clientelistic nature of southern Italian politics is the cultural modification of political structure. In many developing societies, modern political forms perform functions their creators never intended. Bureaucratic organizations become infused with personal and particularistic tendencies. Legislatures, which function as organs of representation in the West, become solidarity-generating institutions. Political parties, bureaucratic and well-articulated in the West, assume the character of broad political movements with poorly articulated organization. Similarly, the interest-group phenomenon, almost synonymous with politics in Western models, assumes a different form and process. All these permutations are important in the political system of the Mezzogiorno, where cultural norms and political structures are not entirely congruent to the institutions of modern politics.

COMMUNISM IN A DEVELOPING SOCIETY

The analysis of the Italian Communist Party in southern Italy takes up a theme of great importance in Marxist dialectics, but one too often ignored in Western political science: the theme of the objective conditions of political party strategy. Lenin and Mao demonstrated that a Communist revolution occurs most readily in conditions of underdevelopment, but that a special strategy is necessary in such settings. Both the Bolshevik party and the Chinese Communist organization were variants of a highly centralized organization that could counterpose the ideology and organization of the leaders to the spontaneity of the masses.

The Italian Communist Party has developed its own response to the "objective conditions" of Italian politics, but its organizational strategy has been attuned mainly to the modern industrial society of the North. Yet objective conditions in Italian politics differ sharply from North to South, and a logical political strategy in the industrial North may be illogical in the South. The basic problem of Italian Communism is that it has chosen to apply the same *Via Italiana al Socialismo* to both regions. Marxist parties have an inherent tendency to embody the social and economic contradictions of a society, and where these contradictions are profound, as they are in northern and southern Italy, the impact upon party structure can be compelling.

Much about the structure of the PCI in southern Italy reflects the social and political configuration of the region. In this respect, I will be concerned with, first, the points of contact between southern Italian society and the PCI electoral constituency, membership group, and leadership cadre; second, the relations between the party's goals and the aspirations of particular social groups; and, third, the links between the party's organization and leadership and the existing political structures.

On the other hand, a simple cause-and-effect approach to the Communist Party in the southern Italian setting misses the real dialectical nature of the relationship between social structure and the strategy of political parties. This relationship can be studied through an analysis of the party's organizational choices, its ideological machinery, and the impact it has upon the society's system of political roles and political structures. If the Russian and Chinese Communists succeeded because their strategies were adapted to political activity in underdeveloped societies, will a political strategy designed for industrial northern Italy fail in the underdeveloped Mezzogiorno?

This issue raises the intriguing question of the nature of political organization in the new nations, where many parties with Leninist goals are unable or unwilling to develop Leninist organization. Are these parties condemned to failure, or, still worse, will they emerge as obstacles to political and economic development? It is a tenable hypothesis that the party that begins with Leninist goals and non-Leninist organization in the developing societies may find itself pursuing non-Leninist goals, whether it wants to or not. The gap that then emerges between its official ideology and its political structure can become paralyzing.

Peasants and Communists

The link between Communism and underdevelopment leads to an equally important problem: the role of a Communist Party in relation to the peasants. Over a century ago, Marx dropped the careless phrase "the idiocy of rural life," [9] a phrase that Western political scientists drag out whenever Communist "manipulation of the peasantry" is discussed. But Marx was neither naïve nor cynical about the peasantry, as we learn from his brilliant *Eighteenth Brumaire,* and Engels was a positive enthusiast about that much-maligned class. It was Engels who first used the incisive phrase "robust vandalism" to describe peasant revolutionary behavior.[10]

Marx's followers, Lenin and Mao, made revolutions in which the peasants played a critical, if not a dominant, role. The enlistment of the peasantry in a revolutionary army whose strategists saw them as merely a secondary force has focused Western attention upon the "instrumental" use of the peasantry by the Communist Party. In the process, we have missed two very critical points. First, the Leninist formula of peasant mobilization is only one possible pattern; other patterns exist, depending upon the status of the peasantry, the strategy of the party, and the objective conditions in which it operates. Second, in our concentration upon Communist "instrumentalization" of the peasantry, we gloss over an equally important point: that under certain historical conditions, as I shall try to show, the peasants, whose wisdom is of a more ancient variety, get the better of the bargain.

DUAL POLITY AND POLITICAL INTEGRATION

This study is based upon a technique of intra-nation comparative analysis which, it is hoped, will eventually prove useful in other settings.[11] Comparative analysis usually involves highly diverse societies, each with its own political tradition and political culture. Yet we still lack a universally applicable conceptual framework that can accommodate all the variables involved in such a complex analysis. In studying Communism in southern Italy, we can find such a framework in the empirical universe itself: in the

9. "The Communist Manifesto," in Lewis S. Feuer, ed., *Marx and Engels, Basic Writings on Politics and Philosophy* (New York, 1959), p. 11.

10. Karl Marx, *The Eighteenth Brumaire of Louis Bonaparte* (New York, 1963), Chap. 7; Friedrich Engels, *The Peasant War in Germany* (New York, 1926), p. 33.

11. See the excellent study "Eight Spains," by Juan Linz and Amando de Miguel in Richard Merritt and Stein Rokkan, eds., *Comparing Nations* (New Haven, 1966).

dualism of the Italian political system. When a single nation is made up of more than one well-defined sociopolitical setting, we can use the divergence as an analytical lever in sorting out important variables. Variations in political structures can be ascribed with confidence either to underlying social structure or to more global factors. In other words, intra-national studies in settings of political diversity within the same society afford the political analyst a bedrock of universals that underlie regional or sectoral differences, enabling him to locate social structural links to politics more readily than in cross-national studies. Such a technique may eventually prove useful in the non-Western world where internal social and cultural heterogeneity is a basic datum of politics.

But political dualism in Italy is a variable in research, as well as a valuable aid in studying the Communist Party in northern and southern Italy. It is a variable in research because political integration is only now coming about in Italy, after a hundred years of merely formal linkage between North and South. Improved communication, urbanization, and industrialization, and even the impact of Fascism, appear to play a role in this process. However, since the major cause of political dualism has been the clientele system in southern Italy, true integration occurs only as new agencies of political expression and representation arise to take its place. The most important agent of this type in southern Italian politics is the Italian Communist Party.

2. The Economic Setting

The division of Italy into North and South is no mere analytical convenience; it has a long intellectual and historical tradition. "Italy," a leading American scholar writes, "represents two distinct cultures, the relatively dynamic and industrial North and the relatively stagnant and traditional South." [1] Italian scholars and ideologists divide the country in two along every dimension, as if a geological fault had once split the peninsula. A classical and rather bizarre example is the nineteenth-century Italian writer, Alfredo Niceforo, who characterized North and South, respectively, as *Italia Civile* and *Italia Barbara*. [2]

Underlying the differences between North and South are a variety of conflicts and prejudices. Derisive Northerners contend that Africa begins just north of Naples. Southerners, in turn, regard the dynamic cities of the North as indelicate and mechanical places whose wealth derives from the exploitation of the Mezzogiorno. So dramatic are the cultural differences encountered in North and South that a sizable number of observers have interpreted the "problem" of the South as the problem of closing its cultural gap with the North. One American student is probably as much a partisan as an observer when he characterizes the North as "European" Italy and the South as "Mediterranean" Italy. [3]

Yet the wide range of differences between northern and southern Italy does not boil down to mere partisanship. Scholars and ideologists both have come to see the gap between the two as a structural gap.

Before Italian unification in 1861, the South of Italy was an independent state; since then, its economic, social, and political structures, nominally integrated with the North, have continued

1. Joseph LaPalombara, *Interest Groups in Italian Politics* (Princeton, 1964), p. 37.
2. Alfredo Niceforo, *Italiani del Nord e Italiani del Sud* (Torino, 1901).
3. John Clarke Adams and Paolo Barile, *The Government of Republican Italy* (Boston, 1961), pp. 13–28.

to present drastic differences from the other half of the country. The complex social configuration of the Mezzogiorno and its isolation within the Italian political community in one sense represents an entire dimension of this study. Its economic structure will be the subject of this chapter.

What are the general contours of the dual economy in Italy? Following unification in 1861, the South's traditional agricultural, low-wage, small-scale economy continued to operate alongside the North's large-scale, high productivity, industrialized sector. However, there was one major difference: the South was opened to the commercial penetration of northern industrial goods while its own industrialization was inhibited. Commercialization was not accompanied by industrialization, as it was in the North. These two processes, closely related in the economic modernization of the West, were not linked in the Mezzogiorno. The difference radically affected the economic, social, and, particularly, political structures of southern Italy.

In industrialized countries, we find, first, large concentrations of labor assembled to take advantage of heavy capital investments, and, second, the distribution of specialized and standardized products over broad geographical areas by a mass organization of consumption. The mere existence of factories does not in itself signify industrialization. Factories may exist even in an economy in which concentrations of capital and labor are small. Such an economy is commercialized but not industrialized when its markets are organized for the consumption of specialized industrial products made elsewhere.[4]

Examples of this type of economy abound in the non-Western world. The African and Asian colonies of the West were consuming the products of Western industry at the same time they produced the raw materials for Western factories. China and Japan represent the classical dichotomy: Japan, closed to Western commercial penetration, was able to make up for its capital shortages by immense concentrations of cheap labor and by imported Western technology; China, with an equally plentiful labor supply, allowed its markets to be organized for the consumption of Western products, stifling its own industrial development.

4. David E. Apter, *The Politics of Modernization*, Chap. 2.

The economic development of the South of Italy is similar in this respect to the developing societies of the non-Western world. Its markets were organized for the consumption of northern goods produced cheaply by a deliberate low-wage policy, and its own industrial development simultaneously lagged far behind. In the absence of industry, the attention of all major southern social groups focused pathologically upon agriculture. Traditional social roles, particularly occupational roles, were unhinged by commercialization, but in the absence of a new logic of industrialization they remained fragmented and transitional. And in its economic relations with the North, the economy of southern Italy assumed the position of a colonial society with respect to its Western rulers.

THE DIMENSIONS OF ECONOMIC DUALISM

In her study of Italian economic development, Vera Lutz contends that Italy has a dual labor market and a dual structure of industry.[5] Other observers are more extreme; as Shepard Clough and Carlo Livi write, "Of all the cases of uneven economic growth in any one nation, one of the most striking and one which is particularly pregnant with lessons of economic development is to be found in Italy." [6]

What is perhaps most revealing about this regional economic split is that it increased after 1900, when economic take-off began in the North. The South, with a traditional economy centered in agriculture and characterized by slow economic growth, was forced still further into agriculture and hampered in its economic growth as a result of its integration in the Italian state. As Lutz observes, "The movement out of agriculture into industry, and especially big industry, took place predominantly in the North and only to a minor degree in the South; and the high-income group is now heavily concentrated in the North, and the low-income group in the South." [7]

Yet a word of caution is in order; it is important to reject the traditional rationalization of southern intellectuals that the South

5. Vera Lutz, *Italy: A Study in Economic Development* (London, 1962), Chap. 5.
6. Shepard B. Clough and Carlo Livi, "Economic Growth in Italy: An Analysis of the Uneven Growth of North and South," *Journal of Economic History*, *16* (1956), 334–49.
7. Lutz, p. 91.

was willfully exploited by the North, as well as the equally naïve idea that a poorer area, integrated nationally with a richer one, will automatically be impoverished by the union. As I shall try to show, it is the particular pattern of national integration which followed that produced the dual structure of Italian society.

The first dramatic index of the poverty of southern Italy is in its share of national income. Whereas 37 percent of the Italian population lives in the South, only 24 percent of national income is earned there. The North, in contrast, with 63 percent of the population, has 76 percent of Italy's national income.[8]

The gross economic product of the South is less than one-third the size of that of the North. In 1951, the gross product of the South was 2,410 billion lire, compared to a gross product of 8,100 billion lire in the North. Growth rates, despite massive state aid to the South, continued to show great regional differences until quite recently; between 1951 and 1962 the annual growth in gross economic product in the North exceeded 6.8 percent while the economic growth of the Mezzogiorno averaged 5.1 percent.[9]

Consumption differs sharply between North and South. With 37 percent of the population, the South accounted for only 27.4 percent of Italy's consumption in 1951; with 63 percent of the population, the North was responsible for 72.6 percent of total consumption. Consumption patterns, moreover, differ sharply from sector to sector. In the relatively basic area of foodstuffs, southern consumption rises to 29 percent of national consumption. However, in expenditures on electricity, transportation, and entertainment, the southern percentage of consumption falls to between 19 and 23 percent of national totals. Per capita consumption of meat is little more than half the consumption of meat in the North.[10]

Wage rates differ widely between North and South, both considered as aggregates and in particular sectors. Per capita income in the South in the 1950s was less than half of that in the North.[11]

8. Associazione per lo Sviluppo dell'Industria nel Mezzogiorno (SVIMEZ), *Un Secolo di Statistiche Italiane: Nord e Sud 1861–1961* (Roma, 1961), p. 772.

9. Comitato dei Ministri per il Mezzogiorno, *Relazione sulla Attività di Coordinamento*, Vol. 1, *Premessa Generale* (Roma, 1963).

10. SVIMEZ, pp. 768, 787.

11. Lutz, p. 91.

Wages differed most sharply in agriculture, the sector in which the largest part of the southern work force is employed. Whereas a steady agricultural worker in the North earns from 340,000 lire to 502,000 lire annually, a corresponding wage earner in the South earns from 250,000 to 303,000 lire a year. In industry, the differentials are narrower, owing to national wage policies and national collective bargaining practices, but wage levels in the South are still significantly lower than in the North, with a typical average wage in industry of 271 lire an hour as opposed to 292 lire an hour in the North.[12]

Unemployment is relatively higher in the South. Its continued high level during the 1950s is testimony to its structural character: 9.5 percent of the work force in the North was unemployed in 1952 and 13.2 percent in the South; in 1960 northern unemployment fell to 6.6 percent, but 11.4 percent of the southern work force was out of work in that year.[13]

In addition to a high level of structural unemployment, southern Italy has a serious problem of structural *under*employment and disguised unemployment. This category of unemployment is made up largely of excess family members in agriculture with neither contractural nor wage status. A survey carried out in 1960 indicates that the percentage of the agricultural population which could be drawn off the farms without reducing output is 10 percent in the South, while the corresponding figure for northern Italy is 2 percent and for central Italy, 4 percent. In other words, a larger number of people working in southern Italian agriculture do not add substantially to its productivity.[14]

The sector distribution of the southern Italian economy also differs sharply from that of the North. Whereas 44 percent of the active population in the North worked in industry in 1960, 24 percent in that region was engaged in agriculture. In the South, in contrast, only 31 percent of the active population was found in

12. SVIMEZ, pp. 730, 737.

13. Ibid., p. 659.

14. GG. Dell'Angelo, *Note sulla Sottoccupazione nelle Aziende Contadine,* ed. SVIMEZ (Roma, 1960). See also the interpretation of Vera Lutz, pp. 137–40, in which she contends that this is *not* as great a potential source of industrial development as is sometimes believed, since the separation of this excess labor from the land would not increase consumption at all in the agricultural sector.

industry, whereas 42 percent worked in agriculture. Service sectors differ less sharply between the two regions, with 32 percent of the active population of the North engaged in service occupations and 27 percent employed in this way in the South.[15] Later in this chapter, I shall describe the internal structure of each sector in the southern Italian economy, and offer an interpretation of the relatively large size of the service sector in the South.

The dual structure of the Italian economy raises structural resistances to integration. As Lutz demonstrates with great clarity, a dual economy composed of a large-scale, high-wage sector and a small-unit, low-wage sector tends to perpetuate itself. Movement from one sector to the other is inhibited, and industry is encouraged in the large sector whereas agriculture is favored in the small sector because of the relative scarcity of capital and redundancy of labor. This explains, Lutz concludes, why "the average income level in the South remained so far below that of the North. In modern parlance we might say that political unification between the two areas failed to bring about a 'common' market between them for labor." [16]

THE CAUSES OF ECONOMIC DUALISM
The Natural Causes

The land and resources of the Mezzogiorno are what Italians call the "natural" cause of its underdevelopment. The land is beautiful: so beautiful that political leaders, bewailing its corruption and poverty, invariably comfort themselves and their listeners by concluding, "But it is beautiful, is it not?"

The topography of the South is one of the wonders of the Mediterranean basin, yet in itself it is a dimension of underdevelopment. In the North, there are three large and distinct geographic zones: the Alps to the north, the Po valley stretching from Turin in the west to the Adriatic on the east, and the rolling hill and mountain country of the central provinces. In the South, mountains are lower and plains are equally flat, but there is a myriad of provincial and regional variations.

15. SVIMEZ, *Un Secolo di Statistiche,* p. 674.
16. Lutz, p. 10. All of Chapter 2 is a discussion of the nature of the dual economy in Italy.

There is far less level land in the South: 15 percent, as opposed to 26 percent in the North. These fertile areas are all relatively small and isolated from one another.[17] The rest of the region shows constant and abrupt topographical changes. To the south of Rome, high barren ridges rise abruptly out of a series of narrow valleys. Further to the east, the mountains of the Abruzzi rise up, broken only by the fertile enclave of the Fucino basin. The Apennine ridge continues irregularly down the western flank of the peninsula, subsiding into densely cultivated hill country and the fertile plains around Naples, rising into the rocky, bitterly poor regions of the Cilento and Basilicata, and still higher into the woods and pastures of the Sila and Aspromonte ranges of Calabria. To the west of the Apennines, the softly undulating tableland of the Tavogliere flattens out into the long plain of Puglia, ending in the flat heel of the Salentine peninsula. These eastern plains, the scene of the most advanced agriculture in the region, are, however, marked by heavily saline soils.

The mountain chain broken by the straits of Messina rises again along the northern coast of Sicily. The central zone of the island alternates between rough hill country of poor soils and high ridges. The southern coast is made up of high mountains, eroded washes, and broad coastal plains with poor soil. Sardinia too is characterized by great contrasts between mountain and valley, and much of the land supports only woods and pastures. Map 1 shows the characteristics of the physical topography of the South.

Rainfall in the Mezzogiorno is only slightly lower than in the North, but it changes enormously from season to season and year to year.[18] The rivers are small and narrow, but vary greatly in their seasonal flow, a factor that makes them a poor source of electric power and useless for inland navigation.[19] The land is subject to heavy landslides and erosion related to the erratic but heavy rain-

17. The topographical zones of Italy are analyzed in SVIMEZ, *Un Secolo di Statistiche,* p. 4.

18. Rainfall in the Mezzogiorno is described by Robert Dickinson in *The Population Problem of Southern Italy* (Syracuse, 1955), p. 38; for statistics on rainfall, North and South, see SVIMEZ, *Un Secolo di Statistiche,* p. 6.

19. The rivers of the North have a seasonal outflow of 308 cubic meters per second, those of the South a seasonal flow of 2,272 cubic meters per second; SVIMEZ, Un *Secolo,* p. 2; also see Friedrich Vöchting, *La Questione Meridionale* (Napoli, 1955), p. 5.

NORTH

SOUTH

MAP 1. THE TOPOGRAPHY OF ITALY

falls and to the deforestation that occurred in the late nineteenth century.[20]

Italy as a whole is quite poorly endowed with natural resources. Yet in this dimension, too, the North far outstrips the South in its potential for economic development. Virtually all the water power sources and most of Italy's navigable streams and canals are in the North. As in many other Western countries, early textile mills were located where these resources could be found. At the time of unification in 1861, numerous textile mills utilizing fairly advanced techniques were found in Lombardy and in the Po valley, but only ten cotton mills existed in the South, and they were mainly founded by foreign capital.[21]

Coal deposits are almost entirely lacking in both regions of Italy, a fact that inhibited the economic development of the whole country when coal was the only fuel used in industry. However, the North had iron ore around Lake Como, in the Val d'Aosta, and in Umbria, which resulted in the establishment of the first mechanical plants at Turin, Milan, and Terni. The South, in comparison, produced only sulphur, zinc, and lead, minerals basically unimportant in the economy of the period. Although sulphur mines were an important industry in Sicily, their inefficient management and the increasing press of American competition damaged their market position in the late nineteenth century.[22] In the absence of coal, electrical energy became an important factor in Italian industry. Yet electrical energy, which finds a ready source in the mountain streams of the North, is almost completely lacking in the South.

The one type of natural resource the South appears to possess in comparable terms to the North is petroleum and natural gas. To match the great petroleum and gas discoveries of the North in the postwar period, there are as yet unmeasured resources in the South in Augusta, Gela, and Ferrandina. These sources of fuel, chemicals, and fabrics controlled by the gigantic state holding company, Ente Nazionale Idrocarburi (ENI), have given rise to a whole complex of industrial and tertiary activities in the "nuclei" of economic de-

20. Vöchting, pp. 6–7; Dickinson, pp. 34–36.

21. Maurice Neufeld, *Italy: School for Awakening Countries* (Ithaca, 1961), p. 146, and Appendix E, pp. 563–67.

22. Clough and Livi, p. 343; also see Neufeld, p. 563.

velopment that surround them. Important as these resources are at the present time, however, they were undiscovered and unimportant during the classical period of Italian industrialization in the second half of the nineteenth century.[23]

An intangible natural resource lay within reach of northern Italy but was lacking in the South during the critical years of the nineteenth century: proximity to the commercial and intellectual centers of industrializing Western Europe. As Maurice Neufeld writes, "The North, blessed by geography, communicated easily—as a result of friendship, conquest, or commerce—with those regions of Europe which had experienced the revolutionary impact of new industrial techniques, commercial institutions, and advances in transportation."[24] As an American historian has shown in a perceptive study, the northern endowment of natural resources, modest as it was, was turned to the purposes of industrialization by the ideas of economic liberalism that filtered into the North following the French Revolution and culminated in the liberal nationalism of the *Risorgimento*.[25]

In the South, in contrast, the impact of the throbbing commercial centers of Western Europe was scarcely felt. Ferdinand II of Bourbon, ruler of the kingdom until 1859, used to boast, "My kingdom is an Island, protected by salt water on three sides and holy water on the fourth."[26] The Papal State, one of the most retrograde in Europe, guaranteed the border of the Mezzogiorno from liberal ideas and aggression, freeing the Bourbon kings from the responsibilities of a modern military and tax administration and from the leavening of modern ideas. Even after unification, the distance of the Mezzogiorno from northern centers of commerce discouraged innovation. Milan was closer to Paris and Berlin in the nineteenth century than to Palermo or Messina.

The Pattern of National Unification

The second factor that caused the development of a dual economy in Italy was the particular pattern of integration embodied

23. Lutz, p. 270.
24. Neufeld, p. 146.
25. Kent R. Greenfield, *Economics and Liberalism in the Risorgimento* (Baltimore, 1934).
26. Quoted in Luigi Barzini, *The Italians* (New York, 1964), p. 241.

in the Risorgimento of 1861. Whole libraries have been written on this rare moment of glory in Italian history. In this context, two general comments are relevant: first, the integration of the Mezzogiorno in the Italian state was effected by a royal conquest from the North and not by local revolution; second, the groups that supported it in the South, and gained in its aftermath, had conservative economic and political aims. These two factors combined in a pattern of unification fatal to the economic future of the South—effecting its rapid commercialization but inhibiting its industrialization.

If Garibaldi's conquest of the old Kingdom of Two Sicilies after the landing of his "Thousand" at Marsala in 1860 had continued undisturbed, the economic and political patterns of the Mezzogiorno might have been radically different today. However, as the British historian Denis Mack Smith has shown, the Risorgimento in the South was quickly appropriated by Cavour and King Victor Emmanuel of Piedmont, who were frightened by the quixotic personality of Garibaldi, the popular unheavals he evoked, and the autonomist leanings of southern liberals. Cavour marched south, dispersing Garibaldi's *Mille,* repressing the peasant uprisings, and placing local authority in the civic committees of the local bourgeoisie.

Political unification, rather than being carefully executed, followed hard upon military victory. Cavour tried to smother autonomist sentiment by the circulation of rumors that the new state would provide adequate safeguards for local autonomy and would be ruled by a decentralized administration. But the instrument of unification was a popular plebiscite engineered by Cavour which gave the country no choice but immediate integration with the North. A unified and highly centralized state was organized in a society hitherto governed by a semifeudal monarchy. Parliamentary representatives were chosen from the smallest of electorates, and were at first hand picked by the Piedmontese from the old ruling groups, as well as from the liberal bourgeoisie.[27]

The bourgeoisie, the main support of the Risorgimento in the South, was a class with conservative aspirations. The northern bourgeoisie, which was already heavily engaged in trade and in-

27. Denis Mack Smith, *Cavour and Garibaldi: 1860* (Cambridge, Mass., 1954).

dustry, had supported the Risorgimento for the sake of economic expansion, but the bourgeoisie in the South, though liberal in politics, was still attached sentimentally and financially to the land. As the Italian historian Rosario Romeo writes, "If the Risorgimento in the North was the social revolution of a bourgeoisie active in the development of capitalism against the old parasitic classes, in the South, on the contrary, it was these old parasitic classes and groups allied to them who fought the battles of the Risorgimento." [28] The socially conservative bourgeoisie of the Mezzogiorno, still tied to traditional symbols of power and prestige, used the Risorgimento to consolidate its control over the land instead of using the movement for the expansion of the southern Italian economy in trade and industry.

The economic impact of this event was to cast the southern economy into a state of stagnation from which it did not begin to recover until recent years. Through the customs union quickly imposed upon the immature southern economy in the wake of unification, cheap and efficiently produced northern products flooded the South and commercialized its economy. High tariffs had traditionally protected weak southern industry. The lowering of internal and external tariffs dealt the factories and cottage industries of the South a severe and lasting blow.[29] None of this hurt the economic interests of the bourgeoisie, who remained in control of the land.

The Piedmontese installed a tax system, based upon their successful French model, which taxed inheritances and liquid assets for the first time. The South, which had a public debt one-quarter the size of Piedmont's in 1860, was now equally responsible for the higher indebtedness of the North. By 1901 Salvemini could write, "The North possesses 48% of the wealth and pays 40% of the taxes; we [in the South] have no more than 27% of the wealth and pay out 32% of the taxes." Central Italy, with 25 percent of the wealth, paid an almost equivalent amount of taxes.[30]

In a gesture of state beneficence, the numerous church and

28. Rosario Romeo, *Il Risorgimento in Sicilia* (Bari, 1950), p. 348.

29. Vöchting, pp. 884–85. Also see Joseph LaPalombara, *Italy: The Politics of Planning* (Syracuse, 1966), Chap. 1.

30. Gaetano Salvemini, *Scritti sulla Questione Meridionale, 1896–1955* (Torino, 1955), p. 73.

public lands of the old Kingdom of Two Sicilies were sold on the open market by Piedmont at bargain prices, enriching speculators and landowners at the expense of the peasants and the Church, and denuding the forests and distorting the water supply of the region. Nitti estimated that the sale of public and church lands in the Mezzogiorno brought the new government 500,000,000 lire. However, as Neufeld concludes, "The cost to later generations in the *Mezzogiorno* defies estimate." [31]

Public works and schools were placed under unified administration. Subsidies to schools varied radically from 13,000 lire for every 10,000 inhabitants in Piedmont to 80 lire per 10,000 inhabitants in Calabria. The rate of illiteracy continued high in the South, while it steadily fell in the North.[32]

The Policies of the National State

The third basic cause of the structural difference between the economies of northern and southern Italy grows from the philosophy and policies of the unified state which emerged in 1861. The government's policies toward the South suffered, first, from misinformation, then from ignorance. A myth of the natural wealth of the Mezzogiorno persisted long after unification. Only the protest of a group of articulate Southerners in the late nineteenth century and the findings of three important parliamentary investigations exploded this myth.[33]

Government policy toward the Mezzogiorno was dominated for most of the nineteenth century by the idea of "normative integration." As a present-day economic planner writes, "The principal objective of the policy of state intervention was that of unifying the framework within which the entrepreneur in the different regions was to operate." [34] Public institutions in the economic field were unified, the structure of land tenure was legally consolidated, and special appropriations were made in the field of public works.

31. Neufeld, p. 78.

32. Salvemini, p. 74.

33. Most important in this regard are the writings of Nitti, Fortunato, Croce, Salvemini, Sonnino and Franchetti, and Stefano Jacini's report, *Giunta per la Inchiesta Agraria e sulle Condizioni della Classe Agricola, Atti, 15,* Fascicolo 1 (Roma, 1881–86).

34. Pasquale Saraceno, "La Mancata Unificazione Economica," in *L'Economia Italiana dal 1861 al 1961* (Milano, 1961), p. 694.

In 1876, a new political group, the Historical Left, took the reins of government amid widespread hope that social and political reforms would follow. Many of its members were Southerners who had been kept out of office by the northern Right between 1860 and 1876, and hopes for the development of the South soared with their arrival in office. The Left did indeed expand the suffrage and increase public spending in the South. However, its efforts to industrialize the country were financed largely by a high protective tariff on grain and industrial goods. Vast public works, particularly in the South, were supported by this device, but its indirect effects were disastrous to the region's economy. It raised the prices on manufactured goods and led southern landowners to increase grain acreage at the cost of crops more suitable to the South, while overall productivity decreased. As LaPalombara writes:

> The policy of the government as far as the South was concerned encouraged an inefficient agriculture, did not significantly benefit the southern peasant or small landowner, and served to aggrandize the *latifondisti,* or exactly that socioeconomic class in the South that had long neglected the problems of economic growth and modernization.[35]

The Left was in fact very successful in providing public works for the South. Disproportionate portions of the national budget were expended for roads and port facilities in the region, and, in 1881, a fifteen-year program of emergency public works was enacted. It is nevertheless true that these programs were not guided by an integral vision of economic development, and that the other activities of the regime—such as its subsidies to industry and banking in the North—negated the impact of its efforts in the South.

Toward the end of the century, a new philosophy began to animate public policy: the philosophy of special legislation. State investment was extended to the construction of aqueducts and public health works. Direct forms of aid were given the small farmers, and attempts were made, albeit halfheartedly, to change the distribution of land ownership. Reclamation projects were begun, but their dependence upon the formation of local cooperatives limited their usefulness in the socially disorganized South. The first in-

35. LaPalombara, *Italy: The Politics of Planning,* p. 5.

vestments were made in the industrial sector; the special law of 1904 created the industrial zone of Naples, and allocated fiscal and tariff concessions to businessmen who would locate factories there. All these special laws were of limited or local impact, and they ignored the structural nature of the economic backwardness of the South.[36]

It was only in the Fascist period that attempts, though primitive, were made to deal with the problem of the Mezzogiorno in an integrated way. Reclamation, for instance, was now conceived as a unified physical-economic operation rather than simply as a matter of providing new land for the still-impoverished peasants. Little was done in the field of industry, apart from the location at Naples of a large steel and mechanical installation by the state corporation Istituto per la Ricostruzione Industriale (IRI). On the negative side, Mussolini's absurd "Battle of the Wheat," the attempt to reach economic autarky in the field of agricultural production, directed agriculture in the South almost completely into the ill-adapted field of grain production.[37]

Despite the innovations of each period, public policy toward the South continued and even aggravated the economic split between North and South. It was not simply the prevailing liberal economic policies and the government's lack of imagination that were to blame, although these factors played an important part. A more basic cause inhibited the Italian government from effectively combating the underdevelopment of the Mezzogiorno: the domination of a highly centralized state by the organized economic interests of the North and the inability of the South to produce political groups that might effectively militate in the national political arena. As Saraceno writes, "Contributing to the already limited efficacy of the politics of unification was the fact that the unifying criteria were inspired by the interests of the stronger and more active economic region, interests that could not possibly coincide with those of the backward region." [38]

A survey of several measures of economic development will indicate the dimensions of the growing development gap between

36. Saraceno, pp. 696–97.
37. Ibid., p. 698.
38. Ibid., p 703.

North and South. A basic index is the growing difference in per capita income; Richard Eckaus estimates that per capita income in 1860 was higher in the North by 15 to 20 percent.[39] Official income figures in 1928 show that per capita income in the North exceeded that in the South by over 40 percent.[40]

Productivity increased more quickly in the North after unification. Eckaus analyzes the growth in the amount of goods transported on major railroad lines as an indirect measure of production. He finds that during the fourteen years from 1872 to 1885, the goods transported in the North rose by 230 percent; in the Center, by 230 percent, and in the South, by 175 percent. Agricultural production may be analyzed more directly. In comparing the gross agricultural production of 1911 with that of the period immediately before unification, Eckaus found that in the North production expanded by 295 percent; in the Center, by 262 percent, and in the South, by 228 percent. The productivity in grain, the most basic item of southern agriculture, declined markedly during the entire period, while in the North it increased.[41]

Industry appears to have been hardest hit by the depression that paralyzed the southern Italian economy after unification, although the data on this phenomenon are scattered and unclear. The textile industry, which is a common barometer of economic development, languished in the South while it grew rapidly in the North, according to statistics on the number of people engaged in the industry and the number of looms in use.[42]

The distribution of the active population changed in *both* regions in the period between unification and the early 1960s, but in the North the active population concentrated in industry, and in the South a large number of people remained in agriculture. More unusual, moreover, is the fact that the work force in industry in the South actually decreased between 1871 and 1951: whereas 12.8 percent of the total population was engaged in industry in the South in 1871, 9.5 percent worked in industry in 1911, and only

39. Richard Eckaus, in Alberto Caracciolo, ed., *La Formazione dell'Italia Industriale* (Bari, 1963), p. 116.
40. SVIMEZ, *Un Secolo*, p. 770.
41. Eckaus, p. 126.
42. Ibid., p. 127.

8.5 percent in 1951.[43] (The percentage increased to 10.7 in 1961.)

The general impact of unification and the economic and political events that followed seem to have retarded the self-starting mechanism of development in the South at a time when the North moved ahead. As Eckaus concludes: "The data make us think of a deepening of the regional division in the last years of the century and later on, with the South remaining ever more backward." [44]

TABLE 2.1

Occupational Distribution of the Population by Region and Sector
(in percentages)

| | 1871 | | 1911 | | 1951 | | 1961 | |
	North	South	North	South	North	South	North	South
Agriculture	34.8	28.6	26.0	26.4	15.7	20.5	9.0	15.0
Industry	12.2	12.8	14.7	9.5	16.2	8.5	18.6	10.7
Other	10.9	11.8	8.8	7.6	11.8	8.1	14.4	14.5
Total Active	57.9	53.2	49.5	43.5	43.7	37.1	42.0	36.2

Source: SVIMEZ, Un Secolo di Statistiche Italiane: Nord e Sud 1861–1961, (Roma, 1961), p. 50; ISTAT, X° Censimento Generale della Popolazione (3 vols., Roma, 1966), 3, 28–39.

THE STRUCTURE OF INDUSTRY

The division of labor in southern Italy is, of course, extensive, as in all Western countries, and in this sense the labor force of the South is relatively modern. However, analyzing the nature of the roles in industry and the relationships between workers and employees, it appears that a modern occupational structure has failed to develop in place of the old system of master and servant.

A predominant part of southern Italian industry is found in what Vera Lutz has defined the "traditional sector." This sector is traditional in the sense that it is concentrated in food production and related fields, tobacco, clothing, furniture, and miscellaneous small manufacturing. It is distinguished from the modern, large-scale sector, which is concentrated in mining, textiles, chemicals, petroleum, metals, and electricity. Most of the southern industrial

43. SVIMEZ, pp. 50, 51, 52.
44. Eckaus, p. 127.

work force lies outside this modern sector, and moreover, much of the South's share of the "modern" sector is in mining—largely of sulphur—and this is a source of industrial employment of a primi-

TABLE 2.2

Industrial Employment in Southern Italy by Section, 1951

Modern	Number Employed in South	Percentage of All Italy
Mining	48,700	41.0
Manufacturing	138,600	6.6
Electricity	14,200	21.1
Total	201,500	8.9
Traditional		
Small Manufacturing	414,200	29.4
Utilities	6,500	32.5
Construction	111,500	21.0
Total	532,200	27.1

Source: Vera Lutz, Italy: A Study in Economic Development (London, 1962), p. 94.

tive nature and in steady decline. With mining excluded, only 152,800 of the industrial work force in the South was employed in the "modern" sector in 1951. "Southern industry," writes Lutz, "still belonged for the most part to the traditional sectors, where very small-scale production is technically more feasible than it is in modern industry." [45]

The size of southern industrial units is very small indeed. Not only does the number of manufacturing firms remain much lower than in the North—117,500 in 1961 as compared to 411,400 in the North—but the average manufacturing firm in the South employs 4.7 workers, as compared with 9.7 workers in the North.[46] The typical southern firm is based upon family management or upon unwieldy multiple partnerships or groups of friends.

The division of positions between managers, technicians, and workers differs sharply in the two regions.

45. Lutz, p. 93.
46. Annuario Statistico Italiano, 1964 (Roma, 1965), p. 195.

TABLE 2.3

Distribution of Personnel in Industry by Position, 1951
(in percentages)

	Owners and Directors	Foremen and Technicians	Workers	Total
North	12.8	7.8	79.4	100.0
South	27.3	4.0	68.7	100.0

Source: SVIMEZ, *Un Secolo di Statistiche*, pp. 337–38.

The smaller percentage of owners and directors in the North suggests that, not only are there more workers per firm, but management is consolidated among fewer people. In the southern firm, the ties of kinship and friendship which continue to permeate economic activity tend to overload the upper echelon, while those in a technical capacity are fewer, and fewer people are employed strictly as workers. A final index of the backward structure of southern industry is that in 1951, 67 percent of southern industrial workers were to be found in firms owned by individuals, while only 13 percent worked for firms in corporate ownership. In the North, in contrast, 30 percent worked for individuals while 44 percent worked for corporations.[47]

The concentration of southern industry in the traditional sector, its low wages, the small size of the firm and the survival of traditional influences in the structure of the firm act as impediments to a modern organization of industry and the success of labor organization. Where paternalistic relations survive between *padrone* and *dipendente* and where the occupation structure is fragmented among a myriad of small firms, communication and organization among the workers is inhibited too.[48]

THE STRUCTURE OF AGRICULTURE

If the failure of the South to modernize is demonstrated by the structure of industry, this failure is still more evident in the agri-

47. SVIMEZ, p. 336.
48. See the analysis of Franco Ferrarotti, "L'Evoluzione dei Rapporti fra Direzioni Aziendali e Rappresentanti Operai nell'Italia nell'Dopoguerra," in *Atti del IV Convegno Mondiale di Sociologia, Aspetti e Problemi Sociali dello Sviluppo Economico in Italia* (Bari, 1959), pp. 137–44.

cultural sector. Whereas northern agriculture was consolidated into efficient economic units of high productivity in the years after national unification, the southern agricultural structure remained backward, fragmented, and unproductive.

Perhaps nowhere in the Western world is there an agricultural system as complicated and confused as in the South of Italy. Crops, tenure systems, and contracts vary distinctly from province to province, from mountain to valley, and from the cultivated areas around the towns to the distant fields. In part, this diversity reflects the topographical diversity of the region. Plains are easily subjected to large commercial farms and modern methods; mountains tend to be parceled into small holdings cultivated with primitive tools. In great part, however, this diversity reflects the failure of the southern economy to complete the transformation from a feudal system to an entirely modern one.

Southern agriculture falls into four more or less coherent zones.[49] The *Mezzogiorno Nudo* consists of areas of extensive agriculture, of grain and pasture, where the classical phenomenon of the great landed estates, or latifundia, dominates. In turn it is divided in two: a small part is organized in large and medium-sized commercial farms (the "Capitalist Latifundia" in Rossi-Doria's terminology), and the rest—in 1948 eight-ninths of the area—remains a florid patchwork of precarious holdings and large and small rentals which are unified only by their low capital investment and peasant operation.[50] This is the zone that Rossi-Doria has appropriately named the "Peasant Latifundia," and it is where the agrarian reform was to have the most solid impact.

The third zone, the *Mezzogiorno Alberato,* is found along the coastlines and in the fertile enclaves scattered throughout the peninsula. It is an intermittent zone of intensive cultivation, producing a great part of the grapes, fruits, nuts, and olives of the country under conditions of surprisingly great productivity. It too is marked by an extreme variety of contractual relations, crop differences, and variations in distribution, all of which leave it

49. The following section is based largely upon the interpretation of Manlio Rossi-Doria in *Riforma Agraria e Azione Meridionalista* (Bologna, 1948), pp. 2–51.

50. According to the estimate of Vöchting, based upon analysis of Rossi-Doria's material in *Riforma Agraria*, p. 265.

internally weakened. "Except in some restricted zones where a precise specialization and uniformity are found, this intensive zone of production has the same anarchy, the same disorder as the rest of the economy of the South." [51]

A fourth area represents an intermediate mixed type of agriculture combining aspects of extensive and intensive cultivation and the contract and tenure types characteristic of each. Here too the agrarian reform of 1950 has caused some rationalization of production, as we shall see. This is Rossi-Doria's *Promiscua* zone.

The relative distribution of these four agricultural areas, the population resident in each, and their productivity in 1950 are summarized in Table 2.4.

TABLE 2.4

Southern Italy: Agricultural Zones, 1950

	Area as a Percentage of South	Population as a Percentage of South	Production as a Percentage of South
Capitalist Latifundia	5	11	7
Peasant Latifundia	42	28	30
Intensive Zone ("*Alberato*")	28	45	44
Mixed Zone ("*Promiscua*")	26	16	18

Source: Manlio Rossi-Doria, *Riforma Agraria e Azione Meridionalista* (Bologna, 1956), p. 57.

Only 5 percent of the area and 7 percent of the production were found in the advanced, capitalist zone. The Peasant Latifundia, on the other hand, contained 42 percent of the area but only 28 percent of the population and 30 percent of production. The Mixed Zone, equally poor, took up 26 percent of the area in 1950 and possessed only 18 percent of production. The single zone whose percentage of production was larger than its percentage of the area is the Intensive Zone of agriculture along the coasts.

While each of these areas has its characteristic structure of enterprise—the commercial farm with hired hands in the Capitalist Latifundia zone and the small family property in the other zones

51. Rossi-Doria, p. 31.

—each contains a large number of marginal properties operated by small renters (*affitti*), share tenants on permanent farmhouse units (*mezzadri*), share tenants on units with no farmhouse or equipment provided (*coloni*), and sharecroppers (*compartecipanti*). These marginal operating units are typically transitional forms between the traditional organization of agriculture and modern, consolidated farms. Most are not "farms" in any significant sense of the word, but merely strips of land operated by a peasant on a short-term, unstable contract with no farmhouse or equipment provided by the owner. The goal of the agrarian reform of 1951 was to stabilize those marginal farms.

The survival of these unstable, unproductive forms of agricultural enterprise would be impossible in a modern economy. In southern Italy, their survival is due to a capital scarcity combined with rural overpopulation and widespread middle class ownership of the land. The latifundia are not so designated because of their size, but because of their uneconomic mode of operation.[52] A large property, usually in absentee ownership, is operated in small strips by a myriad of peasants, each with a short-term contract with the owner. The peasant has to provide his own tools, seeds, and fertilizer, and travels long distances to work the land, since it typically contains no farmhouse.

As Table 2.5 shows, the most fragmented region of the South in 1950 was the Peasant Latifundia, where 21 percent of the land was operated by tenants—often in two- or three-stage rentals; 22 percent was worked by *coloni,* share tenants without tools or a farmhouse provided by the owner; and 6 percent was worked by sharecroppers. Each of these forms of agricultural enterprise was fragmented still further by a tremendous variety of contracts: the percentage of the produce taken by the owner might vary from one-third to two-thirds; the duration of the contract varied from part of an agricultural season to several years; special clauses might reserve the produce of trees to the owner, while the peasant, who

52. "The latifundia is a mode of using the land with a minimum of investment in improvement or equipment. It has a low input of labor per unit of acre and per year, great precariousness of minor settlements, extensiveness and discontinuity of cultivation." From Nello Mazzochi-Alemani, *Direttive di Massima del Piano di Trasformazione del Tavogliere* (Roma, 1946), p. 34.

TABLE 2.5

Southern Italy: Agricultural Zones and Tenure, 1950
(in percentages)

	Peasant Owner	Tenant	Share Tenant (*Mezzadria*)	Share Tenant (*Colonia*)	Sharecropper (*Compartecipazione*)	Hired Help
Capitalist Latifundia	23	24	13	10	4	27
Peasant Latifundia	36	21	2	22	6	14
Intensive Zone ("*Alberato*")	37	22	5	20	4	12
Mixed Zone ("*Promiscua*")	58	18	8	9	2	5

Source: M. Rossi-Doria, "Il Lavoro," in *Annuario dell'Agricultura Italiana, 4* (1950), 369–404.

might be required to tend the trees, took only the produce of the land. These conditions have now been mitigated by the agrarian reform.

Even in the highly productive *Mezzogiorno Alberato,* over 40 percent of the land was worked by renters and share tenants. This zone, particularly in the fertile area of the plain around Naples, is still largely burdened by fragmented, middle class ownership, which dictates the use of the small rental or share tenancy, even though productivity would be aided tremendously by consolidated operation.

Apart from damaging productivity by an irrational system of cultivation, the structure of agricultural enterprise in the South causes a fragmentation of occupational roles. Great numbers of agricultural day workers must integrate their incomes by working a small piece of land on contract or rental. Many small family farmers who cannot subsist on their small holdings are forced to work as day laborers or on contract. As Lutz observes: "the peasant is almost always what is called a mixed figure—small proprietor, tenant, sharecropper, wage earner. In the past at least, the link between him and that part of the land which he farmed but did not own was in many cases a precarious one." [53]

53. Lutz, p. 105.

The Service Sector

As I have indicated earlier, employment in trade and commerce in the Mezzogiorno is almost as high as in the corresponding sector in the North. Moreover, the importance of the service sector expands when we account for the lower value of the total goods produced and the high degree of subsistence production, particularly in agriculture. In other words, the service sector in the South is far larger than its economic position might lead us to expect, given the small amount of goods and services traded in the region.[54]

What explains this unusual phenomenon, and what are the forms it takes? Basically, we see in the Mezzogiorno what occurs in many of today's developing economies when large numbers of people are dislocated from traditional occupational roles and fail to find new places in industry: an inflation of the service sector. To all appearances, moreover, this enlarged service sector in the South has existed for at least a fifty-year period. As Lutz writes: "Large numbers of individuals have left agriculture to swell the already excessive numbers of self-employed trying to scrape a living from some kind of retail trade."[55]

Yet despite the large number of individuals in service positions, or because of it, the service sector takes on the same fragmented character as industry and agriculture. In the villages, barbers, tailors, and artisans are often peasants in disguise; in the provincial capitals, large groups of men and boys fill the piazzas daily, "available" for casual employment; in the metropolitan centers like Naples and Palermo, a good part of the retail trade is carried on in clandestine and informal ways.

Retail trade is carried on predominantly by minute stores and street wagons. The *supermercato,* already a fixture in the North, finds no place in the South. Tradesmen frequently are part-time farmers whose time is divided between producing crops in the countryside and selling them personally in town.

Moreover, the confused organization of southern trade and commerce and its personal character allot a generous role to individuals with the ability to control personal networks of suppliers and

54. Ibid., p. 93.
55. Ibid., p. 125.

distributors. These roles are fortified by family and friendship ties, special concessions by state agencies and, more often than not, by the control or threat of violence. In his searing book on Italian manners and mores, Luigi Barzini compares the respective roles of wholesale fruit and vegetable dealers in North and South. The northerner, he points out, "sits in a modern office, surrounded by dictating machines, graphs on the wall, brisk secretaries. His business is carried out by telephone, with brokers and buyers in Germany, France or Switzerland." The southerner, in contrast, "tours the countryside with his henchmen, bullying and protecting peasants in his well-defined sector, and forcing them to sell their products only to him at the prices he fixes." [56]

Trade and commerce in the Mezzogiorno are more typical of the anarchic, personalized bazaar economies of traditional societies than the well-organized service sectors of modern societies. As Lutz writes, "Many of the commercial enterprises . . . represent a bare escape from unemployment rather than that florid development of 'tertiary activities' which is a feature of prosperous, advanced economies." [57] As Table 2.1 shows, the service sector has grown more rapidly than industrial employment between 1951 and 1961.

ECONOMIC CHANGE

In this chapter, I have analyzed the economy of the South of Italy in terms of the structures that have developed in the region since unification in 1861, and that still predominate there. However, the past twenty years have seen some changes in the economy of the Mezzogiorno that begin to show the outlines of a new economic system.

A critical aspect of the underdevelopment of the Mezzogiorno has always been its scarcity of capital. In 1951, for example, total investment in the South was 400 billion lire, as compared to 1,490 billion lire in the North. Moreover, while the greater part of investment in the North was devoted to industry, southern investment was concentrated in the service sector and in fixed social capital, with very little investment in industry.[58]

56. Barzini, *The Italians*, p. 237.
57. Lutz, p. 95.
58. Comitato dei Ministri per il Mezzogiorno, *Relazione, 1*, 11.

Recognizing the key role investment plays in economic development, the government in 1950 began a massive program of investment and direct intervention in the economy of the South. Special credit agencies for the continental South and for each of the islands were set up. The state-controlled economic sector, through the holding companies of IRI and ENI, was directed to channel a large part of its investment to the South. Most important, an "extraordinary" development agency—the Cassa per il Mezzogiorno—was established to stimulate investment in public works, land development, industry, and education. This agency began its life motivated by a "propulsive" philosophy with efforts concentrated in agriculture and in fixed social capital. However, as the limitations of this approach became clear, attention shifted into industry and to direct intervention in the economy.[59]

Stimulated by these programs, as well as by special government incentives to private industry, per capita income, investment, and economic growth in the South began to rise throughout the 1950s, and the economy began to shift from an almost complete concentration in agriculture to a larger share of the industrial sector.

Investment rose in the South from 400.1 billion lire in 1951 to 1,297.8 billion lire in 1962, an average annual rise of over 12 percent. Investment in the North, it should be noted, rose about 9 percent during the same period, to a total more than twice that of the South. But the pattern of investment in the South shifted radically from agriculture into industry, with an average annual rise in agricultural investment of just over 8 percent, and a corresponding rise in industrial investment of almost 15 percent.[60]

Per capita income has risen in the South in the same period from 100,000 lire annually in 1951 to 172,000 lire annually in 1959, a rise of about 56 percent for the entire period. In the North, however, the same period witnessed a growth in per capita income of over 65 percent.[61]

Finally, the rate of economic growth in the South, represented

59. An excellent summary of the development of the Cassa per il Mezzogiorno and its various stages will be found in Francesco Compagna, *La Questione Meridionale,* Part III (Milano, 1963), and in LaPalombara, *Italy: The Politics of Planning,* Chap. 2.

60. Comitato dei Ministri, *Relazione, 1,* 11.

61. Lutz, p. 127.

by the annual rise in gross economic product, increased during the 1950s. Although the growth rate of the North is still higher, the annual growth rate of the Mezzogiorno was 4.3 percent in the first part of the period and 6.3 percent between 1959 and 1962.[62] However, the recession of 1963–65 hit most heavily in the South.

But while investment was shifting significantly to industry and a large number of new industrial establishments were being created, only a relatively small number of new jobs has been created in industry—just over 200,000, at an annual increase of 2.7 percent. The discrepancy between the growth of industrial employment during these years and the growth of industrial investment is explained largely by the concentration of new investment in capital-intensive industries. To absorb many more workers in industry while still maintaining a high rate of industrial investment, the Cassa per il Mezzogiorno recently decided upon a policy of directing investment "into factories of such dimensions and such sectors that a lower proportion of capital to labor is utilized." [63] For the present, however, even the high-powered investment program on the part of the government has not had notable success in recruiting people into modern occupational roles in industry, which would destroy the old pattern of economic relationships.

Some structural changes are already noticeable in the Mezzogiorno. Observers have marked a lower incidence of minute industrial establishments using few workers and outdated methods. In trade and commerce, national distributors and cooperatives have challenged the traditional marketplace, although this trend is not yet clear in the field of mass consumption. In agriculture, structural changes have been more marked. From the remittances of emigrants and the benefits of government reclamation programs, an increase in both small family farms and large commercial farms began in the 1930s. This trend was accelerated by the massive land reform program of the 1950s, which distributed over 1,600,000 acres of land to the peasants. These developments have caused a more solid clustering of the agricultural population into two modern groups: wage earners and small farmers. However, large numbers of peasants still remain in indeterminate and transitional oc-

62. Comitato dei Ministri, *Relazione, 1,* 10.
63. Ibid., p. 21.

cupational roles, a phenomenon with strategic social and political results.

Along every significant economic dimension, the South of Italy presents an economic structure remarkably different from that of the North. The causes of this economic dualism are found, first, in the region's poor natural resources. Second, the pattern of its inclusion in the new national state in 1861 opened it instantly to penetration by northern industry and a new tax system, lower external tariffs, and a sterner system of administration. A third significant factor was the attitude of the new Italian state, whose economic policies aimed only at normative unification, and whose concepts of unification were framed in terms of the economic interests of the stronger region.

For these reasons, the South of Italy underwent a process of commercialization with no simultaneous industrialization. The effect of that process upon its structure of economic and occupational roles was little short of disastrous: in industry, small-scale, inefficient units dominated by family ownership and paternal labor relations persist to the present day; in agriculture a fragmented system of operations and an atomized structure of occupational roles which is neither traditional nor modern dominates; in the service sector, infinitesimal firms and personalized economic relationships which allot a key role to quasi-criminal organizations persist.

These structural patterns, as I shall attempt to demonstrate, are key factors in the South's system of social and political organization. Moreover, the different scale, shape, and consistency of southern Italian social and political structures have resisted integration in the national political community even after a hundred years of national unity.

Emigration, state investment, and land reform have begun an autonomous process of economic development in the Mezzogiorno. Some observers prophesy the region's gradual integration into the national economy and its ultimate prosperity. However, this change can only be achieved after a long period of economic strain and political conflict. Such a period is currently in progress, and its tensions dominate the social structure and political life of the South.

3. The Social Structure

An old Neapolitan proverb warns the stranger of the nature of the place: "Ca niscun è fesso," or, in acceptable English, "Here there are no suckers." What a perfect country it would be were such a statement true! But life being imperfect, a given number of *furbi* (sly ones) implies at least an equal number of *fessi*.

Who is the sly one and who the sucker? A positively frightening study of southern Italian society, Roger Vailland's *The Law,* suggests an answer: in a society that brags "Ca niscun è fesso," *everyone* is both *fesso* and *furbo,* in a shifting hierarchy of relative advantage. That is the Law. Mastroianni, as the mustached hero of "Marriage, Italian Style," succeeds in divesting himself of an unwanted wife through supreme *furbizia,* only to find his new bride in amorous activity with the first handy sailor.

Can southern Italy really be so distorted, violent, and cynical? Of course it can, but the real question is how it got that way, and how it has managed to survive so long without destroying itself. The interesting point is that "the Law" usually works so well that recourse to violence is the exception, rather than the rule. The real battles in southern Italian society are fought, not with knife and gun, but with the insidious glance, the well-placed rumor, or the triumphant walk across the piazza with someone else's girl friend on your arm, as the whole town watches.

In the last chapter, I presented some indicators of southern Italy's grinding poverty. What is curious is that southerners are not nearly so oppressed by the poverty of the region as they are with one another. The Mezzogiorno has too many people fighting too hard for too few resources—mainly the land and the power it conveys. The problem is that social conflict does not shake down into relatively orderly class or group conflict, but remains festering in the narrow interstices of personal relationships.

Why have broader institutions for channeling social conflict failed to develop in the Mezzogiorno? Because of historical, political, and economic factors, the Mezzogiorno is a *fragmented* society, one in which a new organization of social roles has not yet crystallized to take the place of the system that broke down in the nineteenth century. Thus the characteristics of the society are not traditional, but transitional. These characteristics, complex in themselves, will be analyzed in this and in the following chapters.

THE STRUCTURE OF THE POPULATION

The population of the Mezzogiorno is more urban than industrial, and more agricultural than rural. Population in the South is often regarded as its most basic problem. The population began to grow rapidly in the eighteenth century. One observer estimated an increase of from 3.9 million in 1765 to 4.9 million in 1790 for the continental South alone.[1] Subsequently, the rate of growth of northern and southern populations was roughly similar. At the time of unification in 1861, the South and the two islands, Sicily and Sardinia, contained 9.8 million people, or 39 percent of the total population of Italy, to the North's 15.2 million, or 61 percent. By 1961, the portion in the South had fallen to 36.7 percent with 18.6 million, and the portion in the North had risen to 63.3 percent or 32.0 million.[2]

This population stability disguises several critical variations. Population in the South has maintained its stability only through mass emigration and a very high death rate, with a consequent decline in the size of the productive population. While the number of inhabitants increased steadily, the size of the active population remained virtually constant. Population in agriculture changed little, but the ratio of inactive to active persons has more than doubled.

Since World War I, the birthrate in the North has fallen drastically, while the birthrate in the South has fallen only slightly. No more dramatic measure of the backwardness of the South exists than its failure to control births. During the same time the diffusion of modern medical techniques and the virtual suppres-

1. K. J. Beloch, *Bevolkerungsgeschichte Italiens, 1* (Berlin and Leipzig, 1937), 268–69.

2. SVIMEZ, *Un Secolo di Statistiche,* p. 13; *Annuario Statistico,* p. 24.

TABLE 3.1

Population Evolution in Continental Southern Italy, 1871–1961

Year	Total Population (in millions)	Active Population (in millions)	Percentage Active
1871	6.9	4.1	59.4
1936	10.1	4.1	40.6
1951	11.9	4.4	37.0
1961	12.4	4.7	37.9

Sources: R. Dickinson, *The Population Problem of Southern Italy* (Syracuse, 1955), p. 6; ISTAT, *X° Censimento*, pp. 28–31.

sion of malaria has cut the death rate in the South in half, in contrast to a more gradual decrease in the North. The result is a great drop in the natural population increase in the North and a rise in the South, where 37.5 percent of the population lives, but where 50 percent of all births and 75 percent of the natural increase are found.

TABLE 3.2

Natural Population Increase by Region
(per 1,000 inhabitants)

Region	1881	1912	1951	1961
North	9.6	13.3	3.1	4.8
Center	8.7	13.3	6.4	6.3
South	10.2	14.7	14.7	11.7
Islands	12.6	11.3	13.2	13.8

Sources: *Informazione Svimez*, N. 25–26, Roma, July, 1953; *Annuario Statistico Italiano, 1965*, pp. 29–30.

The distribution of the southern Italian population, moreover, is extremely uneven geographically. The great variations in the amount of arable land, the variety of soils and climates, and the uneven incidence of emigration give the South a population density that varies from a high of 317 inhabitants per square kilometer in Campania—the highest in Italy—to 53 inhabitants per square kilometer in Basilicata and Sardinia.[3] The recent postwar emigra-

3. SVIMEZ, p. 19.

tion has left some communes in the more isolated mountain regions inhabited almost entirely by children, old people, and the
indigent, while population centers like Naples and Catania swell
beyond their capacity to provide employment and public service.

Urbanization in the South, as in many underdeveloped areas, is
a phenomenon seldom accompanied by industrialization. Traditionally, the southern population has clustered in large peasant
cities rather than spreading out in small villages and individual
farmsteads. The Southerner likes to have company in his misery,
even if he sees his fellow townspeople as part of his problem. In
an overcrowded latifundia economy, the village square was an
employment bureau where the fortunate few found a day's labor
while their bitter neighbors looked on.

TABLE 3.3

Size of Population Centers by Region, 1951 and 1961
(in percentages)

| | North | | South | |
Size of Commune	1951	1961	1951	1961
Up to 3,000	15.7	14.5	11.0	10.7
3,000–10,000	30.5	26.1	30.8	28.2
10,000–50,000	22.5	22.2	35.3	34.0
50,000–100,000	7.8	8.8	7.4	8.4
More than 100,000	23.3	28.4	14.5	18.7

Sources: svimez, Un Secolo di Statistiche, p. 22; Annuario Statistico Italiano, 1964, p. 10.

In the North, the population is grouped in small towns up to
10,000 and in the big cities of more than 100,000. In the South, on
the other hand, the population gathers in communes of 10,000 to
50,000 inhabitants. Very few of these cities in the South are centers
of industry and commerce: many are provincial administrative
centers where large numbers of civil servants and peasants live in
uneasy coexistence; others are the dense hilltop clusters originally
built as defense against bandits and malaria; many others are the
large rural "dormitories" of Sicily and Puglia, where peasant populations of over 20,000 live in essentially peasant communities of
abnormal size. The current wave of industrialization in the South

appears to relate more to the diffusion of the mass media and improved transportation than to actual industrialization. Naples,
where the population has risen from 1.0 million in 1950 to 1.2
million in 1960, has an industrial work force of only 125,000, out
of an active population of 356,000.[4] A large portion of the population finds its livelihood in petty trading, in odd jobs, and in the
shady professions practised around the port. The situation in other
southern cities is equally dramatic, and the imbalance between
migration to the urban centers and their potential to provide industrial employment is nearly universal.

Again with great similarity to many other underdeveloped areas,
this imbalance between urban migration and industrialization is
accompanied by widespread seasonal migration between city and
country. Many of the residents of the "boroughs" of Rome, the
"barracks" of Naples and Palermo, and the *sassi* of Matera maintain their family ties and live for part of the year in isolated villages in the provinces. Thousands of others migrate to Switzerland,
southern France, or Germany for seasonal employment and return
home for the remainder of the year.

Alongside this unstable migratory pattern, there is a more permanent resettlement occurring as a result of Italy's economic "mir-
acle" of the past ten years. It has brought hundreds of thousands
of southerners into permanent residence in the thriving industrial
centers of the North. While both these migratory patterns arise
from the same conditions of southern Italian life, they are quite
different in their effects. The seasonal migration results in an uneasy and shifting position in life for the migrant, whereas permanent settlement outside the traditional community leads to new
patterns of life in a mobile situation, and a sudden release from
many of the constraints of village life. Both these patterns have
political results that will be treated in a later chapter.

THE DISSOLUTION OF THE FEUDAL SYSTEM

One of the abiding passions of educated southern Italian gentle-
men has long been the history of their country, from the flowering

4. Istituto Centrale di Statistica Italiana (ISTAT), *X° Censimento Generale della
Popolazione, 1961*, Vol. 11, *Dati Riassuntivi* (Roma, 1963), 500.

of the ancient Greek colonies to the Risorgimento of the mid-nineteenth century.[5] Although the long and pungent historical literature can merely be sampled in this study, one of its major themes is essential: the late survival of feudalism and the failure of a national monarchy to effectively integrate the society socially or politically before its inclusion in a unified Italian nation-state.

Prior to the high period of feudalism in Europe, the South of Italy was fragmented into nine states, several of which—the Byzantine and the Muslim—were outside the Western European tradition. Only the four quasi-independent city-states of Naples, Gaeta, Amalfi, and Sorrento approached the pattern of the city-state then emerging in northern Italy.[6] The region was unified only by the Normans, who began to arrive in the eleventh century, and by the Swabians, who constructed a centralized monarchy during the twelfth century, a period of feudal anarchy throughout Europe.[7] Frederick II, using Norman central administration and adapting Muslim financial techniques, succeeded in bringing all public authority under his own control and destroying the independence of the four city-states, the barons, and the Church. The barons were driven from unrecognized lands and their fortresses were destroyed.[8]

When the Swabian kingdom was destroyed in the thirteenth century, a curious structural reversal occurred in southern Italian history. Domination by successive foreign monarchies allowed the feudal nobility an independence which was then diminishing in the rest of Europe, and which critically retarded the development of a modern state. As Croce observed, "The kings of Naples found

5. The classical sources for the study of the history of southern Italy are: Benedetto Croce, *Storia del Regno di Napoli* (Bari, 1958); Pietro Colletta, *History of the Kingdom of Naples, 1734–1825*, 11 vols. (London, 1858), trans. from the Italian by S. Horner; Rosario Romeo, *Il Risorgimento in Sicilia*; much historical material is collected in Bruno Caizzi, ed., *Antologia della Questione Meridionale* (Milano, 1955) and in R. Villari, ed., *Il Sud nella Storia d'Italia* (Bari, 1962).

6. Luigi Salvatorelli, *A Concise History of Italy* (New York, 1940), pp. 94–120; Giuseppe Pochettino, *I Langobardi nell'Italia Meridionale* (Caserta, 1930), Part III; Janet Trevelyan, *A Short History of the Italian People* (London, 1956), p. 62.

7. Gennaro Monti, *Lo Stato Normanno-Svevo* (Trani, 1945), pp. 10–22; James Van Wyck Osborne, *The Greatest Norman Conquest* (New York, 1937), p. 451; Salvatorelli, p. 178; Gabriele Pepe, *Lo Stato Ghibellino di Frederico II* (Bari, 1951), p. 29.

8. Salvatorelli, pp. 228–32; Pepe, pp. 12, 29.

themselves compelled to grant continual concessions, flattery and toleration to the barons; but with all this, they were unable to halt their constant rebellion . . . While elsewhere, feudalism was declining, in the Kingdom of Naples, and in Sicily in a similar manner, it was taking on new life." [9]

The last independent kings to rule the Mezzogiorno were the Bourbons, who were the first to Italianize, or better, "Neopolitanize." Their efforts at reform, however, were balked by the political and economic power of the barons. Although it succeeded in gaining some control of the Church and its properties, the Bourbon monarchy's reforms in the key financial field were entirely without success. As the Italian historian Rosario Villari writes, the government "was compelled to give in to particularistic forces and to forego the implementation of most of its plans." [10] The barons continued to exercise political and economic jurisdiction in the countryside until the end of the eighteenth century, while the Bourbons eked out a splendid existence in Naples on the proceeds of their royal domains and the taxes they managed to collect from the peasants and the Church.

Locally, a rough sort of balance existed between the autonomous barons and the non-noble classes who were represented in the villages by the *università,* a feudal council. The peasants had common use rights on feudal land and foraged on the communal, ecclesiastical, and royal domains. A few peasants were able to purchase small pieces of land which they operated in freehold. This traditional system began to be destroyed by the decade of French occupation from 1806–15. The French abolished feudalism, modernized the law, and raised the bourgeoisie to the level of landholders and administrators. The kingdom was unified administratively by the creation of a system of intendents, and the bourgeoisie gained control of local government through the establishment of

9. Croce, p. 63; pages 62–66 contain a summary of Croce's famous interpretation of the historical development of the Regno di Napoli; also see Friedrich Vöchting, *La Questione Meridionale,* p. 34; and Colletta, 2, 125–26.

10. Rosario Villari, *Mezzogiorno e Contadini nell'Età Moderna* (Bari, 1961), pp. 18–32, especially for anticlerical reforms; the quotation from Villari will be found on p. 28; also see Pasquale Villani, *Mezzogiorno tra Riforme e Rivoluzione* (Bari, 1962), p. 117; on legal reforms of the Bourbons, see Colletta, *History, 1,* 21.

a new system of city councils composed only of property holders.[11]

The period between the restoration of the Bourbons in 1815 and the integration of the South in the unified Italian state in 1861 completed the destruction of the traditional system. The French had created a new system of local government which the Bourbons inherited but could not integrate nationally. The French had abolished feudalism and mobilized a new class of bourgeois landholders with new aspirations; the Bourbons could not undo the abolition of feudalism, but they were unwilling to grant the aspirations of the bourgeoisie or to give it political representation.[12] Finally, as a result of the Revolution of 1848, public administration, credit, and the courts were paralyzed, police repression was instituted, and public spending was contracted.[13]

The gap between the provinces and Naples and between the bourgeoisie and the Court had a variety of consequences. The attention of the monarchy was lavished on the area around Naples;[14] access to the Crown still depended upon personal and family ties; in the courts, all appeals cases had to be tried at Naples, engendering long and bitter litigation over every business or property dispute and frustrating the aspirations of the bourgeoisie.[15] Most harmful to the bourgeoisie was the Bourbons' opposition to the further division of the public domains.[16]

Yet the Bourbons were unable to brake the growing power of the bourgeoisie, since much of its administrative apparatus was made up of bourgeois individuals who had gained their positions under the French. As Rosario Romeo, an outstanding scholar of

11. Croce, pp. 243–53. An annual income of 48 ducats was required for voting rights in most communes and 24 ducats was required in the villages. See R. Villari, *Mezzogiorno e Contadini*, p. 96, and N. F. Faraglia, *Il Comune nell'Italia Meridionale, 1100–1806* (Napoli, 1883), p. 270.

12. The sources for the study of the collapse of the Bourbon monarchy, apart from the general treatments in Croce and Colletta, are the following: Raffaele De Cesare, *La Fine di Un Regno* (2 vols., Citta di Castello, 1909); Domenico De Marco, *Il Crollo del Regno delle Due Sicilie*, Vol. 1, *La Struttura Sociale* (Napoli, 1960); G. Racioppi, *Storia dei Moti in Basilicata nel 1860* (Napoli, 1868); Romeo, *Il Risorgimento in Sicilia*; Sebastiano Nicastro, *Dal '48 al '60* (Milano-Roma-Napoli, 1913).

13. See Colletta, 2, p. 257.

14. R. Villari, *Mezzogiorno e Contadini*, pp. 202–09.

15. G. Filangieri, *La Scienza della Legislazione*, 2 (Napoli, 1784), 152–70.

16. De Marco, pp. 8, 44.

the Risorgimento, writes, "The new leading groups were strongly entrenched in the army and the bureaucracy and were supported by the [French] division of the feudal domains and the sale of the lands of the state. They had gained a precise consciousness of their power and were at pains not to lose the conquests they had made." [17]

The tension between the Court and the provinces and the Crown and the bourgeoisie resulted in the anarchic breakdown of the system as soon as Garibaldi landed at Marsala in 1860 with one thousand followers. As the British historian, Denis Mack Smith writes, "Political rebellion joined hands with social revolution, and spread from Palermo into the countryside. This in turn brought about the collapse of local authorities all through the Island; police fled for their lives; family feuds and social grievances came out into the open, and society was in a state of more or less complete dissolution." [18]

THE DEVELOPMENT OF SOCIAL CLASSES

With the breakdown of the traditional social system in the first half of the nineteenth century, social groups were loosened from traditional roles, but the absence of a new logic of industrialization left each major group without a clear consciousness of its interests and with a multitude of internal divisions. Where the traditional ordering of social roles has broken down and no modern system of hierarchy has arisen to take its place, status groups are still too fragmented to coalesce into modern social classes. As I shall later show, this phenomenon gives a particular configuration to social values and to political roles in the South of Italy.

It was the independence of the nobility that caused the late survival of feudalism in the South and the failure of a modern state to develop there.[19] This pattern was in turn caused by the cupidity of the foreign monarchies that ruled the country from the thirteenth to the seventeenth centuries. They enfeoffed the greater part of the crown lands to the Church and to the barons, and sold demesnial cities to bankers, lawyers, and tax gatherers, thereby cre-

17. Romeo, *Mezzogiorno e Sicilia nel Risorgimento* (Napoli, 1963), p. 56.
18. Denis Mack Smith, *Cavour and Garibaldi, 1860*, p. 14.
19. Vöchting, p. 40.

ating new baronages.[20] The historian Pasquale Villani estimates that of two thousand communes existing in 1760, over 1,300 were still subject to baronial jurisdiction, assuring the barons' continued domination of economic life.[21]

Unlike the English aristocracy, however, the barons of southern Italy thoroughly disdained trade and commerce and remained concentrated on the land. The abolition of feudalism in 1806 destroyed feudal jurisdictions, but it actually led to an increase in the land owned by the aristocracy as private property.[22] The social prestige of landholding and leisure appear to have outstripped the desire for economic advancement, even in the twentieth century. Evidence on this score is fragmentary. However, a study by Emilio Sereni based upon data collected in 1946 indicates that "the large landed property remains the prevalent economic base of an important part of the nobles." Sereni also found that there was growth in the number of members of the aristocracy on the boards of directors of large corporations, particularly during Fascism, but that such individuals with landholdings in the South were few.[23]

The bourgeoisie was perhaps the most strategic class in the formation of the modern social and political system of the Mezzogiorno. Its most significant feature is its concentration in the traditional professions, in landholding, and in administration, and its detachment from the role-shaping productive process in industry. Even at present, it is a bourgeoisie that is "more intermediary than producer, more lawyer than engineer, more philosopher than inventor, more notary than agronomist, and more functionary than expert." [24]

The origins of this class in the traditional system were typical.[25] What is unusual has been its failure to evolve from an old bourgeoisie engaged mainly in tax gathering, land management, and

20. Colletta, *1,* 26; *2,* 127.

21. P. Villani, *Mezzogiorno Tra Riforme,* pp. 298–99.

22. Ibid., pp. 140–83; see p. 176 on the "embourgeoisement" of noble lands.

23. Emilio Sereni, *La Questione Agraria nella Rinascita Nazionale Italiana* (Torino, 1946).

24. Ibid., p. 268.

25. Gian Maria Galanti, *Nuova Descrizione Geografica e Politica Delle Sicilie* (Napoli, 1789), analyzes the emergence of a legal and administrative class in the land disputes of the eighteenth century; Colletta, *1,* 26, notes the same phenomenon.

litigation into a new bourgeoisie active in trade and industry. Even before the French abolition of feudalism in 1806, the bourgeoisie began to turn its attention to the land, usurping many of the common lands at the expense of Church, Crown, and peasantry. These usurpations, documented by a steady increase in litigation, were fought by the state, but with little success. "Never having measured the legitimate private holdings and seldom marking their borders with permanent signs, the usurpations remained almost completely untouched." [26]

The French reforms, of course, increased the bourgeoisie's opportunities to acquire land. The return of the Bourbons in 1815 braked this process, but could not reverse it. As a historian of the period writes,

> From the new order of property which arose on the ruins of feudalism, the middle class began to flourish. In the new political order, it was the center of gravity of local politics. With the fever for quick gain that took hold of these new and aggressive groups, the domains of the villages were subjected to daily division.[27]

The precipitate fall of the Bourbon monarchy can be largely explained by the disaffection of the bourgeoisie. Indebted to French reforms, it was liberal in politics; prevented from the complete conquest of the land, it was opposed to the regime. Political organization began to appear. Secret societies like the *Carbonaria* were formed. They developed elaborate rituals and infiltrated the army and public administration.[28]

The Risorgimento was greeted in the South as a means of extending and consolidating bourgeois control of the land. The most dramatic impact of the reform of the new state was to liquidate all the vestiges of the former agricultural system to the profit of the

26. Giuseppe Zurlo, *Stato e Storia della Regia Sila*, 2 vols. (Napoli, 1866), *1*, 186; also see Trevelyan, p. 256; R. Villari, pp. 18–21, 45; and Colletta, 2, 39, on the failure of the Bourbon reforms.

27. Racioppi, p. 144.

28. See R. H. Johnston, *The Napoleonic Empire in Southern Italy and the Rise of the Secret Societies* (London, 1904); for primary material from the secret societies of the period, see *Memoirs of the Secret Societies of the South of Italy*, no author (London, 1821).

bourgeoisie. As Rossi-Doria, the foremost expert on the agricultural system of the Mezzogiorno writes, "The bourgeoisie was offered the means to take possession of the greater part of the land, until then unattainable, and to impose its own power in the firmest and widest possible base in all those regions in which the people lived exclusively from the land." [29]

The failure of the South to industrialize after unification left the bourgeoisie settled in landholding, a factor that retarded its emergence as a modern social class. As new strata of the middle class began to emerge from the artisans and peasant groups of the nineteenth century, they too sought ownership of the land, fragmenting ownership among the bourgeoisie and middle class but denying it to the peasants. Hence, both upper bourgeoisie and petit bourgeoisie remained "old" European classes in the midst of social and political changes that were reshaping social values and social roles.

The major occupational change that has occurred within the southern Italian bourgeoisie in recent decades is a partial shift from local politics, law, and landholding into employment in the national bureaucracy. This trend has caused changes in occupational perspectives, opened landholding to the peasants, and left a vacuum in local politics which new groups have been quick to fill.[30]

The peasantry in the Mezzogiorno has developed neither as a class of property-holding small farmers, as in Piedmont and France, nor as a salaried agricultural proletariat, as in the Po valley. As I have tried to show in the last chapter, it is a class with no clear occupational role structure. In fact, so atomized is its occupational structure and so disparate are its interests that it is almost unrealistic to regard the southern Italian peasantry as a class in any concrete sense.

The origin of this structural fragmentation may be found in the peculiar pattern of social and political development of the Mezzogiorno: first, in the late survival of feudalism; second, in the absence of alternate economic opportunities in industry; and, third,

29. Manlio Rossi-Doria, *Dieci Anni di Politica Agraria nel Mezzogiorno* (Bari, 1958); the quotation is from the same author, *Riforma Agraria e Azione Meridionalista*, p. 191.

30. See Alessandro Taradel, "La Burocrazia Italiana: Provenienza e Collocazione dei Direttori Generali," *Tempi Moderni, 6,* No. 13 (1963), Nuova Serie.

in the commercialization of the economy without the reshaping of economic roles that emerges from industrialization.

The late survival of feudalism left the peasantry with no property hold on the land and dependent upon the residue of feudal rights represented by the common use lands and the domains.[31] The breakdown of the traditional system between 1800 and 1860 destroyed this communitarian basis of agriculture, leaving the peasants bereft of the privileges once enjoyed, and embittered against the bourgeoisie. This situation was rendered permanent in the Mezzogiorno by the absence of alternate economic opportunities in industry and by the ambitions of the bourgeoisie toward the land. The expansion of landholding among the middle class only served to fragment economic relationships and landholding still further, increasing the number of people concerned directly or indirectly with the land. The peasants reacted to their unstable relation to the land by a continual series of revolts that culminated in endemic brigandage and alienation from authority.[32]

The peasants are composed, first, of a large number of agricultural day workers whose relation to the land is governed by the need of particular landholders for manpower. These roles, however, are "pure" occupational roles only in the limited zones of commercialized farming. An agricultural expert writes, "The greater part of those who are considered agricultural day workers in the Census are really small farmers who sometimes add to the operation of their own or rented land the money they can earn by doing day labor elsewhere." [33]

Second, a large proportion of the peasants occupy the transitional roles of *coloni*—share tenants whose relation to the land is governed by short seasonal contracts on the latifundia. Unlike the share tenants of the North, these peasants are not provided with

---

31. The analysis of the peasantry is based mainly upon Rossi-Doria, *Riforma Agraria,* and upon R. Villari, *Mezzogiorno e Contadini,* and P. Villani, *Mezzogiorno Tra Riforme.*

32. See especially Franco Molfese, *Storia del Brigantaggio dopo l'Unità* (Milano, 1964), pp. 12–14, 99–102, and Denis Mack Smith, *Italy: A Modern History* (Ann Arbor, 1959), pp. 7, 42–43.

33. ISTAT, *La Struttura della Popolazione Rurale Italiana e le Nuove Figure Agricole rilevate nell' VIII° Censimento* (Roma, 1937), p. 12.

tools, a house, or materials by the landowner. Moreover, this category of peasants is internally divided; the latest census lists eleven basic types of *colonia,* each with a different duration and division of the product.

Third, a large number of peasants rent land for a cash payment. However, so fragmented is the pattern of landownership in the zones where they are found that these peasants work minute or disparate pieces of land. In some areas, the term "rental" also implies a host of middlemen who take a profit before renting the landowner's land to a peasant worker. Moreover, a sizable number of peasant renters are peasants "with several titles," of whom the 1936 census found over 385,000 in the region.[34]

Finally, an increasing number of peasants now own their own land in the South. Although this group was quite small in the years after unification, it has grown in the last thirty years as the result of two distinct phenomena: first, the remittances of emigrants enabled numerous peasant families to purchase land, and a considerable number of emigrants themselves returned and purchased lands; second, government policies since the 1930s have provided peasants with the capital and incentive to acquire small farms. These policies culminated in the agrarian reform of the early 1950s, which distributed over 1,600,000 acres to peasant small owners.

The development of a working class in the South of Italy is very recent. Although numerous workers in cottage industry existed even before unification, a true working class only dates from the early twentieth century. A census report of 1927 shows that, whereas Lombardy had 195 industrial workers per 1,000 inhabitants, in the South the number of industrial workers per 1,000 was much lower: 62.3 in Campania, the most industrialized part of the region, 49.2 in Sicily, and 39.7 in Basilicata.[35]

In the industrial sector, as in agriculture, the failure of the social structure of the Mezzogiorno to coalesce into a modern system of functionally integrated roles is evident. Workers are mostly found in small-scale poorly run firms, bound by patriarchal relations to employers. The history of labor organizations illustrates

34. Ibid., p. 32.
35. Neufeld, *Italy: School for Awakening Countries,* p. 308.

the impact of the backwardness of the working class. In 1910, after the most prosperous decade in Italy's pre-World War II history, only 100,000 workers in the South were organized by the General Confederation of Labor, and these were mainly workers in agriculture.[36] Even today relatively few southern Italian workers are organized in any of the three major labor federations.

In one sense, however, the working class of the South is distinct in the region. First, in a fragmented system of social differentiation, it is the only class with a more or less clear configuration. Second, in a system of social evaluation based predominantly on landholdings, it is the only significant social group that is permanently detached from the land. For this reason, the isolated enclaves of the South where industry has taken hold are virtual oases of social organization and cultural modernity. At Gela, for example, in the backward south of Sicily, the recent development of a working class has transformed social relations; and, in the triangle of Bari, Taranto, and Brindisi, the creation of numerous new jobs outside of agriculture has given these cities an entirely different social configuration from the rest of the South.

THE FORMATION OF VALUES

Cultural values in the Mezzogiorno are perhaps the most exotic aspect of the area's social configuration. Generations of writers have noted the prevalence of violence and the consciousness of death, the modest place of woman in society, and the almost occult role of corruption in economics and politics.

First, values appear to be formed and loyalties to cohere around primary, local, and parochial centers of social life. As LaPalombara writes: "Primary associations are still dominant; family, kinship, neighborhood, village are still the associational forms that have the greatest call on individual loyalties." [37]

Second, the modern values of industrial society, such as rationality, entrepreneurship, and efficiency, have failed to permeate social life in the Mezzogiorno as they do in much of the West.

Third, cynicism and disaffection pervade southern Italian society. It is not the case, as in most backward societies, that individuals

36. Ibid., p. 235.
37. LaPalombara, *Interest Groups in Italian Politics,* p. 38.

participate only in the relatively intimate ties of family and village and not in the secondary associations typical of modern society; in the Mezzogiorno, individuals participate in and directly perceive modern secondary organizations, but for some reason reject them as illegitimate or corrupt.

Many sensitive observers have categorized the culture of the Mezzogiorno as "traditional." [38] Yet traditional cultures generally display more formality, more unanimity, and far less disaffection than is true in the South of Italy. The question for analysis is, Why does the South of Italy display a system of institutional norms and cultural goals that is at the same time more traditional than the North and yet less structured and authoritative than the traditional feudal system?

The answer, it is proposed, lies in the juxtaposition of modern institutions and organizations with a society imbued with traditional values and loyalties. The resulting "dual" culture does not simply combine various degrees of traditional and modern values, but results in cultural patterns that differ both from the traditional feudal system and from modern industrial society. Examination of each major aspect of value formation in southern Italy suggests that it is far from simply traditional.

While the family, the friendship group, and the village play an important role in socialization, this importance is not a simple concomitant of traditionality. Family life demonstrates the unusual situation of a nuclear family that transmits traditional values to its offspring. However, the protective mechanisms of the nuclear family do not function normally; children are socially welcomed as a sign of fertility, but capricious discipline patterns suggest that there are severe psychological resistances to the arrival of new mouths to feed. The press of population on resources instills the fear of death in individuals, and children are imbued with the danger of being "left on the street." The resulting nuclear family solidarity, which Banfield calls "amoral familism," is less the result of traditional loyalties than the fear of destitution, and it internalizes psychological tensions that we do not find in the family patterns of traditional societies.[39]

38. Ibid., p. 61.
39. Banfield, *The Moral Basis of a Backward Society.*

Moreover, the content of family socialization is far from traditional. In a society exposed constantly to the mass media, and where almost every family has relatives abroad, the symbols of modern urban life are communicated just as strongly as the images of tradition. In other words, Southerners do not have parochial values because they are physically isolated or culturally backward; they are dominated by family and local loyalties because more inclusive solidarities have been inhibited by the entire structural development of the society.

Banfield's argument is puzzling in this regard. He demonstrates that the southern Italian is oriented almost pathologically toward the nuclear family; yet he seems to suggest that nuclear family loyalty and loyalty toward other relatives is incompatible. There is no logical reason why this should be so, and empirical evidence shows that southern Italians are strongly oriented toward the extended family as well as the nuclear family. Why else would Southerners go to great lengths to write letters of recommendation for miscellaneous "cousins" and "nephews," even accounting for the fact that nephews in Italy are not always nephews? Moreover, the southern Italian vendetta, a blood feud capable of exterminating whole lineages in Sicily, suggests that family loyalty in most of southern Italy can extend far beyond the nuclear family.

Similarly, Banfield suggests that nuclear family loyalty and loyalty toward other primary and local institutions is incompatible. Again, there is no logical reason to agree, and empirical evidence from all over the region shows that southern Italians are oriented to village, neighborhood, and friendship group as much as to family. Field studies by Moss and Cappannari and by LoPreato are eloquent on this point.[40] In the Abruzzi hill village studied by Moss and Cappannari, not only were loyalties limited to the village, but *within* the village loyalties were divided between "upper town" and "lower town" residents. Clearly whatever operates to inflate nuclear family loyalties exaggerates other parochial loyalties too.

The weakness of entrepreneurship in southern Italy has also

40. Leonard W. Moss and Stephen C. Cappannari, "Estate and Class in a South Italian Hill Village," *American Anthropologist, 64* (1962); Joseph LoPreato, "Social Stratification and Mobility in a South Italian Town," *American Journal of Sociology, 26* (1961).

been a focus of attention for observers. The economic initiative of dynamic Northerners has always been compared unfavorably by them to Southerners who preferred "il dolce far niente." While there is much cultural prejudice in this characterization, it is indeed true that Italy's economic take-off in the late nineteenth century was accomplished by aggressive Northerners, while the South sat on its entrepreneurial hands.

Sample survey evidence verifies this view of southern values, but with some qualification. In a survey of Italian youth in the 1950s, over 55 percent of the Southerners preferred public employment to working for a private firm, mainly for the security it represented. In contrast, a majority of those who expressed a preference in the North (38 percent) preferred work in a private firm.[41]

Northern firms that take advantage of government incentives to locate in the South often find that key personnel are not available. As a sample survey of entrepreneurs carried out by the Associazione per lo Sviluppo dell'Industria nel Mezzogiorno (SVIMEZ) concluded; "In the South we find the danger, noticeable even at the level of local authorities and qualified social groups, that entrepreneurial functions are identified with people from the North. This ascription impedes the formation of new roles necessary for economic development in the region." [42] Along the same lines, it was recently noted that employees of a plant operated by one of the gigantic state holding companies in the South showed that they regarded themselves, not as wage earners in the marketplace, but as government dependents with all the perquisites of civil servants.

On the other hand, economic progress is not only inhibited by the absence of *individual* initiative; the failure is also related to Southerners' inability to act in concert. Just as nineteenth-century attempts to enlist landowners in cooperative reclamation schemes foundered on the lack of group cooperation, twentieth-century planners have had to cope with an excess of individuality too. Projects of the Cassa per il Mezzogiorno are often wasted because local administrators will not cooperate in making use of them. "Of 1150 aqueduct centers located in seven hundred communes, only

41. Joseph LaPalombara and Jerry B. Waters, "Values, Expectations and Political Predispositions of Italian Youth," *Midwest Journal of Political Science,* 5 (1961), 45.

42. SVIMEZ, *Sviluppo Industriale e Imprenditori Locali* (Roma, 1962), p. 16.

218 had actually constructed systems of internal running water, the reason being that taking the water from aqueducts constructed by the *Cassa* and providing it to local residents is at the local community's expense." [43]

Clearly, *both* the lack of individual initiative *and* the inability to organize groups for mutual advantages inhibit economic growth in southern Italy. Banfield, with his concept of "amoral familism," accounts for only the latter. But if southern Italians are prevented from joining with their fellows in cooperative ventures because of their suspicion of those outside the nuclear family, why then are there few signs of *individual* entrepreneurship either, a pattern that would be perfectly compatible with amoral familism?

Any explanation of entrepreneurship in the South must take account of the fact that southern Italians *do* routinely and skillfully form groups for certain purposes: to fool the government, to carry on black market activity, to send relatives as immigrants to America, and even, on occasion, to storm the land of the latifundia in unison in the name of social justice. In other words, when it fits in with their values, southern Italians form groups by the thousands, but their values are those of people living in a developing society and bear little resemblance to entrepreneurship. Both individual initiative and group-forming propensity flourish when the situation warrants it.

Finally, it is puzzling that the nuclear family should be causally associated by Banfield with economic backwardness. The nuclear family is the dominant type of family in most highly developed societies today (with the possible exception of Japan). That economic development is lacking despite the prevalence of the nuclear family suggests that far deeper factors are present to differentiate southern Italy from most of the Western world.

Entrepreneurship is a typical property of the "new" middle class of Western Europe. Its absence in the Mezzogiorno is really explained by the "old" nature of southern Italian social classes. Individuals who seek control of the land, power in local politics, and leisure in the liberal professions do not normally perceive eco-

43. Joseph LaPalombara, *Italy: The Politics of Planning* (Syracuse, 1966), p. 45; also see Gabriele Pescatore, *Dieci Anni di Esperienze della Cassa per il Mezzogiorno* (Roma, 1961).

nomic life in the same manner as a modern middle class in trade and commerce.

A third cultural factor often stressed in discussions of southern Italy is cynicism. It is interesting that Banfield's *The Moral Basis of a Backward Society,* which begins as a study of a structural factor —the nuclear family—is full of commentary on a cultural factor— the cynicism of southern Italian public life.[44] The cynicism and corruption of southern Italy do not result independently from the structure of the family either, but from the juxtaposition of modern organizations and institutions with a society where a modern system of social roles has failed to develop. It is not simply true that primary and secondary structures remain apart. On the contrary, the interpenetration of these units means that values born of primary and personal groups infiltrate the world of impersonal modern social organization. The result is cynicism, often expressed as corruption.

Yet the values that lead to cynicism and corruption are really functional in terms of the basic relationships that dominate southern Italian society. The state of mind engendered is less akin to the *anomie* (normlessness) described by Durkheim than the *ressentiment* described by Scheler.[45] One rejects the authenticity of the institutions that dominate the society, but one continues to operate within their framework. Such is the real meaning of Banfield's *The Moral Basis of a Backward Society,* a documentation of the distrust, disaffection, and cynicism rife in southern Italian society.

SOCIAL STRATIFICATION

The central role of social stratification in political analysis has often been noted. As David Apter writes: "The values and ideas of a changing social system can be expressed in the activities which take place to modify or protect the given pattern of stratification in a particular area. Stratification is, as well, a useful way of indicating the degree of internal flexibility in a system." [46] Paradoxically, the stratification system in the Mezzogiorno is both inflexible and fragmented. The activities of most major social groups

44. Banfield, Chap. 5.

45. Max Scheler, *Ressentiment* (Glencoe, 1950).

46. David E. Apter, "A Comparative Method for the Study of Politics," *American Journal of Sociology, 64* (1958), 223.

are aimed at ownership of the land, at best a limited and inflexible source of status, and yet these groups are fragmented into a myriad of poorly articulated occupational categories, a factor that confuses social evaluation and has a critical impact upon the conflict between social groups.

During the last decades of the nineteenth century, under laws requiring the equal division of lands among a proprietor's children, a fragmentation of bourgeois landholdings began, slowing up and suspending their improvement and maintenance. With a smaller land base, families were often forced to move to the cities and to seek professional or bureaucratic employment. The lands— even the larger latifundia—were left in the hands of renters or managers.[47] Through such a process, the landholders "came always more clearly to assume the figure and the characteristics of simple *rentiers* with no real function in production and in agricultural progress." [48] The latifundia system is based upon two- or three-stage rentals without the provision of equipment, and not upon large-scale commercial farms. The proprietor is economically removed from production because he hires a manager or large renter, who in turns parcels out the land to the peasants on yearly rentals. This phenomenon dates from the nineteenth century. "A large part of the property of the bourgeoisie, whether large or small, was fractioned into infinite divisions which the peasants took in rental . . . increasing the precariousness of the enterprise and the anarchy of the agrarian organization of the region." [49] Soon after national unification, a great number of petit bourgeois city dwellers began to turn to the land for investment: "Every doctor, storekeeper, public official, up to the last *carabiniere,* felt that with the purchase of a piece of land, he could make his own economic position more stable, and in any case raise himself a grade on the social scale." [50]

These new owners, far from the scene and ignorant of agriculture, contributed both to the state of disorganization of the agricultural economy and to its continued backwardness. Equally im-

47. Rossi-Doria, *Dieci Anni di Politica Agraria,* p. 20.
48. Ibid., p. 21.
49. Rossi-Doria, *Riforma Agraria,* p. 204.
50. Rossi-Doria, *Dieci Anni di Politica Agraria,* p. 22.

portant, they contributed to the fragmentation of its occupational structure. The incessant division of bourgeois property and the rise of a class of urban *rentiers* gave many peasants who were formerly simple agricultural day workers the chance to rent a small piece of land, to become sharecroppers, or even to buy a "handkerchief of land." The differentiation among the agricultural population was extreme:

> Each became different from the other; he came to find himself even more involved in a bitter battle of competition to obtain work or to be able to cultivate a little land, and thus participated less in class solidarity and in the life of the collectivity, and appeared exclusively interested in the progress of himself and his family.[51]

This process established a fragmented structure of contractual ties between proprietors and peasants:

> Little by little, every southern bourgeois became the absentee landlord of every southern peasant. There is to be found in this one of the major roots of the many surprising phenomena of social and political life in the South.[52]

The social status that accrues to landholding, however, differs from class to class. Peasants who own their own land are seldom accorded high status, for alongside possession of the land, the ability to live without performing manual labor remains an important element of prestige. This is demonstrated by the vast number of middle class individuals who live on their scanty incomes from the land, as well as by several almost unique symbolic aspects of southern Italian social life.

The *galantuomo* of the ninetenth century emphasized his position in life by wearing the *giamberga*, by prefacing his name with a title, and perhaps joining one of the rival lay religious fraternities, organizations that combined the functions of conspicuous consumption with religious zeal. The southern bourgeois of the present still uses the appelation "Don" in some zones of the South, and a host of other titles, conferred and imagined, follow his name on

51. Ibid., p. 23.
52. Ibid., p. 22.

his visiting card. He wears a suit and tie for virtually every occasion, and in the smaller towns he will not bring home packages from the store, but gives them to some peasant boy to carry.[53]

The predinner stroll—the *passeggiata*—fills the streets of every southern city during the hours from seven to nine with all the residents except the very rich and the hopelessly poor. In a society with a scarcity of resources, conspicuous leisure becomes a meaningful social activity. Cafés are forever full of lounging men *in borghese* (wearing suits and ties), whose slow steps and round, expansive gestures offer a sharp contrast to the intense, agitated conversation of the peasants.

Education is an important index of power and prestige in the South, but southern universities are notorious for training very few students in technical and business pursuits, and for concentrating their efforts on the learned professions. In the absence of sophisticated studies of occupational ranking, probably the best index we have of the evaluation of various professions and occupations is in the enrollment records of the schools. In the North of Italy, we find a great many students engaged in technical and economic studies, while in the South literary and professional studies predominate. The classic example, of course, is the law. The lawyer, it should be pointed out, is the South's classical figure of an educated gentleman of leisure. He is nothing like the busy, efficient individual scurrying about the halls of industry; he specializes in kinship manipulation, petty favors, and land disputes. The last gives him a strategic political position in the South.

TABLE 3.4

University Enrollment by Region and Major Field, 1963

	Science	Engineering	Economics	Law	Literature, Philosophy	Total
North	18,634	16,286	39,202	18,646	26,833	119,601
	15.6	13.6	32.8	15.6	22.4	100.0
South	7,383	4,205	17,016	14,677	21,444	64,725
	11.4	6.5	26.3	22.7	33.1	100.0

Source: Annuario Statistico Italiano, 1964, p. 109.

53. Banfield; also see the description in LaPalombara, *Interest Groups in Italian Politics*, pp. 42–43.

The educational values in school enrollment are demonstrated too by the distribution of younger students among the four types of secondary schools available. Students preparing for college in Italy may attend the literary and humanistic *Liceo Classico* or the technical and scientific *Liceo Scientifico*. Secondary school students who do not plan to go on to college can attend the general, humanistic courses of the *Istituto Magestrale*—a typical normal school— or terminal technical and vocational schools. In the North, almost 20 percent of all students at the secondary level attend the *Liceo Classico*, while 11 percent are found in the *Liceo Scientifico*. In the South, the differential between the two is far greater, with 28 percent in the *Liceo Classico* against 5 percent in the *Liceo Scientifico*. As regards the noncollege preparatory schools, a larger percentage in the South attend the humanistic *Istituto Magestrale*, and a smaller percentage are found in the technical and vocational schools.

TABLE 3.5

Secondary School Enrollment by Region and Institution, 1958–59

	Percentages in North	*Percentages in South*
Liceo Classico	19	28
Liceo Scientifico	11	5
Istituto Magestrale	14	22
Technical, Vocational	56	45

Source: SVIMEZ, *Un Secolo di Statistiche*, p. 923.

In the North, where industrialization has helped to organize social roles primarily around the occupational hierarchy, career-oriented studies are prevalent; in the South, where strategic social roles remain in landholding and are removed from the productive process, many individuals choose fields of study with less practical and more prestige value.

SOCIAL MOBILITY AND GEOGRAPHIC MOBILITY

In contrast to traditional societies, geographic mobility in southern Italy is quite high. Peasants travel long distances to find day labor during harvest time, returning to their families in the winter months. More recently, a pattern of seasonal and yearly migration to the cities has begun by individuals whose social roots remain in the countryside. A large number of transitional figures who are urban-based but rural-oriented have resulted.

Among high status groups, spatial mobility is somewhat greater and more permanent. A study of a national sample of professionals showed that only 53 percent of those born in the South still resided there permanently in 1955.[54] But many of these individuals—in large part, bureaucrats in Rome—retain land and family ties in the provinces. For both low and high status groups of this type, it might be said that the city is the place to earn a living and find amenities, but the town remains the point of social reference.

Shifting population patterns and the lack of industry give southern provincial cities a peculiarly unstable structure in which modern secondary associations are absent and the piazza becomes the central focus of activity.

> The city of the South is a typically political and administrative center in which economic activity is prevalently artisan, in which an entrepreneurial class and an industrial proletariat are lacking . . . The southern city does not have the propulsive function for the surrounding countryside of modern markets and great service centers, but only has the function of "permanent fair," where one goes to buy and to spend a little in diversion.[55]

Social mobility in an overpopulated country with little economic opportunity outside of agriculture is of course quite limited. The peasant, who generally does not own the land and is condemned by his manual labor to lowest status, has little opportunity for advancement. Moreover many of the peasants who do own small, family properties are frequently weighted down by obligations and debts on a plot of land too small to yield profit. These "pseudoproperties," which are very widespread in the South, are seldom independent enough to distinguish the owner from nearby peasants who do not own their own land.[56]

54. *Informazioni SVIMEZ, 9,* Nos. 9–10 (1956), 212.

55. Goffredo Zappa, "Aspetti Sociali e Culturali," *Il Veltro* (special issue on the problem of the South), *6* (1962), p. 1019.

56. Vöchting, pp. 308–19.

Beginning in the 1930s, a small group of peasants were able to buy their own farms and to save enough to train their sons as teachers, priests, and petty professionals. For many years, land-ownership was the single entrance to high social status.[57] More recently, peasants whose relatives have succeeded in America have gained symbols of status bought with the emigrants' remittances,[58] and have even been able to buy enough land to send sons to college. A third somewhat smaller group is composed of repatriated emigrants who have worked for years in the New World for the privilege of returning to their home town to sit in the piazza at leisure and speak a few words of English in the local "Club Americano."

Apart from these groups, the peasants are separated by a real mobility rift from high and middle status groups. Their speech, dress, manners, and attitudes are sharply distinguished from those of middle and upper status town dwellers, despite the fact that many of them live in the towns and cities. A recent anthropological study of a small hill town in the Abruzzi concluded:

> The disjunctive nature of the stratification system is seen most clearly at the upper and lower levels of the hierarchy. Social contacts between the upper echelon and all others in the community are limited by prescribed patterns of behavior. Visible manifestations of status include such obvious symbols as clothing and style of life. Less obvious, perhaps, the little fingernail is extended—indicating that one does no manual labor.[59]

Another study of the South found that members of the upper class "perceive a social chasm" between themselves and the rest of the population, and interact with other classes only on a purely contractual-legal basis.[60]

This disjunctiveness in the stratification system gives some idea of the strategic function of middle class professionals in communicating between high and low status groups and in handling dis-

57. Joseph LoPreato, "Social Stratification and Mobility in a South Italian Town," p. 587.

58. Ibid., p. 593.

59. Moss and Cappannari, "Estate and Class in a South Italian Hill Village," p. 293.

60. LoPreato, "Social Stratification," p. 587.

putes over the land. These middle groups, made famous through the political journalism of Salvemini,[61] arose originally out of the land disputes of the last years of the Bourbon monarchy and as administrators of the lands of absentee landowners. They are the most mobile group in southern Italian society, and, lacking opportunities for advancement in industry, their peculiar domain is politics.

Middle class groups find mobility opportunities in the public services too. With the growth of the bureaucracy begun under Fascism and accelerated during the postwar years, the Italian bureaucracy has been overwhelmed by Southerners, both in Rome and in the provinces. Far from reflecting a dedication to public service, however, the trend appears merely to shift the aspirations of the southern professional bourgeoisie from local politics to national politics. A 1958 study of Italian youth asked nearly 3,000 respondents ranging in age between 18 and 25 whether they preferred private or public employment. The results, distributed by geographic regions, are as follows:

TABLE 3.6

Preference for Private or Public Employment by Region
(in percentages)

Preference	North	Central	South	Islands
Private Firm	38.0	28.6	21.4	17.0
Public Agency	31.8	46.9	55.2	59.2
No Preference	29.8	24.5	23.3	23.8
No Response	0.4	—	0.1	—

Source: Joseph LaPalombara and Jerry B. Waters, "Values, Expectations and Political Predispositions of Italian Youth," *Midwest Journal of Political Science*, 5 (1961), 45.

The fragmentation of social groups and the dominant emphasis upon landholding in the stratification system of the Mezzogiorno gives a peculiar character to social conflict. There is a great deal of social conflict, as any popular novel about the South suggests. However, in the absence of strong occupational classes, there is little of what could legitimately be considered *class* conflict. Where the

61. Gaetano Salvemini, "La Piccola Borghesia Intelletuale," in Bruno Caizzi, ed., *Antologia della Questione Meridionale,* pp. 383–404.

traditional ordering of social roles breaks down and a modern system of hierarchy has not yet been consolidated, status groups are too fragmented to coalesce into social classes. Social conflict, instead, focuses upon ascriptive memberships, family and parafamily tensions, and in the interstices of personal relationships, in manners, speech, and symbolic systems of ranking. This diffused and poorly articulated pattern of social conflict gives an abnormally important role to personal and primary relationships, and shapes secondary and bureaucratic group behavior in unusual ways.

PRIMARY AND SECONDARY ASSOCIATION: PARENTELA AND CLIENTELA

Although much of the color of social relations in the South of Italy involves kinship relations—*parentela,* as they are called—very little has come to light about the place of the family in social structure in general. Slum children in America became accustomed to hearing southern Italian immigrant children threaten, "I'll get my big brother after you," but only in their native habitat have southern Italians developed to the fullest the more militant manifestations of family solidarity.

Banfield, in *The Moral Basis of a Backward Society,* traces the dominance of the nuclear family to fragmented tenure conditions. Probably of equal importance is the Catholic Church and relatively high geographic mobility.[62] Although family units and economic units seldom correspond, even in industry, kinship is important in all contractual and business relations. Families, nuclear and extended, are installed in the *management* of many small firms, even when doing so overburdens slim profits. Southerners are often prevented from making capital investments by the weight of the family on their profits. In a society of great fragmentation and underdevelopment of secondary associations, an individual is "recognized" as a family member before he is identified as the member of some group or occupation. So close are the reputed links between family members that a family's prestige in a village will be based in part upon the wealth of its relatives in America or on the influence of a cousin in Rome.

The southern family tenaciously preserves the amount of land it

62. Banfield, pp. 153–54.

holds, for land is the most effective measure of status, and the only sure guarantee that daughters will find husbands. One of the most important impediments to the rationalization of agricultural cultivation is the grasp families have on fragmented and separated holdings. As land is inherited through division among all the heirs, losses in landownership must be made up in the marriage of male children. Individual marriages are seldom contracted by the family, but a formal bargaining session often follows an engagement. Until quite recently, family land fragmentation was fought by the delegation of many younger sons to the clergy.

Family-linked roles of a secondary nature play an important role in the South. The *compare* system is similar to the *compadrazo* of rural Spain, but far less important.[63] The godfather in southern Italy is usually a friend of the parent who does not have business ties with the family. He is a protector and confidant to the godchild, but his role may extend to eventual economic or political patronage.

Far more important is the system of patronage between a peasant's sons and a landholder for whom the peasant works or with whom he has contractual relations. The landholder is a support in time of famine, his advice will be formally sought before marriages and land purchases, and he is asked for recommendations in the peasant's frequent encounters with the bureaucracy.

A given landholder or professional may have such clientele relations with several peasants and their families, but each of these patterns is independent and vertical, discouraging horizontal organization of a permanent nature among the peasants. *Clientelismo*—as it is called—permeates southern Italian society. It is the basis of the shifting and temporary contractual relationships in agriculture and in industry. Until recently, for example, even on the relatively modern commercial farms of Puglia, labor was hired on a day-to-day basis. The *braccianti* (agricultural day laborers) would mill about in the central piazza of a town, and the landowner or one of his henchmen would circulate among them, giving a day's labor to those they knew and trusted.

In the widespread criminal and vendetta organizations that permeate southern Italian society, clientele and family relation-

63. See Julian Pitt-Rivers, *The People of the Sierra*, pp. 136–59.

ships predominate. It is not an accident that the local groups of
the Sicilian Mafia are today known as *famiglia*. An individual's
vendetta applies to all the male members of his family, because
they are considered responsible with him for his actions. The
leader of a given Mafia *famiglia* is in a choice position for the dis-
pensation of favors. His is an eminently political position, and he
is a specialist in obligation and compensation.[64] The clientele relationship is dominant as well in the semicriminal organizations
that organize agricultural commerce. Acquaintance and obligation
determine to whom the peasant sells his produce, and not price or
quality.

Observers often confuse the clientele relationship with feudalism; in reality it is quite different. In feudal society, social relations were formalized, hierarchical, and legally sanctioned. A
logical pyramid of mutual obligations was built up which was
congruent with the requirements of the society for defense and
solidarity.[65] These were functions of particular importance for the
time. Clientelismo, on the other hand, is shifting and informal,
and has no institutional recognition in concrete institutions.
Equally important, it is antithetical to modern society's emphasis
on scale, horizontal solidarity, and large-scale organization. This
has particular significance in the patterns of politics that evolve.

Modern secondary associations, on the other hand, have been
very slow in developing. The previous chapter has shown the surprisingly small size of the typical industrial unit in the South; agricultural units, because of the fragmented landholding system
and tenure arrangements, are equally miniscule. Labor organizations, which depend upon large production units and homogeneous occupational groups, are far more powerful in the North and
Center of Italy than in the South or the Islands. As I shall show
in the next chapter, the panoply of organized secondary associations that abound in Western politics is largely lacking in the
Mezzogiorno.

Related to the weakness of organized secondary association in

64. Michele Pantaleone, *Mafia e Politica* (Torino, 1962). See especially Chaps. 8
and 9.

65. See Marc Bloch, *Feudal Society*, trans. from the French by L. S. Manyon (Chicago, 1961).

the South is the interpenetration of primary groups with the institutionalized groups of business, government, and religious life. Unlike the typical Western setting, where secondary associations are insulated from the ascriptive and particularistic influences of primary groups, in the South, the activities of business, bureaucracy, and Church are dominated by the narrower logic of *clientela* and *parentela*. In many of these units, formal organization and operation are observed only as ritual; their real operation is highly informal. For those with good connections, the system works smoothly; for the unconnected, the bureaucracy is impassive and unresponsive.

Yet even for the participants of *clientela-parentela* pyramids, the increasing complexity of modern social life makes this form of social action unwieldy. Rather than coalescing into more broadly based associations, the chains of individuals become longer and longer, and less and less flexible. Economic opportunities that require large-scale functional organization are squandered, and social conflicts are expressed as friction between clienteles, a factor that guarantees they are never truly resolved. This explains the great significance of the appearance for the first time, after World War II, of mass political organizations. They could either break down this immobilist structure of personal ties or be absorbed by it. Or was some other alternative possible?

4. The Political System

In his great novel, *The Leopard,* Lampedusa explores the subtle relationships between Italian national unification and the evolution of his native Sicily. A monarchy is replaced, an aristocracy humbled, elections are held, and local control passes from lordly princes to social-climbing bourgeoisie. The *Risorgimento,* a fresh wind from the North, appears to have swept away centuries of tradition and brought progress and liberty.

Yet everything in the Mezzogiorno, we soon learn, is not as it seems. Another autocracy—Rome—replaces the old one, but rules far more remotely. Elections are held, but ballot boxes are stuffed and paid retainers cheer in the village square. The new bourgeoisie apes the old princes, but with more cupidity and less refinement. And the fresh wind from the North becomes a dry, hot Scirocco from the South. As Tancredi, the young hero, says, as he goes off to fight with Garibaldi against the old regime: "It is necessary to change everything, so that everything will remain the same."

Has everything, in fact, "remained the same" in southern Italy? As I have suggested in the previous chapters, everything has indeed changed, in the sense that the old organization of social roles has broken down. On the other hand, nothing has changed completely, in the sense that no new, modern organization of social roles has yet crystallized. Politically, the same thing is true; the Bourbon monarchy and its trappings are long since gone, but the liberal, democratic institutions imported after the Risorgimento function in a manner their founders never intended.

POLITICS AND ORGANIZATION

For generations, observers have noted that politics in the Mezzogiorno is poorly organized. As in the case of economic life and social organization in general, the political system in southern Italy reveals a weakness of the familiar panoply of parties and groups that characterizes politics in most of the West. Most observers look to the social structure as the cause, but interpretations differ.

One school of thought turns to the structure of the family and to patterns of primary socialization in the formation of political values and organization. The most articulate spokesman for this view is Edward Banfield, whose book *The Moral Basis of a Backward Society* has become justly famous in the study of developing societies. Banfield interprets the low organizational capacity of the South of Italy as the result of poor goal articulation: "the inability of the villagers to act together for their common good." [1] In explaining this incapacity, he lays great stress upon family structure and upon socialization processes. Children see their parents as their only possible source of protection, and parents raise their children through a general indulgence that is interspersed with indiscriminate reliance on blows.[2] The people in the village, Banfield writes, "act like selfish children because they are brought up as selfish children." [3] They behave in society as if they were following the basic rule: "Maximize the material, short-run advantage of the nuclear family; assume that all others will do likewise." [4]

This ethos, according to Banfield, leads to an organizational and political vacuum in local public life. No one will further the interest of the group unless it is to his private advantage to do so; private citizens take no interest in public affairs, and public officials are apathetic; organization—political and otherwise—is difficult to achieve and impossible to maintain; cynicism and corruption are rife; there are no leaders and no followers; there are no strong and stable political machines; and party loyalty is constantly shifting.[5]

Several comments should be made with regard to Banfield's work. First, he allots an unusually important role to the family in the formation of political and organizational patterns.[6] Second, he allots little independent value to the institutionalized norms of the

1. Banfield, *The Moral Basis of a Backward Society,* p. 10.
2. Ibid., pp. 150–63.
3. Ibid., p. 161.
4. Ibid., p. 85.
5. Ibid., Chap. 5.
6. See Gabriel Almond and Sidney Verba, *The Civic Culture* (Princeton, 1963), p. 35, for a critique of such an approach.

society in forming behavior patterns; in the family itself, the socialization patterns Banfield posits have no institutional content.[7]
Third, in seeking the source of organizational incapacity of a
society in the structure of the family, Banfield is forced into a position where he calls the nuclear family in the South of Italy a dis-
incentive to political and economic organization. Yet comparative
experience indicates it is the nuclear family that is dominant in
those societies which have gone furthest in their degree of political
organization and economic development.[8]

There remains another important point of disagreement with
Banfield's observations as well as with his interpretations. The
organizational incapacity that rifles southern Italian society, of
course, has a heavy influence upon patterns of politics. Banfield
concludes from this that the village he describes has a *political*
vacuum as well:

> What accounts for the absence of organized action in the face
> of pressing local problems? Why, for example, is nothing done
> about the schools? . . . Why are the political parties them-
> selves so unconcerned about local issues? Why is there no
> political "machine" in Montegrano, or even any stable and
> effective party organization? What explains the erratic behav-
> ior of the electorate in a single town from one election to the
> next? And why do those elected to office at once lose credit
> with their supporters? . . . *What accounts for the political
> incapacity of the village?* [9]

I have characterized the South of Italy repeatedly as a developing
society. Does it not seem odd that such a society should suffer from
political incapacity? A society undergoing rapid change might be
expected to have a great deal of political activity and expertise. As
David Apter writes: "Where active modification of the stratification system is going on, members characteristically are (1) status-
conscious . . . ; (2) are engaged in role-testing . . . ; and (3) are
future-oriented . . . Where these conditions prevail, the implications for political development are great." [10]

7. Banfield, p. 161.
8. Bernard Barber, *Social Stratification* (New York, 1957), p. 364.
9. Banfield, pp. 30–31. Italics added.
10. David E. Apter, "A Comparative Method for the Study of Politics," p. 223.

Although it is clearly true that the political system of the Mezzogiorno is characterized by a weakness of the organizational forms typical of modern Western society, there is no evidence that this organizational vacuum signals the absence of political capacity altogether. It is more nearly true that both family structure and disorganization result from the same factor—the fragmentation of social roles described in the last chapter. This structural configuration produces great political interaction in definite patterns of political organization. In a sense, it is the absence of organizational capacity that makes politics more important to the individual than would otherwise be the case.

Clientelismo is a pattern of political integration that is linked directly to the inflexibility, disjunctiveness, and fragmentation of the stratification system of the Mezzogiorno; it is characteristic of fragmented systems passing from a traditional to a modern organization of social roles. It allocates key political roles to those who, through control of the land, have a network of vertical relations with numerous individuals. It excludes a large number of individuals from political roles because of their low status, and it severely restricts the range of interest aggregation because of the narrow, personal nature of its internal relationships. An individual is linked to the authority structure through personal ties of obligation and loyalty, rather than through the merger of his interests with others of the same social group or ideological persuasion. Hence, politics is nonideological, broad functional interests cannot be expressed in politics, and access to authority can expand only through the further vertical extension of clientele links, a type of expansion that lengthens obligation beyond the scope of effective political allocation.

Clientelismo differs structurally from a true system of representation, although it can adapt to an electoral system, and it deals in the satisfaction of personal interests. But rather than locating the broad common interests of social groupings or interest associations, the clientele system links a distinct chain of individual and personal interests through the benefits of patronage. As a result, broader interests remain unrepresented, and immobilism is built into the system. Demands remain locked in the recesses of the stratification system, leaving all social relations abnormally colored by the status-seeking and status-testing that is normally expressed in politics. Courtship, leisure, and friendship, although removed from politics in most Western societies today, are linked to the blockage in the structures of political aggregation; their intense, almost theatrical quality in the Mezzogiorno take up some of the slack of the status interactions that find no effective outlet in politics.

Personal acquaintance is the most notable aspect of this phenomenon. Where political organizations of a specifically political character are limited, the structure of acquaintance has distinctly political implications. An individual seeking employment in a fragmented economic system must be available on all sides; this need leads to the formation of a broad circle of personal acquaintances that merges with the clientele system at its upper level. One "reaches" the structure of authority, not by merging one's demands with the parallel demands of others, but by linking oneself to a hierarchical chain of personal acquaintance that reaches power holders at the higher level.

This system of personal acquaintance and its relation to authority is strikingly similar to the system of rural southern Spain. As Pitt-Rivers writes: "The institution of friendship, based upon the moral notion of equality and the free exchange of favour, builds up, in situations of moral inequality, a structure of patronage which links up the authority of the state through the economic power of certain individuals to the network of neighborly relations." [11]

The individual is to an unusual degree a negotiator in the market place. He is at once both highly political and resistant to horizontal secondary organization. Gramsci observed this phenomenon in the Mezzogiorno: "The mass of rural workers and the lumpenproletariat," he wrote, "have always been 'volunteers,' in a certain sense displaced persons, and never, or hardly ever, are they homogeneous social groups." [12] The individual, forced to seek various forms of employment constantly in a context of overpopulation and scarce resources, becomes a negotiator. In this sense, all his social relations are "political." He has many possibilities, none of

11. Julian Pitt-Rivers, *The People of the Sierra*, p. 154.
12. Antonio Gramsci, *Il Risorgimento* (Torino, 1955), p. 196.

them certain, and his success or failure requires him to be as available as possible to many potential employers, or to find a patron on whom he can depend on the basis of personal obligation.

Political knowledge becomes especially crucial to individuals engaged in a search for work in a marketplace in which the criteria for their employment are ascriptive or particularistic. It is an individual's "business" to find out about the preferences and alliances of various employers and landowners, and to know the structure of influence in the community. Far from feeling Banfield's "political incapacity," Southern Italians have great interest in politics, broadly understood.

This dimension of politics is difficult to document, but it is possible to gain some measure of southern Italians' consciousness of politics by using the data of Almond and Verba in *The Civic Culture*. In this study, published in 1963, the authors collected survey data on participation in five countries—the United States, Great Britain, Germany, Mexico, and Italy. I have broken down the Italian data according to region, to gain some insight into the differences in political culture between northern and southern Italy.

Regarding the problem of political knowledge, respondents in the Almond and Verba study were asked: "How about local issues in this town or part of the country? How well do you understand them?" Although many Italians in both regions expressed little understanding, more than twice as many Southerners as Northerners maintained that they understood local issues very well. Moreover, if we consider together those Italians who maintained that they understood local issues "not so well" and "not at all," we

TABLE 4.1

Understanding of Local Issues by Region
(in percentages)

Understand Issues:	North	South	Italy
Very well	11	23	15
Moderately	21	27	23
Not so well	21	16	19
Not at all	30	20	27
Depends; no answer	17	14	16

find 51 percent in the North and only 36 percent in the South. It may be that Southerners know little of local politics; but the fact that they say they are well informed suggests the importance of political knowledge.

In much the same way, although many Italians of both regions pay little attention to electoral campaigns, almost twice as many Southerners as Northerners declared that they pay great attention to campaigns. Nothing is more corrective to the vision of the South as a traditional society full of "parochials" who pay no attention to politics. Table 4.2 records this aspect of political consciousness in North and South:

TABLE 4.2

Attention to Electoral Campaign by Region
(in percentages)

Amount of Attention	North	South	Italy
Much attention	13	24	17
Little attention	26	22	25
No attention	57	50	54
Other; don't know	4	3	4

Clientelismo has a critical impact upon participation too. Participation in a clientele system, while nominally similar to representation, is completely different from participation in a representative system. Voting consistency is very low, since loyalties and obligations are personal and shifting. The lack of consistency in clientele politics is documented in a study conducted in Italy by an American research group. In seventy-six communes of the Mezzogiorno where the vote had shifted greatly compared to the vote in the previous election, the study found, "That the voters were motivated by strictly *local* and personal economic issues, that ideology and national issues played little part in determining voting behavior, and that many shifts were simply the result of *clientelismo,* voters following a personal leader from one party to another." [13]

Clientelismo finds another expression in the use of the *pre-*

13. Joseph LaPalombara, *Interest Groups in Italian Politics*, p. 65. The citation is to a field study of International Research Associates, mimeograph, n.d.

ferenza or optional preference vote for an individual candidate on a party's list. The *preferenza* is used in the South almost twice as much as in the North, indicating that in the South there is more tendency to vote for a familiar name, rather than for a party list.[14] A related phenomenon is the tendency of neighboring villages with similar socioeconomic characteristics to show tremendous differences in the votes gained by the various parties, because of the influence of powerful local figures in each commune.

Elections, in such a milieu, combine the attributes of the bazaar and the smoky back room. One sensitive student of the South, LoPreato, vividly documents this characteristic in a study of social classes and conflicts in a Calabrian town. After pointing out that ideology is hardly an issue in local elections, LoPreato comments upon the basis of political interest:

> Politics in *Motta Nuova* is a matter of patronage interest: interest in being able to control jobs such as town doctor, cemetery attendant, town guards, and street cleaners; interest in receiving favors or gifts for a vote; interest, at least, in not being subjected to a "spiteful enemy." Political realignments and hostilities are, therefore, a never ending process.[15]

The candidates are active, but not in terms of the ideological issues. Attention focuses upon the personal attributes of the opposition:

> In the village square they [the candidates] alternate in singing each other's faults and defects—real or imagined. They might begin by reminding each other of their respective origin, passing quickly to accusations of robbery while in office or of intention to achieve public office in order to defraud the public. Then they might discuss the motives behind their marriage to their respective wives.[16]

14. Giovanni Schepis, "Analisi Statistica dei Risultati," in Alberto Spreafico e Joseph LaPalombara, eds., *Elezioni e Comportamento Politico in Italia* (Milano, 1963), p. 337.

15. Joseph LoPreato, "Class and Achievement in a Developing Society: Causes and Effects of Emigration," unpublished MS, 1966, p. 393. I wish to thank Professor LoPreato for generously consenting to let me quote extensively from his manuscript.

16. Ibid., p. 394.

The party supporters are also active, according to LoPreato, but they appear to be members of the personal following of each leader, rather than a disciplined ideological cadre:

> Small sections of the population—the faithful clientele of each leader—engage in behavior during political gatherings that substantially adds to the public caricature. While the speaker is engaged in publicizing the inglorious nature of his opponent, the faithful followers laugh, applaud, and cheer, or they tune up on "Bronx cheers" and shout back courtesies in kind, as the case may demand.[17]

But what of the electorate? The voters, LoPreato notes, take part enthusiastically in the politics of the piazza, but with a curious twist; in a political system in which cynical leaders manipulate cynical followings for their own advantage, no one is more cynical than the ordinary voter:

> The bulk of the population listens and laughs, enjoying it all, for this situation created by the leaders is not only amusing, but it also serves the function of undermining the aura of social superiority that they are intent upon building around themselves . . . if conflict is particularly marked in times of political elections, it is because the political arena is a legitimate, public, almost sportsmanlike context within which to give vent to the pent-up emotions and hatreds accumulated during centuries of endless shame and economic insecurity.[18]

Southern Italians, in other words, are very conscious of politics, but for reasons that go back to the social and economic substructure of the society.

The relatively high degree of political consciousness in the South of Italy does not make it a "participant culture" in the Anglo-American sense of the term. Southerners may be very conscious of politics, but they do not discuss them as freely as does the "ideal" citizen. On a question regarding the fear of discussing politics, the Almond and Verba data show that almost 60 percent of the southern respondents will discuss politics with no one or with very few

17. Ibid.
18. Ibid., p. 395.

people, as compared to 46 percent of the Northerners. Clearly, *all* Italians are suspicious of discussing politics openly, but greater suspicion marks the southern sample.

The development of political parties in the South presents an unusual picture. It is certainly true, as Banfield pointed out, that secondary political organizations in the South of Italy are severely limited in their development. LaPalombara states in his interest group study, "Secondary associations that are economically or politically based, such as interest groups, have failed to attract southerners except in the rarest cases." [19] But at the same time, political *parties* have made great strides in the South since World War II. Often the poorest, most backward village will have its party offices on the main street of town. This development of parties, while interest groups and other secondary organizations remain stagnant, is expressed in the answers of Italian respondents in *The Civic Culture.* The respondents were asked to choose which among the following possibilities would be the most effective method of influencing government: "working through personal and family connections; writing to government officials; getting people interested, or forming a group; working through a political party; organizing a protest demonstration." [20]

The results are not completely predictable. Though *all* the Italian respondents gave great weight to family and personal influences and written contacts with officials, Northerners stressed the formation of groups and Southerners emphasized working through a party:

TABLE 4.3

Preferred Methods of Influencing Government by Region
(in percentages)

Methods of Influence	North	South	Italy
Personal, family connections	12	12	12
Writing to officials	13	15	14
Forming a group	15	9	13
Working in a party	12	25	16
Protest Demonstration	7	5	6
None, Other, Don't know	41	34	39

19. LaPalombara, *Interest Groups in Italian Politics,* p. 38.
20. Almond and Verba, Appendix B, p. 529.

The validity of the data is damaged by the large number of residual "No answer, Other, Don't know" responses, but the high percentage of Southerners who would work through a party (25 percent), and the low percentage who would use a group (9 percent), strongly indicate that in the South, modern group formation and parties have almost no correlation.

Apart from challenging a latent assumption of political scientists that there is a positive correlation between group-forming propensity and party association, these data perhaps help us in interpreting the nature of political party organization in southern Italy. Clientelismo, rather than dying out as parties have come into prominence, has infiltrated the political party in the South. In the case of the governing party—the Christian Democrats—this occurred as government agencies came in to spend vast development funds, and turned automatically to the local Christian Democratic politicians for personnel. The other parties as well, however, are infiltrated by clientele groups. Strong, ideological groups in the North are reduced in the South to congeries of local notables who mouth the slogans of their party with little sincerity. Politicians change party label at will, and their constituents join them with dispatch. A respondent in LaPalombara's interest group study reported:

> Families which wish to prosper will place family members in several of the political parties. Thus, one will go into the Christian Democracy, another into the Communist Party, another to the Monarchist party or the Italian Social Movement as a means of hedging against all of the probable or possible political eventualities of the country.[21]

The myriad of local party organizations are often little more than locales for friendship cliques, replete with soccer teams and pinball machines. The organizational success in the mid-1950s of the Monarchist Party of Achille Lauro, the Neapolitan shipbuilder, was due largely to the technique of placing television sets in each local party office. As television became more common in bars and in people's homes, however, the Monarchist offices were abandoned.

21. LaPalombara, p. 345.

THE POLITICAL ELITE

The political elite of the Mezzogiorno is centered in the professional groups Salvemini characterized as the "intellectual petit bourgeoisie." [22] This group, which arose in the early nineteenth century as retainers of the landowners and the legal class of the Bourbon monarchy, was the prime beneficiary of the reforms of the political unification of Italy. It is a political elite almost by definition because of its strategic economic role as intermediary between the landowners and peasants. The emergence of a national bureaucracy in this century has reinforced the intermediary role, for this class now mediates between the illiterate peasants and the state as well as between peasant and landowner. Lawyers, notaries, and profit seekers are recruited into intermediary roles in the everyday transactions carried out with the public administration and with the courts. This is particularly true of lawyers, who have a key role in litigating the land disputes that persist to the present day. The mediatory positions are often institutionalized; the peasant can have fruitful contact with the government only through particular middlemen who have established special monopolies of these functions either by bribery, special competence, or personal influence.

Recruitment into political roles is merged with recruitment into the intermediary professional positions. Individuals are co-opted into political roles through the courts, through their relations with the government of the communes, and through personal relations with the bureaucracy in the provinces. The Church, with its long-term boycott of Italian nationhood, was not a notable recruiting ground for politics until Fascism reconciled it to the state. Since the end of World War II, the Church has represented one of the basic recruiting sources and checkpoints of the political system in the South, although this role is far more limited in the North.

The southern Italian politician is at once a dilettante and a professional. His recruitment into strategic liberal professions and land management automatically confer political status upon him,

22. Gaetano Salvemini, "La Piccola Borghesia Intellettuale," in Bruno Caizzi, ed., *Antologia della Questione Meridionale,* pp. 383–405.

and yet his political function is carried out simply as an expansion of his personal economic life. He seeks only the support of his own clientele, and does not seek out the broad interests of particular social groups or ideological blocs. As a result, the system produces fewer fulltime professional technicians than is true in the North. Particularly with regard to the parties of the left, this situation is changing sharply in the Mezzogiorno, a subject that will be discussed later.

Culturally, the southern Italian political elite is distinct from that of the rest of the country. The level of education of political leaders is exceptional, probably because of the high value placed upon intellectual attainment in their social class. Remarkably, despite the cultural isolation of many parts of the South and its variety of dialects, the political elite is characterized by quite a homogeneous political culture. Many are versed in the writings of Croce and Salvemini, who once provided a focal point for their aspirations. Further, since the end of the last century, a few great southern Italian statesmen have made an intellectual mark on the thinking of the political elite that orients most toward the problem of the South. The ideological sophistication of their thinking is not notable, and their ideas about political change vary greatly, but most of the political elite is united in considering the Mezzogiorno the colonial possession of the marauding North.[23]

Fascism, with its need for petty functionaries in the provinces, gave the professional middle class the opportunity to firmly entrench itself into these positions of local power too, and to move into the national bureaucracy. These changes had very powerful effects upon the political system. The middle class was freed from dependence upon the land, and internal migration opened landholding to new peasant groups. Local clientele politics was integrated into national political patterns, since provincial officials, although they derived their positions from local prestige, were

23. See the writings of Fortunato, collected in *Il Mezzogiorno e lo Stato Italiano* 2 vols., (Bari, 1911); Croce's most important work on the South is *Storia del Regno di Napoli*. The importance of the Crocian school of philosophy among the southern intelligentsia is analyzed by Gramsci in his article "Alcuni Temi sulla Questione Meridionale," which is reprinted in C. Salinari and M. Spinella, eds., *Antonio Gramsci, Antologia degli Scritti* (Roma, 1963), p. 68.

now responsible to Rome. Finally, the movement of the professional middle class into the bureaucracy and from the provinces to the major cities opened political possibilities to new middle class groups for the first time, and many of them were the sons of peasant families.

However, while changes in social origins, career patterns, and political orientations have become apparent since the end of Fascism, the southern Italian political elite remains basically a class of upper middle class professionals whose participation in politics is part of their personal economic activity. These aspects of the political elite may be examined through the analysis of the Italian parliamentary delegations from 1946 to 1958 made by Giovanni Sartori and a group of associates in their study *Il Parlamento Italiano*.[24]

In terms of their social origins, southern political leaders differ markedly from the political elite in the North. Although a large number of Italian leaders are from upper class backgrounds, most of these leaders (61 percent) are from southern Italy, with 39 percent from the Center-North. Forty-seven percent of the upper middle class leaders in Parliament are from the South, compared to 53 percent from the Center-North. On the other hand, 71 percent of the middle middle class leaders, 85 percent of the lower middle class leaders, and 87 percent of the lower class leaders are from the Center-North, whereas in the South only 29 percent are of middle middle class background, 15 percent are of lower middle class origin, and 13 percent are of lower class background.[25]

In terms of their education, southern leaders include a much larger number of well-educated individuals than Northerners. Although 55 percent of northern Italian leaders and 56 percent of central Italian leaders hold college degrees, 75 percent of political leaders in the South and 77 percent in the Islands hold college degrees and a far larger number of Southerners than Northerners hold the *libera docenza,* a higher degree that confers academic status. Furthermore, whereas 9 percent of northern leaders and 8.5 percent of central leaders have only an elementary school edu-

24. Giovanni Sartori et al., *Il Parlamento Italiano* (Napoli, 1963).
25. Ibid., p. 61.

cation, these groups compose only 1.5 percent and 1.1 percent of the leadership group in the South and the Islands.[26]

In their occupational distribution, the southern political elite is found predominantly in the liberal professions. Slightly more than half of the southerners are found in these fields, while approximately one-third are professionals in the North. A second large group in the South are public officials (10 percent), as compared to about 5.7 percent in the North. Half as many in the South are industrialists, businessmen, or managers (6.6 percent, compared to 12.8 percent in the North).[27]

The most interesting fact about the professional distribution of southern political leaders in comparison to northern is the weakness of full-time political professionals in their ranks. In a political system that is dominated by large-scale bureaucratic parties, less than 15 percent of the southern leaders list their professions primarily as political party careerists, whereas approximately 30 percent of the Northerners look upon themselves primarily as political professionals.[28]

Data on ideology are not found in the Sartori study, and, in any case, this dimension of the political elite will be analyzed in detail in later chapters. However, the prevalence throughout the postwar period of parties of the far right in the South suggests the ideological backwardness of the political leaders. If these groups had possessed coherent Fascist or Monarchist ideologies, some political maturation would at least have been demonstrated by comparison. But they are for the most part vaguely nostalgic negativist movements whose major contribution is to deny the legitimacy of both the governing parties and the extreme left. The word *qualunquismo,* which may be roughly translated as "know-nothing populism," has been coined to designate the attitudes of these groups.

The character of the press in the Mezzogiorno suggests the ideological weakness of the political elite. A study by the southern Italian journal *Nord e Sud* found an overwhelming political conformity among the provincial newspapers of the region, with little

26. Ibid, p. 51.
27. Ibid., p. 50.
28. Ibid.

or no ideological coloring.[29] Opposition is almost always expressed as a cavil to particular policies or to particular individuals, but almost never on ideological grounds. This is most unusual in a country whose political parties have strong ideological traditions.

PATTERNS OF POLITICAL ALLOCATION

In Chapter 2 I analyzed the unequal regional patterns of economic allocation during the development of the national Italian state. These patterns resulted to some extent from the failure of the Mezzogiorno's integration into the unified state, and to some extent from the unequal distribution of political power between the elites of North and South in the national political arena. However, it is not a simple case of northern "colonial exploitation" of the South; it is more nearly true that, while the North produced powerful political groups that geared the activities of the government to the region's capitalistic expansion, the South produced political structures that served only the rather narrow personal interests of the clienteles they represented.

Local politics became the fulcrum of these political structures. Far more than in more advanced areas, local government in the Mezzogiorno is a vital instrument of political and economic allocation; it controls a large number of public positions, the assignment of the communal lands, and the assessment of taxes. Salvemini records how the control of local government became a source of local rivalry among local political leaders in the South. He writes, "The party of the doctor would fight with that of the pharmacist, that of the municipal clerk with that of the teacher, to be able to reach into the heart of local administration where the opportunity lay to distribute favors and express resentments."[30]

Parliamentary elections in the South were won by those who controlled local government and, therefore, patronage. Parliamentary deputies were the delegates of dominant local clienteles, who "bought" national patronage by making their votes available to successive ministries. Southern deputies were the mainstays of the "transformist" ministries that dominated Italian national poli-

29. Nello Ajello e Giovanni Cervigni, "Giornali di Provincia," *Nord e Sud*, 2, No. 7 (1955), 64.

30. "La Piccola Borghesia Intellettuale," pp. 383–405; see also Vöchting, *La Questione Meridionale*, p. 30.

tics from 1876 until the First World War. The existence of a corps of ideologically flexible southern deputies allowed national leaders like Crispi and Giolitti to form ministries out of disparate and poorly organized groups. During the ministries of Giolitti, the techniques of creating rotten boroughs, using the prefecture in elections, and manipulating state patronage to preserve this reservoir of ready votes from the Mezzogiorno were developed. The political dualism of the Italian political system was symbolized in the running of electoral campaigns; while in the North, elections came to depend upon well-organized political and labor groups, in the South the allocation of patronage was sufficient to dominate large numbers of clienteles.

Political allocation in the South, consequently, took the form of patronage and personal favors that individual deputies could channel to their constituencies. The bitter complaint of statesmen like Nitti, Fortunato, and Salvemini was not that these deputies were unsuccessful delegates, but that they sought only personal and narrow goals for their constituents. Their highest achievement was a large protective tariff on wheat to protect large landowners, while the products of small farmers were left unprotected and the price of manufactured goods rose.

Scientific data on parliamentary behavior is only now being collected. A recent study by a research group at Bologna unearthed an interesting fact about Italian parliamentarians.[31] These researchers report that the parliamentary *interrogazione* (a private member's inquiry to a minister) is utilized in Italy predominantly and increasingly by southern deputies. In other words, it is mainly the southern representatives who take advantage of their privilege of asking for information on behalf of constituents. Ironically, they make better delegates for their constituents than Northerners, although most *interrogazioni* involve narrow local interests.

The bureaucracy in the Mezzogiorno, after an early period of disaffection, soon institutionalized the clientele patterns that dominated the political system. In the years following unification, the

31. I wish to thank the Carlo Cattaneo Research Institute for allowing me to refer to this material, which will appear in Italian in *DC e PCI nel Parlamento*, to be published subsequently in an English version in the United States. For an initial treatment, see Giorgio Gulli, *Il Bipartitismo Imperfetto* (Bologna, 1967).

missionary zeal of the Piedmontese administrators evoked bitter
response from individual Southerners unaccustomed to regimen-
tation. But gradually local politics appears to have dominated the
functioning of the state apparatus in the South, rather than vice
versa.

The prefecture is the fulcrum of local public administration in
Italy. Prefects are chosen in Rome, but in the South they are routinely co-opted into local clienteles. In the North, the prefect is a
humble functionary whose duties are performed quietly and apo-
litically. In the South, in contrast, the prefect is the ruler of a petty
kingdom. He is invited to marriages and baptisms, his advice is
sought in business matters, and he is a formidable political figure.
The political ties between local clienteles and the prefects reached
their apex during the ministries of Giolitti in the early twentieth
century, but they remain a typical aspect of southern Italian politics today.[32]

The field offices of the national ministries in the South are per-
meated with clientelismo. This pattern could be noted during the
pre-Fascist era, but the Fascist destruction of Parliament closed off
the center of political allocation in which the southern deputies
had suffered from their lack of cohesion, and elevated the bureaucracy, where Southerners' special talent for informal personal politics was compelling. Second, the increased domination of Southerners in public administration has filled it with officials whose
personal style and political attitudes make them receptive to the
personal demands of southern clienteles. It is ironic that, although
the South had virtually no role in the origin or development of
Fascism, it received a large share of the public works and patronage
allocated by the Fascist regime.

With the massive increase in state expenditures and public
works in the South which began in 1945, the unbalanced regional
allocation of resources has apparently ceased. Yet, ironically, the
domination of bureaucratic practices in the South by cultural
norms of a particularistic and ascriptive cast increases the leverage
of local clienteles in the allocation of state benefits. The result has
been to deflect many policies for regional economic development

32. See the vivid, though exaggerated description in Luigi Barzini, *The Italians*,
"The Problem of the Mezzogiorno," and Robert Fried, *The Italian Prefects* (New
Haven, 1963).

to the advantage of local political groups. A respondent in LaPalombara's study of interest groups underscores this phenomenon; the Cassa per il Mezzogiorno, he maintains, "has become a gigantic patronage organization which employs people and awards developmental contracts strictly on the basis of political considerations." [33] The same is true of the agencies of agrarian reform established in the wake of the massive land reform of the early 1950s.

AUTHORITY AND LEGITIMACY: THE INVERSION OF IDEAL ROLES

The juxtaposition of the institutions of a modern state with the social structures and cultural patterns of southern Italy has resulted in an oblique confrontation of traditional and modern norms and institutions. In a system that denies political access to a majority and confers it upon a minority through structures of questionable legitimacy, the authority of the system is destroyed for the politically inherited and disinherited alike.

The development of this legitimacy vacuum in the Mezzogiorno may be traced historically to the unification process and its aftermath. The identification of the conservative bourgeoisie with the liberal Risorgimento from the North was completed by the new state's allocation of vast landholdings to this group shortly thereafter, at the expense of the remainder of the population. The clientele structure of southern Italy derives from that period and not from feudalism and derives its power from the landholdings conferred upon the bourgeoisie at that time. Moreover, the new state invoked norms and practices alien to the traditional patterns of the South, and spoke a foreign dialect—Italian. The majority of the southern Italian population actually felt an economic loss resulting from unification, while the political elite was established upon a power base whose legitimacy was never accepted. Even today, court cases deriving from the land disputes of the Risorgimento are still being contested.

So poor is the legitimacy of the government in the South that a type of authority adheres to individuals and groups who work outside its sphere or deny its norms. To a great extent, authority roles are actually inverted in the Mezzogiorno. Institutional rules are

33. *Interest Groups,* pp. 344–45. See Chapter 12 below, for a fuller discussion.

followed to the extent that they can be enforced. However, individuals who deny the authority of the institutions gain an authority of their own which extends to the establishment of an antisystem authority system. This inversion of authority roles sustains the development of antistate solidarity and mobility groups and apolitical modes of dissent.

The classical example of the first phenomenon is, of course, the *Mafia*. Much controversy is found regarding the pedigree of the Mafia, and some scholars have tried to establish a relationship to the *compagni d'arme* of the Renaissance. The phenomenon actually arose economically out of the system of estate caretakers on the Sicilian latifundia, and is intimately related to the bourgeois conquest of the land. Culturally, its popularity derives from the myth of the outlaw as the protector of the oppressed; the word itself, as Salvatore Francesco Romano writes, "expressed the idea of quality, valor, superiority, excellence and even graciousness and perfection." [34] The Mafia possesses a very significant hold upon the popular imagination in Sicily and a degree of legitimacy denied the state and the Church.

Contrary to popular belief, the Mafia is not simply an organization of crime or terror. In a political and social system characterized by mobility chasms unassailable by conventional means, the Mafia, like the Neapolitan *Camorra*, provided a mobility channel for aggressive individuals of middle class background. A writer of the late nineteenth century spoke of "the necessity of using the *Mafia* to succeed in life." [35] Its particular pattern of success depended upon its ability to use diversified means to attain its purposes: political power, prestige, or violence.

From the nineteenth century on, the Mafia was political. It merges with the structure of acquaintance that feeds the clientele system of the Mezzogiorno and politicizes social life. Romano, for example, describes his return to a Sicilian town after many years' absence to run as a Communist candidate in a local election. "It is well known," he writes, "that in the provincial centers, one cannot

34. Romano, *Storia della Mafia* (Milano, 1963), p. 31.

35. Sebastiano Cammarari Scurti, in *Critica Sociale* (April 16, 1898). Also see the excellent treatment in Eric Hobsbawm, *Social Bandits and Primitive Rebels* (Glencoe, 1959), Chap. 2.

avoid going to the central piazza, and there meeting with everyone, greeting friends and enemies, family and strangers, and that every encounter and every greeting . . . is observed, noted, commented upon." [36]

The Mafia is political because it is linked to the same intermediate economic roles as the southern political elite. The investigation of Franchetti and Sonnino in 1876 discovered in the Mafia all the characteristics of an intermediate economic group settled in the countryside and involved in all phases of economic activity. Its connection with the government was always oblique. It denied the legitimacy of the norms prescribed by the state, prescribing its own instead while it penetrated public agencies and co-opted political leaders to gain economic ends. Although Fascism had debilitated the Mafia, the appearance of American Military Government in 1943 raised it to immediate power through the appointment of numerous political officials from Mafia ranks. In those early postwar years, the Mafia was dispersed among most of the political parties, and even in the extreme left, but the eventual domination of the state by the Christian Democrats directed Mafia leaders into the higher echelons of that political party.[37]

The Mafia represents an antistate structure of authority, solidarity, and mobility with its own cultural system, a structure that merges with the family structure and the clientele system, and a political orientation that uses the state while denying its legitimacy. It is inaccurate, however, to regard it as opposed to the dominant clientele system; the Mafia is a system of clienteles only distinguished from the norm in the degree of its organization and the extent of its rejection of authority.

Forms of dissent take on unusual configurations in a system of inverted authority roles. Eric Hobsbawm, in his book *Primitive Rebels and Social Bandits,* has shown the relationship of forms of apolitical dissent in southern Italy to the impact of commercialization in the economy. Hobsbawm's analysis also brings out a unique feature not found in typical political modes of dissent: the moral authority of the brigand as a Robin Hood figure. This factor is more closely related to the legitimacy of the state than to the com-

36. Romano, *Storia della Mafia,* p. 24.
37. Michele Pantaleone, *Mafia e Politica, 1943–1962* (Torino, 1962), pp. 95, 231ff.

mercialization of the economy. As a result, all movements of social revolt in the Mezzogiorno from national unification to the present display the same antisocial, anarchic character.[38]

The relation of brigandage to bourgeois domination of the land was evident even before national unification in 1861. In the last decades of the Bourbon regime, bourgeois usurpations of the common lands began to destroy the feudal remnants upon which the peasants depended. A historian of the period writes,

> The landless, seeing themselves disinherited, grew insistent about reclaiming the public land that had been occupied without payment by the new bourgeoisie . . . Not finding support among local leaders who had been elected by the bourgeoisie, frequent uprisings and abandonment to violence recur periodically and at every crisis in the political order.[39]

Peasant uprisings greeted the arrival of Garibaldi at Marsala in 1861, emerging into a full-scale guerrilla war against the hastily formed national guard units of the bourgeoisie. But rather than disappearing with the formation of the new state, brigandage continued as the common domains were parceled out to the bourgeoisie, and a bitter regime of absentee landlordism and government tax increases began.[40]

The brigands were no mere bandits. They actually did repay the abuses of the landowners against the peasants, and these events are an important theme in popular legendry in the South. The brigands occupy a position in popular memory where statesmen, politicians, and clergymen are notably absent. Moreover, the sustenance of the brigands from the villages indicates that theirs was a movement of revolt shared by much of the society. As a parliamentary commission reported,

> The brigand becomes something different, a fantastic being, a symbol of their [the people's] frustrated aspirations, the vindicator of the wrongs done them. He is no longer the assassin, the thief, the man of sack and rapine, but the person whose powers suffice to attain for himself and for others the justice

38. Eric Hobsbawm, *Social Bandits and Primitive Rebels*.
39. Giacomo Racioppi, *Storia dei Moti in Basilicata nel 1860*, p. 144.
40. Franco Molfese, *Storia del Brigantaggio dopo L'Unità*, pp. 99–102.

which the law fails to give. And the man who protects him becomes a hero.[41]

These anarchic modes of dissent were succeeded by a series of agricultural rebellions in the 1890s. The most famous of these, the *Fasci Siciliani*, were spontaneous groups of workers and peasants who attempted work stoppages and stormed the usurped common lands. They were quickly suppressed by groups of proprietors, and their organization was destroyed by the repressive ministry of Crispi.[42]

The First World War and the dislocations it brought caused a series of violent agricultural upheavals in the South which were fanned by the government's hollow promise to appease the peasants by dividing the latifundia. Similar uprisings followed the Second World War with equal fervor. However, in the second case, a modern revolutionary party harnessed the movement. Except for this recent phenomenon, peasant dissent in the Mezzogiorno has preserved the disorganized, antipolitical, antistate quality of early brigandage. Its prevalence is an indication of the depth of the alienation that separates the mass of the population from the national state.

This background of political dissent gives even present-day political movements in the Mezzogiorno an unusual quality. The prevalence of nostalgic fascist movements and separatist parties gave political life just after 1945 the air of unreality. Even the Christian Democrats, pillar of tradition, were compelled to pretend their dedication to the cause of Sicilian separatism in order to establish a following in Sicily. More bizarre still was the momentary glory shortly after World War II of the bandit Salvatore Giuliano, who established a bandit army dedicated to the cause of dislocating Sicily from the Italian state.

The legitimacy vacuum of the Mezzogiorno and the persistence of apolitical modes of dissent presents an intriguing problem: in a political system characterized by the inversion of ideal authority roles, what role will be assumed by a revolutionary mass party? Does it retain the Leninist structure of a party of cadres with a

41. Quoted in Denis Mack Smith, *Italy: A Modern History*, p. 7.

42. Ibid., p. 173; detailed treatment is provided by Salvatore Francesco Romano (pseud. S. Marsilio), *I Fasci Siciliani* (Milano-Roma, 1954).

sophisticated ideology and rigid organization, or does it assume the role of a modern Robin Hood, an ultimate brigand who captures the imagination of the peasantry through a daring challenge to the legitimacy of the state?

THE PROBLEM OF POLITICAL DUALISM

The narrow, personalistic structures of political organization and allocation of the Mezzogiorno reflect the social structure of the region and inhibit its economic development. They prevent the expression of the broad demands of much of the population, and inhibit the expansion of political elites and participation. Moreover, the persistence of apolitical modes of dissent and groups that challenge the authority of the state indicate that disjunctions remain between the aspirations of the society and the structures the social system has produced for their representation.

It is precisely these characteristics that have created and reinforced the dualism of the Italian political system. While interest groups, parties, and electorates have developed in Northern Italy along the lines of most Western European countries, southern Italy has displayed political structures and norms of an entirely different variety. Even an eminently national institution—the bureaucracy —functions differently in North and South.

Political dualism can persist indefinitely in a political system. To an extent, it is a corollary of economic dualism, but like most historical structures, as Schumpeter points out, it develops a logic of its own. The lesson is clear; economic development may result in an integration of the dual economy, but the dual polity may continue to prosper. Not only does political dualism exacerbate existing problems; it *creates* political problems, simply because it exists.

The tensions and problems created by political dualism are of a character and intensity unknown in integrated systems. Tension arises between members of each sectional group; the progress of one sector is seen, with some justice, as a concomitant of the depression of the other. And special governmental efforts on behalf of the more backward sector are resented by the members of the other sector, since they have to pay for whatever programs are created.

Another result of political dualism is to leave the system prone to highly mobilized political movements that claim a special vocation to unify the system. The drama of the appearance of the Communist Party in southern Italy is directly related to the PCI's self-proclaimed unifying mission. Much of the progress of the last twenty years in Italy toward unifying North and South in an integrated political system has been caused by the disturbing presence and pressure of the Italian Communist Party. History, however, is often ironic, for the party's success in bridging the political gap has been gained at the expense of a more fundamental goal.

5. The Italian Communist Party: History and Theory

Of the many cleavages that crisscross Italian politics, regional dualism is but one. It must be understood in combination with deep class divisions, Church-state conflicts, and institutional tensions, all of which paralyze Italian politics, particularly in moments of difficulty. Such a paralysis occurred in 1922, making conciliation between traditional forces of left and right impossible, and allowing the advent of Fascism. So stable are these cleavages that Italian politics may be understood as "stable instability, far more so than politics in the French Fourth Republic, where the sources of cleavage shifted constantly.

As a corollary of the structural cleavages that divide their political system, large numbers of Italians provide social scientists with a favored specimen: the alienated citizen. Gabriel Almond has called Italy an "isolate political culture," and the Italian respondents interviewed by Almond and Verba in *The Civic Culture* were unique for the degree of their political suspicion, cynicism, and disaffection. Interpreting these results, Joseph LaPalombara writes,

> In his attitudes toward government, his identification with the nation and its political institutions, his reactions to public policy, his views concerning third persons and voluntary organizations and his sense of involvement in the political process, the Italian is far removed from the kinds of citizens one finds in countries like the United States or Great Britain.[1]

Italian political institutions buttress the divisions. The multiparty system, for example, institutionalizes alienation, polarizing opinion and creating relatively unstable majorities. As Giovanni

1. Joseph LaPalombara, "Italy: Fragmentation, Isolation, Alienation," in Lucian W. Pye and Sidney Verba, eds., *Political Culture and Political Development* (Princeton, 1965), p. 282.

Sartori writes, "The net result is a byzantine and undecipherable party system whose end product is overcomplication and confusion. . . . The complexity of the political system is in itself a powerful agent of alienation." [2]

Italian Communism is the major expression of the deep social and territorial cleavages that mark Italian society. For over 25 percent of Italy's voters, Communism represents a legitimate alternative to the country's present government; almost half, on the other hand, consider it the embodiment of the antichrist. In a curious way, however, it contains many of the country's most salient cultural features: its ideology has strong national features; its goals appeal to broad strata of the population; it crystallizes the alienation and disaffection that permeate every major group in the society. In other words, in a society in which lack of consensus is virtually universal, and alienation is a norm, a political party that makes dissent into a science has an almost mythical appeal even to those strata of the population that oppose its ideology.

THE THEORY OF DEVOTION AND COMBAT

Our present body of theory about Communist parties in the West helps little in understanding the Partito Comunista Italiano, the PCI. Western political scientists have often ascribed a ferocity and discipline to Communist parties in advanced capitalist countries that the parties' leaders might wish they possessed. Curiously, the factors often emphasized are precisely those that have become less salient in Marxist parties in the West.

For example, in *Political Parties,* Duverger presents a model of what he at one stage calls a "devotee party," and which he describes as a modification of the "conception of the party as a class; it is the party conceived as the elite." [3] The devotee party therefore differs fundamentally from the old-fashioned party of notables (or "cadres," in Duverger's lexicon) and from the mass party. Its members pledge their "whole human being" to their party, a commitment "which admits of no distinction between public and private life,"

2. Giovanni Sartori, "European Political Parties: The Case of Polarized Pluralism," in Joseph LaPalombara and Myron Weiner, eds., *Political Parties and Political Development* (Princeton, 1966), p. 152.

3. Maurice Duverger, *Political Parties* (2d rev. ed., New York, 1965), p. 70.

and fosters "an irrational attachment, founded on myths and beliefs of a religious nature." [4]

Devotee parties have a distinctive structure, for Duverger. "In contrast to the semi-decentralization of the socialist (mass) parties, they have in common a very strict centralization, a system of vertical links ensuring that the elements at the base are strictly divided into cells," and they have a "leadership based on autocratic methods." [5] The mass parties, on the other hand, depend upon the branch or section at the capillary level. While they have "authentic separation of powers," they too are highly centralized, for inside them "powerful oligarchic tendencies manifest themselves." [6]

The strategy of the devotee party is also distinctive, for Duverger, for it specializes in "unceasing propaganda and agitation, using direct and sometimes violent methods, strikes, sabotage, incidents, etc." It operates in the parliamentary arena, but the instrumental nature of this participation is demonstrated by the weakness of its parliamentary representatives within the party in contrast to the "apparachiki," who pull the strings.[7]

Closely related to Duverger's formulation is the theory of the "combat party," developed by Philip Selznick in *The Organizational Weapon*. Although he cautions the reader that this model is most relevant where Communist doctrine is unappealing to the population set up as a target, Selznick nevertheless maintains that it "provides a fair interpretation of the Communist vanguard or combat party, wherever it is found." [8]

Whereas Duverger's description is directed toward the outward structure of the party, Selznick is more interested in what he calls "latent structure," a concept based upon the combat party's distinctive ability "to turn members of a voluntary association into disciplined and deployable political agents." [9] As a result, the essence of the party is found not in the straightforward data of the organizational chart, but in the shadowy world of manipulation and deception.

4. Ibid., p. 2.
5. Ibid.
6. Ibid., pp. 1–2.
7. Ibid., p. 2.
8. Philip Selznick, *The Organizational Weapon* (Glencoe, 1960), p. vi.
9. Ibid., p. xii.

The combat party is defined by its capacity for infiltration and subversion, in particular by (1) its capacity "to deploy members as controlled agents within target groups," (2) its use of techniques of indoctrination and mobilization that withdraw the member from other group loyalties," (3) "its adoption of subversion," and (4) "the penetration and manipulation of institutional targets." [10]

Selznick's model is related to Duverger's, particularly in the importance attached to the party's control of the "total being" of the militant and in its concentration upon conspiratorial activity. Both are deeply indebted to Lenin's *What Is to Be Done?*, but Selznick's is the more extreme version, since its emphasis upon deception gives it an occult quality. In his view we cannot subscribe to anything a Communist leader says about his intentions, since his "operational code" depends upon deception. The combat party is thus something of a self-fulfilling prophecy.

A third attempt to characterize Communist parties, and one closely related to Selznick's, is Gabriel Almond's *The Appeals of Communism*. Here, again, the cue is provided by Lenin, for Almond concentrates on revealing the distinction in the Communist operational model between the party elite and its mass following. The leader is seen as a "power-oriented tactician" (a characterization with which it would be difficult to quarrel when dealing with *any* politician), whereas the mass following is seen as being primarily an object of agitation.[11] Almond analyzes the content of Communist Party internal and external literature to demonstrate that two fundamentally opposed communication systems—an esoteric and an exoteric one—divide elite cadres from mass following.[12] There is probably nothing about *The Appeals of Communism* with which Lenin would have disagreed.

When we turn to the Italian Communist Party, probably the best treatment is Giovanni Sartori's paper "European Political Parties: The Case of Polarized Pluralism." [13] But instead of Selz-

10. Ibid., p. xv.

11. Gabriel Almond, *The Appeals of Communism* (Princeton, 1957), pp. 5–6.

12. Ibid., Chap. 3. Note that, whereas Almond's theoretical treatment of the Communist Party "model" is quite close to those of Duverger and Selznick, his empirical materials in the second half of the book suggest that the French and Italian parties must be understood in a less rigid framework.

13. In LaPalombara and Weiner, eds., *Political Parties*, pp. 144–48.

nick's emphasis on the party's capacity to withdraw members from other group loyalties, Sartori speaks of "the ability of the party's organizational network to produce a culturally manipulated isolation of given social groups in given areas." [14] He shares Almond's concern with "the dual nature of Communist organization—a party of elite with mass following," but he disagrees with Duverger's emphasis upon the cell by speaking of the organizational incapsulation and cultural saturation that a Communist *network* is capable of producing." [15] The term "network" applies to party front groups and mass organizations.

However, Sartori goes a lot further than any of the other three writers in his conception of the Communist Party's role in the political system. Although Duverger, Selznick, and Almond do indeed discuss the subversive aspects of Communist activity, Sartori writes, "We thus come to the uncomfortable paradox that the Communist party would make for an excellent opposition if it were an opposition, i.e., a possible alternative government. But since it would replace the *system* as well as the people, the net result is that the country is deprived of its best potential elites." [16]

Although no one would deny the Italian Communist Party's opposition to the present Italian regime, it is quite another story to consider it outside the system. Sartori presses home the point in his series of manipulative hypotheses. He maintains, first, that "an extreme centrifugal development is very likely wherever the political system accepts not only as legal but also as a legitimate and somewhat equal and normal competitor a party (or parties) which oppose the very system, such as a Communist Party." Second, he adds, "Such a centrifugal development will not necessarily follow . . . if the existence of anti-system parties is legally prohibited." [17]

Apart from the fact that these "hypotheses," if realized, would not make for a very democratic theory,[18] Sartori's article (which,

14. Ibid., p. 145.
15. Ibid., pp. 145–147. Emphasis added.
16. Ibid., p. 147. Emphasis added.
17. Ibid., p. 170.
18. See Sartori's excellent *Democratic Theory* (New York, 1965). The problem of the efficacy of legal prohibition may perhaps be settled by a consideration of the history of the German Social Democratic Party in the nineteenth century; the party's illegal status first, and its legalization after, seemed to have made no difference either

incidentally, is a brilliant treatment of the Italian party system) raises the following question: Are we justified in regarding the Italian Communist Party as an antisystem, as well as an antigovernment, party? Does the PCI confirm or deny the basic characteristics of the party of devotion and combat described by Duverger, Selznick, Almond, and other writers? Do its history, ideology, membership, leadership, organization, and behavior within the system justify us in identifying the PCI as the close-knit elite Leninist model that is the basis of so much Western writing on Marxism? In this chapter and the next, I will deal with this problem in some depth as a general introduction to the analysis of the PCI in southern Italy which follows.

HISTORICAL DEVELOPMENT

Like most of the Communist parties of Western Europe, the Italian Communist Party (PCI) was a product of the inner conflicts of a socialist movement. The Socialist Party, founded in Italy in 1894 by Filippo Turati, had long been divided between a group of reformists and a radical "maximalist" wing influenced by the teachings of Bakunin and the anarchosyndicalists.[19] Underlying doctrinal disputes was a dichotomy in the composition of the party; although its leaders were drawn mainly from the intellectuals of Turin, Milan, and Genoa, its most substantial support came from the agricultural proletariat of the Po valley, members of the National Federation of Workers of the Land (Federterra). Between 1900 and 1926 these agricultural workers were far better organized than Italian industrial workers, and were far more militant than the bourgeois leaders of the Partito Socialista Italiano (PSI).[20] In the resulting intraparty factionalism, control of the leadership passed from the reformists to the maximalists, of whom Benito Mussolini was an important leader.

---

to its growing membership or its tendency to support the system in 1914; see Douglas A. Chalmers, *The Social Democratic Party of Germany* (New Haven, 1964), p. 5.

19. A. Romano, *Storia del Movimento Socialista in Italia* (3 vols. Milano-Roma, 1954), *1*, Chap. 3; *3*, Chap. 1.

20. See the Introduction by Renato Zangheri in the Congressional Records of the Federazione Nazionale dei Lavoratori della Terra, collected in *Lotte Agrarie in Italia* (Milano, 1960); G. Procacci, "Geografia e Struttura del Movimento Contadino della Valle Padana," *Studi Storici, 5*, No. 1 (1964), 45.

World War I and the Russian Revolution crystallized these conflicts and gave rise to a third group within the party which favored the exploitation of the war for internal revolution. It later advocated complete abstention from parliamentary activity after moderate leaders had gained 156 seats in the Chamber of Deputies. Foremost among these elements in the party were the strident group headed by Amedeo Bordiga in Naples, and a number of creative young intellectuals at Turin, led by Gramsci, Togliatti, Terracini, and Tasca, whose ideas had emerged from the industrial movement in that most modern of Italian cities.[21]

The immobilism of the moderate Socialist leadership and the immaturity of the maximalists led this new group to prepare to leave the party during the chaotic years following World War I. This determination was only heightened by the postwar success of the moderates at the polls, when Turati had said: "Universal suffrage, when it is used self-consciously, is the most formidable weapon . . . for every conquest.[22] The radical Italian Socialist delegation to the 1920 Congress of the Third International accepted the International's Twenty-one Conditions, among which was the requirement that parties belonging to the International should expel reformists. At the Seventeenth Congress of the PSI in Leghorn in January 1921, this motion was rejected by the delegates and the radicals walked out to form the *Partito Comunista d'Italia* as a section of the Communist International.[23]

The paroxysm of schism and foundation gave the party an immediate élan of unity, evident in its Organic Act of Constitution, which accepted all of Lenin's theses. The theses proclaimed the imminent dissolution of capitalism and the necessity of armed conflict between the workers and the bourgeois state, the hegemonic role of the proletarian party, and the goal of the destruction of the bourgeois state and the immediate establishment of a dictator-

---

21. Mario Einaudi, Jean-Marie Domenach, and Aldo Garosci, *Communism in Western Europe* (Ithaca, 1953); Giorgio Galli, *Storia del Partito Comunista Italiano* (Milano, 1958), pp. 28–29.

22. Filippo Turati, "Discorso detto al Congresso Socialista di Bologna, 7 ottobre 1919," p. 29, *Atti del Partito Socialista Italiano*, n.d.

23. Einaudi, Domenach, and Garosci, pp. 158–59; Galli, *Storia del Partitio*, pp. 44–47; the relative documents are collected in *Come si Costituii il Partito Comunista d'Italia*, Roma, n.d.

ship of the proletariat.[24] However, this declaration disguised great differences in ideology and style within the new party. Bordiga and his group, centered in Naples where industry barely existed, saw the conquest of the state as the first step in the construction of socialism.[25] The other axis of the new party, the group around Gramsci and *L'Ordine Nuovo* of Turin, was unorthodox in a different way. Gramsci's experiences, gathered in the industrial ferment of Turin, showed him means by which the capitalist state could be transformed *from within* as a preparation for the workers' revolution. Here, Gramsci's group had established the *Consigli di Fabbrica,* workers' councils which aimed at workers' gradual assumption of the control of production. In 1919, Gramsci wrote: "The socialist state already exists potentially in the institutions of the social life of the exploited working class. To tie these institutions together . . . to centralize them powerfully . . . means creating from then on a true and real worker's democracy." These concepts, which developed logically from Gramsci's interpretation of the nature of Italian society, met the immediate opposition of Bordiga, who wrongly called them "reformist experiments." [26]

Gramsci, seeking to lay the groundwork for an "Italian" road to Communism, soon moved closer to the positions of the International in order to remove Bordiga and the extremists from power and to become the political and intellectual leader of the party. The evolution of Gramsci's ideas in this early period and his relation to the International are summed up in his theses for the Lyon Congress of 1926. In this document he set out his interpretation of the "conditions" of Italian society, adopted the organizational principles for the "bolshevization" of the party, and also adopted the Leninist tactic of "partial actions," even when "such actions would not directly better the workers' conditions." [27]

24. Galli, pp. 23–24.

25. "L'Estremismo, Malattia Infantile del Comunismo," in V. Lenin, *Opere Scelte* (Mosca, 1948), pp. 617–18.

26. Antonio Gramsci, *Antologia degli Scritti, 1,* 36–49; for Bordiga's reactions, see *Il Soviet,* Napoli (11 giugno 1920).

27. The theses of Lyon can be found in *Trent' Anni di Vita e Lotta del PCI* (Roma, 1952); an interpretation that sees the period as a submission to orthodoxy is found in Galli, *Storia del Partito,* pp. 117–23; however, that there were real doctrinal issues between Gramsci and the left seems clear in his *Verbale della Com-*

But it was already too late. In a critical respect, Gramsci and the Turin faction differed little from Bordiga and the extremists: they failed to appreciate the radically new nature of Fascism. Mussolini had taken power in 1922 by means of the social convulsions of lower middle class groups with the support of large industry and the complicity of the police and the monarchy. Continuing for several years to operate through parliament, Mussolini nevertheless began to dismantle traditional guarantees of speech and political organization. Yet in May 1925, Gramsci could still characterize Fascism simply as another version of the conservative Italian liberal state: "The old agrarian social forces, originally anticapitalist, and coordinated traditionally with capitalism although not absorbed by it, have taken control of the organization of the state." [28] He expected that capitalism had merely been pushed a step further toward catastrophe and would surely reach its crisis in a few years' time.

Failing to understand the radically new nature of Fascism, the PCI did not recognize the need to band together with other anti-Fascist groups. These groups, foremost among them the Socialists and the Christian Democrats of Don Luigi Sturzo, seceded from parliament and met in "exile" on the Roman Aventine. The PCI eventually joined the Aventine secession, but refused to seek the reestablishment of constitutional government, and continued to make violent attacks against the non-Communist parties.

The failure to interpret Fascism correctly also led to an inadequate preparation for clandestine activity. When, between 1926 and 1929, Mussolini was powerful enough to "relieve" anti-Fascist deputies of their parliamentary rank and to declare the PCI illegal, all the party's national leaders and hundreds of provincial leaders were arrested and imprisoned.

Some preparation for illegal activity was begun during the late 1920s. A foreign center was established, first in Switzerland and then in Paris, and a system of couriers was set up to assure the party a communications network in the event of its going underground.

missione Politica per il Congresso di Lione, reproduced in Critica Marxista, 1, Nos. 5-6 (1963), 302-26; the quotation on "partial actions" is from Einaudi, et al., pp. 166-67.

28. Trent' Anni di Vita, pp. 93-94.

At the same time, a secret domestic center was maintained which was continually destroyed and reestablished until 1932, when the party executive declared it to be too dangerous.[29]

The organization of the PCI during the twenty-two years of Fascism was under great strain, with constant defections and arrests, and long periods with no communication between the various regional groups and the leadership. After 1932, the PCI concentrated its activities on the Italian émigrés in France and on support for the Loyalists in Spain. Domestic work in Italy was limited by breakdown of regular communication between the leadership and the regional cadres. This had two important results for Italian Communism. First, the bewildering series of shifts in party line emanating from Moscow in the 1930s was read by few Italians as a reflection on the Italian Communist Party. The Hitler-Stalin Pact, which crippled many European Communist parties, was signed while the Italian Communists were working clandestinely. By the time the party renewed domestic activity, Russia had been invaded and the International had returned to an anti-Fascist line. Thus when legal political activity began again after World War II, the PCI, unlike its French, German, and American counterparts, had a relatively clean slate. It has never ceased to profit from this record.

Second, the long period of underground activity left the control of local activity in the hands of regional groups. This was of little importance in the 1930s, but when partisan activity began in 1942, local PCI leaders were ready to take control of local resistance groups. The PCI was therefore identified forever after as the leader of the armed Resistance, one of the few glorious chapters in modern Italian history. Moreover, PCI regional cadres developed an expertise and an independence that helped them rapidly build a territorial organization after the war. It remains true today that the PCI is virtually the only Italian political party with a creative and efficient regional leadership.

Italy entered the Second World War in 1940, and by 1942 the PCI was in control of the factories and of the partisan brigades in

29. Einaudi, et al., p. 180; Galli, pp. 220–26. The activities of the PCI in World War II are documented in Giorgio Amendola, ed., *Il Comunismo Italiano nella Seconda Guerra Mondiale* (Roma, 1963), pp. 3–19.

the North, and had begun to infiltrate Fascist mass organizations. Between 1942 and 1944, a series of successful strikes were carried out in Turin and Milan, and contact was reestablished with myriads of party cells which had patiently awaited liberation in isolation. The arrest of Mussolini and the formation of the Badoglio provisional government in 1943 led to the liberation of surviving political prisoners from Fascist jails. A Communist was made co-leader of the national labor organization taken over from the Fascists and, before long, the party was in active control of this important parapolitical organization.[30]

The Soviet Union's strategy in 1943 aimed at sublimating the revolutionary aims of the movement to the war effort against Hitler, and mollifying the Allies by nonrevolutionary policies in liberated areas. Thus, the Comintern was dissolved, a moderate stance was taken at Yalta, and Communist Party leaders returning from exile sought the formation of national front governments.

On his return to Italy in 1944, Palmiro Togliatti took over the leadership of the PCI and appeared to develop this strategy. Speaking to the recently liberated people of Naples, he said: "We are the party of the working class: but the working class has never been foreign to the interests of the nation. We will no longer be a small, restricted association of propagandists for the general ideas of Communism." [31] Accordingly, the party's activities from 1943 forward were directed at: (1) pursuing the war effort and beginning national reconstruction; (2) developing a policy of collaboration and conciliation with other parties and classes in the name of national solidarity; and (3) holding in check the revolutionary potential of the workers and preventing the formation of other parties which could exploit this potential.[32] Its dual goals were preventing isolation from the right and upstaging from the left, and it formulated a program of national solidarity and renewal rather than working class militance and revolution.

In the meantime, a Committee of National Liberation (CLN) of various political parties had been formed to coordinate the Resistance in the North and to form a provisional government in Rome.

30. Einaudi, et al., p. 177.

31. *Rinascita* (29 agosto 1944), p. 4.

32. Galli, p. 219; also see *Il Comunismo Italiano nella Seconda Guerra Mondiale,* pp. 20–34.

So anxious was the PCI to build ties across the whole political spectrum during that period, that its policies in the CLN risked the alienation of the Socialists and the center-left Action Party.[33]

As the war drew to a close, a government was formed in Rome, first with the participation of all six anti-Fascist parties, and from 1946 onward with a triparty coalition of Communists, Socialists, and Christian Democrats. Although a Unity of Action Pact had brought the PCI and the Socialists into close collaboration, the PCI was unable to gain control of the government through this alliance. The Christian Democrats emerged as the strongest party in the country, and ultimate control of the government rested in the hands of the Allied Control Commission, which carefully excluded the left from critical cabinet positions.[34]

The Communist leadership, firmly believing that the party could come to power by electoral means, strove to keep militant elements under control to avoid the wrath of the Allies and to gain the allegiance of the demoralized middle class. Many radicals, often heroes of the Resistance, were removed from positions of leadership, and arms caches were surrendered to the state. As a result of the PCI's moderation, many Fascist functionaries remained in the Italian bureaucracy, and some industrialists who had been heavily compromised by their association with Fascism regained their positions. Frustration with these moderate policies within the party was symbolized in the general strike that followed the attempt on Togliatti's life in 1948, when party leaders refused to use the opportunity for an insurrection. The Roman crowds shouted "Dacci Via" ("Show us the way"), and party leaders sent them to their homes.[35]

Contrary to the party's high expectations, the PCI and its Socialist allies received only 31.0 percent of the vote in the general elections of 1948. The Christian Democrats, aided by the massive

33. Galli, p. 223.

34. For the events of this interesting period, see Norman Kogan, *Italy and the Allies* (Cambridge, Mass., 1956), and H. Stewart Hughes, *The United States and Italy* (Cambridge, Mass., 1953). Both works indicate that the doctrinal and political innovations in Italian Communism that later became the *Via Italiana al Socialismo* had their origin in the international situation at the end of World War II.

35. In the North, where factories had been protected from Nazi sabotage by Communist units of the partisan movement, an attempt was made to operate these factories by workers' groups, but it was shortly dropped by the party in favor of a policy of reconstitution of capitalism. Einaudi, et al., pp. 185–87; Galli, pp. 291–93.

intervention of the Church and the lavish expenditures of American intelligence, gained 48.4 percent of the vote. From 1953 to 1963, the Christian Democrats received between 42.3 percent and 38.3 percent of the vote. They were enabled to govern by means of shaky coalitions with the minor parties of the center-left or the right, who were united on little else than their opposition to Communism. The Communists, simultaneously, raised their percentage of the vote with each general election, but their alliance with the Socialists eroded to the point that now a Communist-Socialist government would be unthinkable. Since 1963, the country has been governed by a center-left government which has succeeded in involving the Socialist Party in a regime that has made few structural reforms. Table 5.1 summarizes the division of the electorate among the various parties in the general elections between 1948 and 1963.

TABLE 5.1

General Elections to the Chamber of Deputies

Percentage of Vote by Party

	1948 (1946)[a]	1953	1958	1963
Mass Parties				
Communists (PCI)	19.0	22.6	22.7	25.3
Socialists (PSI)	20.7	12.8	14.2	13.8
Christian Democrats (DC)	48.5	40.1	42.4	38.2
Minor Parties				
Social Democrats (PSDI)	7.1	4.5	4.5	6.0
Republicans (PRI)	2.5	1.6	1.4	1.4
Liberals (PLI)	3.8	3.0	3.5	7.0
Monarchists (PNM and PDIUM)	2.8	6.9	4.9	1.7
Neo-Fascists (MSI)	2.0	5.8	4.8	5.2

[a] For the Communists and Socialists, 1946 figures are provided since the two parties presented a unified slate in 1948.

Source: *Elezione della Camera dei Deputati*, Vol. 1, *Risultati desunti dai Verbali Elettorali di Sezione* (Roma, 1950, 1955, 1960, and 1965).

In the meantime, within the Communist Party the national front policy of the immediate postwar years has been expanded into the *Via Italiana al Socialismo*. Despite its failure to gain power legally, the PCI still foreswears revolution. It seeks "a form of socialist society based upon . . . our traditions of a multiparty system, on full respect for constitutional guarantees, and for religious and cultural liberties." [36] The theme of "rebirth" has been heightened to attract the entire population to Communism, particularly the "productive middle classes."

Dissatisfaction with these policies and with the PCI's failure to gain power smoldered among the party's lower and middle leadership from 1948 onward. The party's internal polemics concentrated most sharply upon these "sectarian elements" for whom Marxist revolution and Stalinist bayonets were indissolubly linked in their conception of the proper Via Italiana al Socialismo. These groups had formed the backbone of the party's organization since the clandestine period, an experience that led them to be less patient with Togliatti and more devoted to the Soviet model of revolution than was he. Many of them were expelled during these early years, and many others were relegated to relatively obscure posts in the party bureaucracy. Their existence underscored the party's basic strategic problem: establishing itself as a legitimate force within the Italian political system while maintaining the vision of the future socialist society. Or, as stated by one acute analyst of the PCI, the dilemma was "how to move in the directions necessary to increase its prestige and influence in the circumstances of Italian life without at the same time losing the qualities that give it special advantages and distinguished it so sharply from other participants in the political game." [37]

The death of Stalin and events in Poland and Hungary in 1955–56 brought about a series of defections and expulsions. The rebels complained that "the PCI is no longer the vanguard of the Italian democratic and socialist worker's movement . . . but the organized ideological expression of the most miserable and discontented strata." [38]

Although it was clear that much of the tension generated in the Italian party came from the sectarians, an increasingly articulate "new left" began to criticize Togliatti's leadership after 1956. As

36. See the *Promemoria* of Togliatti in *Rinascita* (settembre 1964), p. 1.

37. Donald L. M. Blackmer, *Italian Communism and the International Communist Movement* (Cambridge, Mass., mimeograph, 1966), pp. 179–80.

38. Fabrizio Onofri, *Classe Operaia e Partito* (Bari, 1957), p. 183.

the sectarians were more and more isolated as a result of the de-Stalinization campaign, the new left became the major disruptive factor in the PCI. But unlike the old left, its members did not criticize the fundamentals of the Via Italiana. Instead they put more emphasis on trade union action and upon workers' democracy, seeking legitimacy in the early writings of Gramsci and finding concrete support in the Communist youth movement.[39]

The important fact about the new left is that it did not share the sectarians' faith in the Soviet model and criticized Togliatti, not for his participation in the Italian system, but because this participation was not sufficiently dynamic. In this sense, there is a common purpose in the criticisms leveled at the party bureaucracy from left and right within its ranks. This convergence and opposition should be borne in mind when we consider the PCI's behavior within the system.

Succeeding years brought into clearer focus the fact that sharp cleavages divided the party as to its goals and methods and its relations with the international Communist movement. The elements on the right want to look more deeply than Khrushchev (or Togliatti) into the causes of Stalinism, and to bring the PCI into closer alignment with the rest of the Italian political spectrum. The left, still weak in the highest councils of the party, seeks more internal democracy in order to make its views better known. Its leaders would like a far stiffer line in labor disputes: "The bosses are *still* the bosses," they are fond of saying.

The party's conflicts have grown continually. Every party congress and conference since 1956 has been full of ominous rumblings. The 1956 Congress, which met shortly after Khrushchev's epochal revelations on Stalin, forced changes in the party structure that allowed more internal discussion. Similarly, the debate of the Central Committee on the Twenty-second Congress of the Soviet Communist Party was marked by outright dissatisfaction with the noncommittal report of Togliatti.[40]

The political genius of Togliatti—whom his enemies called the

39. Blackmer, pp. 329–33.

40. Reprinted in "Report on the Debate of the Central Committee of the PCI on the Twenty-second Congress of the CPSU," *New Left Review*, Nos. 13–14 (April–June 1962), pp. 152–92.

greatest brain in Italian politics—kept the storm from breaking. By carefully balancing his statements, using persuasion rather than the expulsion of dissident elements, and focusing attention upon the country's deteriorating political situation, he was able to preserve party unity. But so attentive was he to antagonize neither left nor right that his speeches and writings often give an impression of great confusion and casuistry. For example, in his *Partito Comunista Italiano,* he wrote: "The advance toward socialism cannot and will not not occur in our country in a way that is different from the way it has occurred in the Soviet Union and elsewhere." [41]

Togliatti's death in August 1964 has left the PCI in the hands of his long-time collaborator and friend, Luigi Longo. Longo's administration is generally seen as an interim one before the party decides which of its two factions will succeed to power. Longo attempted to keep the Via Italiana alive by the surprise publication of Togliatti's *Promemoria on the Problems of the International Workers' Movement and Its Unity.* Its messages are fourfold: (1) The Chinese question is being badly handled; (2) the Communist movement in the West is stagnating; (3) polycentrism in world Communism must increase; and (4) freedom in the U.S.S.R. is too slow in coming.[42] The impact of the "Promemoria" both in Italy and abroad was dramatic. It has created the conviction among many that Togliatti's Italian road to socialism is a lasting concept and that the Italian Communist Party is the most liberal force in world Communism today.

Is the Via Italiana simply a sophisticated Russian ploy in the Cold War, or does it constitute a serious theoretical revision in Marxist strategy? Is it "outside" the Italian system, or has Togliatti succeeded in finding a formula to make the working class "of" the society as well as "in" it? There is a good deal of evidence that, in its theoretical structure as well as in its behavior within the Italian system, the PCI represents something new in world Communism, something that attempts to synthesize revisionism and Leninism, democracy and socialism, liberty and progress. The shape of this "new party," as will appear in both its ideology and behavior, is not

41. Palmiro Togliatti, *Il Partito Comunista Italiano* (Roma, 1961), p. 70.
42. *Rinascita* (settembre 1964), p. 1.

unambiguous, and in many ways it has failed to maintain the delicate balance it has attempted to establish.

PATTERNS OF IDEOLOGY

The measure of the internal revolution the PCI has undergone since its formation is the theoretical distance that separates its earlier leaders—in particular, its founder Gramsci—from its present-day leaders. This is paradoxical, since the official PCI view is that both in theory and practice the party is faithful to all of Gramsci's teachings. But except in several crucial particulars that will be elaborated below, the difference between Gramsci and Togliatti is the difference between Leninism and something else, something we should hesitate to call "revisionism" because "revisionism" is such a slippery concept.

The difference between Gramsci and Togliatti appears particularly in three essential aspects of Communist Party theory: (1) in the acceptance or rejection of particular institutions of bourgeois society, (2) in the conception of the role that various groups and classes have to play on the road to socialism, and (3) in the strategy for the conquest of power.

The Institutions of Bourgeois Society

Although neither Gramsci nor Togliatti reject the need to utilize the institutions of bourgeois society—a position that would be thoroughly unmarxist—they differ fundamentally in their conceptions of where the forces of production end and bourgeois institutions begin. For Gramsci, law, parliament, and the ordinary administration of the state were artifacts of bourgeois society and therefore to be rejected. In 1919, while still a leader of the old PSI, Gramsci wrote:

> We are persuaded . . . that the socialist state cannot be embodied in the institutions of the capitalist state, but is a fundamentally new experience with respect to that state, if not with respect to the history of the proletariat. The institutions of the capitalist state are organized for the goals of free competition: it will not suffice to change its personnel to move off in another direction.[43]

43. Antonio Gramsci, *L'Ordine Nuovo, 1919–1920* (Torino, 1955), p. 17.

Not only were Italian political institutions unchangeably bourgeois; they did not even arrive at the standards of free competition of most advanced Western states. In fact, in the failure of its institutions to provide an "equilibrium" between various social groups, Gramsci thought Italian society was strikingly similar to society in Czarist Russia.

> The Italian state . . . has never even tried to mask the open dictatorship of the propertied classes. . . . In capitalist states which are called liberal-democratic, the major institution for the protection of popular liberties is the judicial power: in the Italian state, the law is not an independent power, it is an instrument of executive order, an instrument of the Crown and of the propertied classes.[44]

The liberal state is born from the equilibrium of the forces of industry and agriculture, an equilibrium that operates through the institution of parliament. Czarist Russia, governed by an autocracy, suffered from a disequilibrium between the power of landed property and the weakness of industry. Liberal Italy was formed by the "brutal subjection of agriculture to the interests of industry; the Italian state was never liberal, because it wasn't born from a system of equilibrium."[45] In its internal dynamics, therefore, Gramsci thought the Italian state was more like the backward Russian autocracy than its Western European neighbors.

In much the same key, Gramsci rejected the traditional parties and trade unions as being artifacts designed to serve the working class only during the capitalist period. In 1920, he wrote,

> The real process of the proletarian revolution cannot be identified with the development and the action of revolutionary organizations of a voluntary and contractual type such as the political party and the professional trade unions: organizations born in the field of bourgeois democracy, born in the field of political liberty as an affirmation and development of political liberty.[46]

44. Ibid., p. 73.
45. Ibid., p. 75.
46. Ibid., p. 103.

It should be added that this criticism was aimed mainly at traditional parties, but that for Gramsci a fundamental revision in the nature of the proletarian party was necessary to make the revolution.

For Togliatti, on the other hand, not only the trade unions and a system of political parties, but also parliament and the ordinary administration of the state are institutions that can be included in a socialist society. He writes, "It is impossible, in Italy, to conceive realistically of the advance toward socialism outside the fabric of Italian democratic life, outside of the struggle for the objectives that interest the entire society." [47] And in his famous polemic against the Chinese, Togliatti writes:

> To say then, as they [the Chinese] do, that we will be reduced to social democratic opportunism because we see the passage to socialism by means of the conquest of 51 percent of the votes, is a fatuous statement. *Parliament is part of the political structure of a democratic society and can have a higher or a lower degree of representativeness and of democratic functionality,* a factor which either reduces or increases its importance and the possibility to carry out in it an activity that is more than simply one of denunciation or agitation.[48]

There is a developmental emphasis in Togliatti's willingness to work within parliament. The delicate basis of modern industrial society would be destroyed were its political institutions to be overthrown. The result, for Togliatti, would be tragic for the working classes. He affirms,

> In Western Europe . . . a socialist solution that destroys the bases of the economic and political power of the capitalist bourgeoisie must not only secure bread and work, but must be able to guarantee a high rhythm of productive development, to set in motion an economic plan in which individual initiative finds a place, to lead the society while still guaranteeing an ample system of political liberties and autonomies." [49]

47. *Rinascita* (29 agosto 1944), p. 1.
48. Palmiro Togliatti, *Sul Movimento Operaio Internazionale* (Roma, 1964), p. 343. Emphasis added.
49. Ibid., p. 344.

The emphasis upon higher stages of development and its contrast with Gramsci's conviction that Italy was as backward as Czarist Russia, is notable. For Gramsci, the revolution in Italy was justified in part by the country's underdevelopment and the oppressiveness of its bourgeois institutions; for Togliatti, parliamentary and other bourgeois institutions are accepted precisely because of the advanced nature of Italian society. Between the two conceptions lies not only forty-five years, but also a fundamentally different way of viewing reality.

Groups and Classes

It may seem curious to distinguish between two Marxist thinkers in terms of their attitude toward social classes, but in fact Gramsci and Togliatti differ fundamentally in this crucial aspect of their ideology. Gramsci conceived social groups in selective but dialectical terms; Togliatti's thinking is marked by inclusive and additive concepts of class.

For both thinkers, of course, the working class forms the necessary basis of the party. Yet in both there appears to be an initial ambivalence between the concept of the worker and that of the laborer (*classe operaia* and *classe lavoratrice*). Gramsci resolved the problem, natural to a proletarian party seeking a wider network of support, by pointing out that the party "vulgarizes its doctrine" by appealing to the entire laboring class. The vulgarization is justified by the fact that "the entire laboring class is destined to become like the factory worker, to become a class without property and mathematically certain that it will never have property." [50]

But Gramsci was quite clear on the issue of who will make the revolution. In 1920 he wrote,

> Only the working class, taking in hand the power of the State, will operate a radical change . . . not collaborating with the bourgeoisie, it will cause the outright division of classes in the countryside, dividing the poor and small peasants from the rich, and making them auxiliaries for the creation of a workers' state. [51]

50. Gramsci, *L'Ordine Nuovo,* p. 91.
51. Ibid., p. 79.

The peasants, in other words, would be used instrumentally under the direction of the working class. If the image recalls Lenin, it is no mere coincidence.

Gramsci was even more explicit in characterizing the petit bourgeoisie, and in rejecting it as an ally of the working class. Like Marx, he saved his most pejorative commentary for his own social class. He wrote: "The small and medium bourgeoisie is in fact the corrupt, dissolute, putrescent barrier with which capitalism defends its economic and political power." [52]

As for the factory owner, the rich bourgeois, in the age of imperialism and concentration, his economic role has been destroyed, and his power has been overcome by the power of state capitalism. Gramsci asks:

> Where has the economic figure of the entrepreneur-owner gone, the captain of industry who is indispensable to production, who makes factories flower with his ingenuity, his initiative, with the stimulus of his own interest? He has vanished, liquefied in the process of development of his own forces of labor.

The state thus has become "the single proprietor of the forces of labor, assuming all the traditional functions of the entrepreneur." [53]

Gramsci posed these classes in relation to one another with dialectical incisiveness. He saw alliances as necessary under certain conditions—for example, between the workers and the peasants in making the revolution—and opposition as inevitable in others —for example, in the capacity of the peasants to oppose the proletariat after the revolution. Alliances are always posed as conditional, and it is quite clear that in a changing universe, yesterday's partner is tomorrow's opponent.

In Togliatti's thought, we do not find anything like this scalpel-like technique. Instead, there is an inclusive concept of groups and classes which poses alliances in additive terms. First of all, no clear theoretical distinction is ever made between workers and laborers, and the two terms are in many cases used interchangeably. This is

52. Ibid., p. 61.
53. Ibid., pp. 82, 83.

important because Gramsci's emphasis on the growing property-lessness of the laboring class is never explicit.

Second, the peasantry is seen as an equal partner in the venture of the Via Italiana al Socialismo. Gramsci's highly instrumental use of the peasantry is replaced by the idea of "the real unity between workers and peasants in the common battle for the structural renewal of the Italian state." [54] Within the peasantry, Gramsci had concentrated upon the land-hungry semiproletariat and the small poor peasants. For Togliatti, the middle group of peasants, who could merely be neutralized for Lenin, are now drawn theoretically into the alliance by policies in favor of their interests. Finally, the rich peasants are also appealed to by the PCI, for "sometimes occasional alliances are necessary." [55]

Finally, the petit bourgeoisie—the "productive middle class"—is drawn within the ambit of this theoretical system of alliances, because, as a result of changes afoot in Italian society, "today it is possible to construct a new system of . . . alliances which has at its head the working class of old and new industrial groups, and is based upon the peasants and the urban middle class." [56] It is conceivable for Togliatti, as it was not for Gramsci, that a socialist conscience will develop among these groups despite their property-holding interests.

Again, it is the high stage of development of Italian society that justifies these radical changes. The direction is clear; Togliatti and the PCI have built up such a tissue of theoretical alliances that virtually no one is safe. As a result, Italian Communism must direct itself only against large, monopolistic industry and foreign imperialism. Togliatti writes: "At the head of the battle there must be the working class guided by its revolutionary vanguard; in the course of the same battle, the front of the advance toward socialism must gradually extend itself to new social groups, and from them must come an ever stronger socialist conscience." [57]

54. Giorgio Amendola, "Come si Pone la Questione Meridionale dopo il Voto del 7 Giugno," *Rinascita, 10,* No 7 (1953), 402.

55. Ruggiero Grieco, *I Comunisti e la Lotta per la Riforma Agraria* (Roma, 1949), pp. 16–17.

56. Partito Comunista Italiano (PCI), *Il PCI e la Battaglia Meridionalistica* (Roma, 1963), p. 13.

57. Palmiro Togliatti, *La Via Italiana al Socialismo* (Roma, 1964), p. 183.

As a close observer of the PCI writes, "All 'democratic' elements of society—the individual peasant landowner, the small industrialist, the intellectual, the white collar technician—were now presumed to have a common interest with the industrial proletariat and the landless farm worker in the fight against monopoly capital." [58]

The Strategy for the Conquest of Power

Their divergent perspective on bourgeois institutions and on the role of various groups and classes in the Italian revolution is capped by a third fundamental difference between Gramsci and Togliatti: on the nature of the revolutionary party and its path to power.

For Gramsci, the superstructural nature of bourgeois institutions and their oppressive quality in Italy excluded them as the primary locus of activity of the revolutionary party. The revolution, he stated many times, would be made in the factory, since the factory is the only institution in bourgeois society that is not mere bourgeois superstructure. Consequently, the party must be organized around the factory through "the cells of the new order," the factory councils. He wrote, "The socialist state already exists potentially in the institutions of social life characteristic of the exploited laboring class." Therefore, "it is necessary to develop and give more power to the proletarian institutions that already exist in the factory, making others like them grow up in the villages and making sure that the men who make them up will be Communists who are conscious of the revolutionary mission that the institution has to carry out." [59]

Since the party was to be based on its units in the factory, its own bureaucratic superstructure must be limited. Time and again he criticized the old Socialist Party and its trade unions as bureaucratic institutions so tainted by their foundation and growth in bourgeois society that they are incapable of directing the factory councils. What then is the role of the central party organization outside the factory? The party is an "institution of Communist education, the fulcrum of faith, the depository of doctrine, the

58. Blackmer, *Italian Communism*, p. 383.
59. Gramsci, *L'Ordine Nuovo*, pp. 5, 10, 18.

supreme power that harmonizes the organized and disciplined forces of the working class and the peasants and leads them to their goal." [60] The party, in a tumultuous and pregnant metaphor, "expropriates the first machine, the most important instrument of production, the working class itself." [61]

The most creative elements in Gramsci's concept of the party emerged only after his political career was ended by his imprisonment, when he wrote *Notes on Machiavelli*. Here Gramsci elaborated on the idea of the political party as a center of education and integration. He wrote,

> The modern prince, the myth-prince, cannot be a real person, a concrete individual; it can only be an organism; a complex element of society in which the formation of a recognized general will and its partial affirmation in action has already begun. This organism has already been developed historically. It is the political party: the first cell in which are collected the germs of the general will which will tend to become universal and total.[62]

Again, as in his earlier writings, Gramsci saw the party as the pristine nucleus of the new society in the bosom of the old. The difference, of course, is that the earlier version applied only to the factory councils; now Gramsci spoke of the whole party in these terms. The cause of this difference is that in his earlier writings Gramsci referred to the old Socialist Party whereas in *Notes on Machiavelli* his focus is the Communist Party.

To create the general will, the party must educate the working class. But it cannot achieve this colossal task through agitation alone; it solves the problem of education by organization and by the formation of a new group of intellectuals. Right from his factory council days, Gramsci showed an unusual preoccupation with organization. In 1919, he wrote, "The Communist revolution is essentially a problem of organization and discipline." [63] In *Notes*

60. Ibid., p. 61.
61. Ibid., p. 126.
62. Antonio Gramsci, *Note sul Machiavelli, sulla Politica e sullo Stato Moderno* (Torino, 1955), p. 5.
63. *L'Ordine Nuovo*, p. 126.

on Machiavelli, he elaborated three levels of organization: (1) a "diffuse element, whose participation depends upon discipline and faith, and not on an organizational and creative spirit"; (2) "the principal cohesive factor," which organizes and centralizes "a number of forces that, left to themselves, would count for little or nothing"; and (3) a "middle element that articulates the first element with the second, putting them into not only physical but moral and intellectual contact." [64]

While this formulation recalls Lenin's *What Is to Be Done?,* it is important to note, first, that the lowest element—the mass element—was *inside* the party for Gramsci, rather than outside, as it was for Lenin. Second, whereas Lenin's line of command was largely downward, that is not completely true in Gramsci, who attached great importance to the middle element's role in the internal education of the party. Moreover, the middle element had the critical role of preserving the party should the cohesive element at the top be destroyed.

The key to the formation of the middle element of leadership lay in the problem of the intellectuals. For Gramsci, the political party was "a collective intellectual." It was the representative of a class, and "for many social classes, the political party is nothing else than a way of elaborating its own category of organic intellectuals." [65]

The intellectuals were to come from two sources: first, from the social class itself—the organic intellectuals; second, from the traditional class of bourgeois intellectuals. "The political party . . . assures the link between organic intellectuals of a certain group, the dominant group in the party, and traditional intellectuals. . . . An intellectual who joins the political party of a particular social group is merged with the organic intellectuals of the group itself." [66]

Herein lies one of the basic ambiguities in Gramsci's thought and one of the core problems in Marxism. Recognizing from his prison cell that his party had failed because it was insufficiently

64. *Note sul Machiavelli,* pp. 23–24.

65. Antonio Gramsci, *Gli Intellettuali e l'Organizzazione della Cultura* (Torino, 1955), p. 12.

66. Ibid.

prepared for the revolutionary moment in 1922, Gramsci tried to devise a theoretical system to make the party a collective intellectual that would train itself for revolution. But since he insisted implacably on the working class basis of the party, he was faced with an absence of intellectuals to start up and run the machine of education. Some of these individuals had to come from the traditional source of teachers, publicists, and technicians: the bourgeoisie. Upon entering the party, Gramsci assumed, they would merge with the working class' own intellectual product: the organic intellectuals.

When we counterpose this formulation with Gramsci's earlier delineation of the three stages of party hierarchy, the paradox of his theory of the intellectuals becomes clear. A proletarian party which is to achieve the level of preparation necessary to carry off a revolution must co-opt intellectuals from the bourgeoisie; yet there is no guarantee that these traditional intellectuals will not, by virtue of their superior training, dominate the upper level of leadership, leaving the working class "organic" intellectuals to man the secondary posts at the middle level of leadership.

It is not clear whether Gramsci anticipated this problem or not, but he certainly saw the intellectual as a leadership function and not as a simple service activity. He wrote, "A party can have a larger or a smaller group of the higher or the lower level [of intellectuals]; that isn't what really matters. What matters is their function, which is directive and organizational, and therefore educative, therefore intellectual." [67]

What does Togliatti have to say on the problem of the nature of the party and its path to power? To his acceptance of the legitimacy of operating primarily within the institutions of bourgeois society and his theoretical broadening of the alliances of the working class, Togliatti adds what amounts to a concept of a new mass party. "What is the new party?" he asks in 1944, and responds, "The new party is a party of the working class and the people that doesn't limit itself only to criticism and propaganda, but intervenes in the life of the country with a positive and constructive activity." [68]

67. Ibid.
68. Palmiro Togliatti, *Il Partito* (Roma, 1964), p. 69.

The new party is, first of all, a national party; "The new party that we have in mind must be a national Italian party, that is a party which poses and resolves the problem of the emancipation of labor in the framework of our national life and liberty, making its own all the progressive traditions of the nation." [69]

But the national idea is not simply rhetorical; it takes Togliatti into what will become his major theme, the theme of solidarity. "When we speak of nation," he asks, "what do we mean? . . . we mean the working class, the peasant class, the mass of the intellectuals, the mass of laborers of the thought and not only of the arm— white collar employees and professionals," in other words, everyone but the ruling class. [70]

It is curious that Togliatti invokes Gramsci to legitimate this theme of national solidarity. He writes:

> The central idea of the political action of Gramsci was the idea of unity: unity of the working class parties in the battle for the defense of democratic institutions . . . unity of the working class parties with the democratic forces which began to organize particularly in the South; unity of the socialist working masses with the Catholic working masses of the city and countryside; unity of the workers; unity of workers and peasants; unity of workers of the arm with those of the mind, for the creation of a great bloc of national forces. [71]

Togliatti has interpreted Gramsci's emphasis on the party's formation of a new unified state as an emphasis on national solidarity! [72]

But Gramsci actually uses the image of the Prince as a symbol of organization, not of solidarity. What does Togliatti have to say about the organization of the new party? The organizational character of the party follows logically, for Togliatti, from its multiclass composition: it must be a mass party. He writes, "It is necessary to attract into the party all the active elements that are in

69. Ibid., p. 70.

70. Ibid., p. 79.

71. *Rinascita* (29 agosto 1964).

72. In its popular anthology of Gramsci's writings, the party has emphasized this point, perhaps to excess. See Salinari and Spinella, eds., *Antonio Gramsci: Antologia degli Scritti, 1, 220.*

the working and intellectual classes, and to make of our party a party with a mass character." [73] Hence, recruitment is loosened, ever new groups of party members are made party cadres, and the broad, geographical party section overtakes the functional party cell in importance.[74] For Gramsci, organization had been logically prior to composition of the party, and less flexible.

In a curious, almost Parkinsonian manner, Togliatti calls for the broadening of the party's activities in order to give all the new members something to do. "If we want to realize the directive that in the party there is work for all and that everyone in the party must work, it is essential to multiply the most elementary forms of the work of broadening the contacts of the party with all the strata of the population." [75] Like his concept of class, therefore, Togliatti's ideas on the organization of the party are additive and inclusive, rather than selective and dialectical.

The fundamental policy directive that emerges from these ideas is the policy of presence: the idea of participating wherever the demands of broad groups of the population are made and wherever an opportunity exists for the creation of a new organization that will involve a new social group in the activities of the party. As a leading labor intellectual of the party writes, "The CGIL [*Confederazione Generale Italiano dei Lavoratori*] does not try to prevent the modernization of Italian capitalism. Instead of opposing neo-capitalist solutions *a priori,* we each time oppose more advanced and equally realistic and concrete solutions of our own." [76]

We find little in Togliatti's writings to parallel either Gramsci's incisive theory of the three levels of organization or his formulation regarding the organic intellectuals of the working class. Presumably, the mass in Togliatti's mass party refers to Gramsci's "diffuse element" of party members, but we nowhere find a theoretical distinction between mass and elite that corresponds to Gramsci's. What we *do* find, however, is that from 1947 onward Togliatti and other party leaders complain of a failure of the party to create a sufficient number of cadres—Gramsci's middle

73. *Il Partito,* p. 91.
74. Ibid., pp. 111–25.
75. Ibid., p. 125.
76. Quoted in *New Left Review* (April–June 1962), p. 153.

level. "We are already a mass party; we must now acquire also the basic qualities of a party of cadres, which means that we must increase the number of cadres of the party decisively." [77]

It is interesting that in an article called "Leninism in the Thought and Action of Antonio Gramsci," Togliatti never mentions Gramsci's three-level theory of party organization. Moreover, while an essential part of Gramsci's thought on the organization of the party regards the factory councils, Togliatti downgrades Gramsci's insistence on their primacy as "a few propositions written in 1919." [78] Nor have we any mention of Gramsci's condemnation of the primarily parliamentary activity of the old PSI.

When we contemplate the overall relationship of Togliatti's thought to Gramsci's, it is hard to believe that the PCI's ideological roots lie in the second writer. In his concepts of class, party, and the road to power, Gramsci is a Leninist, although his writing represents a real creative advance over Lenin's rumbling prose. In many of these dimensions, Togliatti has moved sharply away from his predecessor. If Gramsci is the dialectical surgeon, Togliatti is the general practitioner.

But it would be a gross error to dismiss Togliatti as a revisionist like Bernstein. His concept of the party as a mass force of leadership, his subtle ideas on the reform of structure, and his counterposition of democracy and socialism are both more complex and less straightforward than the reformism of Bernstein. If anything, Togliatti's formula of the Via Italiana al Socialismo recalls Lenin's great enemy Kautsky. For example, Togliatti's insistence upon the need for a multiparty system in Italian politics, and the need for internal democracy in the Soviet Union, recall these words of Kautsky's written long ago in polemic against Lenin: "Socialism and democracy are therefore not distinguished by the one being the means and the other the end. Both are means to the same end." [79]

Is there then no theoretical connection between Gramsci, Leninist leader of the PCI in the 1920s, and Togliatti, Italian polycen-

77. *Il Partito*, p. 113.
78. Ibid., p. 155.
79. Karl Kautsky, *The Dictatorship of the Proletariat* (Ann Arbor, 1964), p. 5.

trist in the 1960s? Are they united only by their Italian citizenship? As a matter of fact, the common thread that runs through the writings of both theorists regards precisely the nature of the proletarian revolution in a country like Italy.

In his political writings in the 1920s, Gramsci was at great pains to show that Italy was a backward country. Italy was like Russia in, (1) the oppressiveness of its so-called "liberal" institutions, and (2) the lack of equilibrium between its internal social forces—particularly between the industrial monopolies of the North and the semifeudal agriculture of the South. In combatting the claims of the revisionists that the highest stage of capitalism had to be reached in order for the revolution to succeed, Gramsci continually pointed to the similarities between the backward Italian and Russian economies. In fact, his favored weapon, the factory councils, were for Gramsci a kind of soviet.[80]

This aspect of Gramsci's writing, like many others, is diametrically opposed to Togliatti, who justifies the Via Italiana as a version of socialism adapted to the *advanced* economic and political conditions of a modern Western state. Togliatti's approach is the fruit of the bitter experience of Communism in Western Europe between 1920 and 1945, an experience in which a strategy developed successfully in backward Russia had proven radically unfit for advanced countries. If the strategy of the small vanguard party using shock tactics achieves a revolution against an archaic autocracy in a backward country like Russia and fails in the West, it seemed to follow that the proper strategy to adopt in the West would be a large mass party achieving socialism through parliamentary institutions.

The story would end with the transformation of a revolutionary vanguard party into a mass parliamentary party were it not for a curious intermediate stage in the analysis that we owe to Gramsci. For in about 1930, brooding in his prison cell on the failure of the Italian revolution, Gramsci arrived at a formulation that might well bridge the theoretical gap between his earlier writings and those of Togliatti.

He began by contemplating the failure of the revolution in the West, recognizing first that, although fundamental historical crises

80. Gramsci, *L'Ordine Nuovo*, pp. 25, 54, 67.

are economic, only the presence of an organized force of will (that is, the party) can produce fundamental *events* out of crises.[81] In advanced countries, however, "civil society has become a complex structure that is resistant to the catastrophic eruptions caused by immediate economic elements such as crises or depressions." [82] In modernized countries, "the superstructure of civil society is like the system of trenches in modern warfare," where "the first artillery attack seems to have destroyed the adversary's system of defense, but has destroyed only the external perimeter." [83] In a backward country like Russia, in contrast, the state is everything, and with the destruction of the state, all of civil society crumbles too.

What lessons can be drawn from this for Communism in advanced societies? Gramsci designs two military metaphors to deal with the problem, making clear by his use of hidden citations of Luxemburg, Trotsky, and Lenin that he is dealing with internal revolution and not external war. The first metaphor is the "war of movement," in which the army uses guerrilla tactics to destroy the superstructure of society with lightning blows at key points in the superstructure. The second is the "war of position," in which a drilled, disciplined regular army confronts the enemy on the stable field of trench warfare. To hammer home the difference between the two strategies, Gramsci uses the analogy of the Italian Risorgimento, when the war of movement was fought by Mazzini, Garibaldi, and their semiguerrilla bands, and the war of position was fought by Cavour, the state of Piedmont, and a regular uniformed army.[84]

The point of all this Aesopian language, which recalls the military metaphors Machiavelli used to deal with Florentine politics, is to show the differences in revolutionary strategy necessary in backward and advanced societies. The war of movement is "in the last analysis the reflection of the general economic, cultural, social conditions of a country in which the structures of national life are

81. Gramsci, *Note sul Machiavelli*, p. 49.
82. Ibid., p. 67.
83. Ibid.
84. Ibid., pp. 62–84. This entire section must be read carefully for an understanding of the structure of Gramsci's "Machiavellian" writing technique.

embryonic." [85] Trotsky's error, for Gramsci, was in assuming the "permanence" (or universality) of a war of movement strategy that was actually adapted only to underdeveloped conditions.

Lenin, on the other hand, was a true European, since "he understood that it was necessary to change from the war of maneuver, applied victoriously in the East [Russia] in 1917, to the war of position, which was the only one possible in the West." In passing, we should note that it is not at all clear that Lenin would have agreed, but it is interesting that Gramsci should have cited him as an authority.

What does the war of position mean in political terms? If in military terms, it meant "the united front" led by career officers and staffed by regular soldiers,[86] then in political terms it meant a long campaign of "passive resistance" inside the superstructure of bourgeois society. The revolutionary party is therefore required to deal with parliamentary democracy on its own terms. He writes, "The massive structure of modern democracies, their state organizations and complexes of civic associations, constitute for political art the 'trenches' and permanent fortifications of the front in the war of position." [87]

In other words, if the lesson of the Russian Revolution is that a backward country requires the war-of-movement strategy, the lesson of Communism in the West is that an advanced country primarily requires a war-of-position strategy—for example the institutionalized trench warfare of parliamentary and electoral life. We see here Gramsci's divergence from his earlier "underdeveloped" strategy, and his approach to positions to be assumed by Togliatti in 1945.

The basic difference between this vision of political strategy in advanced countries and Togliatti's Via Italiana is Gramsci's insistence that the war of position must continue to be supplemented by the war of movement if parliamentary success is to be converted into revolution. Using the parallel of the Risorgimento, and likening it to an unidentified "restoration," which could only mean the overthrow of Fascism, Gramsci sets the following dialectical di-

85. Ibid., p. 67.
86. Ibid., pp. 68, 72.
87. Ibid., p. 84.

lemma: *both* the war of position and the war of movement were necessary for final military victory.[88]

If we can translate the metaphor into political terms, Gramsci admitted the need to achieve success primarily in parliament, but wanted to continue the war of movement in the factories, in the fields, and at the railroad junctions to convert success into revolution. In other words, to achieve the revolution in the West, the party must be essentially two parties fighting two different battles at the same time. The secret in maintaining the balance is in organization.

Why do we find so little reference to the war-of-movement strategy in Togliatti's writings? (One reference curiously misinterprets it as a description of the confrontation between the U.S.S.R. and the West.) It is not clear whether, on the one hand, Togliatti disregarded the war-of-movement theme to cloak an untarnished revolutionary will, or, on the other, he simply abolished it as unrealistic over the long run.

Two points of general interpretation should be made here. First, the double strategy of position and movement is *made possible* by virtue of Gramsci's organizational schema (that is the Leninist three-stage structure described above and the factory councils designed in his early career). Second, the double strategy *necessitates* a double leadership, and this is perhaps the framework in which we ought to see his critical distinction between organic and traditional intellectuals. Just as it is difficult to conceive of the traditional intellectuals directing the war of movement in a factory setting, it is hard to imagine the organic working class intellectuals as generals in the war of position in parliamentary democracy.

The real value of Gramsci's dual strategy is that it allows us to understand Italian Communist behavior against a theoretical background. It points our attention to several aspects of PCI life that might otherwise escape our notice: first, the problems of organization that were to plague the party after 1945, for example, the problem of a middle level of cadres; second, the problem of sustaining a revolutionary politics in an arena—parliament—that deals primarily in a politics of interest; and, third, the problem of

88. Ibid., p. 70.

the unusual leadership needed for the dual strategy of movement and position. It is interesting, for example, that every left-wing opposition to the Via Italiana both inside and outside of the PCI has recalled Gramsci's writings on the factory councils and the organic intellectuals.

In other words, there is a built-in dilemma in Gramsci's strategy of position and movement. He convinces us that revolutionary strategy in advanced countries must utilize both the parliamentary war of position and the guerrilla war of movement. But to sustain both, the party must be two parties, its organization must be geared to both the war of position and the war of movement, and its leaders must be divided between two types of party intellectuals.

The theoretical, not to mention political, problems of this strategy are immense. They are the starting point both for an analysis of the political thought of Palmiro Togliatti and of the organization, leadership, and behavior of the Italian Communist Party. Togliatti's party represents the almost inevitable victory of one Gramscian tendency over another, since the dialectical tension he establishes in theory is virtually impossible in practice except over the very short run.

6. The Italian Communist Party: Structure and Behavior

In comparing the concrete characteristics of Italian Communism with the political thought of its present-day leaders, we are faced with a paradox: not only do the party's following, organization, and leadership reflect the salient aspects of the Via Italiana al Socialismo; they perhaps reflect it too well. While Gramsci's balance between the war of position and the war of maneuver requires that the party retain the capacity to shift suddenly from one strategy to the other, in practice the PCI has adapted so completely to the first that its transformation to the second appears virtually impossible. The PCI, in a manner of speaking, has *institutionalized* certain aspects of its strategy in the Italian political system, so much so that a shift in strategy would undoubtedly destroy much of its popular support.

Voters, Members, and Leaders

The success of Togliatti's strategy can be measured in one dimension by the party's electoral constituency and membership group, both of which exhibit the strategy of broad-ranging alliances that is the most salient characteristic of Togliatti's thought. The Communist electorate, which represented 19 percent of the vote in 1946, grew to 25.3 percent in the 1963 parliamentary elections, and it has grown slightly more in local and provincial elections since then. An increase of over one million in the total electorate between 1958 and 1963 was converted to a 2.6 percent rise in the Communist vote in 1963, at a time when the Christian Democrats lost over 700,000 votes.[1] The general impression in Italy after this unpredicted success was that the Communists were gaining the lion's share of young voters who were voting for the first time.

1. "Analisi del Voto del 28 Aprile," *Tempi Moderni, 6,* No. 13 (1963), p. 75.

Other reasons widely circulated in Italy for the PCI's electoral success in 1963 were the following: Pope John's conciliatory attitude toward Marxism; the gradual alleviation of cold war tensions; the final demise of the far-right Monarchist Party which had controlled many lower class votes; and the surge of southern Italian immigrants into the crowded outskirts of northern cities like Turin, Milan, and Bologna. The last phenomenon was most striking; in Turin, for example, the rate of in-migration in various zones of the city and its surroundings corresponds in an almost linear fashion to the increment of Communist votes.[2]

The social composition of the Communist vote appears to be distributed broadly among the population, with a natural concentration among lower income groups. We have two sources for these conclusions: first, ecological conjectures made by the French social scientist, Mattei Dogan; and, second, several sample survey sources. Both these sources leave something to be desired in the way of precision and significance, but they appear to verify the success of the electoral aspects of Togliatti's Via Italiana.

The PCI is not merely the party of the working class. According to Dogan's estimates, only one-third of the working class vote of the Northern Industrial Triangle goes to the PCI, while three-fifths of the workers in this region vote for the Socialists, the Social Democrats, and the Christian Democrats. A slightly larger vote is registered for the PCI among the lower class *Lumpenproletariat* and the urban unemployed, a phenomenon that is probably linked to the large proportion of displaced immigrants among these groups according to Dogan.[3]

In the small towns and rural districts of less than 10,000 residents, the PCI receives an estimated 20.1 percent of the vote, about 5 percent below its present national average. These figures may be doubly deceptive, however, for a large part of Italy's agricultural population lives in cities of more than 10,000 inhabitants.[4] By far the strongest group of PCI voters are among the share tenants (*mezzadri*) and agricultural workers of the central regions—the so-called

2. Ibid., p. 87.

3. Mattei Dogan, "La Stratificazione Sociale dei Suffragi," Spreafico e LaPalombara, eds., *Elezioni e Comportamento Politico in Italia*, pp. 420, 429.

4. Ibid., p. 433.

"Red Belt"—two-thirds of whom appear to Dogan to vote for the left. It is ironic that these relatively prosperous tenants and farm workers should support the Communist Party to a greater degree than either the industrial workers of the North or the poorer peasants of the South. Among small family farmers, the PCI rural vote is lowest of all; Dogan estimates that 12 percent of them vote for either the PCI or the Socialists.[5]

Middle and upper class urban groups vote overwhelmingly for the parties of the center and right, but Dogan estimates that 7 percent give their votes to the PCI and 12 percent divide their loyalty among the two socialist parties. As Table 6.1 indicates, the urban middle and upper classes are the largest source of support for parties other than the four major parties—in other words, parties that are mainly on the far right.

TABLE 6.1

Social Groups and Political Parties:[a] Estimated Votes (in thousands)

	PCI	PSI	PSDI	DC	Others	Total
Industrial Working Class	3,300	2,250	450	2,300	450	8,750
	38%	26%	5%	26%	5%	100%
	49%	53%	34%	18%	10%	29.6%
Urban Lower Class	400	110	—	220	280	1,010
(nonindustrial)	40%	11%	—	22%	27%	100%
	6%	2%	—	2%	5%	3.4%
Agricultural Groups	2,400	1,350	350	5,600	1,300	11,000
	22%	12%	3%	51%	12%	100%
	36%	33%	26%	45%	27%	37.2%
Urban Middle and	600	500	550	4,400	2,750	8,800
Upper Class	7%	6%	6%	50%	31%	100%
	9%	12%	40%	35%	58%	29.8%
Total	6,700	4,210	1,350	12,520	4,780	29,560
	22.7%	14.2%	4.5%	42.4%	16.2%	100%
	100%	100%	100%	100%	100%	100%

[a] PCI: Italian Communist Party   PSDI: Italian Social Democratic Party
PSI: Italian Socialist Party   DC: Christian Democratic Party
Source: Mattei Dogan, "La Stratificazione Sociale dei Suffragi," in Joseph LaPalombara e Alberto Spreafico, eds., *Elezioni e Comportamento Politico in Italia* (Milano, 1963), p. 454.

5. Ibid., p. 439.

As the table indicates, although the largest part of the PCI vote comes from the lower classes of city and countryside, its almost seven million votes are by no means solely drawn from the industrial proletariat. As Dogan concludes, "The expression 'the Communist Party is *the* party of the industrial proletariat' does not correspond to reality, since, we repeat, half of its electors do not belong to the industrial working class, and more than three-fifths of this class do not turn to the PCI." [6]

Sample survey evidence gives an even more dramatic indication of the social diversity of the PCI vote. Utilizing a 1963 survey of the CISER (the only Italian public opinion institute that carefully probes the political preference of its respondents) we find a broad distribution of the Communist vote among various occupational classes. Table 6.2 shows the occupational distribution and party preferences of a male subsample of the CISER survey computed by the Carlo Cattaneo Institute of Bologna.

Table 6.2 is striking, first, because of the large proportion of agricultural workers who prefer the PCI: 37 percent as opposed to 29 percent of the urban working class respondents. Second, it is interesting because of the large number of middle class rural and urban voters—small farmers, office workers, artisans, people in trade, and white-collar workers—who report a preference for the PCI. Third, low status occupational groups show an increasing preference for the PCI, but the converse is not true for the Christian Democrats (DC), whose support is strongest among small farmers, white-collar workers, and salaried office workers, in that order. The only Italian party that shows a completely positive correlation with increasing social status is the right-wing Liberal Party (PLI).

The PCI's broad occupational support may indeed fulfill a condition of Togliatti's strategy—the theme of alliances—but a negative factor emerges from the same data: that the strongest electoral support for the PCI comes from the agricultural workers, a social group that lacks organization, discipline, and geographic concentration, and appears to be diminishing within the population. As an obvious corollary, the PCI has failed to increase its share of the urban working class vote to a level above its support among agri-

6. Ibid., p. 467.

TABLE 6.2

Occupational Classes: Percentage Preferring Various Parties[a]
(CISER Survey 1963, male subsample)
(N = 1,537)

Occupation	(N)	PCI	PSI	PSDI	PRI	DC	PLI	PDIUM	MSI	DK, NA	TOTAL
Agricultural Workers	(131)	37	22	6	1	21	3	2	6	2	100
Urban Manual Workers	(513)	29	25	9	2	25	3	1	4	2	100
Small Farmers	(247)	18	13	6	1	44	8	2	3	5	100
Salaried Office Workers	(91)	19	14	10	2	37	9	1	4	3	100
Artisans	(155)	19	23	8	1	31	9	1	6	1	100
Trade, Commerce	(132)	17	18	6	3	35	11	0	6	4	100
White Collar	(194)	13	12	11	1	38	11	3	8	3	100
Professional, Managers, Owners	(74)	11	9	7	1	33	26	0	8	5	100

[a] PCI: Italian Communist Party DC: Christian Democratic Party
PSI: Italian Socialist Party PLI: Italian Liberal Party
PSDI: Italian Social Democratic Party PDIUM: Italian Monarchist Party
PRI: Italian Republican Party MSI: Italian Social Movement (Neo-Fascists)

Source: Istituto Carlo Cattaneo, *Il Comportamento Elettorale in Italia alle Luce di Alcune Ricerche Condotte Direttamente sugli Elettori* (Bologna; unpub. analysis). This analysis will be partially reported in Giorgio Sivini, ed., *Il Comportamento Elettorale*, Quaderni dell'Istituto Carlo Cattaneo, No. 1 (Bologna, Il Mulino, 1967).

cultural workers, despite the fact that the number of urban workers is increasing rapidly in Italy.

This problem is linked to the problem of the regional imbalance of the PCI vote. As is well known, the party is much stronger in the predominantly agricultural regions of central Italy than it is in the highly industrialized North. For example, in the 1963 elections, it controlled 23.4 percent of the vote in the northern provinces and over 32 percent in the central Red Belt. In agricultural southern Italy too, the PCI vote is now higher than in the North. In the northern provinces with the highest degree of industrialization—Piedmont and Lombardy—the PCI controls only 23.2 percent and 20.1 percent of the vote respectively.[7]

It is the regional imbalance of its vote that largely explains the influence of the PCI among nonproletarian agricultural groups. Although 12 percent of these groups support the party in the North and 11 percent do so in the South, 47 percent of the nonproletarian agriculturalists (mainly mezzadri) in central Italy support the PCI. Among the agricultural workers, on the other hand, the PCI is most strongly represented in the North, with 30 percent in the South, 32 percent in the Center, and 41 percent in the North.[8]

The urban working class is more strongly in favor of the PCI in central Italy too, according to the CISER survey. Whereas 25 percent of urban manual workers report a preference for the party in the North and 31 percent do so in the South, 40 percent of the working class respondents in central Italy prefer the PCI to the other parties.[9]

The same is true among some middle class groups; 30 percent of the artisans interviewed in central Italy expressed a preference for the PCI, as opposed to 14 percent in the North and 11 percent in the South. In these two regions, artisans are strongly attached to the Christian Democrats (38 percent in the North and 48 percent in the South), a factor that probably relates to the Church's traditional paternalism toward artisans.[10]

7. "Analisi del Voto del 28 Aprile," p. 76.
8. CISER data, 1963, p. 93.
9. Ibid., p. 67.
10. Ibid., p. 117.

The heavy concentration of the PCI vote in central Italy raises important questions about Communist strategy. If the policy of alliances leads to the relative strength of the PCI in agricultural central Italy and its relative weakness in highly industrialized northern Italy, this suggests two things: first, that there is perhaps a traditionalist logic in the Via Italiana al Socialismo; and, second, that increasing industrialization in central Italy may erode the power base of the PCI in that region. In actual fact, much of the party's success in the region derives from two things: first, traditional leftist and anticlerical sympathies, and second, the party's success in closing the gap between the region's backward agricultural structure and world markets by a network of cooperatives and lending facilities. It is ironic that the Tuscan sharecropper is attached to the PCI in large part because its economic service agencies allow him to make a profit.

Three other aspects of the structure of the PCI vote underline the problems that arise from its self-consciously sought broad support. First, the PCI is the party of the lowest status members of each occupational class it represents. This is particularly striking in the case of both major agricultural groups; almost twice as many poor agricultural day workers support the PCI as do those whose income is higher; much the same is true of nonproletarian rural groups. The appropriate statistics for each occupational and socioeconomic status group are reproduced in Table 6.3.

TABLE 6.3

Occupational Classes: Percentage Supporting PCI by Socioeconomic Status
(CISER Survey, 1963)

				Occupation			
SES Level	Workers	Agric. Wkrs.	Other Rural	Artisans	Trade, Commerce	Salaried, Office	White Collar
High	—	—	—	—	—	—	9
Medium-High	—	—	—	10	13	13	9
Medium	13	—	10	10	13	13	11
Medium-Low	30	26	17	21	18	17	17
Low	35	46	32	21	18	17	17

[a] Upper class occupations (Professionals, Managers, Owners) are omitted because of insufficient subsample size.

Source: CISER data, 1963, pp. 51, 84, 106.

Related to the lower income level of those in the CISER sample expressing a preference for the PCI is their lower level of education. Working class support for the PCI increases from 23 percent for those with more than five years of education to 30 percent for those with less than five years of education. While virtually no difference is encountered along this dimension for artisans and tradesmen in the CISER sample, a sharp educational cleavage marks the political preferences of salaried and white-collar workers; of this group 28 percent of those with one to five years of education support the PCI, as compared to 10 percent with six to eleven years of training and 8 percent of those with twelve or more years of schooling. It is interesting, however, that upper class respondents with fifteen or more years of education were far more likely to support the PCI (18 percent) than upper class individuals with less than fifteen years of schooling (3 percent). However, the absolute number of upper class PCI supporters in the sample is so small that these indications are hardly significant.[11]

The low educational level of the PCI supporters in the CISER sample cannot be surprising. But there is very little evidence that PCI mass supporters show any sign of producing that class of organic intellectuals of which Gramsci wrote, at least if intellectualism is at all measurable by formal education.

A final dimension of the structure of the PCI vote is even less positive than the data on occupation, income, and education: in the two largest occupational groups—the urban and rural workers —the percentage supporting the PCI increases with age. Among respondents of the urban working class, the old-age PCI vote is most dramatic. Table 6.4 represents this aspect of the CISER data, but without the data for the upper class, which are too fragmentary to be of significance. The relatively low PCI support among younger industrial and agricultural workers suggests that the party's massive gains between 1958 and 1963 may not have come from voters voting for the first time, but from former supporters of the two parties that lost heavily in 1963, the Christian Democrats and the Monarchists. We have no data with which to explore this conjecture, but the old-age weighing of the PCI supporters in the CISER

11. Ibid., pp. 59, 112, and 127.

TABLE 6.4

Occupational Classes: Percentage Supporting PCI by Age Group
(CISER Survey, 1963)

	Age Group				
Occupational Class	21–30	31–40	41–50	51–60	60 plus
Urban Workers	27	28	30	31	45
Agricultural Workers	26	32	31	42	40
Other Rural Groups	21	15	22	16	19
Artisans, Tradesmen	16	16	19	12	17
Salaried, White Collar	10	11	15	14	15

Source: CISER data, 1963, pp. 60, 89, 111.

sample, particularly among workers and farm workers, speaks
poorly of the potential militance of PCI voters in any case.

When we turn from the PCI's electoral constituency to its mass
membership, similar problems emerge. Although the party's registered membership reflects a broad social background, its inconsistency, decreasing size, and decreasing ratio to PCI voters takes
the edge off the party's revolutionary image.

The number of PCI voters has increased steadily in the past
twenty years, but the number of party *members* has fluctuated
with shifts in the party's political fortunes. The end of World War
II saw a tremendous rise in membership as the PCI virtually assumed the mantle of the Resistance. Between 1944 and 1947, party
membership rose from 400,000 to 2,245,000. By 1952, the breakdown of the national coalition and the advent of the Cold War
caused registration to fall to 2,100,000. The catastrophic events in
Poland and Hungary and the secret Khrushchev speech of 1956 had
even more negative results; party registration fell from 2,036,000
in 1956 to 1,790,000 in 1959 and to 1,615,000 in 1963.[12] This rapid

12. The following analysis is based upon these official Italian Communist Party
documents: *Forza ad Attività del Partito,* Dati Statistici Preparati per la IVª Conferenza Nazionale del PCI (Roma, 1954); *Organizzazione del PCI,* Dati Statistici Elaborati dalla Sezione Centrale di Organizzazione (Roma, 1961); *Dati sull'Organizzazione del PCI,* Dati Statistici Elaborati dalla Sezione Centrale di Organizzazione per
la Vª Conferenza Nazionale di Organizzazione (Roma, 1964). An early source, less
reliable than these documents, is *L'Attività del Partito in Cifre,* VIº Congresso
Nazionale (Roma, 1948).

rise and decline in membership suggests that the vast majority of Communist Party members in Italy are not dedicated militants, but are so loosely attached to the party that their adherence depends upon the political situation of the moment.

Equally significant, membership fluctuates from year to year, with a large number of newly recruited among the dwindling files of the party. New recruits amounted to 7.9 percent of total membership in 1961 and 6.4 percent in 1962. In other words, not only did the party suffer a net loss of 45,000 members a year, but many of the remaining members were untrained new members.

At the same time, the ratio of PCI members to voters has decreased sharply. In 1956, the party controlled three times as many votes as it had members. In 1959, there was one PCI member for every 3.7 PCI voters. By 1963, the ratio had become 1 to 4.5. This trend occurred in every Italian region but one—Lucania—and was relatively greater in the highly industrialized regions than in the less industrialized regions.[13]

The social composition of the membership reflects the PCI's working class orientation, but reflects as well the leadership's vigorous attempts to give the party a national cast. The percentage of industrial workers in the party ranks is 39.5; 12.7 percent are agricultural workers; nearly 11 percent are *mezzadri;* 5.6 percent are small farmers; 5.2 percent are artisans and tradesmen; 12.4 percent are housewives; and 2.2 percent are office workers. The social composition of party members has changed somewhat in the years since World War II, with the greater emphasis given by the PCI to the "productive middle classes." Table 6.5 summarizes changes in the structure of party membership from 1948 to 1962.

As the table shows, the percentage of industrial workers and agricultural workers in the PCI has declined between 1948 and 1962, with a smaller decline in the number of sharecroppers and artisans. Gains have been registered among small family farmers, housewives, and many of unspecified occupation, a category composed mainly of the retired and the unemployed. This shift in distribution certainly gives PCI membership a national character,

13. *Dati sull'Organizzazione,* p. 21; and "Modificazioni Strutturali e Politiche del PCI al suo IX° Congresso," *Tempi Moderni,* 2 (aprile 1960), 99–100.

TABLE 6.5

Social Composition of PCI Membership, 1948–62
(in percentages)

	1948	1950	1956	1962
Urban Workers	45.0	42.0	39.8	39.5
Agricultural Workers	17.0	18.0	17.1	12.7
Sharecroppers ⎱	16.0	11.8	11.9	10.7
Small Farmers ⎰		3.5	4.7	5.6
Artisans	5.6	4.3	5.0	5.2
Professionals	0.8	0.6	0.5	0.6
White Collar Workers	3.3	2.5	2.1	2.2
Students	0.7	0.5	0.3	0.3
Housewives	9.5	11.4	14.0	12.4
Others	2.1	5.4	4.2	9.8

Source: Official party statistics (1948, 1954, 1961, 1964).

but it has also led to a sharp decrease in militance, particularly in the agricultural categories.

Although we know a good deal about the structure of the PCI electorate and the composition of its mass membership, we have little precise information on the next level, that of the middle category of militants. This class of party activists includes the leaders of the factory cells, the secretaries of party sections, and other activists. The party affirms that "the overwhelming majority of the cells and the sections are directed by workers," but we might wish this declaration to be more precise. We know that the party's leaders periodically launch campaigns to arouse these groups to greater participation, complaining that their activities trail off between electoral campaigns. The recent emphasis given to the zonal committees can be understood largely as an attempt to stimulate activity at the base.

There is scattered evidence to suggest that this level of leadership—which corresponds to Gramsci's "middle level"—is by far the weakest in the PCI's structure of support. The party stopped publishing even the rudimentary data on the numbers of middle-level cadres in 1954, and the data we possess up to that time are approximate and probably inflated.[14] We do know, however, that

14. *Forza ed Attività del Partito,* p. 58.

great dissatisfaction exists in the party regarding the amount and level of ideological education given to local cadres throughout the country. For example, in 1961 party leaders complained that several of the most important regional federations had not sent students to the party's national schools at Bologna and Rome, and that the problem of party education for both workers and women had still to be overcome. The provincial federations appear to have given only a total of twenty-six local regular courses to a total of 444 students in 1959 and 1960.[15]

A report of 1962 is equally critical. "The problem of launching an elementary activity of ideological education in the party on a wide scale remains an urgent one." And a report in 1964 points out that "only eighteen federations have sent us incomplete data [on education]." and that "sixteen courses and seminars are held in ten federations on varied political and ideological problems, with the participation of 449 comrades, of whom seventy were women." [16]

The intellectual activity of these middle-level members appears to have dropped sharply between the party's postwar period and the present day. Using as an index of intellectual activity the number of newspapers of at least weekly circulation published on a provincial or local level, we find a sharp drop in activity between 1948, when forty-four local and provincial weekly journals were being published, and 1964, when only twenty-four such journals were being regularly published.[17] The latter figure however excludes a large number of factory journals of obviously limited circulation.

We should recall, at this point, Gramsci's emphasis on the formation of a large group of "organic" working class intellectuals and the importance of the middle level of organization. In questionnaires sent out to PCI federation secretaries in 1964, only 46 percent of these party leaders reported that more than 15 percent of the members in their federation were carrying out a regular party function; 28 percent reported that 10 to 15 percent were carrying out a regular function; and 23 percent reported that less than

15. *Organizzazione del PCI,* pp. 57–58.
16. Ibid., pp. 59–62; also see *Dati sull'Organizzazione del PCI,* p. 77.
17. *L'Attività del Partito in Cifre,* p. 79; *Dati sull'Organizzazione,* p. 79.

10 percent were carrying out some continuous party function. (Of the eighty respondents, 3 percent did not answer the question.)

Above the middle level of cadres, we find the PCI's provincial and national leadership cadre. This is the group who may be said to direct the implementation of the party line and who give the party its image in Italian society. In the main, these leaders are an intellectual elite of lower middle or middle class origin whose families were socially mobile and who received a degree of education greater than their social origin would normally suggest. Relatively few are workers or are of working class background. Many received their first political experiences in the Resistance movement, and large numbers fulfill their primary activities in the labor union field. They possess experience and training far more extensive than that of other Italian party leaders, and they are far and away the most professional group in Italian politics.

On the provincial level, we find that 37 percent of the members of the provincial Federal Committees are workers; on the next level, that of the provincial Direction Committees, 35 percent are workers; and at the highest provincial level, that of the party secretaries, 34 percent are workers.[18]

Moreover, the figures relating to the 113 party secretaries are open to dispute. In questionnaries and interviews carried out in 1964, I found that, of the 80 secretaries who responded, 26.4 percent were of working class background, 8 percentage points lower than the figure released by the PCI in 1960; 48.6 percent were of lower middle class origin; and the remaining 25 percent came from white-collar or professional families. The discrepancy between the two sets of figures results either from a radical change in the composition of the provincial leadership or from differences in the definition of "working class."

Moreover, many of the provincial leaders have been educated above a level normal for their social origin. Of the total responding to my survey, 19 percent had only an elementary school education, 29 percent had attended a junior high school or technical school, 19 percent had a secondary education, and 35 percent had attended or graduated from college. Many were trained as special-

18. E. Berlinguer, *Relazione al Comitato Centrale del PCI* (2 marzo 1960).

ized workers, some served briefly as technicians or in the public service, and a large number studied for university degrees in the traditional Italian fields of philosophy and jurisprudence. In other words, relating their educational level to their social origins, the provincial leadership cadre of the PCI appears to be made up predominantly of socially mobile individuals of middle class status. Most of them had entered the party through the Resistance movement; 8 percent became Communists before 1942, 69 percent had joined during the years of the Resistance, and 22 percent had joined since 1945.

At the very highest level—that of the parliamentary group and members of the central apparatus—we possess very detailed information from a study of the Italian parliament directed by Giovanni Sartori. These leaders are of higher social origin than those in the provincial cadres, and they have had longer political experience and a broader political background. Table 6.6 analyzes the social origin of Communist leaders and compares it to relative data for the PSI and DC.

In regard to their social origin, using paternal occupation as an index, 31.6 percent of PCI national leaders are sons of "dependent workers" (industrial and agricultural); 13.3 percent are sons of public officials; 11.2 percent are sons of artisans; 11.9 percent are sons of doctors, lawyers, teachers, and other professionals; 9.5 percent come from families in trade and commerce; and 4.8 percent are sons of white-collar workers. Remarkably few leaders (2.7 percent) are the sons of peasants.

This distribution of the PCI leaders stands in marked contrast with the leadership of the other major Italian parties, which include many more sons of landowners, public officials, and lawyers than the PCI. Particularly striking is the contrast with the Socialist Party, which is presented as a typical party of opinion, and is led by many sons of professionals, bureaucrats, and tradesmen.

However, although the Communist leaders by and large have come from a lower social origin than the leaders of the other parties, they appear to have experienced a relatively high degree of social mobility in their formative years. Using a different grade of social status, also taken from the Sartori study, we find a consid-

TABLE 6.6

Paternal Occupation of Italian Legislators, 1946–58, by Party
(in percentages)

Paternal Occupation	PCI	PSI	DC	All-Party Average
Landowner	3.1	4.5	11.8	8.9
Peasant Owner	2.7	0.6	4.5	2.8
Industrialist	1.7	3.9	3.5	3.9
Commerce, Trade	9.5	10.6	10.6	9.8
Lawyer	5.8	7.2	8.2	9.4
Doctor	3.7	5.0	4.0	4.6
Other Professionals	1.4	3.3	2.9	2.4
Journalist	1.0	2.2	.2	.9
White Collar	4.8	5.5	6.9	5.6
Public Official	13.3	18.3	13.6	15.0
Teacher	3.4	2.2	4.7	5.6
Professor	.3	1.1	1.3	1.9
Political Career	—	1.7	—	.2
Artisan	11.2	5.6	8.2	7.4
Dependent Worker	31.6	15.6	8.4	12.9
Other	6.5	12.8	11.1	11.3
Total (N)	294	180	549	1,358

Source: Giovanni Sartori et al., Il Parlamento Italiano (Naples, 1963), p. 89.

erable proportion of the Communist Party's leadership cadre had a middle or upper middle class status upon entering politics; 59.8 percent list their social status upon entering politics as middle and upper middle class, with 39.9 percent remaining in the lower and lower middle classes. As a single index, whereas 31.6 percent were born the sons of dependent workers as shown in Table 6.6, only 25.9 percent listed themselves as of lower class status upon entering politics, as shown in Table 6.7. These figures, like the data presented on the PCI electorate and its membership group, suggest that the party is not a proletarian party in its leadership composition. The only largely proletarian level is the middle one, and that is probably the weakest level ideologically.

The educational level of the Communist deputies shows radical differences from that of the other parties. A large number of them (21.8 percent) attended only elementary school, and only one-third

TABLE 6.7

Social Class of Italian Legislators on Entering Politics, 1946–58, by Party
(in percentages)

Class	PCI	PSI	DC	All-Party Average
Upper	0.3	1.1	3.3	4.4
Upper Middle	22.4	50.0	59.8	53.4
Middle	37.4	33.9	31.1	28.5
Lower Middle	14.0	11.1	4.7	7.0
Lower	25.9	3.9	1.1	6.7
Total (N)	(294)	(180)	(549)	(1,358)

Source: Sartori et al., p. 93.

graduated from college. However, as in the case of the party's provincial leadership, PCI national leaders received more education
than is typical of their social origins in Italy; 27 percent reached
the middle and upper level of the secondary school system, and 42
percent attended or graduated from college or graduate school.
These figures are presented in Table 6.8.

TABLE 6.8

Educational Level of Italian Legislators, 1946–58, by Party
(in percentages)

Educational Level Completed	PCI	PSI	DC	All-Party Average
Self-taught	2.7	2.8	0.6	1.3
Elementary	21.8	2.8	1.8	6.0
Junior High[a]	14.7	8.8	5.1	7.5
Technical	8.5	4.4	4.7	5.4
Magistrale[b]	3.7	3.9	0.9	1.9
College (No degree)	5.8	1.7	1.8	2.9
College (Degree)	33.0	61.7	75.0	63.2
Ph.D.	3.7	4.4	8.4	7.0
N.A., Other	6.1	9.5	1.7	8.8
Total (N)	(294)	(180)	(549)	(1,358)

[a] Includes Scuola Media Inferiore and Scuola Media Superiore.
[b] Terminal secondary school.
Source: Sartori et al., p. 95.

With regard to their experience, technical capacity, and professionalism, PCI leaders differ markedly from the leaders of the other Italian parties. Politics in Italy is dominated by intellectuals and professionals of a "humanistic" and "liberal" training and background. Italy, in fact, is the last country in Western Europe to preserve in its political elite the figure of the upper class notable or political dilettante who was common in English and French politics in the nineteenth century. This group is rapidly being replaced by a professional elite, but many of them still operate in the traditional parties.

The Communist leaders, in contrast, are an intellectual elite of a much different character. They are organizational technicians with long and varied experience in the political arena, who regard politics as their profession. Their varied experiences in the party and in its affiliates bring them in contact with different groups of people and increase the internal communication in the PCI far above that of the other Italian parties.

In terms of length of experience, more than 50 percent of PCI leaders joined the party before the age of twenty-one, compared to 39 percent of the Socialists and 20 percent of the Christian Democrats. More significantly, over 50 percent of the Communists held party office before the age of twenty-five. Since the majority of the PCI respondents were between the ages of thirty and fifty in 1958, on the average they have had about twenty years of active political experience. Many (40.8 percent) were politically active during the period of Fascism. This figure is considerably higher than that of the PSI, with 22.8 percent, and higher again than that of the Christian Democrats, with 4.2 percent.

Communist leaders exceed the leaders of the other parties in the *breadth* of their experience, too. Whereas 31 percent of the Christian Democrats and 40 percent of the PSI leaders have held positions as provincial or city councilmen, 48.3 percent of the Communists have done so.[19] In labor organizations as well, the multiple roles of PCI leaders are evident; 63.3 percent are also members of labor organizations, compared to 43.3 percent of the Socialist leaders and 43.9 percent of the DC.[20]

19. Giovanni Sartori et al., *Il Parlamento Italiano,* p. 101.
20. Ibid., p. 104.

TABLE 6.9

Age of First Party Registration and First Party Office
of Italian Legislators, 1948–58, by Party
(in percentages)

Age at First Party Registration	PCI	PSI	DC	All-Party Average
Not registered before 1st Elec.	0.8	0.8	1.4	1.5
Before 18	29.6	20.2	5.9	14.5
18–21	20.2	18.7	13.6	16.0
22–25	21.4	17.2	16.2	15.8
26–30	14.4	17.9	18.8	15.6
31–35	4.9	8.9	16.2	11.4
36–40	1.6	3.7	13.2	8.7
41–50	4.1	8.2	8.9	8.3
Over 50	0.4	0.8	3.1	3.7
N.A.	2.5	3.7	2.6	4.1
Age at First Party Office				
Never held office	0.8	6.0	14.8	10.5
Before 25	52.3	35.3	23.0	30.0
25–30	12.0	16.5	15.8	12.9
31–35	7.5	6.8	13.4	10.0
Over 35	8.7	13.5	21.5	18.0
N.A.	18.7	21.9	11.5	18.6
Total (N)	(241)	(133)	(419)	(1,008)

Source: Sartori et al., p. 87.

Moreover, the PCI parliamentary party and its bureaucratic apparatus are more interrelated than is the case in the other parties; 72 percent of all PCI parliamentarians have held a party post on the provincial level, as compared to 44.5 percent in the PSI and 54 percent in the DC. It is interesting, however, that the number of PCI deputies who have held positions in the *central* office of the party (9.9 percent) is lower than the average of all the parties (13.9 percent). This fact can be attributed to the routinized recruitment system available to the PCI through its extensive provincial bureaucracy. The other parties, in contrast, are often forced to find suitable parliamentary candidates in their central organizations.

Table 6.10 summarizes the experience of parliamentarians of the three major parties in their respective party bureaucracies.

TABLE 6.10

Positions Held by Italian Legislators in Party Bureaucracy, 1946–58, by Party
(in percentages)

Party Position	PCI	PSI	DC	All-Party Average
Provincial Organs	71.8	44.5	53.7	48.0
Central Apparatus	9.9	14.4	6.7	13.9
Provincial and Central	13.9	23.9	14.4	14.7
No Positions	2.0	9.4	16.6	14.4
No Response	2.4	7.8	8.6	9.0
Total (N)	(294)	(180)	(549)	(1,358)

Source: Sartori et al., p. 97.

The professionalism of the Communist leader far exceeds that of his non-Communist counterparts. As I have shown above, in a political system dominated by lawyers and professors, the PCI leaders include only one-third as many lawyers as the other parties and one-fourth as many teachers and professors. They are mainly party professionals and labor leaders with long political experience.[21] Sartori's summary of the degree of professionalism in the major parties is reproduced in Table 6.11.

TABLE 6.11

Party Professionalism Among Italian Legislators, 1946–58, by Party
(in percentages)

	PCI	PSI	DC	All-Party Average
Nonprofessional	0.7	1.7	4.9	7.1
Semiprofessional	24.5	62.8	83.4	64.6
Professional	74.8	35.5	11.7	28.3
Total (N)	(294)	(180)	(549)	(1,358)

Source: Sartori et al., p. 106.

21. Ibid., p. 89.

As in the case of its electoral constituency and its middle-level leaders, one cannot easily categorize the top-level leaders of the PCI as proletarian. In the inclusion of traditional intellectuals in the leadership, the minimal conditions for Gramsci's war of position are met. But does the organization of the party permit the coexistence of the war of position with the war of movement? In this respect the PCI has clearly overadapted to its current strategy.

THE ORGANIZATIONAL PATTERN

The PCI is structurally a *mass* party, and not a party of devotees, both in Duverger's terms and in Marxist terms of reference.[22] Devotees are highly trained cadres of militants whose lives are dedicated to a political cause; the revolutionary party operating in illegality or semilegality is inevitably such a party. However, the party that seeks power by electoral means cannot gain power through such a vanguard. It requires a small number of bureaucrats and politicians, a larger group of part-time militants, and a much larger group of voters and sympathizers to bring it to power.

In Italy, the change from a devotee party to a mass party occurred suddenly with Togliatti's return from Russia and the opening of his theory of the Italian road to socialism. In a postwar theoretical piece, the Communist leader wrote: "The battle for the liberation of the country from Fascism and the construction of a democratic regime . . . will be implemented in the party's policies and activities, and, therefore, in a transformation of its organization." [23]

The first symptom of change was the recruitment of Catholics into the party ranks and the extension of membership to illiterates. On a symbolic level, the change in character of the party was demonstrated by a subtle change in the meaning of the word "cadre" or *quadro;* in popular Communist parlance the word is now used to mean an individual militant rather than a group of such individuals.

The classical weapon of the Leninist devotee party is the party

22. Duverger, in *Political Parties,* has codified this view in his classification of devotee parties and mass parties.
23. *Rinascita, 1,* No. 4 (1944), 25.

cell. Although the immediate postwar years in Italy were characterized by attempts to strengthen the party's cell structure and to
increase the number of cells, in fact the number of party cells soon
began to decrease (from 54,000 in 1950 to 41,000 in 1960 and to
33,600 in 1963). The trend was combatted by a rule of 1950 requiring all party members who work in factories to belong to the
cell in their place of work. The attempt was largely unsuccessful,
and, according to one observer, "the cells in the places of employment have virtually ceased to function almost everywhere." [24]

Simultaneously, the party sections—territorially based units
much larger and more unwieldy than the cells—have increased
from 10,200 in 1951 to 11,000 in 1961.[25] In effect, the shift in emphasis from revolutionary and resistance activity to the parliamentary and electoral arena has made the section rather than the cell
the basic working unit of the party. The PCI organization secretary
in 1950 wrote: "Now that the party is new and different, organizes
different social classes and has new tasks of government and local
administration, the functioning of the *section* becomes much more
important than in the past." [26]

The sections, which usually contain from 100 to 500 members,
are typical Italian political clubs, rather than militant cadre organizations. In most of the smaller towns there are no cells at all,
and a single section will contain all the party members in the area.
In many areas, leaders complain, there are more sections than cells,
and the cells themselves "are virtually only administrative units in
which the cell leader is simply a distributor of newspapers and col-
lector of dues." [27]

Above the level of the cells and sections, the PCI is organized
geographically into provincial federations whose basic organs are
federal committees, directory committees, secretariats, and secretaries. Each federal committee, composed of thirty or more pro-

24. This evolution is documented in the official party statistics cited in note 12;
Celso Ghino, "Osservazioni sul Partito," in *Rinascita, 1,* No. 10 (1950), 459; "Modificazioni Strutturali e Politiche del PCI al suo IX° Congresso," p. 50.

25. *Forza ed Attività del Partito,* p. 7; *Dati sull'Organizzazione del PCI,"* p. 3.

26. Pietro Secchia, "L'Arte dell'Organizzazione," *Rinascita, 3,* No. 12 (1945), 267.

27. Celso Ghino, "Aspetti della Struttura dell'Organizzarione," *Rinascita, 7,* No.
3 (1950), 263.

vincial leaders, elects its own directing committee, secretariat, and secretary. In reality, the secretariat has most of the power, and the federal committees merely ratify choices reached at that level.[28]

A surprising degree of flexibility, if not independence, marks the activities of these provincial organs of the party, dating to their long period of isolated action under Fascism. Federal secretaries are generally born in the region in which they work. Their contacts with the central office are intermittent, unless they also happen to be members of the Central Committee, which meets in Rome at regular intervals. When we compare the provincial strength of the PCI to the imperious power of the Federation of the Seine in the French Communist Party, we see a sharp difference in internal dynamics.

These provincial units originally duplicated the provincial organization of the country. Gradually, however, a number of new federations have been created within the territory of existing provinces, raising the total number from 92 in 1948 to 99 in 1956 and to 113 in 1960. These new federations are vital in understanding the inner dynamics of the PCI. They have been formed either to divide a strong Communist zone from a weaker one (Melfi), to isolate an economically homogeneous zone (Avezzano), or to accede to the demands of a group of militants for autonomy from an imperious federation (Monza). This organizational flexibility suggests that the PCI possesses means of internal reconciliation and is responsive to the demands of its local cadres.

During the same period, intermediate party organs began to proliferate between the sections and the provincial federations, and between the federations and the central office. These units are city committees, zonal committees, occupational category committees, and regional committees. In some cities, in addition, units

28. PCI, *Statuto*, Articolo VII, in *VIII° Congresso del PCI, Atti e Risoluzioni* (Roma, 1957), p. 994. The federal committee parallels the role of the Party Congress on the national level. The directory committee "directs the federation in the interval between meetings of the federal committee." The provincial secretariat "assures the continuity of the work, the execution of the decisions of the Federal Committee and the Directory Committee, and the fulfillment of day-to-day tasks." In reality, however, the secretariat has most of the power, and the federal committee merely ratifies choices reached at that level. See "Modificazioni Strutturali e Politiche del PCI al suo IX° Congresso," *Tempi Moderni*, 2 (aprile 1960), 40 and n. 39.

that organize various parts of the city have been formed. In the cities of large-scale immigration, centers of immigrants have been created.[29]

These new organizations give the PCI structure an even more marked territorial bias and decrease even further the importance of the functional and occupational party cells. As the cells disappear and the sections show signs of weakness and demoralization, the PCI has attempted to govern them with the interposition of various types of intermediate bodies. The result is a decidedly top-heavy organization in each province. The following table gives some idea of the structural evolution of the past decade.

TABLE 6.12

Changes in PCI Organizational Structure, 1954–63

	1954	1959	1963
Cells	57,000	39,800	33,600
Cells in the Place of Work	11,500	7,115	4,700
Communal and City Committees	529	526	474
Zone Committees	185	226	334
Federations	97	99	113
Regional Committees	18	18	18

Source: Official party statistics (1954; 1961; 1964).

Although the number of party cells decreased between 1954 and 1963 by approximately 80 percent, the number of *cells in the place* of work—the classical devotee organization—decreased by about 125 percent in the same period. The evolution of its capillary organization gives the PCI a structure that approximates that of the other parties in the Italian political arena and changes the nature of the relationship between the party and its members. The new organizational techniques described above, in the words of a leading critic, "are all measures through which the PCI seeks to adapt its organized structure to the needs of electoral competition, and contribute involuntarily to cause a transformation at all levels into an electoralistic party." [30] Moreover, these territorial units

29. *Statuto,* Arts. 9, 11, 12, 14; also see the "Rapporto del Attività" in *l'Unità,* No. 17 (1960).

30. "Modificazioni Strutturali e Politiche," p. 30.

are less susceptible to organizational control than the classical party cell, for they give dissenting elements the opportunity for stable organization and communication, and they strengthen the regional bias in the party power structure.

On the national level, the party is composed of a Central Committee of 128 members and a Central Control Commission of 62 members, both elected by a congress of provincial, parliamentary, and bureaucratic party leaders who meet every four years. In recent years, both the Central Committee and the Central Control Commission have been expanded greatly in response to demands from below for more equitable representation. A secret vote was established at congresses in 1956. The Central Committee and the Central Control Commission in turn elect the national secretary and vice-secretary, the Direction, and the Secretariat. Frequent shifts in both the Direction and the Secretariat suggest that the Central Committee has very real powers, and its published debates often demonstrate great internal dissent.

This national organization is highly bureaucratic and centralized, with many of the same leaders holding posts in several of the top decision-making bodies as well as in the parliamentary group. What is remarkable about this structure in the context of the Italian political system is not its *difference* from the organization of the non-Communist parties, but its *similarity* to them.[31] The major difference is the organization of factions in the other parties and their lack of organization in the PCI. Despite this absence, each of the PCI's major factions, with the notable exception of the "Chinese" faction, is represented in its highest bureaucratic organs. For example, the debate on Togliatti's report on the Soviet Twenty-second Party Congress brought a clear split of opinion in the Central Committee. Similar debates have marked the PCI's entire reaction to the "Chinese" question, and to the critical issue of the powers of the Central Committee.

The PCI, finally, operates, or has a dominant influence in, a number of important mass organizations, such as the CGIL, the national labor organization, a peasant group (the Alleanza dei Contadini), a national cooperative organization, a women's organization, an

31. John Clarke Adams and Paolo Barile, *The Government of Republican Italy,* p. 157.

association of former partisans, and a peace organization.[32] These groups all carry the party line or some suitable modification of it, and they no doubt contain cells of militants who attempt to control their policies.

However, in a critical respect these mass organizations and front groups do not operate as Leninist dogma would dictate. First, Italy's political system is one in which various ideological traditions each organize a world of secondary organizations around themselves. Thus, when it appeared that the PCI in 1947 would soon control the National Confederation of Labor (CGL), the Catholic unionists and the Social Democrats broke off to form the CISL and the UIL, two rival federations.[33] Similarly, a Christian Democratic organization, the Coltivatori Diretti, opposes the Communist peasant group, a Christian Democratic women's group opposes the PCI women's organization, and a rival cooperative group organizes a number of cooperatives throughout the country. As a result, the PCI mass organizations are in competition with other groups that are equally well organized. They are required to compete for the workers' alliance, often in ways that go against the party's direct interest. The CGIL, for example, often reminds the PCI that it is not merely a "transmission belt" for the party.

Second, many of these organizations develop their own organizational and recruiting structure and gain independence from the PCI. The Federation of Young Communists (FGCI), for example, is a youth group of some 173,700 members organized into 4,600 clubs. It has its own publication, *Nuova Generazione,* its registration cards and finances, and it holds its own national congresses. It is often sharply critical of the leadership of the PCI, and the left faction in the PCI uses the Young Communists' publications as a mouthpiece.

Both in the mass organizations and in the party's central and provincial organizations, operating legitimately in a representative system in competition with other groups, *once the burdens of legitimacy have been accepted,* leads inevitably to the internal differentiation characteristic of political parties in these systems.

32. Joseph LaPalombara, *Interest Groups in Italian Politics,* Chap. 5.
33. Joseph LaPalombara, *The Italian Labor Movement: Problems and Prospects* (Ithaca, 1957).

POLITICAL BEHAVIOR: THE CONFUSION OF POLITICAL ROLES

In its policies in the national political arena, the Italian Communist Party has the dubious virtue of confusing its friends as well as its enemies. Because of its strategy of alliances, the party has developed an ideology of solidarity, rather than one of revolution. Its organizational structure has lost its revolutionary rigidity and gained a territorial and an interest bias. Moreover, its leadership cadre and its membership group are drawn from diverse parts of the stratification hierarchy, dulling the party's militance while extending the range of the interests it must seek to satisfy.

These characteristics of the Italian Communist Party's ideology, organization, and membership have a definite impact on the policy level. Party leaders have institutionalized the PCI as a new type of radical party in a capitalist society, seeking the transformation of the society through the utilization of its present political structures. It has largely shifted from a politics of revolution to a politics of interest, proposing many reforms that are un-Marxist and even anti-Marxist in the process. This is not simply Lenin's scheme of "partial actions"; in fact, Togliatti made clear quite soon after his return to Italy in 1944 that the party was revising the Leninist dictum that transitional slogans may be used only in time of crisis. The PCI has institutionalized its role within the system to such an extent that turning suddenly toward revolution would cause a loss in its mass support and bring about critical internal dislocations.

Communist organizations participate in the political and economic life of the country in diverse ways and cooperate with non-Communist power groups when it is essential to further their goals or the interests of their members. For example, the party administers many cities in the central provinces. These local governments are required to perform all the functions of local government and to maintain majorities that are by no means wholly dependent upon workers and party members.

The PCI administers a whole range of profit-making cooperative ventures which are essential in tying the loyalties of workers and peasants to the party economically. In Emilia, numbers of cooperative stores, credit agencies, and businesses are run with party backing and participation. These are essentially businesses that buy and sell agricultural products at market prices. The party is rumored to gain a large source of revenue from this source. Whatever their political role, these cooperatives allow the peasants of the central provinces to compete in European markets with producers from richer and more modernized agricultural areas than Emilia and Tuscany. Were they to be destroyed by a revolutionary shift in strategy, thousands of PCI members and voters would instantly lose their reason for supporting the party.

Most compromising, perhaps, are the PCI's policies toward the Church. As part of its policy of alliances, the party has looked toward an eventual understanding with progressive Catholics. As a result of this policy, Togliatti acceded to the inclusion of the Fascist Lateran Treaty in the Constitution of 1948. As a further result, the party has been politically crippled from agitating publicly for the removal of the Church's stranglehold over secular education or for the promulgation of modern marriage laws. And since the Church continues to dominate Italian culture and training, Italy has been unable to produce the progressive, openminded group of lower level militants that Gramsci called the organic intellectuals. This is perhaps the major explanation for the relative weakness of that level of party members.

When we turn to analyzing the behavior of PCI leaders in the political system, we have few quantitative indexes to utilize. We know definitely that PCI deputies all vote predictably in the Chamber of Deputies, and that they are by far the most disciplined group in Italian politics. When questioned on party discipline, only 7.8 percent of Communist leaders thought it was excessive, as compared to 36.7 percent of Socialist leaders and 46.1 percent of Christian Democratic leaders.[34]

On the other hand, we know that PCI leaders use parliament actively for purposes more concrete than propaganda and opposition. For example, in parliamentary committee voting, the PCI apparently votes with the government on most issues, since unanimity or near unanimity is usually recorded in committee deliberations. Although these parliamentary organs do not handle matters of general national policy, they *do* legislate on problems of local

34. Sartori, et al., *Il Parlamento Italiano*, p. 105.

government and private members' requests—in other words, in areas where the parties are virtually required to cooperate.[35]

Equally important, the PCI deputies in parliament are frequent users of the right of written interrogation of ministers, Italy's closest equivalent to the question period. These written interrogations usually pertain to private members' inquiries on behalf of constituents or inquiries into possible administrative irregularities. Their increasing use by the PCI since 1948 certainly has nothing to do with the use of parliament as a propaganda platform, and suggests that PCI deputies are among the most serious delegates for their constituents in parliament.[36]

All this activity would still be compatible with an untarnished dictatorial will, were there not evidence that PCI national leaders express democratic preferences and attitudes. A study of Italian parliamentarians carried out in 1963 revealed that Communist deputies scored lower on the Rokeach dogmatism scale than Christian Democratic deputies.[37]

It would be naïve to force the issue of the PCI's adaptation to democracy in the absence of evidence about the internal life of the party. What is certainly clear, however, is that the party strategy— a strategy of broad, democratic alliances in the name of the structural reform of the system—has had a great impact on the party's following. I have shown that great social diversity marks the PCI's voters, mass members, and leaders; what remains to be shown is the wide diversity of attitudes among these groups. Experience is never neutral; a twenty-year strategy of alliance, reform, and democracy cannot fail to awaken corresponding attitudes among the party's followers.

For interesting evidence on this score, we need only consult the same CISER 1963 survey described above. When PCI supporters were separated from the general sample, it was found, first, that their attitudes reflect the reformist doctrinal line of the party, and, second, that within the sample, certain key divergences may be seen.

35. Istituto Carlo Cattaneo, *PCI e DC nel Parlamento* (Bologna, mimeograph, n.d.), p. 100.

36. Ibid., pp. 87–88.

37. Gordon Di Renzo, *A Social Psychological Analysis of Personality Structures of Members of the Italian Chamber of Deputies*, unpublished Ph.D. thesis, University of Notre Dame, 1963.

For example, when confronted with three unidentified left-wing slogans, 69 percent of the total subsample showed strong approval of a popular alliance slogan ("unity of the working class"), 51 percent approved of a sectarian slogan ("all power to the forces of labor"), and only 26 percent showed approval of a Social Democratic slogan ("realizing the socialism of democracy"). The first slogan corresponds most closely to Communist Party alliance slogans.[38]

The alliance strategy appears to influence Communist supporters' choice of a governmental coalition formula, for when asked, "What form of governmental coalition do you think is preferable in Italy?" only 61 percent of the Communist respondents were in favor of a government of the left, 15 percent were in favor of the government as it was then (a modest center-left coalition), 16 percent favored a government with Socialist support, and 9 percent favored some other formula or did not answer.[39]

More striking still was the equivocal attitude of PCI supporters toward a possible bipolar party system in Italy. They were asked: "It is said that in truly democratic countries only two political parties exist. If in Italy there existed only the PCI and the DC, for whom would you vote? And if there existed only the PSI and the DC, for whom would you vote? And if there existed only the PCI and the PSI?" Only 78 percent of Communist supporters would choose their own party in a bipolar choice between the PCI and Christian Democracy; 83 percent would choose the Socialists between the PSI and the DC; and only 60 percent would choose their own party in a choice between the PCI and the Socialists.

It is not certain that the question was phrased in a completely clear manner, but the lack of potential support for the PCI if it were one pole in a bipolar system is quite dramatic. The diversity of opinion among the Communist supporters in the CISER sample appears even more starkly when we consider the results of the same questions when asked of Christian Democratic supporters; 100 percent would choose their own party over either the PCI or the Socialists, and none would choose the Communists over the Socialists in a bipolar system between those two parties.

38. CISER data, 1963, Istituto Carlo Cattaneo analysis, pp. 150–51.
39. Ibid., p. 153.

Perhaps even more interesting than these statistics is the internal diversity of the Communist sample when controlled for socioeconomic status and for sex. Sharp differences mark the attitudes of those in manual and nonmanual occupations, and, in some cases, the attitudes of those in urban and rural occupations. Housewives, and particularly high-status housewives, are sharply differentiated from the male respondents on many issues. Table 6.13 analyzes the

TABLE 6.13

Attitude Profiles of PCI Supporters by Occupation and Sex
($N = 599$)
CISER, 1963 Survey

Percentage:	Urban Manual	Agri-cultural	Urban Non-Manual	High-Status House-wives	Low-Status House-wives	Total
Finding economic situation good	27	24	46	41	29	31
Finding economic situation improving	22	23	47	27	33	29
In favor of "unity of working class" slogan	74	87	43	60	66	69
In favor of "all power to the forces of labor" slogan	58	69	25	43	43	51
In favor of "realizing the socialism of democracy" slogan	23	20	45	18	26	26
Favoring government as is, 1963, (DC, PSDI, PRI)	13	7	17	20	21	15
Favoring government with PSI ministers	17	12	39	13	6	16
Favoring coalition of DC and the right	0	0	1	0	2	1
Favoring centrist government	1	2	6	9	6	4
Favoring left-wing government	67	78	30	46	46	61
Don't know	1	1	7	13	5	4
In two-party system:						
Choosing DC between DC and PCI	15	7	45	32	25	22
Choosing PSI between DC and PSI	85	95	82	77	76	83
Choosing PCI between PSI and PCI	66	82	29	45	59	60

Source: CISER data, 1963, Istituto Carlo Cattaneo analysis, pp. 142–54.

attitudes of the PCI CISER subsample toward (1) the economic situation, (2) the choice of slogans, (3) the coalition choice, and (4) the choice of a party in a hypothetically bipolar system.

Three points in particular stand out about the attitudes of PCI supporters. First, there is a sharp cleavage between urban manual and rural supporters on the one hand, and urban nonmanual and women party supporters on the other. Second, the strongest left-wing attitudes are found, not among the urban proletariat but among the rural respondents (a category that includes farm workers, share tenants, and small farmers). And, third, the relatively small percentage favoring a left-wing government and choosing the PCI over the other two parties in a hypothetical two-party system, suggests that the PCI profits from a large protest vote that would vanish were the party to have a serious chance to come to power. What is most revealing about this third factor is that the protest vote is registered most strongly not among the poorest urban and rural workers, but among those in urban nonmanual occupations and among high-status housewives. But even among urban working class respondents, only 67 percent would prefer a left-wing government and only 66 percent would choose the PCI between the Communists and Socialists in a two-party system.

In other words, the following of the PCI is far more pluralistic than has been generally acknowledged. It is not clear whether the PCI supporters' diversity of attitudes, like their social diversity, is a direct result of the party's strategy of "war of position," or if it results from confusion at the complex rhetoric of a party trying to institutionalize itself as a new type of radical party in a capitalist system. In either case, the findings of this CISER attitude profile lend strength to the conclusion of Almond and Verba regarding the Italian sample reported in *The Civic Culture,* when they discovered that supporters of the left are more likely to be "open partisans" than supporters of the right. They write,

> Italy thus presents us with the curious anomaly of a political system in which the formal democratic constitution is supported in large part by traditional-clerical elements who are not democratic at all. . . . Opposed to the constitution is a left wing, which, at least in part and at the rank-and-file voter

level rather than among the party elite, manifests a form of open partisanship that is consistent with a democratic system.[40]

The theoretical paradox of the strategy Gramsci outlined in 1930 thus appears as a practical political paradox as well. The "war of position" within parliamentary institutions leads to attitudes on the part of the party's supporters that would prevent a sudden switch to a "war of movement" strategy. The PCI has adapted to the Italian political system more completely than its leaders might have wished. That is why Togliatti appears to us today as a revisionist and Gramsci, despite his acute understanding of the changes in strategy necessary in advanced political systems, was still a Leninist.

In one sense, however, the dialogue between the "war of position" and the "war of movement" has not been resolved. It persists within the PCI in the tension between its two major factions—the new left and the reformists. The left represents Gramsci's insistence upon the primacy of the factory and the active strategy of the war of movement. The revisionists embody the passive strategy of the war of position in parliament and in elections. It is the left that seeks more internal democracy (publication of the proceedings of the Central Committee and the empowering of party congresses to make theoretical decisions). The right, which is much more advanced in its adaptation to the Italian system, proposing the creation of a unified party of the left and denying the hegemonic position of the working class, is more conservative in its unwillingness to loosen up the party's internal life.[41] This is the final paradox of Gramsci's dual strategy; since each strategy is embodied in a concrete faction, we see an internal opposition in the leadership, precisely the accommodation to democratic life that Gramsci, as a good Leninist, hoped to avoid.

40. Gabriel Almond and Sidney Verba, *The Civic Culture* (Boston, 1965), pp. 115–16.

41. See Pietro Merli-Brandini, "La Crisi del Pensiero Comunista," in *Conquiste del Lavoro, 18* (14–20 novembre 1965), 9–20.

7. The Communist Vote: North and South

Revolutionary Marxism was the child of a particular place and time: Western Europe during its early period of industrial development in the nineteenth century. The combination was explosive, for it presented history with a bourgeois intelligentsia that had yet to find an economic function, and an uprooted lower class whose economic function was all too clear.

Marx's vision of revolution was deeply imbedded in that moment of history. When the moment passed—when both intellectuals and lower classes were integrated in society—then the assumptions of the Communist Manifesto were outdistanced and Marxism took a social-democratic turn. These assumptions, as George Lichtheim writes, had "presupposed a pattern of events which experience had shown to be no longer possible in Europe—*or indeed in any advanced country.*" [1]

Such a pattern, however, was still dominant in Russia in 1917. For just as economic and political development in the West had transformed European socialism, "the obverse also applied: where the pre-1848 situation still existed, the fire that had gone out in the West might still burst into flames." [2] Lenin's double-edged contribution was to recognize the connection between political backwardness and revolution, and to develop an organizational weapon and a strategy tailored to these conditions.

But if Lenin's strategy in Russia in 1917 represents a successful adaptation of Marxism to conditions of economic and political backwardness, Togliatti's strategy in Italy turns the tables once again: it attempts to adapt Marxism-Leninism to societies with a

1. George Lichtheim, *Marxism: An Historical and Critical Analysis* (New York, Praeger, 1963), p. 125. Emphasis added.
2. Ibid.

high level of development. As I indicated in the last chapter, it is senseless to pass Togliatti's strategy off as mere deception, since its implementation has required certain crucial changes in structure and behavior.

The paradox of the Italian Communist Party lies precisely in its relation to the developmental dialectic outlined above. For if the Via Italiana al Socialismo reflects an accurate reading of a politically advanced industrial society, it is almost by definition not an accurate reading of a politically backward agricultural society. The paradox lies in the fact that Italy in the 1960s is both—a politically advanced, industrialized North and a politically backward, agricultural South.

It is here that the dimensions of Italian political dualism become highly relevant. The problem is, once again, dialectical. Does a dualistic political setting require a Marxist party to elaborate two entirely different strategies? If so, will the party be torn apart by internal schizophrenia? On the other hand, if the same strategy is applied to two entirely different political settings simply because they happen to be included in the same nation-state, will it succeed in one and fail in the other?

These are some of the problems that will be analyzed in the following chapters. In its organization and leadership, its mass membership, and its ideology, the Italian Communist Party has had to face essentially the same problem: the problem of the implicit contradiction between Marxism's original affinity for societies in early stages of development and a national strategy designed for a society in an advanced stage of development.

Although it is in the internal life of the party that these problems can be most fruitfully studied, even the structure of the Communist vote shows the far-reaching effects of political dualism. The PCI began its postwar career in Italy as the child of the Resistance—a mainly northern phenomenon. As a result, its vote in the North in 1946 was more than twice the size of its vote in the South.

The last two decades have witnessed a dramatic shift in the balance of Communist electoral power. Whereas the Communist vote in the North has increased only slightly, in the South it has more than doubled during the same period. Moreover, the highest

Communist vote in the North is now concentrated on the periphery of the big cities, where much of the population is made up of recent rural immigrants!

This dramatic shift in Communist electoral support, although it is welcomed by PCI leaders, creates a new dilemma: that a party with a strategy designed primarily for a highly developed urban society now attracts a large proportion of its votes from a backward, rural society. Is it possible that the party places a subjective limit on its electoral expansion in the South—where the chances are most fecund—because its strategy was designed for the North—where potential support may be tapering off?

Moreover, the political setting of a backward society places certain *objective* limits on a proletarian party's capacity for action. When we examine the structure of the Communist vote in North and South, we see sharp differences in its concentration, its consistency, and its sources. These differences are related to distinct styles of campaigning, bases of support, and types of candidates. In other words, despite the elaboration of a unified strategy for a Via Italiana al Socialismo, the Italian Communist Party may be hampered by the same problems of political dualism that have affected Italian politics since the Risorgimento.

VOTING AND POLITICAL DUALISM

Students of American politics have for many years been entranced by the different structure of nominations, campaigning, and voting in North and South in the United States.[3] Italian scholars have confronted the same problem, but with more emotion and less analysis. Typically, for example, studies of Italian voting behavior focus on the limited property franchise in the nineteenth century and its effects in reducing the eligible electorate in the poverty-stricken South.

This is a trivial consideration, for in 1870 the percentage of the population eligible to vote was almost the same in North and South: 2.05 per hundred in the North and 1.87 per hundred in

3. V. O. Key, *Southern Politics in State and Nation* (New York, 1949); for a more recent treatment of southern politics see Avery Leiserson, ed., *The American South in the 1960's* (New York, 1965).

the South.[4] Roughly 40 percent of the voters were found in the South, a figure almost exactly proportional to the region's share of the general population.

By 1919 these proportions had shifted, but not, as historians have imagined, in favor of the expanding northern population. Although it had barely 36 percent of the Italian population in 1919, the South had 43.3 percent of the voters. In other words, the expansion of the franchise between 1870 and 1921 favored the South in relation to the North, although the South had never really been disfavored by the relatively narrow property franchise in force until then.[5]

A more important factor in Italian electoral history is that, under the limited suffrage in force until 1882 and the slightly enlarged suffrage in force until 1919, the voting turnout in southern Italy was proportionally much higher than in northern Italy. Turnout in the North in 1870 averaged 44.4 percent and ranged from a low of 31 percent in Umbria to a high of 47 percent in Piedmont. Turnout in the South averaged 60.5 percent and ranged from 43.5 percent in Lazio to 62.5 percent in Sicily. Regional statistics for 1892, when the electorate had been enlarged from 530,000 to 2,900,000, are even more significant. While 51.1 percent of registered voters were voting in the North, 65.4 percent were voting in the South.[6]

It was only when the suffrage had been extended to the entire male population in 1919 that these proportions shifted. With an increase in the total electorate to over ten million voters, participation in the North increased to over 60 percent in most regions, while participation in the South declined to just over 50 percent of all registered voters. Voting after 1945 expanded greatly in both regions, with a national turnout of over 90 percent. But participation in the South remains lower than in the North, with a postwar average of just over 90 percent, compared to a northern

4. SVIMEZ, Un Secolo di Statistiche Italiane: Nord e Sud 1861–1961 (Roma, 1961), p. 1028.

5. Ministero dell'Interno, Compendio dei Risultati delle Consultazioni Popolari dal 1848 al 1954 (Roma, 1955), pp. 36–39; population figures are from SVIMEZ, Un Secolo di Statistiche, pp. 14–15.

6. SVIMEZ, p. 1028.

average of 94 percent. The number of registered voters and the percentage voting by region are presented in Table 7.1.

TABLE 7.1

Number of Eligible Voters and Percentage Who Voted in
Selected Elections, 1870–1948, by Province and Region

	1870[a]		1890[b]		1919[c]		1948[d]	
	Eligible Voters	% Voting	Eligible Voters	% Voting	Eligible Voters	% Voting	Eligible Voters	% Voting
North								
Piedmont	75,738	47.0	443,303	45.7	1,051,094	63.0	2,554,878	93.1
Liguria	25,819	41.6	122,094	45.1	354,470	60.5	1,107,816	91.5
Lombardy	68,961	40.8	393,646	45.2	1,343,223	67.4	4,272,578	94.1
Veneto	39,960	40.9	269,931	47.7	939,892	51.5	2,399,258	93.3
Center								
Emilia	42,180	32.7	190,771	48.4	777,223	71.5	2,350,338	95.3
Tuscany	48,035	32.0	206,665	58.6	785,285	61.3	2,128,937	94.7
Marches	13,956	38.0	79,090	57.5	333,915	47.6	860,020	94.3
Umbria	8,272	31.1	47,429	52.3	215,809	56.2	505,414	94.3
South								
Lazio	12,725	43.5	79,974	56.6	376,355	47.5	1,982,749	90.2
Abruzzi	20,923	57.6	110,993	63.1	556,145	51.3	1,004,370	91.1
Campania	56,326	50.9	247,105	62.8	919,502	49.9	2,409,666	88.8
Puglia	29,994	55.0	125,636	68.0	605,539	54.2	1,715,640	93.6
Basilicata	8,788	58.2	37,811	62.6	162,884	50.9	334,845	91.7
Calabria	19,760	57.6	98,966	65.9	434,786	47.9	1,094,685	88.2
Sicily	41,645	62.4	255,635	61.3	1,149,950	44.5	2,594,903	88.0
Sardinia	16,936	46.8	43,609	64.3	233,254	55.5	686,624	90.1
Total	530,018	45.5	2,752,658	53.7	10,239,326	56.6	29,117,554	92.2

[a] Restricted suffrage and single-member districts.
[b] Slightly enlarged suffrage with two-, three-, and four-member districts.
[c] Manhood suffrage, list system, and proportional representation.
[d] Universal suffrage, list system, proportional representation with optional preference vote.
Source: Ministero dell'Interno, *Compendio dei Risultati delle Consultazioni Popolari dal 1848 al 1954* (Roma, Istituto Poligrafico dello Stato, 1955), pp. 38–49.

How can high participation before 1919 in the very backward South be explained? In order to understand it, we must take note of the fact that, before 1919, the narrow suffrage was accompanied by single-member colleges of the size of French cantons or American counties. When universal manhood suffrage was established in 1919, the electoral college was expanded to provincial size or greater. There were now fifty-four large circumscriptions electing party lists in place of over five hundred smaller ones, each of which had elected one, two, or three individual candidates.

Moreover, the development of the structure of political parties differed from North to South. By 1919, there were four well-organized parties in the North: the Communists, the Socialists, the Catholic Popular Party, and the Republicans. In the South, in contrast, politics was still the domain of freewheeling notables supported by informal groups of followers, a type of electoral structure entirely suited to the narrow suffrage and the small, single-member district. High southern voting turnout before 1919 was a concomitant of this pattern. Voters were mainly landowners, professionals, and rich peasants who were involved in close networks of personal ties; since the range of the electorate rarely extended beyond the limits of these clientele groups, high participation was a rather obvious corollary.

When, in 1919, the suffrage was expanded, the electoral college broadened, and the party list replaced the single candidate, the efficacy of these old clientele structures in getting out the loyal vote was severely damaged. Further, most of the new southern voters were isolated peasants, sharecroppers or farm workers whose participation tended to be low in any case. In the North, on the other hand, there were already well-organized parties in existence which could reap the benefits of proportional representation and of an expanded suffrage that now included large numbers of urban industrial workers.

The sharp regional differences in party structure, somewhat obscured before 1919, were now emphasized by the candidates' obligation to join together in provincial party lists. The Socialists had always been a party of the North, but the electoral reforms had the effect of forcing dissident Socialists to present lists of their own. Two of these lists, which were opposed to the official Socialist Party, received most of their votes in the South (over 90 percent in the elections of 1921) while the PSI received 86 percent of its support in the North.[7]

7. *Compendio*, p. 75.

The largest group elected to parliament from the South under the new system were the Liberals, a miscellaneous collection of notables whose ideology derived from the old liberal beliefs of the Risorgimento; in the elections of 1921, 70.2 percent of the Liberal votes and 76 percent of Liberal-Democratic votes came from the South as opposed to 29.8 percent and 24 percent in the North.[8]

Support for the other Italian parties and electoral groups was equally polarized between North and South. The Republicans received 96 percent of their support in the North and 4 percent in the South; the Catholic Popular Party received 80.6 percent of its support in the North and 19.4 percent in the South; the Veterans' Party (Combattenti) received only 15.4 percent of its support in the North and 74.6 percent in the South; the right-wing National Bloc and the Communists were predominantly Northern, the former with 86.7 percent and the latter with 91.5 percent of their vote located in the North. The only political party that received electoral support approximately proportional to the regional division of the population was the small, highly explosive Fascist Party of Benito Mussolini, which came to power on a wave of reaction one year later.[9] The distribution of regional voting by party or electoral group in the elections of 1921 is analyzed in Table 7.2.

Southern Italian politics was dominated by clientele groups from the time of unification on. However, in the amorphous Italian political scene, many southern politicians were not part of the historic right, but formed the backbone of the "Sinistra," a loose alliance of diverse political elements. Their leftism referred not to ideological radicalism, but to their having been in opposition between 1861 and 1875. In the 1865 elections, for example, 240 of the 276 successful "ministerial" candidates had come from the North, 152 of the 232 successful "opposition" candidates were from the South.[10]

What is perhaps most incongruous about the "leftism" of the

8. Ibid.

9. Ibid.

10. Giuliano Procacci, *Le Elezioni del 1874 e l'Opposizione Meridionale* (Milano, 1956), p. 9.

political leaders of the left in the South is that they were mainly large landowners, professionals, and aristocrats. In Sicily, for example, many of the opposition deputies were barons and princes. In the province of Naples, the prevalence of propertied groups was assured by the great weight of those who had become electors by virtue of education. Out of an electorate of barely 8,000, 37.5 percent had received the right to vote in this way. The result, of course, was that when the left came to power in 1875, no significant changes were made in public policy toward the South.[11]

What did change in 1875 was that southern notables began to profit hugely from state patronage, particularly in the form of municipal posts for their followers and a large protective tariff on wheat that was won in exchange for a large tariff for northern industry. From 1875 onward, southern deputies were the most consistent *ministrabili*. A surprising number of southerners like Nitti, Crispi, and Salandra gained power through their lack of fixed ideology and the flexible clientele character of their following. The prime ministry of Crispi, whose followers constituted the largest clientele group in the country's history, was particularly notorious in this regard.

The broadening of the franchise, to a limited extent in 1882 and much more in 1919, had been expected to lead to a radicalization of southern Italian politics. But so ingrained was the clientele system that the mass of new voters, most of them rural and all of them dependent economically on the political elite, were easily integrated into the existing system.

Campaign techniques differed radically from North to South, especially after the rise of organized mass parties in the North in the 1890s. During the Giolittian era from 1899 to 1911, which was one of the country's most progressive, majorities in the South were gained through the formation of rotten boroughs, the manipulation of state patronage, and the use of the regional prefecture to control the ballot box. At the same time, politics in the North was already shaped by cohesive party groups, and Giolitti's major-

11. Ibid., pp. 60–82, for the social composition of the Sinistra in the South. On government policy toward the South under the rule of the Sinistra, see Joseph La-Palombara, *Italy: The Politics of Planning*, Chap. 1.

ities there depended upon concessions to the labor movement and the Socialist cooperatives. But Socialism, as Salvemini complained, busied itself fighting for the rights of the northern proletariat to the ultimate disadvantage of the southern peasant.[12] The backwardness of southern politics was also evident in the failure of a peasant and a Catholic party to take root in the region at a time when both would have found a natural constituency there.

The long interregnum of Fascism is usually passed over by observers of Italian electoral politics. But the Fascist regime had an important effect upon Italy's political integration and political organization. In the South, local clientele structures continued to exist, but with a critical difference. Local leaders who had formerly held power under the loose denomination of Liberals were now forced to legitimate their rule through Fascist Party membership and control of the local Fascist *podestà*. Thus the end of World War II saw many formerly independent clientele groups identified with the Fascist Party.

Yet, in contrast to the North, where liberation saw Fascist collaborators purged, in the South, where local leaders held their power by virtue of local influence, they continued undisturbed. The loyalty of their clienteles, which had never depended upon allegiance to Fascism, but to economic, familial, and parafamilial ties, was undamaged, and many of these leaders turned immediately to the postwar parties of the right. The only significant group of local leaders in the South who lost power under Fascism was the Sicilian Mafia.

A second lasting impact of Fascism in the Mezzogiorno was to elevate the Catholic Church to political consciousness. Throughout Italy, Mussolini's desire to legitimate his regime encouraged him to give the Church a position of leadership similar to the role of the Catholic Church in Spain today. The Church, which had enjoyed little sympathy from the pre-Fascist liberal state, now controlled education and culture. It had transferred its economic interests from agriculture to stocks and bonds, and could act as a

12. Gaetano Salvemini, "Riforme parziali e riforme generali," in Rosario Villari, ed., *Il Sud nella Storia d'Italia* (Bari, 1961), pp. 480–93. On the "management" of southern elections, see Robert Fried, *The Italian Prefects* (New Haven, 1963), pp. 122–27.

powerful channel of access for ambitious individuals seeking state contracts or economic subsidies.

This entirely new political influence of the Church was muted in the North by the similar progress of other organized groups and institutions—particularly large industry. In the South, however, the kind of economic interest groups that were maturing in the North were almost completely absent. Hence, the end of the Fascist regime saw the Church in the Mezzogiorno fortified by a network of organizations ready to spring directly into politics. Its prestige—in a traditionally anticlerical region—was heightened by twenty-two years of officiating at the opening of public works and at the departure of soldiers and emigrants for Ethiopia and the New World.

When we turn to the regional distribution of the Italian vote just after the fall of Fascism, we must confront a striking fact: whereas liberation in the North restored the organized parties of 1921 to power, liberation in the South transformed the political forces of the right into electoral forces, and gave the Catholics an importance they had lacked before Fascism. Comparing the distribution of the vote in the North in the elections of 1921 and 1946, we see the solid progress of the left, despite its long exile, and of the Catholics, who controlled over 25 percent of the vote in 1921 and 37.3 percent in 1946. These gains were registered mainly at the expense of the right-wing liberals and the far right, which appear to have been totally discredited by Fascism. Much the same situation may be observed in central Italy.

In the South, in contrast, the elections of 1946 show only a moderate rise on the left, a rather large jump in Catholic support, and a turnout of almost 20 percent for the far right. The major losses have been registered by the miscellaneous left-wing groups, which have almost disappeared, and the Liberals, who controlled 40.4 percent of the vote in 1921 but only 14 percent in 1946. In other words, while the dominant pattern in the North was a return to the political forces that had been most popular before Fascism, the dominant pattern in the Mezzogiorno was the continued popularity of the political forces that had gained power over the past two decades—mainly the Church and the far right. These results are analyzed in Table 7.2.

Table 7.2

Comparison of Party Votes in 1921 and 1946, by Region
(in percentages)

Party or Tendency	North 1921	North 1946	Center 1921	Center 1946	South 1921	South 1946	Total 1921	Total 1946
Communists	5.9	22.4	7.1	24.7	1.2	10.2	4.6	19.0
Socialists[a]	33.5	28.5	27.4	17.7	10.7	10.5	25.3	20.7
Misc. Left[b]	0.1	1.4	0.4	1.6	20.1	1.5	6.6	1.4
Republicans	1.6	2.4	5.9	11.0	0.2	3.4	1.9	4.4
Catholics	25.1	37.3	21.0	30.0	12.4	35.0	20.4	35.2
Liberals[c]	8.3	3.2	2.0	3.9	40.4	14.0	17.5	6.8
Far Right[d]	21.5	3.3	36.0	8.0	13.1	19.8	21.2	11.1
Total[e] (N)	(3,423,059)	(11,273,998)	(1,082,980)	(4,392,986)	(2,102,702)	(7,301,302)	(6,608,141)	(22,968,286)
(%)	100	100	100	100	100	100	100	100

[a] For 1921, includes Official Socialists (PSI) and Independent Socialists; for 1946, only PSI, then called PSIUP.

[b] For 1921, includes Democratic Socialists and Democratic Reformists; for 1946, includes Action Party only.

[c] For 1921, includes Liberals and Liberal Democrats; for 1946, includes Democratic National Union only.

[d] For 1921, includes Combattenti, National Bloc, and Fascists; for 1946, includes Uomo Qualunque Front, National Bloc of Liberty, Sicilian Independence Movement, and Sardinian Party of Action.

[e] Excludes minor parties; for 1921, excludes Dissident Catholic Party, Economists, and Slav and German parties; for 1946, excludes Democratic Republican Concentration, Italian Unionists, Christian Social Movement, Italian Peasants' Party, and Democratic Party of Labor.

Source: Ministero dell'Interno, *Compendio*, pp. 75–79.

The conservatism of southern voters was also evident in 1946 in the results of the referendum on the character of the new constitution. Italians, who were asked to choose between a republic and a constitutional monarchy, chose a republic by a vote of 12,700,000 to 10,700,000 (54.3 percent to 45.7 percent). Had the vote been limited to northern and central Italy, support for a republic would have been as high as 65 percent; had the vote been limited to the South or the Islands, monarchy would have won by the same margin! [13]

It is important to reject the plausible hypothesis that conservatism in the South was mainly located among the small farmers in isolated villages, and that the big cities were centers of modern ideas on constitutionalism. This thesis works quite well for small villages in the North, where the largest vote for the monarchy in that region was found. Whereas the average vote in favor of monarchy in the North was 35.2 percent in the villages of less than a thousand inhabitants, 44.6 percent voted for a king. Conversely, the highest vote in favor of a republic (67.6 percent) is found in the North in the largest cities, those of more than 500,000 inhabitants.

In central and southern Italy, on the other hand, there was no linear correlation between size of commune and voting in favor of a republic or a monarchy. In these regions, and particularly in Sicily, the strongest support for a republic was found in the communes of 30,000 to 100,000 in population, whereas support for a monarchy was equally strong in the small villages and in the big cities. On the southern mainland, for example, the highest vote for the monarchy was in the city of Naples (79.9 percent) and the weakest support for monarchy came from the communes of from 30,000 to 100,000 inhabitants (64.2 percent). The regional distribution of the percentage vote in favor of a republic or a monarchy is analyzed by size of commune in Table 7.3.

The strong sentiment in favor of monarchy in large southern cities, and the fact that the main republican sentiment was found in medium-sized communes, should alert us to the fact that left-wing voting in Italy south of the Po River is not a simple concomitant of city size and industrialization. It is not in the big cities

13. *Compendio*, pp. 146–54.

that the Communist Party must seek potential supporters, but in the less advanced milieu of medium-sized cities. In fact, as we shall see, the strongest Communist Party support in southern Italy is found within this range of communes.

TABLE 7.3

Percentage of Vote for Republic or Monarchy in the Referendum of 1946 by Region and Size of Commune

Region and Percentage of Valid Votes

| | North | | Center | | South | | Sicily | | Sardinia | |
Size of Commune	Rep.	Mon.	Rep.	Mon.	Rep.	Mon.	Rep.	Mon.	Rep.	Mon.
0–1,000 inhabitants	55.4	44.6	39.8	60.2	29.2	70.8	—	—	33.9	66.1
1,001–3,000	59.6	40.4	54.2	45.8	31.8	68.2	14.2	85.8	39.8	60.2
3,001–5,000	61.8	38.2	64.2	35.8	32.6	67.4	28.2	71.8	43.6	56.4
5,001–10,000	65.2	34.8	66.4	33.6	33.3	66.7	34.3	65.7	43.3	56.7
10,001–30,000	68.0	32.0	71.3	28.7	34.7	65.3	36.7	63.3	39.3	60.7
30,001–100,000	69.9	30.9	70.3	29.7	35.8	64.2	44.0	56.0	28.3	71.7
100,001–250,000	66.4	33.6	80.5	19.5	34.0	66.0	40.4	59.6	27.8	72.2
250,001–500,000	65.3	34.7	63.4	36.6	—	—	16.9	83.1	—	—
500,000 and over	67.6	32.4	46.2	53.8	20.1	79.9	15.8	84.2	—	—
Total	64.8	35.2	63.5	36.5	32.6	67.4	35.3	64.7	39.1	60.9

Source: Ministero dell'Interno, *Compendio*, pp. 156–59.

The greater part of the southern electorate in 1946 turned to the parties of the right, and the composition of this right-wing vote was particularly interesting. The old pre-Fascist Liberal Party had been revived in the form of the Democratic National Union, a group of old liberal notables under the spiritual leadership of Benedetto Croce. They were strongest in the most backward part of the region, Basilicata, where generations of liberals like Nitti and Salandra had controlled large personal machines.

Today's Neo-Fascist and Monarchist parties did not yet exist, and rightist sentiment was distributed among a variety of fascist, nationalist, and separatist groups. Two of these groups were ephemeral but important. The Sicilian Independence Movement, which gained almost 9 percent of Sicily's votes in 1946, was made up of traditional landowning groups who subsequently financed the bandit army of Salvatore Giuliano. It was Giuliano who sought to make the island the forty-ninth American state.

The major Fascist phenomenon on the mainland in 1946 was the Uomo Qualunque Party, a name that can be most faithfully rendered into English as "Anybody's Party." As an American observer wrote, its leader, Guglielmo Giannini "wore a monocle and no necktie and professed equally inconsequent politics." [14] What is interesting about this party is not that it should have existed in 1946, since vague nostalgia for the fallen Fascist regime led logically to some such development. What is more significant is its regional distribution; the Uomo Qualunque gained 2.7 percent of the vote in the North, but its share of the southern vote was over 9 percent, with nearly 10 percent in Sicily.

Since 1946, the traditionalism of southern voters appears to have diminished greatly. As we can see in Table 7.4, the Liberal vote has

TABLE 7.4

Chamber of Deputies Elections, 1946–63, by Party and Region
(by percentage)

	1946		1953		1958		1963	
	North	South	North	South	North	South	North	South
Communist (PCI)	23.9	10.2	23.2	21.4	22.9	22.2	25.7	23.7
Socialist (PSI)	26.9	10.5	14.9	8.2	16.0	10.6	14.3	10.8
Social Democratic (PSDI)	—	—	5.6	2.4	5.6	2.5	6.7	3.1
Christian Democratic (DC)	35.5	35.0	41.0	38.3	41.3	44.4	37.2	41.2
Liberal (UDN-PLI)	3.1	14.0	2.6	3.8	3.5	3.6	4.5	3.1
Far Right	2.8	19.8	12.9	22.5	6.9	15.2	3.9	9.8

Source: Francesco Compagna e Vittorio de Caprariis, *Studi di Geografia Elettorale, 1946–1958* (Napoli, 1959); ISTAT, *Elezioni Della Camera dei Deputati*, Roma, for 1953, 1958, and 1963.

declined from 14 percent to 3.1 percent in the South, and increased from 3.1 percent to 4.5 percent in the North, where it has become identified as the mouthpiece of big business. The far right has fallen from almost 20 percent of the southern vote in 1946 to 9.8 percent in 1963, whereas the Socialist and Social Democratic parties are now supported by 13.9 percent of the southern voters, as opposed to a Socialist vote of 10.5 percent in 1946. In the North,

14. John Clarke Adams and Paolo Barile, *The Government of Republican Italy*, p. 156.

simultaneously, the Socialist vote has fallen from 26.9 percent in 1946 to a combined Socialist and Social Democratic vote of 21 percent in 1963.

The Catholic vote has continued to rise in the South from its early level of 35 percent in 1946 to 44.4 percent in 1958, with a decline to 41.2 percent in 1963. In the North, in contrast, the Christian Democratic percentage of the vote rose sooner (to 42.1 percent in 1953) and has declined more rapidly (to 37.2 percent in 1963). The strength of Catholic voting in the South is related both to the increase in Church authority in the Mezzogiorno during Fascism, and to the extension of the suffrage to women in 1946. Southern women remain a strongly traditional group of voters, much more so than women in the North, who hold jobs in industry and commerce and have been exposed to modern ideas of family life. Estimates made by Mattei Dogan suggest that southern women vote in very great proportion for the Christian Democrats, even single women under twenty-five years of age. Left-wing leaders like Togliatti have long complained about this fact, for "it has been very easy to conduct an anti-Communist agitation among the women." [15]

The most important development in the South since the fall of Fascism has been the phenomenal rise of the PCI from just under 11 percent of the vote in 1946 to 20.7 percent in 1953, 22.4 percent in 1958, and 23.7 percent in 1963. The subsequent provincial elections of 1964 brought it above 25 percent in the South and therefore substantially even with the Communist vote in the North. Maps 2 and 3 illustrate the changes in the PCI vote by province between 1946 and 1963.

THE STRUCTURE OF THE COMMUNIST VOTE

Three factors stand out about these maps, aside from the very obvious rise in PCI support in the South and its stability in the North and the Center. First, in both 1946 and 1963 the northern vote was divided sharply between a low Communist vote (from zero to 25 percent) above the Po valley and a very high Communist vote (from 25 percent to over 50 percent) in the provinces below

15. Mattei Dogan, "Le Donne Italiane tra il Cattolicesimo e il Marxismo," Spreafico e LaPalombara, eds., *Elezioni e Comportamento Politico in Italia*, p. 485; for Togliatti's comments, see his *Discorsi alle Donne* (PCI, Roma, 1953).

the Po. The distinction is important, for it is only in some of the provinces north of the Po that Italy has an economy that is highly specialized between industry and agriculture, a highly skilled industrial population earning high wages in large firms, and an agricultural sector divided between stable small farms and efficient commercial farms.

In central Italy, on the other hand, where the Communist vote is very high, only in four provinces out of twenty-three is more than 20 percent of the population engaged in industry! Hence we cannot deduce high Communist voting in the central Red Belt directly from industrialization. It goes without saying that, above the Po, the strongest Communist vote is found in industrial cities like Turin, Genoa, and Pavia, but below the Po, the strongest Communist vote is not found in the central cities at all, but in the newly settled urban periphery and the countryside.[16]

Second, in southern Italy the Communist vote is generally higher than in northern Italy above the Po valley, but lower than in central Italy. But nowhere do we find a consistent zone of provinces where there is very high Communist voting as in Emilia-Romagna and Tuscany; and nowhere do we see a large area of very low Communist voting as in the Alpine and Venetian regions to the northeast.

Very few northern or central provinces are found near the regional average of a Communist vote of 25.7 percent. In almost one-third of them, the PCI vote is less than 18 percent; in two-fifths of them it is over 30 percent; and in less than one-third of them is Communist voting in the intermediate range between 19 percent and 29 percent of the vote. These distributions are shown in Table 7.5.

In the South, in contrast, more than two-thirds of the provinces are found in the intermediate range, and less than one-fifth have a Communist vote below 19 percent; even fewer have a Communist vote above 30 percent. Curiously enough, however, when the Communist vote in the South is divided into ranges of five percentiles —as is illustrated in Map 3—for 1963 there is no bloc of provinces where we may see consistent PCI strength or weakness.

16. Achille Ardigò, "Il Volto Elettorale di Bologna," in Spreafico e LaPalombara, eds., pp. 828–30.

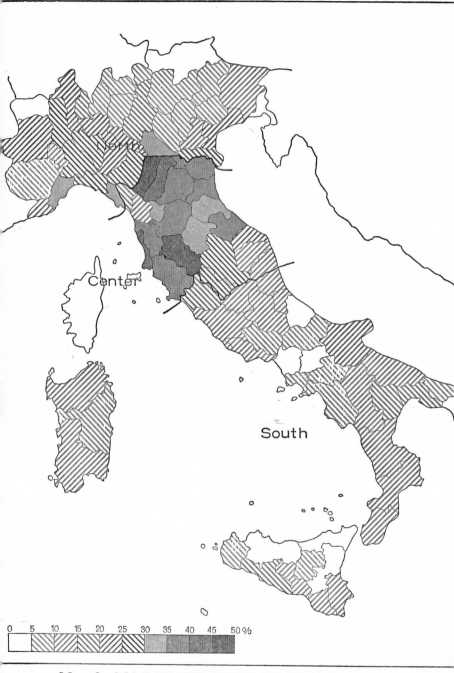

North

Center

South

0 5 10 15 20 25 30 35 40 45 50 %

MAP 2. COMMUNIST VOTE BY PROVINCE, 1946

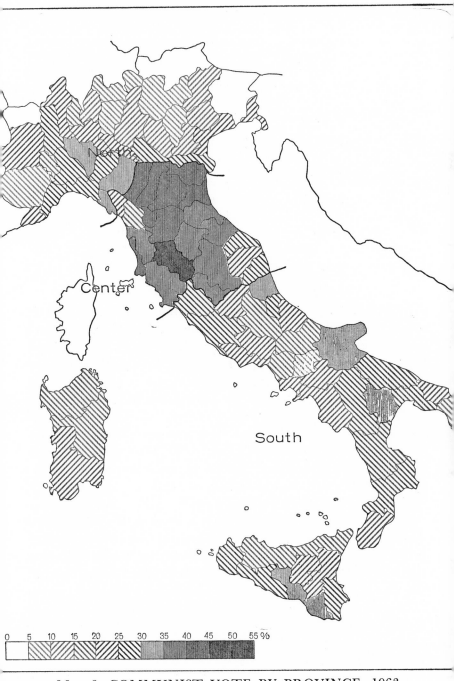

North

Center

South

0 5 10 15 20 25 30 35 40 45 50 55 %

MAP 3. COMMUNIST VOTE BY PROVINCE, 1963

TABLE 7.5

Consistency of Communist Vote in 1963,
by Province and Region

| | Provinces | |
PCI Vote	North	South
0–18%	17	7
	31%	19%
19–23%	8	10
	14.5%	27%
24–29%	8	14
	14.5%	38%
30%+	22	6
	40%	16%
Total	55	37
	100%	100%

Third, the electoral consistency of the Communist vote in southern Italy differs radically from the North when it is related to the strength of the other major political forces: the Christian Democrats, the Socialists, and, in part, the far right. The increase in Communist voting in the South since 1946, although far more dramatic, has been matched by a simultaneous increase in the Catholic vote. At the same time, however, the vote has not polarized geographically within the South into areas of high Communist vote and areas of high Catholic vote. The paradox of party polarization in a multiparty system is that it can allow the two major forces great strength within the same constituency. This appears to be the case in the Mezzogiorno.

In northern Italy, as in two-party systems such as the United States and Great Britain, the vote is highly polarized geographically. In the strongly Catholic regions of the North, the PCI is quite weak. Conversely, in the "Red Belt" of Emilia and Tuscany, the Christian Democratic Party has little popularity. In 78 percent of the northern provinces where the Communist vote is low, the Catholic vote is high. Similarly, in 93 percent of the provinces where the Communist vote is high, the vote of the Christian Democrats is low.

In the South, in contrast, the situation is more ambivalent. Although it is certainly not the case that high Communist voting correlates positively with high Catholic voting, a large number of southern provinces combine a high Communist vote with an above-average Catholic vote. Forty percent of the southern provinces with a high Catholic vote have a high vote for the Communist Party, and 35 percent with a low Catholic vote have a low Communist vote as well. These relationships are represented in Figures 1a and 1b.

Similar relationships are presented in the provincial capitals. In the North, in 97 percent of the cities where the PCI has an above-average vote, the DC runs below average. In the South a high PCI vote is accompanied by a low DC vote in only 50 percent of the provincial capitals. In the remaining 50 percent in which the DC is popular, the DC has an above-average vote with respect to its national average.

The contrasting relationship between PCI and DC voting in northern and southern Italy is strongest in cities of 20,000 to 50,000 in population. In a one-in-three sample of such cities in the North, 100 percent with an above-average Communist vote have a below-average Catholic vote; correspondingly, 84 percent with a low PCI vote have a high DC vote. In the South, in comparison, the two parties are less polarized. A high Communist vote is accompanied by a low Catholic vote in only 60 percent of the cities; a low PCI vote is matched by a high DC vote in only 63 percent. In other words, the growing polarization of the vote in the South between the Communist Party and the Christian Democrats is not expressed, as it is in the North, by a geographic division between Communist areas and Catholic areas. Where this negative correlation exists, it is not particularly strong.

In interpreting this phenomenon, we must note that the Christian Democratic Party in the South, as in the North, has launched its most powerful campaigns against the Communists, and that Communist leaders perceive the DC as their bitterest foe. Why then do many provinces with high Communist voting present a picture of Catholic strength as well?

It is suggested hypothetically that in many ways the two parties are symbiotic. Both are concerned with the problems of modernization; both were involved positively in the land reforms of the early 1950s; and both are relatively new in the area. Probably if

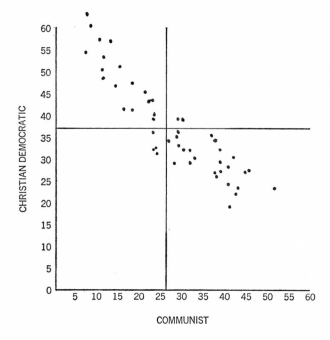

COMMUNIST

Figure 1a. Size of Communist and Catholic Vote, Northern
Italy, by Province

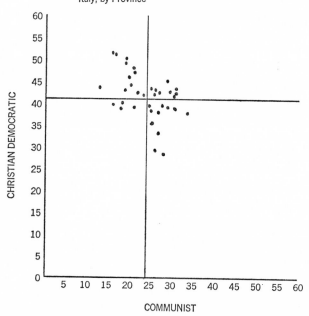

COMMUNIST

Figure 1b. Size of Communist and Catholic Vote, Southern
Italy, by Province

there is an overall explanation for the presence of high Catholic voting in provinces with high PCI voting, it is that both are the harbingers of a new style of organized mass politics in the South— the DC somewhat less so than the PCI. The relationships of the PCI and the DC in the Mezzogiorno, and the inroads of both upon traditional clientele politics, will be analyzed at length in the following chapters.

In contrast to Catholic-Communist voting relationships, the relationship between the Communist vote and that of the far right in the South is far more polarized than the same relationship in the North. In northern Italy, Neo-Fascism and Monarchism appear to be generic expressions of the same widespread disaffection as Communism, and therefore appear in the same areas as the PCI. In the South, in contrast, the political setting differs: the reactionary parties express the preferences of traditional groups of landowners and their clienteles. They appear to have little to do with either generic dissent or the desire for a return to a Fascist regime on the part of large numbers of Southerners.

In the North, there is no geographic polarization between the PCI vote and the vote of the parties of the far right. In 54 percent of the provinces where the PCI vote is above the regional average, there is a below-average vote for the extreme right; in the remaining 46 percent of the provinces with a high PCI vote, the far right's portion of the vote is above average. In the South, in comparison, in 75 percent of the provinces with a high Communist vote, the far right scores quite poorly; in 25 percent of these Communist-dominated provinces, the far right has a higher percentage of the vote than its national average. These relationships are represented graphically in Figures 2a and 2b.

The link between the southern reactionary vote and traditional patterns of clientele politics is suggested strongly by the concentration of far right in the provincial capitals. Almost 80 percent of the cities of the South that are the bastions of the far right are cities in which the PCI vote is below average.

A final important relationship is that of the votes of the PCI and the Socialist Party. In the North, between 1953 and 1963, a net 2.5 percent Communist gain has been accompanied by a net 1.3 percent Socialist loss. In the South, a Socialist gain of 2.5 per-

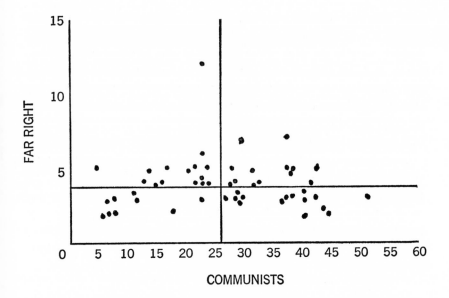

Figure 2a. Size of Communist and Far Right Vote, Northern Italy, by Province

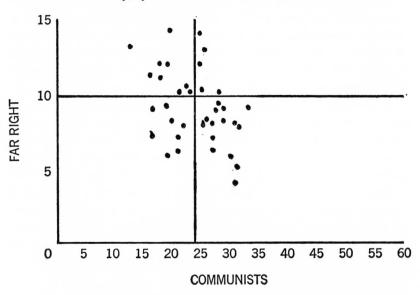

Figure 2b. Size of Communist and Far Right Vote, Southern Italy, by Province

cent has accompanied an equal Communist rise in the same period. Only in Sardinia has a reversal of these relationships occurred, with a PSI gain and PCI loss. In the North, only in Lombardy has the Communist gain been accompanied by a Socialist gain. In other words, northern voters seem to distinguish between the two parties and choose one at the expense of the other, whereas in the South the PSI has profited from the greater increase of the PCI and vice versa.

The geographic structure of the Socialist vote correlates positively with the Communist vote in the South, attaining high levels in areas where the PCI is popular, and low levels where the PCI is weak. In the North, in contrast, no correlation of this nature appears. Figures 3a and 3b represent the relationship of Communist and Socialist electoral success in the North and South in the 1963 elections.

These relationships suggest that, whereas in the North voters will choose the Communist Party at the expense of the Socialists, or vice versa, in the South party politics is not yet sufficiently differentiated for the two left-wing parties to be perceived as in opposition. However, the installation of the PSI in a center-left government in 1963 may radically change this situation. The PSI, for its part, has lost little time in exploiting its patronage opportunities in the South, a factor that has already been reflected in the results of the 1966 local elections.

Turning now to a consideration of the Communist vote in relation to demographic and socioeconomic variables, a single factor appears to dominate all others: the PCI in the North has a higher vote in the cities than in the countryside, while in the South it gains a higher percentage of the vote in rural than in urban areas. Using the ninety-two provincial capitals as a crude index of "urban," we find that 51 percent of these cities in the North have an above-average Communist vote. In the South, in contrast, only 27 percent of the provincial capitals have an above-average vote for the PCI. In other words, most of the PCI vote in the South comes from areas other than its largest cities.

The relationship of PCI electoral support in the provincial capitals to PCI voting in the provinces is represented graphically in Figures 4a and 4b for northern and southern Italy. As may be

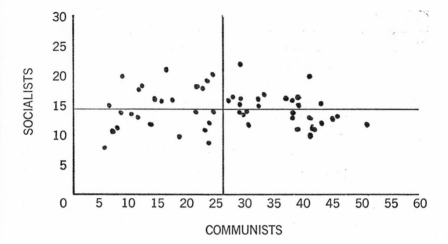

Figure 3a. Size of Communist and Socialist Vote, Northern Italy, by Province

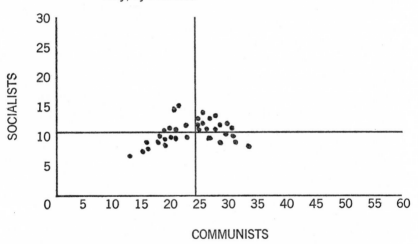

Figure 3b. Size of Communist and Socialist Vote, Southern Italy, by Province

seen, in the vast majority of southern provincial capitals, the Communist vote is considerably lower than in the province as a whole.

This division of the vote in the South is a clear indication that the appeal of the Communist Party in the region is basically a peasant appeal, and that its large cities, populated as they are by large numbers of landowners, professionals, and artisans, do not have the necessary working class composition to contribute strongly to the Communist vote. However, the structure of the PCI vote in the South is somewhat more complex than a simple urban-rural confrontation. For while the largest PCI vote is found outside the southern provincial capitals, it is extremely weak in the smallest villages. These villages, dedicated to semi-subsistence agriculture, suffering pathological depopulation, and largely undisturbed in their traditional value patterns, are tied to the immense political power of the Church, and have responded slowly to the appeals of Communism.

The Communist vote in the South is highest, in contrast, in small and medium-sized peasant cities from 20,000 to 50,000 in population. In these communes, famous in Puglia and Sicily but important throughout the region, a self-conscious group of organized agricultural workers has begun to form. A large percentage of the population is engaged in light industry and trade, and the social transformations typical of a society in an early phase of industrialization have filtered in, even though the actual benefits of industrialization are still absent. In 77 percent of the cities sampled in the South, the PCI vote is above the national average. In the North, in contrast, the PCI vote is above the national average in only 56 percent of these medium-sized cities. As Table 7.6 shows, North and South are more or less equal in the distribution of provinces above and below the national PCI average; in the provincial capitals, the South falls below the national average in a large majority of cases; but most of the sample of medium-sized cities in the South are above the national average.

It is in central Italy south of the Po, of course, that the PCI vote is highest in this range of medium-sized cities—an average of 36.4 percent as opposed to 20.4 percent north of the Po and 31.9 percent in the South. It is interesting, however, that this figure is *lower* than the 38.4 percent average Communist vote in central

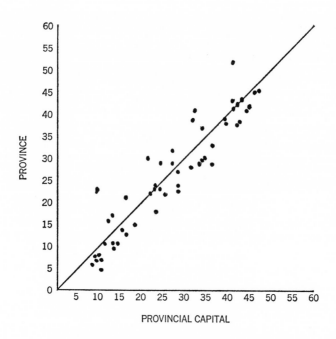

Figure 4a. Communist Vote in Provinces and Provincial Capitals,
Northern Italy

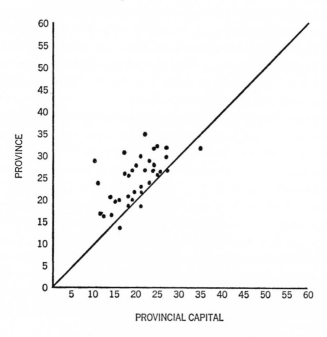

Figure 4b. Communist Vote in Provinces and Provincial
Capitals, Southern Italy

Italy. It is only in the South that the Communist vote in medium-sized cities is higher than in the region as a whole (an average of 31.9 percent as opposed to the regional average of 23.7 percent).

TABLE 7.6

Distribution of Communist Party Vote, by Provinces, Provincial Capitals, and Medium-Sized Cities in the 1963 Elections, by Region
(in percentages)

	Provinces	Provincial Capitals	Cities,[a] 20,000–50,000
North			
Low	51	49	44
High	49	51	56
South			
Low	46	73	23
High	54	27	77

[a] Based on a one-in-three sample of cities 20,000–50,000 in population analyzed by the author.

The fact that the highest Communist vote in southern Italy is found in medium-sized cities of 20,000 to 50,000 inhabitants raises interesting theoretical problems about the nature of left-wing voting. Herbert Tingsten long ago pointed out that the highest working class turnout (in industrial cities) is found where the working class is highly concentrated residentially.[17] Our data on Communist voting in southern Italy suggest the hypothesis that in societies in early stages of industrialization, left-wing voting is highest in small and medium-sized cities that are only partially industrialized and in which a large sector of the population is still engaged in agriculture.

In fact, if we look carefully at the sample of communes in southern Italy, we find that their portion of the population in industry (12.2 percent) is well above the regional average (8.5 percent) but that substantial numbers of individuals are engaged in agriculture (13.1 percent as opposed to a regional average of 20.5 percent). Naturally, these aggregate figures do not convey the great diversity among the units in the sample, but they do indicate

17. Herbert Tingsten, *Political Behavior* (London, 1937), p. 154.

two things: first, that the presence of a sizable working class cadre among an agricultural population raises the left-wing vote substantially; and, second, that as urbanization and industrialization increase the number of cities where we find a mixed industrial-agricultural population, Communist voting will almost certainly increase.

Here is perhaps the key to understanding the phenomenal rise in PCI support in the South since 1946; while the heavily urbanized provincial capitals and the small villages continue to oppose the PCI, the transfer of part of the population to industry in the medium-sized communes has brought about a disproportional rise in left-wing voting among the population in these communes as a whole.

When we turn to industrialization on its own, we find virtually no correlation with the Communist vote in either North or South. In the North, only half of the provinces with an above-average percentage of the population engaged in industry have an above-average PCI vote, whereas two-thirds of those northern provinces with a small population in industry have an above-average PCI vote. In the South, 56 percent of the provinces with a relatively large industrial population have a large PCI vote, and roughly even numbers of provinces with a small population in industry vote strongly for the Communist party.

The situation in the provincial capitals is no more polarized. In the North, there is virtually no correlation between industrialization and high Communist voting. The capital cities with the highest Communist voting record (between 30 percent and 45 percent) are found mainly south of the Po, where the degree of industrialization is only intermediate. Relatively low Communist support (between zero and 25 percent) is found in the North in provinces with low, intermediate, and high ranges of industrialization.

In southern Italy, the entire range of industrialization is low, but within that range no correlation between a large portion of the population in industry and high Communist voting is found. In the fourteen southern provincial capitals in which more than 10 percent of the population is employed in industry, the average Communist vote is only 19.6 percent, well below the regional average. Only three of these cities have a Communist vote above the national average of 24.7 percent.

The relation of the PCI vote to urbanization in the South is far more interesting. In the North, the Communist vote is about the same in provinces where the population is stable or in decline and in those where population gain is significant. In the South, however, the PCI vote is quite low where there is a sharp population loss; it is high where population is stable or gains slightly, and much higher where there is significant population gain. Table 7.7

TABLE 7.7

Relation of Communist Provincial Vote to Urbanization
in the 1963 Elections, by Region

	Northern Provinces with Population:			Southern Provinces with Population:		
PCI Vote	Loss	Stability	Gain	Loss	Stability	Gain
Low	4	16	7	8	7	2
	50%	47%	54%	80%	37%	25%
High	4	18	6	2	12	6
	50%	53%	46%	20%	63%	75%

expresses these relationships in terms of the number of provinces with above-average or below-average Communist votes.

A special case of urbanization that reinforces the connection between population growth and the PCI vote is the immigrant vote in the urban centers of the North. Although it would certainly be unreasonable to assume that such groups instantly become "northern," there is a far greater dislocation for them than for the Southerners who move to southern urban centers. In terms of the value patterns they encounter, emigrants to Turin, Bologna, and Milan are far more challenged than those southerners who find their way to Naples or Rome. Italian studies indicate that it is in the teeming, outer *borghi* and *baracche* of Milan and Turin, where southern immigrants cluster, that the Communist vote is strongest in those cities.[18] In most other sections of those cities, the Communist vote has suffered a decline.

18. G. Bonazzi, P. Brea, A. Livi, "Il Voto degli Emigranti nel Triangolo Industriale," *Tempi Moderni, 6,* No. 5 (1963), 87–95.

Three factors in the structure of the Communist vote in southern Italy draw particular attention: first, the party's poor showing in the highly urbanized capitals as opposed to the provinces as a whole; second, its concentration in medium-sized cities with mixed industrial-agricultural bases; and third, its correlation with population growth. The process of industrialization now under way and the probability of much more population growth in the South both suggest that PCI support in the region will continue to grow. However, two factors must condition our prediction in this regard. First, population growth is highest in the provincial capitals, precisely the class of communes in which the Communist vote is lowest; and, second, if the medium-sized communes become almost entirely industrialized—as indeed they may—the present basis of their support may wane, for it is generally true that industrialization per se has no direct relation to high Communist voting.

Underlying these problems lies a basic problem less closely related to electoral trends and more closely related to the nature of Marxist movements. If we may understand organized Marxism-Leninism as a combination of close-knit organization and broad popular support, then the PCI in southern Italy presents us with a paradox: its electoral map depends mainly upon medium-sized cities with a mainly peasant population, whereas its organizational structure is clustered heavily in the provincial capitals, where electoral support is low. Much more will be said later on the problem of the imbalance between small Communist support in the provincial capitals and high support in the countryside.

The consistency of the PCI vote *within* individual provinces is quite low. There are far greater differences in the PCI vote from commune to commune than in the North, where the PCI either suffers a general unpopularity or enjoys great support. In most cases, economic or demographic variables do not appear to explain southern intraprovincial divergences. For example, in the Marsica, the bitterly poor zone made famous in Silone's *Bread and Wine* and *Fontamara,* a great homogeneity of political and demographic conditions exists. The eleven communes of the area all surround the Fucino basin, a lake drained in the late nineteenth century and divided into the most notorious latifundia in the entire country.

The land was rented to large *affittuari,* who then sublet it to the peasants. In 1950 a dramatic Communist-led uprising of the peasants forced the government to concede to the division of the latifundia. The local population shares a common dedication to agriculture, a history of common oppression by the agents of the Torlonia latifundia, and, in large part, the benefits of the agrarian reform. Yet the towns of the region, all between 1,000 and 5,000 voters (except for Avezzano), and all within forty miles of one another, display a bewildering diversity in the vote accorded to the Communists. This lack of consistency in the voting patterns of the Marsica is portrayed in Table 7.8. Similar intraprovincial

TABLE 7.8

Communist Party Vote in the Marsica by Commune, 1963 Elections

Commune	Valid Votes	Percentage of Communist Vote
Avezzano	16,433	15.6
Celano	5,145	35.6
Gioia dei Marsi	1,607	5.0
Lecce dei Marsi	1,289	46.1
Luco dei Marsi	2,833	53.3
Magliano	1,914	13.1
Ortona	1,341	17.9
Ortucchio	1,128	24.7
Pescina	3,032	42.7
S. Benedetto Marsi	2,312	32.4
Trasacco	3,088	20.9

voting diversity is found in the South in other "natural" geographic or economic areas: the "conca d'oro" around Palermo, the Naples-Vesuvius-Amalfi coast, and the Sila zone in Calabria.

In interpreting this lack of voting consistency, Communist leaders usually turn to distinct historical events as causal factors: for example, the Tuscan origin of the founders of one town with a high PCI vote, or the tradition of self-help of another. It is probably more reasonable to turn to the prevailing personalism and localism of southern Italian politics as the explanation of the great voting inconsistency. In the Marsica, for example, Avezzano has long been controlled by the Torlonia family, and

remains an administrative center under their control with virtually no industry. Luco, in contrast, in which the PCI enjoys an
absolute majority, is the birthplace of the regional Communist
federation's secretary. Celano, another PCI stronghold, was the
scene of the killing of two peasants by the state police during the
battle for the land in 1950. In the Sila region of Calabria, similarly, whether individual communes have a large or a small Communist vote appears to depend largely upon the government's
ability to corrupt or employ the local PCI leaders. In other words,
despite Communism's obvious organizational unity and discipline, it has had a hard time breaking down the barriers of personalism of traditional southern Italian politics.

An important index of the personalism of the southern Italian
Communist vote is the *preferenza,* or the optional preference vote
Italian voters may use in addition to their vote for a party list.
The national index of preference votes actually used in relation
to the total preference votes available is 29.8 percent. As pointed
out in Chapter 4, the index of preference voting rises from a
median of 21.3 percent in the North to a median of 37.9 percent
in the South. The index of preference voting for the Communist
Party follows a similar course: whereas the index of PCI preferences is 14.7 percent in the North, it is 36.3 percent in the South,
or more than double the figure for the North. Table 7.9 represents this aspect of the structure of the PCI vote.

Related to the personalism of the Communist Party vote in
the South is its decline in local and provincial administrative
elections. In the North, it is common for the Communist Party
to receive more votes in local and provincial elections than in
national elections. In the South, in contrast, voters in provincial
and local elections tend to perceive their vote more in terms of
local patronage than in terms of ideological attachments. The
PCI, consequently, fares worse in these administrative elections in
the South than in national elections, in which little is at stake in
personal terms. Table 7.10 demonstrates the variation of the
Communist Party vote between the national election of 1958
and the provincial elections of 1960, both in North and South.
(A similar dichotomization of North and South occurred in the

TABLE 7.9

Index of Preference Voting for the PCI by Electoral College

Electoral College	Index of Preference Votes	Electoral College	Index of Preference Votes
North		*South*	
Turin	17.5	Rome	32.3
Cuneo	18.7	L'Aquila	30.9
Genoa	18.4	Campobasso	22.0
Milan	10.6	Naples	43.0
Como	20.0	Benevento	40.2
Brescia	14.1	Bari	35.7
Mantova	12.6	Lecce	36.8
Trento	8.8	Potenza	29.3
Verona	17.8	Catanzaro	40.3
Venice	9.6	Catania	41.2
Udine	11.4	Palermo	50.6
Bologna	21.9	Cagliari	38.5
Parma	22.2		
Florence	16.2		
Pisa	31.5		
Siena	16.2		
Ancona	18.2		
Perugia	26.5		

Source: Giovanni Schepis, "Analisi Statistica dei Risultati," in Alberto Spreafico e Joseph LaPalombara, *Elezioni e Comportamento Politico in Italia* (Milano, 1963), p. 397.

provincial elections of 1966, when the Socialists and Social Democrats made use of their new position in the government to take votes from the PCI in the Mezzogiorno.)[19] Since the overall trend of the election was a gain of 1.5 percent for the PCI, provinces in which the Communist vote remained unchanged or lost ground have been grouped together.

Local issues and personalities still appear to dominate elections in the South, and the PCI, despite its national ideology and goals, has had to adapt to campaigning in such a milieu. In a 1953 study of communes where the Communist vote had either increased or decreased sharply, it was found that the vast major-

19. Lino Iannuzzi, "Quando la Lepere Vuol Farsi Prendere," *L'Espresso* (July 9, 1966), pp. 6–7.

TABLE 7.10

Provincial Elections, 1960: Variation in Communist Voting Patterns
from Last National Election, by Region

| | | *Provinces* | |
Variation		North	South
Rise	(N)	*39*	*8*
	(%)	71	22
Stable and Fall	(N)	*10*	*15*
	(%)	18	41
Inappropriate	(N)	*6*	*9*
	(%)	11	24

ity of voting shifts had been caused by local, personal, and clientelistic issues, *even in those communes where the Communists had gained substantially.* In the few communes in which interviews were carried out in the North, in contrast, class hostility, Communist organization, and propaganda are cited as the most frequent causes of electoral change. Table 7.11 represents the reasons cited for left-wing increase and decrease in the sixty southern communes. (The northern communes are not included because they are only sixteen in number and are mainly located in the far north of the country.)

As Table 7.11 shows, the most important reasons for left-wing gains were (1) personal prestige or animosity; (2) the government's allocation of or failure to allocate patronage and welfare benefits to local residents; and (3) poverty, unemployment, and class hostility.

That the PCI in the South has adapted to the region's highly localized and personalized political structure may be accounted a credit to the party's leaders. But widespread localism and personalism injure the consistency of the Communist vote. The harm done is more than instrumental; can a Marxist party, which seeks solid bases of support and draws upon long-term grievances in the population, achieve success where the basis of its support is local or personal and the grievances that sustain it are shifting and inconsistent?

The shifting, localistic, and personalistic basis of Communist

TABLE 7.11

Causes of Voting Shifts in Southern Italian Villages Showing Large Shifts
Between the Elections of 1948 and 1953

Causes of Voting Shifts		Left-Wing Increase (Number of villages: 30)	Left-Wing Decrease (Number of villages: 30)
Personal			
Shifts in personnel;	(N)	17	24
Personal prestige or hostility	(%)	25.0	27.8
Patronage, Welfare	(N)	18	23
	(%)	26.5	26.8
Inefficiency, Corruption	(N)	5	8
	(%)	7.4	9.3
Poverty, Unemployment, Class hostility	(N)	16	8
	(%)	23.5	9.3
Land Reform Benefits or Failures	(N)	8	12
	(%)	11.8	13.9
Party Organizational Success or Failure	(N)	4	11
	(%)	5.8	12.9
Total	(N)	68	86
Causes	(%)	100.0	100.0

Source: Calculated by the author from an unpublished report prepared by International Research Associates, Inc., of New York, no date, mimeograph. (*Note:* The percentages are calculated on the total number of causes of voting shifts, rather than the number of villages, because several causes are listed for each village, and it is impossible to calculate the most important.)

support is related to the problem posed earlier: the imbalance between PCI organizational centers in the provincial capitals and strong electoral support in the medium-sized cities. If the party is forced to dissipate its energies seeking momentary or shifting electoral support in various places, what is the effect likely to be upon its organizational structure? Second, if the techniques of campaigning call up local and personal issues, what will the impact be upon the character of the leaders and the skills they possess? Third, what is mass membership and commitment like in a political setting in which electoral support is shifting and discontinuous? These questions will be taken up in the next chapter.

8. The Party Structure:
North and South

The Italian Communist Party constitutes an organizational revolution in the South of Italy. It has brought the region those forms of political organization—the party section, the secretariat, and the secondary association—that have been developed in more advanced environments. Virtually unknown in the South under Fascism, the party began to filter into public life only in 1944. It stimulated great masses of the population of the region to a degree of participation never before known.[1]

Wherever the party went, labor organizations, peasant associations, front groups, and cooperatives appeared. Wherever it went, the Church began to organize politically under the banner of anti-Communism. Encouraged by the early successes of Christ and Antichrist, two traditional movements—Monarchist and Socialist—rose perceptibly out of the morass of clientelism to wave the faded banners of almost-Communism, and of authoritarian anti-Communism. Party sections, chambers of labor, and flamboyant political literature and propaganda began to saturate the region, making of every village square a circus of red flags, blue crosses, and even golden fasces.

The Communist-inspired mass organization of politics in the Mezzogiorno has dislocated traditional clientele structures, created new means of representation for formerly unrepresented social groups, and caused a radical shift in patterns of political allocation. Yet on close examination of the structure of the PCI in the South, it is clear that the instruments and symbols of modern political organization do not necessarily convey their spirit. Despite its importation of all the paraphernalia of the mass party, the PCI in southern Italy is something very different from the "New Prince" of Gramsci or the "party of a new type" of Togliatti.

1. Compare Edward Banfield, *The Moral Basis of a Backward Society*, pp. 30–31.

The Party's Composition

The composition of the Communist Party in southern Italy can be traced to its earliest days of proselytism and recruitment. Soon after 1944 and the end of Fascism, organizers from the North and from the large cities of the South were dispatched to the remotest parts of the region, even to the desolate interior zones of Sicily and Sardinia. Their task of organization was impeded by the usual difficulties of proselytizers in a backward society—hunger, privation, incomprehension. However, they suffered others of a more chilling nature. In the 1948 elections, Communist speakers in the piazza of Villalba, Sicily, were riddled by Mafia bullets; in Piana degli Albanesi in 1950, a peasant group on an outing was massacred by bandits; in the Calabrian hills in 1949, a pathetic group of *braccianti* in search of land was attacked by a platoon of state police. The government had more subtle means at its command; northern organizers in the South were sometimes exiled from the region on the basis of a Fascist statute that limited movement from province to province.

Under such conditions, organizational work was extremely difficult. In numerical terms, the party grew more modestly than in the rest of Italy. Approximate postwar party statistics show a rise in southern membership from 278,000 members in 1944—the first year of active PCI organizational work—to 430,000 in 1948. During the same period, Communist membership in northern and central Italy increased six times over, from 223,700 in 1944 to 1,637,000 in 1948.[2] By 1950, growth began to stabilize, with membership in the Center-North decreasing to 1,600,000, and membership in the South increasing to 504,000.

The southern portion of the party at this time composed 23.9 percent of the national membership, as compared to 41 percent for the Center and 35 percent in the North. However, the political disillusionment of the early 1950s and the catastrophic events in Eastern Europe during those years caused a decline of over 100,000 in the North and Center. In the South, in contrast, membership continued to rise from 504,000 in 1950 to 536,000 in 1956. Membership in the Communist Party in the South is far less responsive

2. PCI, *L'Attività del Partito in Cifre*, 1948.

to national and international events than membership in the more advanced and literate sections of the Center-North. Only after 1956 did it begin to reflect the national decline, decreasing by 22.4 percent between 1956 and 1963, as compared to a decrease of 13.5 percent in the Center-North in the same period.

In the North, where the population is divided between densely settled industrialized provinces like Milan and Turin and isolated Catholic provinces around the Swiss border, the party now has 27.8 percent of its members, or 2.4 percent of the population of the region. In the three industrialized provinces of Milan, Turin, and Genoa alone there are 156,000 members, fully one-third the membership in the thirty-two provinces of the North. In the thirteen provinces of the agricultural Veneto, on the other hand, the party organizes 93,500 members, or only 21 percent of the total.

In the central provinces, the so-called "Red Belt" of Italy, the PCI has its largest membership. Although only 19 percent of the Italian population lives in these provinces, 46 percent of all Communist Party members are found there. This is equally true among the agricultural proletariat of the Po valley and among the *mezzadri* (share tenants) of the Tuscan hills as well as the industrial workers of Florence and Bologna.

TABLE 8.1

Evolution of PCI Membership by Region, 1950–63[a]

		1950	1956	1963
North	(N)	739,675	625,403	449,533
	(%)	35.0	40.7	27.8
Center	(N)	868,768	873,530	748,761
	(%)	41.1	42.9	46.4
South	(N)	504,150	536,419	416,818
	(%)	23.9	26.4	25.8
Total	(N)	2,112,593	2,035,353	1,615,112
	(%)	100	100	100

[a] The breakdown of the three geographic regions in this chapter differs from the official PCI statistics, which group Emilia-Romagna with the North and Lazio with the Central Provinces. Emilia-Romagna is more logically part of the Central "Red Belt" and Lazio, the region around Rome, is culturally and economically a part of the South.

Source: PCI, Official party statistics.

In the South, where 44 percent of the Italian population lives in conditions of the greatest poverty, only 25.8 percent of the Communist Party's membership is found. Although the party's political influence is perhaps now most intense in the South, it has succeeded in organizing only 1.9 percent of the population of the region, compared to 2.4 percent in the North and 8.3 percent in the Center. In other words, no organizational victory has followed the dramatic electoral impact of Communism in the South of Italy.

TABLE 8.2

Geographic Profile of PCI Party Membership, 1963

	Regional Distribution of Party Members		Regional Distribution of Population Percent	Percentage of PCI Members in Population
	Number	Percent		
North	449,533	27.8	37.9	2.4
Center	748,761	46.4	18.8	8.3
South	416,818	25.8	44.0	1.9
Total	1,615,112	100.0	100.0	3.2

Source: PCI, Dati Sull'Organizzazione del PCI (Napoli, 1964).

The distribution of Communist Party membership within the provinces varies greatly from North to South. In the North, where the population is predominantly urban or lives in dispersed rural communes, the Communist Party is an urban phenomenon. The percentage of members in the provincial capitals is 34.5 in the North and 22.1 in the South. The remainder in the South are dispersed among the large peasant cities of 20,000 to 50,000 population and the small, mountain villages.[3]

But rather than being evenly distributed over the entire region, Communist Party membership in the South, like the PCI vote, is extremely discontinuous. There are numerous enclaves of organizational strength and great barren areas without Communist presence. These enclaves, as we shall see, have only a partial relationship to urbanization or industrialization, and do not vary according

3. PCI, Dati Sull'Organizzazione del PCI, 1964, pp. 11–14.

to the relative wealth or poverty of the people. In the most industrialized centers of the South—Messina, Catania, and Siracusa—
less than 1 percent of the urban population is enrolled in the PCI.
Similarly, in some of the most destitute areas—such as in Benevento, Avellino, and Potenza—the percentage of population registered in the party is also low. Communist party membership in
the South is highest in three classes of communes: (1) in the large
peasant cities scattered throughout the eastern tableland of Puglia
and Lucania and in the interior of Sicily; (2) in the mountain villages of Calabria, where the historical legacy of the great latifundia
is most oppressive; and (3) in a scattering of villages and towns in
Lucania and Calabria, where Communism was propagated by notable local individuals or Northerners exiled to the South by the
Fascists.

When we relate the percentage of PCI members in the population
of each province to the PCI vote in that province, we find an interesting confrontation between North and South. In the North, there
is (1) a strongly positive correlation between the number of PCI
members and voters in a particular province and (2) a rising curve
of membership compared to voting increase. In other words, although PCI members increase slowly when the party vote increases
from 5 percent to 25 percent of the provincial vote, PCI membership increases phenomenally as the vote increases from 25 percent
to 50 percent of the provincial vote. Figure 5a represents the relationships between PCI voters and members in the provinces of the
North.

In the South, as Figure 5b shows, the PCI membership is far
smaller than in the North, both in absolute terms and as a percentage of total population. The range of membership strength varies
only slightly from province to province, regardless of PCI voting
strength in the province. The province with the highest PCI vote
in the South has a membership strength of 3.5 percent of the population, only 0.8 percent higher than the province with the lowest
PCI electoral support. The flat cluster of provincial voting and
membership strength in Figure 5b contrasts significantly to the
sharp curve in Figure 5a.

The true significance of these diagrams for the problem of Marx-

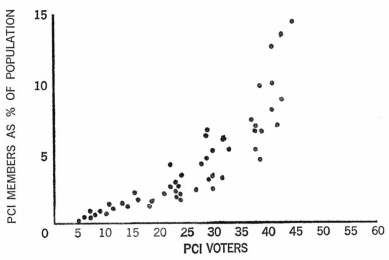

Figure 5a. Communist Voters and Members, Northern Italy, by Province

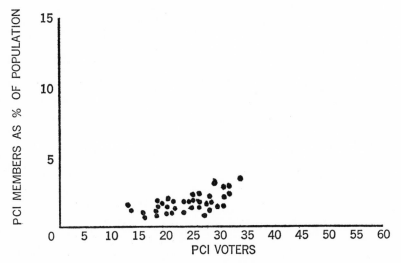

Figure 5b. Communist Voters and Members, Southern Italy, by Province

ist party strategy emerges only when we examine PCI membership in northern provinces in which the PCI controls more than 25 percent of the vote. In these provinces, party membership increases almost geometrically. The obverse also applies: the most important correlate of the *low* Communist membership in the South (in absolute terms) is that the geometric effect does not take hold. In other words, in the North there is evidently a close relationship between organizational strength and voting strength in the PCI. In the South, there is a very weak correlation between voting strength and membership strength, and neither one is high enough for the other to increase rapidly.

These data are difficult to interpret, but provocative enough to warrant the attempt. When we consider voting strength as the independent variable, and membership as the dependent variable, the data suggest that Communist membership in the South is subjectively limited by the party's failure to gain more than 25 percent of the vote in any but a few provinces. But when we consider membership strength as the independent factor, and electoral success as dependent, we arrive at the following proposition: the organizational incapacity of a developing society places an *objective* limitation on the party's vote-getting ability.

While both these propositions are tenable and neither can be rejected with the data in hand, an additional factor makes the second proposition more interesting to examine: namely, that PCI membership in the South is lower than the North in an *absolute* sense, even considering provinces where the party's percentage of the vote is similar, and particularly in the upper range of the southern provinces (between 25 percent and 35 percent of the vote). In the North, this range of provinces has already begun an organizational breakthrough that raises the ratio of members to voters considerably. In the equivalent range of provinces in the South, in contrast, organizational strength is still fairly low.

These considerations go back to the dialectical problems posed by the Via Italiana al Socialismo. In northern Italy we find a strong relationship between "the organizational weapon" and the prestige of the party among the electorate: a concrete demonstration of the vitality of Togliatti's strategy. In the South, we see a small group of cadres diffused throughout the society without relation to the party's general popularity with the electorate, *precisely the result that Lenin feared a Menshevik strategy would lead to in Russia.* The strategic validity of the Via Italiana in an advanced society like northern Italy is demonstrated by its strategic weakness in a backward society like the Mezzogiorno.

Moreover, the PCI in the South suffers from an almost pathological membership turnover. This reflects something of the spirit with which the peasant joins the movement: not with lasting commitment, but with intense, temporary enthusiasm caused by a dramatic struggle or a general crisis. New members in the South amounted to 13.9 percent of the total in 1961, as opposed to 6.2 percent of total members in the North and 5.2 percent in the Center. Considering that the entire membership of the party in the South fell from 409,000 in 1960 to 369,000 in 1961, these figures indicate that new membership in the Mezzogiorno was more than 15 percent of the total, while in the North it was stabilized at about 6 to 7 percent.[4]

The social composition of the party in the South is perhaps its most interesting dimension. As Table 8.3 indicates, a great portion of the party's membership in the South is made up of agricultural day workers, sharecroppers, small farmers, and artisans, thereby reflecting the occupational distribution of the population. However, it is not a "popular" party in any sense of the word, for the PCI in the Mezzogiorno has failed to make the small working class its solid organizational nucleus. In traditional industrial centers such as Catania and Messina, the PCI organizes less than 5 percent of the industrial workers. Throughout the South, workers in all types of industry, who constitute 30 percent of the active population, amount to 31.5 percent of the membership as opposed to 54 percent in the North and 35 percent in the Center.

The largest bloc of members in the party are poor peasants and agricultural workers. This group, which constitutes nearly 35 percent of the active population and 42 percent of the membership, has been drawn to the party because of its emphasis upon a land reform. However, as party leaders well know, the peasants' aims

4. Ibid., p. 21.

Table 8.3

Social Composition of the PCI by Region, 1963

		Urban Workers	Agricultural Day Workers	Sharecroppers	Small Farmers	Shopkeepers and Artisans	Students and Intellectuals	White Collar	Housewives	Others	Total
North	(N)	240,151	37,000	7,163	14,996	23,209	3,470	10,718	55,439	59,909	440,533
	(%)	54.4	8.3	1.6	3.4	5.3	0.7	2.4	12.5	12.7	100.0
Center	(N)	269,537	66,160	138,960	32,730	54,238	3,565	17,338	104,976	67,806	755,281
	(%)	35.7	8.8	18.4	4.3	7.2	0.4	2.3	13.9	8.9	100.0
South	(N)	134,046	103,525	27,852	43,648	24,367	7,760	8,772	40,912	33,166	424,048
	(%)	31.5	24.5	6.5	10.3	5.7	1.9	2.1	9.6	7.8	100.0
Italy	(N)	643,733	206,684	173,975	91,374	101,818	14,809	36,828	202,327	159,002	1,619,862
	(%)	39.5	12.7	10.7	5.6	5.2	0.9	2.2	12.4	9.8	100.0

Source: PCI, Dati Sull'Organizzazione del PCI, 1964.

are hardly revolutionary, and their participation is limited to those aspects of party activity that bring them closer to ownership of the land. In other words, the Communist Party has as its largest membership bloc the group with the very poorest organizational potential—the poor peasants and agricultural semiproletariat.

Agricultural workers—the *braccianti*—constitute one-quarter of the region's active population and almost one-quarter of the PCI membership, more than three times the weight of the same category in the Center-North. In some provinces of the South, moreover, this group has a near-predominance. In the provinces of Foggia, for example, it comprises almost half the work force and 56 percent of the party. In Sicily, similarly, more than 40 percent of party members are agricultural workers. The size of the agricultural workers' group in all the provinces of Puglia and its comparison with the percentage of industrial workers in the party is analyzed in Table 8.4. In every province of the region but one, the percentage of agricultural workers is far greater than the proportion of industrial workers in the party, and in three cases is more than three times higher. An analogous situation exists in Sicily.

TABLE 8.4

Social Composition by Province of the PCI in Puglia, 1954

Province	Total Membership	Number of Workers	Percentage of Workers	Number of Agricultural Workers	Percentage of Agricultural Workers
Bari	32,157	4,000	12.4	14,000	43.5
Brindisi	9,731	1,040	10.7	4,501	46.2
Foggia	30,182	2,600	8.6	17,000	56.3
Lecce	13,740	2,918	21.2	4,700	34.2
Taranto	15,186	4,353	28.7	3,557	23.4
Total Puglia	100,996	14,911	14.8	43,759	43.3
Total South	559,192	172,914	30.9	138,643	24.8
Total Italy	2,145,317	856,315	39.9	382,257	17.8

Source: PCI, *Forza e Attività del Partito*, 1954.

In large part, these braccianti do not work in mechanized "factories in the field," which themselves induce a great degree of organization. The southern Italian bracciante is usually an isolated figure whose contractual relations with landowners are short-term and unstable, and whose work takes him far out into the countryside. Only in some parts of Puglia are large-scale commercial farms in operation which allow the braccianti to be organized in industrial-like units by the PCI. In the broad zones of the peasant latifundia and the mixed peasant-commercial zones which comprise 42 percent and 26 percent respectively of the area of the South, the bracciante is a dispersed, disorganized, and, more often than not, part-time small farmer. One begins to understand somewhat the organizational difficulties of a militant mass party in the milieu of a developing society, when it is dependent for its largest cadres upon groups of undisciplined, poorly organized agricultural workers.

The PCI has had less success in organizing the sharecroppers and share tenants of the South who operate 28 percent of the acreage under cultivation in the region. This category accounts for 6.5 percent of party members in the South. In Central Italy, in contrast, the sharecroppers account for 18.5 percent of the membership. Small property farmers, at one time unimportant in the South, now comprise 10 percent of PCI membership, compared to less than 5 percent in the Center-North, where they are virtually the major agricultural group.

Intellectuals and students comprise a relatively small percentage of party membership throughout the country, particularly since young people are organized separately in the FCGI (Federation of Young Communists). However, it is interesting that twice as many intellectuals and students are found in the southern membership cadre than in either the Center or the North (1.9 percent in the South as opposed to 0.4 percent in the Center and 0.7 percent in the North).

Middle class groups have not responded to the PCI's call for social solidarity by joining the party. Despite the fact that 35 percent of the work force is in service, the party has failed to attract significant numbers of white-collar workers and technicians, and the number of women in the party is far less than in the Center-North. Even the artisans, whose role in backward southern industry remains important, have not marshaled to the PCI. Their interest in the land is decreasing, and, at the same time, they are threatened by modern industry for perhaps the first time. As a result, elections find them turning more and more to the parties of the right.

With a small working class cadre, large numbers of poor peasants and agricultural day workers, and a grouping of miscellaneous middle class groups, the PCI has certain characteristics of a party of the masses in that it reflects the social composition of the South, but its failures among the workers and the middle classes leave it with a significant weakness in its cadres. Rather than a working class party with peasant support, the PCI has the shape of a poor peasant's party with a scattering of worker and middle class groups on both sides.

Two special groups are of particular interest in analyzing the composition of the PCI in the Mezzogiorno: women and youth. In a backward society such as the South, the role of woman remains traditional, and accordingly, as already mentioned, a smaller percentage of women belong to the PCI in the South than in the Center-North. Young people, in contrast, are more likely to join the Young Communist Federation (FCGI) than in the remainder of the country. This perhaps reflects the despair of youth in a developing society, where the symbols of affluence have recently become visible but the means of achieving them are not yet available. The distribution of these two groups within the PCI and their respective positions in the three regions of the country are represented in Table 8.5.

What are the causes of the particular social composition of the PCI in the South? Clearly, the present social complexion of the party is the result of the interplay of the system of social classes in the South with the strategy of the party. The industrial proletariat in the South is small, dispersed, and poorly organized. A prevalence of urban workers in the party would be difficult to achieve in any case. Moreover, the value system of the South turns political interest toward the land at a time when urban workers have generally broken that pervasive link. As a result, the *braccianti*—the landless—predominate, along with the small peasants. The PCI, rather than seeking to shape new societal values, has attached itself to the land. Consequently, it has attracted some of the least progressive forces in the region and alienated some of the most advanced.

TABLE 8.5

Geographic Distribution in the PCI of Women and Youth, 1962–63

		Regional Distribution		
Region		Women	Youth (FCGI)[a]	Total
North	(N)	101,274	38,722	449,553
	(%)	24.8	22.3	27.8
Center	(N)	235,072	75,749	748,761
	(%)	57.8	43.7	46.4
South	(N)	71,426	58,918	416,818
	(%)	17.4	34.0	25.8
Italy	(N)	407,772	173,389	1,615,112
	(%)	100	100	100

[a] Federation of Young Communists of Italy.
Source: PCI, Dati Sull'Organizzazione del PCI, 1964.

The prevalence of poor peasants and the scarcity of workers in the PCI in the South of Italy is a phenomenon that reproduces itself through the weakness of working class cadres. While working class membership groups and unions in northern and central Italy produce disciplined and dedicated lower and intermediate leadership cadres, poor peasants and agricultural day workers in the South make poor organizers. Dispersed physically and socially in their work, they lack the discipline of the factory process and retain the cultural particularism typical of the South. This perhaps explains why the "geometric effect" described above does not occur.

THE PARTY ORGANIZATION

Why has Communist registration in the South of Italy lagged so far behind in the face of the movement's great political impact and rising electoral success? In part, it is the result of a curious reversal of political roles, which links the Mezzogiorno to the developing societies of the non-Western world. In advanced Western societies, it is generally the labor unions that organize first, involving large numbers of the poor in the general aims of labor agitation, thereby developing cadres of experienced organizers capable of militating politically. Only then have working class parties been formed, fortified by an existing substructure of experience and a ready group of disciplined cadres.

In many developing societies today, political movements have preceded well-developed labor organization. The eminently political appeals of the movement are launched in a vacuum, and organizational drives proceed without the benefit of a trained, local cadre of worker-organizers. Communism in the South of Italy exhibits this historical reversal of roles. As I shall suggest later, the weakness of the unions in the South—a factor only partially related to industrialization—creates a structural weakness in the leadership of the party as well as in its organization.

A second characteristic of the organization of the PCI in the South is its spontaneous methods of recruitment. In the tumultuous years after World War II, the party, lacking trained cadres, recruited with improvised techniques. "The party," a southern leader wrote, "not having behind it a strong organizational tradition, was not completely prepared for the great spontaneous influx of the masses." [5] The party very quickly "took on the physiognomy of a movement, preventing it from acquiring the character of the organized and self-conscious vanguard of the working masses." [6] Many members, it later appeared, were seeking local office or political patronage, since the party was then part of the national government. A surprising number were lawyers and landholders whose membership in the party actually impeded further organization and lent the movement a personalistic character typical of the South. In areas where the party remains in power locally, such elements are still prominent in its organizations.

Great fluctuations in membership followed this early period of spontaneous recruitment. With the PCI's loss of national govern-

5. No author, "Partito e Organizzazione di Massa," *La Voce del Mezzogiorno*, 2, No. 22 (1950), 7.

6. Pietro Secchia, "Relazione," in PCI, VII° Congresso Nazionale, *Atti e Risoluzioni* (Roma, 1951), p. 165.

mental responsibility, many middle class elements quickly turned to the Christian Democrats and the far right-wing parties. The peasants, their adhesion depending upon the battle for the land, would enter the party and leave it with little compunction, depending upon the relative success or failure of the battle. The party retains the careless, improvised character of a movement. As Togliatti said in an almost brutal speech in Sicily, "If you want to achieve wider contacts with peasants, farm workers, small businessmen, professionals and artisans, you must lose a little more of what still remains prominent in our party, its plebeian character. . . . I allude to the plebeian state of mind which is one of blind rebellion, impotent rebellion, almost a prelude to submission." [7]

The inability of the party to draw significant numbers of women to its banners is caused in part by this plebeian character. As Togliatti, a little snobbishly, writes, "Those who frequent our organizations are so poor, so badly dressed, that the Sicilian woman, with her century-old pride, finds herself a little ill at ease." [8] To a great extent, however, the party's continued failure to recruit women is the result of the persistence of traditional paternalism and diffidence. As one party leader has written, "Conceptions that assign to women a subaltern and marginal role in society are not yet overcome in the PCI." [9]

A third organizational theme in the Communist Party in southern Italy relates to the same structural features of the society that have traditionally inhibited political organization: the fragmentatation of social roles. As a PCI document states, "Experience has shown the great difficulty in organizing the masses of the southern peasants and, above all, of grouping them in organizations by category, because of their indeterminate social character." [10] Not only are roles fragmented geographically, economically, and contractually, but great numbers of individuals occupy several economic roles simultaneously. A Sardinian leader has written, "Every social category is fragmented in a guise difficult to isolate.

7. Palmiro Togliatti, "I Compiti Nuovi nella Lotta per la Rinascita del PCI," *Cronache Meridionali, 4,* Nos. 7–8 (1957), 437.

8. Ibid.

9. Pietro Valenza, "Alcuni Problemi del Rinnovamento del PCI nel Mezzogiorno," *Cronache Meridionali, 4,* Nos. 1–2 (1960), 7.

10. PCI-Comitato Centrale, *Documenti, 1951,* p. 197.

. . . More then twenty or thirty people in a village who are tied to a clear identity of interests do not exist." [11]

This fragmentation and confusion of social roles mainly inhibits organization of the peasants, but it also creates a critical obstacle in the organization of the new groups of women workers in industry now emerging from traditional roles in the home and on the farm. Women in the South, a party leader in Rome wrote, "cannot easily be characterized with exactitude, and the various categories of female workers are not easily defined with precision. The female agricultural worker, for example, is not always that; she is also an artisan or a worker in industry. In between times she is a housewife again." [12]

The strategy of the PCI in the South has emphasized Togliatti's stress upon solidarity. The party has self-consciously concentrated on "the development of those forms of organization which have the character of movements and have a broad, unifying force." But the party has not been blind to the impact of the social structure of the region upon party organization.[13] The tactic of solidarity is phrased so as to relate both to the Via Italiana strategy *and* to the requisites of an underdeveloped area. A resolution of the Central Committee in 1951 isolates the link between social structure and party organization. "A multiplicity of popular assemblies, of committees for the land and other democratic organizations of an elementary type are necessary to give a primary and simple form of organization to masses of the people who are not socially concentrated and homogeneous." [14] After their first contacts with southern Italy, party leaders soon concluded that the society "would respond to a broad political appeal such as the movement for the occupation of the land whereas it would not respond to stable labor organizations." [15] *In other words, the party's strategy and the social objective conditions in which it operates in the South are closely linked by party leaders despite the fact that the*

11. Velio Spano, "La Sardegna alla Vigilia delle Elezioni Regionali," *Rinascita, 6*, No. 3 (1949), 103.

12. Luciana Viviani, "Il Lavoro Femminile nella Società Meridionale," *Cronache Meridionali, 20*, No. 6 (1955), 375.

13. PCI, VII° Congresso Nazionale, *Atti e Risoluzioni*, p. 352.

14. PCI-Comitato Centrale, "Risoluzioni della Direzione," *Documenti, 1951*, p. 230.

15. Interview, February 7, 1964.

*broad alliance strategy was first designed for a highly developed
society in the North.*

Its character as a broad popular movement has given the PCI in
the South a dramatic appeal and a power of mass mobilization
never before known in the region. However, at the same time, it
has *institutionalized* the party's initial organizational disabilities
and left it chronically unable to consolidate its political influence
in stable, effective organizations. First, organizational articulation
was inhibited by undertaking many tasks that logically should have
fallen to labor organizations, peasant groups, and cooperatives;
second, in its orientation toward the battle for the land, the movement actually impeded the permanent organization of urban workers; third, it also impeded the stabilization of peasant groups into
solid self-conscious categories, by unceremoniously dumping them
into hazy and amorphous organizations that mirrored their indeterminate social status. As a party directive read, "It is necessary to
find all the forms of organization capable of involving the larger
mass of peasants in our struggle, and to avoid fixing any schemes
for the organization of the semiproletarian and small and medium
peasants." [16] For a time even the relatively homogeneous braccianti
were organized together with sharecroppers, share tenants, and
small property owners. Now organization by category is more ra-
tional.

The quantitative dimensions of PCI organization in the South
which demonstrate its differences from the party in the North are
particularly dramatic. The PCI has *fewer* units in the South than
in the Center-North, but within its organization there is a lower
degree of articulation at each level. Although 30 percent of the
party's sections are found in the South, only 11.4 percent of all its
cells—less than 8 percent of its factory cells and 7 percent of its
women's cells—are found there. The diminishing articulation of
the PCI in the South from level to level, and the contrary phenomenon in the Center-North, is analyzed in Table 8.6.

It is notable that only one category of the party's capillary organizations in the South, the *Circoli* of the Communist Youth
Federation (FCGI), possesses a level of organization approaching
the political influence of the party in the South. Young people in

16. Ruggiero Grieco, *La Lotta per la Riforma Agraria* (Roma, 1949), p. 21.

the South—students, recent migrants to the cities, the unemployed —have begun to react to the chasm between their expectations and the possibilities open to them by widespread involvement in politics. Their response differs sharply from past circumstances in the Mezzogiorno, when embittered youth turned typically to the clergy, the Mafia and Camorra, and to brigandage.

TABLE 8.6

Organizational Structure of the PCI by Region, 1962

		Sections	All Cells	Women's Cells	Factory Cells	Youth Circles (FCGI)
North	(N)	4,348	8,685	1,322	2,405	1,111
	(%)	39.1	23.0	16.5	53.0	24.1
Center	(N)	3,486	24,957	6,093	1,777	2,475
	(%)	31.3	65.6	75.4	39.1	53.8
South	(N)	3,286	4,352	670	356	1,015
	(%)	29.6	11.4	7.1	7.9	22.1
Total	(N)	11,120	37,994	8,085	4,538	4,601
	(%)	100	100	100	100	100

Source: PCI, Dati Sull'Organizzazione, 1964, pp. 29–75.

The functioning of the PCI capillary organizations is illustrative of their problems. To some extent, these organizations are artificial, either existing only on paper or as mere administrative units for the diffusion of propaganda or the collection of dues. In some communes there are more sections than cells, and the existing cells are far too large to permit their political use. An early study indicated the national average to be thirty-nine members per cell, but the regional average of cells in the South was one hundred and fifteen members.[17]

The sections have often had an artificial life as well. In part, this results from their predominantly peasant character. Party leaders

17. Celso Ghino, "Aspetti della Struttura della Organizzazione," Rinascita, 7, No. 3 (1950), 163; also see the observations of Togliatti in "L'Azione Democratica e Socialista nel Mezzogiorno," Cronache Meridonali, 1, No. 6 (1954), 404. He complains, "During the immediate struggle, the forces are well organized; but I would like to know what remains of the organization after the struggle and how we succeed in constructing something that is not simply a generic and spontaneous movement of protest after the battle."

have continually complained that the geographic and social dispersion of the braccianti and sharecroppers in the South leaves their local party organizations detached from their economic lives. Under these conditions, the party section is reduced to a recreational facility. In the North, a host of secondary organizations, both party and nonparty, draw the attention of party members. Some, such as the Casa del Popolo, exist solely for purposes of recreation. The South is organizationally far less differentiated. Even the churches do not possess the panoply of social and recreational branches common in most countries of the West.

The single physical manifestation of the pci in southern villages is the party section. The party member goes there to meet his friends and gossip, to play cards, and to watch television. Surprisingly, 42 percent of the pci sections in the impoverished South have television sets, as opposed to 16 percent in the Center-North.[18] Other instruments of recreation also make their appearance in party sections, to the dismay of old-line militants. The pinball machine and the billiard table are the most common.

The artificial character of the capillary organizations and the dispersal of the membership in the countryside puts an unnatural burden on the provincial federations. The federation must often substitute for work normally carried out by the sections. Since there are almost never the financial means to reimburse functionaries at the capillary level, the most dynamic cadres tend to gravitate to the federation, where they find paid positions and far greater social prestige. These individuals, who often transfer their employment to the provincial capital, cannot then return to unpaid positions in the villages, since they are dependent upon both the financial rewards of federation work and the social status that accrues to a political figure in the *capoluogo*.[19]

There is a sharp division between the great mass of the registered party members and the leadership, with the former spread out in the villages and the latter concentrated in the provincial capital. In this regard, the peculiar stratification system of the South plays a decisive role. The villages are generally great expanses of peasant

18. pci, *Dati Sull'Organizzazione del PCI*, p. 45.
19. Pietro Valenza, "Alcuni Problemi del Rinnovamento del pci nel Mezzogiorno," p. 10.

dwellings with a social life dominated by the need to find work. The cities, though they lack industry, are centers of leisure and diversion, each with its sparkling bars and broad piazzas. Throughout the South, the PCI found that dispersing cadres in the villages slowed up the process of formation of a leadership group, for organizers forced to live in the villages became demoralized and isolated, and frequently involved in clientelistic relationships with local figures.[20]

A disproportionate number of the full-time cadres in the South are now stationed in the provincial capitals, and many village sections have a merely formal existence. So concentrated is the party around its federation headquarters, and so artificial the operation of the cells and sections in the village, that an accurate diagram of the party's effective organization in the South would be an inverted pyramid.

THE PARTY AND THE MASS ORGANIZATIONS

Organized Marxism appeared in northern Italy in the first half of the twentieth century in the wake of the trade unions. In the factories of Turin and Milan, on the commercial farms of the Po valley and in the shipyards of Genoa, autonomous working class associations paved the way for the appearance of the Italian Socialist Party in these northern regions. When the Communist Party was founded in 1921, its basis was the most militant of these working class organizations—the factory councils of Turin.

In southern Italy, no trade union movement worthy of the name existed before Fascism. This initial disadvantage created a radical imbalance between the popularity of the party and the weakness of the trade unions. In many areas the classical relationship between mass organization and party was reversed: the party was a reservoir for the sustenance of the trade unions, rather than vice versa. As a PCI national leader complained in 1951, "One of the defects in our organization [in the South] is that the party today pursues many of the activities which should be fulfilled by the mass, secondary organizations." [21]

20. Pietro Valenza, "Lo Stato del Partito nell'Italia Meridionale," *Rinascita, 14,* No. 6 (1957), 226.

21. Pietro Secchia, "Relazione," VII° Congresso Nazionale, p. 146.

The converse was apparently also true. The balance of strength between party and mass organizations depended largely upon which of the two arrived first in a particular area, the party or the unions. In some areas, the labor union does not complement the programs and activities of the party, but takes their place. Local party leaders in agricultural areas complain that the braccianti may often be found in the offices of the agricultural workers' union when they should be at party meetings.

The unions and the chambers of labor themselves suffer organizational problems similar to those of the PCI. In the early years, they forced together fragmented and incongruous groups of individuals in the same units. In many parts of the South, the chambers of labor—the horizontal union organizations—operate only as peak associations with little or no division of labor by occupational category. As a Northerner writes of his experience in the South before 1955, "The chambers of labor were almost never structured into unions or leagues, and they limited themselves to representing the workers as a whole. The agricultural cooperatives, for example, united agricultural workers, sharecroppers, small renters and small property owners together in the same programs." [22]

Not only were the mass organizations poorly articulated internally, there were many cases in which the same personnel were in charge of different sectors of the movement. They would simply change hats (and, presumably, demands) according to the role they were playing at the moment. "Very often, the Communist Party, the Socialist Party, the chambers of labor and the cooperatives were nothing but different faces of a single popular movement." [23]

In the CGIL, the recruitment of urban southern workers and farm workers is still behind the non-Communist unions even though some progress has been made in the last two decades. The CGIL was initially heavily weighted in the North, with relatively few of its members in the Center or the South. Between 1948 and 1962, the confederation suffered losses in the North which were far greater than its losses in the rest of the country, thereby redressing

22. P. De Pasquale, "Dalla Politica di Salerno alla Crisi del Frontismo Meridionale," *Rinascita, 13,* No. 10 (1956), 548.
23. Ibid.

the balance between regions. However, it is notable that the effect of this redistribution was to raise the number of workers registered in the CGIL to regional parity only in the Center, for the CGIL in the South is still far below its share of the population. Table 8.7 reppresents the distribution of CGIL membershp by region in 1948 and 1962.

TABLE 8.7

CGIL Membership by Region, 1948 and 1962

		1948	1962
North	(N)	2,824,926	1,360,464
	(%)	53.2	38.9
Center	(N)	1,505,880	1,210,382
	(%)	28.4	34.6
South	(N)	975,824	925,114
	(%)	18.4	26.5
Total	(N)	5,310,630	3,495,960
	(%)	100.0	100.0

Source: Istituto Carlo Cattaneo, Le Organizzazioni di Massa (mimeograph, Bologna, 1965).

The relative growth of the CGIL labor movement in the South over this fourteen-year period is incontestable, but it has still failed to keep up with the non-Communist unions in the South, even though it continues to dominate the trade union scene in the North. In figures released in 1965, using a different regional breakdown, the editors of Tempi Moderni find that the CGIL is far behind its Catholic and Social Democratic competitors in its organization in the South; according to these figures, only 21 percent of the CGIL members are found in the South, as opposed to 32 percent of the Catholic CISL members and 31 percent of the Social Democratic UIL members.[24]

More important perhaps than the CGIL's numerical inferiority in the South is its continued failure to develop a strong capillary organization. In the province of Matera, for example, the movement still depends heavily upon agricultural day workers and construc-

24. Luciano Visentini, "I Dirigenti Sindacali nel Processo di Sviluppo del Mezzogiorno," Tempi Moderni, 8, No. 23 (1965), 21–49.

tion workers for its largest categories; over 50 percent of its members are braccianti and another 25 percent are in the building industry. The CGIL has failed to organize large numbers of workers in commerce, in local government, in the new sugar factories and cement works, and in food processing, leaving a free hand in these areas to the Catholic CISL. It is perhaps indicative of the confederation's difficulties that 10 percent of its members in Matera province in 1955 were designated "old people." Despite the fact that the PCI polled 31 percent of the vote in the province in the elections of 1963, its mass organizations there remain weak and disorganized.[25]

The organizational weaknesses of the CGIL in the Mezzogiorno may be attributed to several sources. First, it suffers from the same objective problem as the PCI: it is attempting to organize workers and peasants in a society that has been dominated by clientele relations for centuries. A second "objective" factor is that southern Italy is still in transition between a subsistence and a commercial economy. It is difficult to urge workers to seek an eight-hour day or equal salaries with workers in northern Italy when they have just emerged from conditions in which they worked a sixteen-hour day for less than 12 cents an hour.

But these objective problems appear to be reinforced by equally powerful subjective weaknesses. The weakness of cadres and organizations in the CGIL makes it dependent upon the party for direction and staffing. It is curious, for example, that more southern leaders of the party have at some time held local positions in the CGIL than northern leaders, despite the fact that the CGIL is far weaker in the South. While an average of 24.8 percent of the national leaders from the Center-North had held local CGIL posts in 1964, 31.6 percent had been CGIL leaders in the South.[26]

Related to the weakness of autonomous CGIL cadres in the South is another subjective factor: the lack of faith of party leaders in the peasants' and workers' capacity to organize trade union activity on their own. This factor was revealed dramatically in a report made by the secretary of the CGIL, Novella, to the confederation's

25. Leonardo Sacca, "I Sindacati dopo la Riforma Agraria," *Nord e Sud, 13* (maggio 1966), 104.

26. I wish to thank Dr. Gianfranco Poggi, of the University of Edinburgh, for making these data available to me.

third national conference on the South in 1965. His remarks are worth quoting at length. He says:

> On the regional structuring of our organization, I want to say one thing; it seems to me that we are proceeding much too slowly in this direction. One can obviously not ignore the *objective* difficulties that impede the realization of our decisions, but I maintain that at the base of our backwardness there are also *subjective* difficulties—the underestimation and even resistance which we find and must overcome especially in the Mezzorgiorno.[27]

When we consider objective and subjective difficulties together, we may understand the PCI's dilemma in a backward society like southern Italy. Guided by its vision of a Via Italiana al Socialismo, the party seeks the economic development of Italy as well as the advancement of the workers. Yet, since economic development in the South is almost entirely in the hands of the state, cooperation with the developers would be tantamount to supporting the government. On the other hand, total opposition would prevent the economic development which would eventually lead to higher salaries.

Once again, the PCI is caught between the objective conditions of the underdeveloped setting of the South and the subjective factor of its national strategy. As a result, a critic writes, the CGIL "cannot move beyond the generic representation of popular aspirations and expectations, without leading to political gains that are not its own." The result, according to the same critic, is "primitivism" in collective bargaining, "which, on the one hand, recognizes the need for capital accumulation but on the other attempts to equalize the contracts of workers in North and South." [28]

Objective difficulties appear to be the major problem of the Communist peasant association—the Alleanza dei Contadini—which attempts to organize peasants other than agricultural workers. At first the organization attempted to group together small family farmers, sharecroppers, share tenants, and renters. Today

27. "IIIᵃ Conferenza Meridionale della CGIL," *Rassegna Sindacale; Quaderni,* Nos. 11–12 (dicembre 1965), 27.

28. CISL, *L'Azione Sindacale nel Mezzogiorno* (Roma, 1962), p. 27.

its emphasis is the growing class of small property farmers, but it still attempts to organize the remaining groups, since each of them seeks the ownership of the land. In trying to organize the *coloni* (the share tenants) for example, the Alleanza is involved in a bitter conflict with the agricultural workers' union, the Federbraccianti. Each affiliate of the PCI maintains that the coloni should be organized in its own organizations. The Alleanza contends that the coloni are producers, but the Federbraccianti leaders contend that they are agricultural workers and therefore should be unionized. The conflict is not merely jurisdictional. So pervasive is the structural fragmentation of southern Italian society that there is indeed great confusion as to the occupational roles of great numbers of southern workers and peasants.

Finally, the nature of the PCI appeal to the peasants condemns the peasant organizations to a fluctuating and ephemeral character. The party is oriented to the dramatic issues of the agrarian reform, pursuing the theme of the "land to whoever works it." The peasant organizations have, as a party critic writes, " a necessarily fluctuating character in the sense that their existence is tied to a succession of agitations on single themes." [29] Twenty years after the Communist Party began its activity in the South, its peasant organizations and labor groups still suffer from an amorphous and fluctuating character typical of political movements in developing societies, and lack both the "organizational weapon" of the Leninist party and the broad participation characteristic of the mass party.

If objective difficulties are the major problem of the Alleanza dei Contadini, the PCI's cooperative movement seems to suffer largely from subjective problems. The Lega delle Cooperativi, powerful in northern and central Italy, might be expected to find fertile ground in the South also, for two important reasons. First, the distribution network of the South is incredibly backward, and cooperatives would prove very useful in distributing consumer goods and agricultural raw materials. Second, since the agrarian reform, there are many small farm owners in the South who lack the resources to operate their land in anything like an effective

29. Giuseppe Vitale, "Il Movimento Democratico e la Riforma Agraria," *Cronache Meridionali,* 2, No. 11 (1956), 686.

fashion. Cooperatives of production and marketing could provide tractors and trucks to enable these small farmers to compete effectively in European markets.

The PCI has either been unable or unwilling to exploit these opportunities in the Mezzogiorno. In fact, the number of Communist cooperatives active in the region has actually decreased from 1,466 in 1950 to 1,447 in 1962. At the same time, cooperatives of the Lega delle Cooperativi have increased in number in northern and central Italy. Table 8.8 represents the evolution of

TABLE 8.8

Number of Cooperatives in the *Lega dei Cooperativi* by Region, 1950–62

		1950	1962
North	(N)	1,529	2,332
	(%)	28.0	34.3
Center	(N)	2,458	3,017
	(%)	45.1	44.4
South	(N)	1,466	1,447
	(%)	26.9	21.3
Total	(N)	5,453	6,796
	(%)	100.0	100.0

Source: Istituto Carlo Cattaneo, *Le Organizzazioni di Massa.*

the regional distribution of PCI cooperatives in 1950 and 1962.

The failure of the Communist cooperative movement appears especially puzzling in the light of the powerful force the left-wing cooperatives had in the occupation of uncultivated land in 1946. Since that time, the party has placed great emphasis upon the "autonomy" of the small family farm, an autonomy that cannot possibly be achieved without the economies of a strong cooperative movement like the one the Communists have successfully developed in central Italy.

The logic of the situation is puzzling. On the one hand, the party continues to put forward plans for the stabilization and "valorization" of the small family farm, as in the Sereni-Milillo bill for a four-year plan of support for changes in cultivation, particularly on small family farms. On the other hand, the party has failed to develop the instruments with which the small family farmer can find the technical and economic resources to utilize these resources.[30]

The perplexities aroused by this contradiction are not ours alone. A powerful polemic has been waged within the Communist Party and its affiliates on precisely the question of the party's failure to activate the cooperative movement in the South. Leaders of the cooperative movement itself have protested loudly against their failure to make headway in the South. One leader suggests that the party ought to have created cooperatives out of all the peasant organizations in the South, because of these organizations' instability and lack of economic function. Such suggestions met the immediate and violent opposition of the leaders of the peasant organizations, and the polemic appears to have been settled in favor of the latter.[31] The problem of the failure of the PCI to advance cooperation in the Mezzogiorno will be discussed at greater length when we turn to analyzing the peasant movement.

In both the Communist Party and its important mass organizations in the South, we see the same order of organizational problems. Nowhere more than in organization does the Leninist model of the vanguard party find support. On the other hand, Togliatti's vision of the road to socialism is partly an organizational strategy too. But neither the vanguard party nor a successful mass party can be said to exist in the PCI in southern Italy. Rather, we are dealing with a political movement of the type found most frequently in underdeveloped countries, one in which poor organization, a personal relationship between leaders and followers, and a shifting, discontinuous membership reflect the unstable nature of the society and the ambiguous goals of the leaders.[32]

Particularly in the failure of its mass organizations to provide the party with a solid basis of cadres and experience, the PCI resembles the experience of political movements in underdeveloped areas outside Western Europe. The vacuum is not simply organizational; there is no real educational transition belt of the type

---

30. Sacca, "I Sindacati," p. 102.
31. Vitale, "Il Movimento Democratico."
32. See the description in David E. Apter, *The Politics of Modernization*, p. 205.

Gramsci envisioned between backward peasants and workers and the "collective intellectual" of the party. And, as the next chapter will make clear, the failure of the party to provide itself with substantial numbers of "organic intellectuals" in the South has left a power vacuum within the party which can be filled by only one class, and that class is distinctly not the proletariat.

9. The Party Leadership:
North and South

When asked what he thought of the Italian Socialists—who were then under the influence of his great enemy, Bakunin—Karl Marx replied that they were "lawyers without clients and doctors without patients." And, in fact, if we look back at the Socialist movement in southern Italy in the second half of the nineteenth century, nothing is more striking than the absence of the peasants and the abundance of bourgeois professionals in the leadership.[1] The irony was not lost upon Marx; these political leaders differed from the rest of the Italian political elite only in their opinions. In Gramsci's phraseology, they were traditional intellectuals who had discovered the poor, but had not yet been absorbed within the collective intellectual of the vanguard party.

One would be hard pressed to find romantic bourgeois figures of this type in Italian politics today, or, for that matter, anywhere in Europe. However, as was indicated in Chapter 6, in southern Italy politics is still dominated by a highly educated class of bourgeois political amateurs who, in their social origins and professional training, resemble the old nineteenth-century Italian elite. Our first important problem for analysis is how southern Italian *Communist* leaders compare to these characteristics of the southern Italian political elite as a whole.

A second important question concerns Banfield's assertion that there is in southern Italy a *political,* as well as an *organizational,* incapacity. We have seen that in its membership structure and organization, the PCI in the South is neither a successful mass party nor a vanguard party; it remains to be seen whether its structural weakness leads to a political weakness, too. We can approach this

1. See Aldo Romano, *Storia del Movimento Socialista in Italia* (3 vols., Milano-Roma, 1954).

question in two ways: first, by an analysis of the party leadership and ideology, and, second, by an analysis of the party's behavior and activities. The nature of the leadership and its political role in North and South is the subject of this chapter.

One can learn a great deal about the leadership of a party simply by reflecting upon its origin. In Russia, for example, long years of exile and opposition gave Bolshevik leaders a negative outlook which can still be found in their rhetoric after fifty years of government.[2]

The most meaningful experience in the formation of a leadership cadre in the Italian Communist Party was their long period of clandestine activity and the Resistance movement they directed against the Germans. One can scarcely underestimate the impact of years of secrecy and months of battle upon leaders of a political movement who then enter everyday politics.

The relevant point in this context is that, although most of the leaders of the Resistance were Communists at one time or another, not all Communist leaders were in the Resistance. As a matter of fact, PCI leaders in northern Italy came mainly from the Resistance movement, whereas southern leaders arose only later and in an entirely different context. In other words, not only did the Resistance differentiate northern from southern Communist leaders at the outset; it provided the party with a national elite which was at first overwhelmingly northern and only later began to include significant southern components. Table 9.1 represents the evolution of the regional distribution of Communist *national* leaders between 1946 and 1963. It is based upon questionnaires sent out to living members of the national party elite in 1964 by the Istituto Carlo Cattaneo.[3]

When we turn to the provincial leaders of the PCI, the distinction between northerners and southerners is much sharper. The majority of today's provincial leaders in the North joined the party from the Resistance movement during World War II. In the South, in contrast, the largest group of today's provincial

2. I am indebted for this observation to my colleague Leon Lipson of the Yale Law School, who is currently engaged in a study of Soviet political rhetoric.

3. I wish to thank the Istituto Carlo Cattaneo, and particularly Gianfranco Poggi of the University of Edinburgh, for making these data available to me.

TABLE 9.1

Regional Components of PCI National Leadership by Year of First National Office
(percentage)

	1946 (127)	1950 (229)	1953 (283)	1957 (268)	1961 (281)	1963 (323)
North	75.2	73.4	68.6	68.7	64.8	63.2
South	22.4	25.3	29.1	29.5	32.4	33.1
Foreign	2.4	1.3	2.3	1.8	2.8	3.7
Total	100.0	100.0	100.0	100.0	100.0	100.0

Source: Istituto Carlo Cattaneo, unpublished data.

leaders came to the party through the peasant and labor movement
or from an intellectual or professional career. These data, which
are taken from questionnaires solicited by the author from PCI
provincial secretaries in 1964, are presented in Table 9.2.

TABLE 9.2

Route of Party Recruitment of PCI Provincial Secretaries by Region
(in percentages)

		Resistance Movement	College or Professional Career	Labor or Peasant Movement	Other	Total
North	(N)	25	5	9	8	47
	(%)	53	11	19	17	100
South	(N)	8	9	12	4	33
	(%)	24	28	36	12	100

Even those southerners who participated in the Resistance
fought a different kind of war than was fought in the North. The
Resistance in the South involved relatively small bands of partisans
carrying out harassment tactics and reconnaisance against the
Germans. But the war in the South ended with the liberation of
Rome, while the armed resistance in the North involved full-scale
military operations supported by the Allies and giving Communist
and other leaders a real exposure to commanding large groups of
militants.

A side product of this historical situation, but one that held
great importance for the South, was that in the early postwar years

the PCI in the South was largely directed by Northerners, many of whom had begun their political careers in the Resistance or in exile and then traveled South along the dirt roads and across the mountains to militate politically in the isolated villages of the Mezzogiorno.

It was a highly romantic enterprise. The Italian journalist, Marco Cesarini Sforza, recalls its spirit in the center-left journal *Nord e Sud*. "They took off their shoes and walked barefoot in the hills, eating the food offered by the poor population and sleeping in haystacks." [4] A Communist observer, Giorgio Amendola, who eventually led these cadres, invokes the same mood of evangelism:

> The North furnished thousands upon thousands of cadres who could operate methodically in the organizations of the laboring masses of the South. They were revolutionaries who accepted their coming to the South not as functionaries being punished with exile, but with enthusiasm, as brothers helping their brothers, living in sacrifice, introducing into the political life of the South a new style of politics and a serious attention to concrete issues. [5]

Yet enthusiasm quickly met the primitive realities and stubborn cultural obstacles of peasant society. Organizers who had succeeded in establishing contact and rapport with villagers were subjected to countless difficulties. They were generally workers or intellectuals operating in peasant societies. To them the peasant dialects were inscrutable and peasant mores were foreign. To the peasants, in turn, these visitors from an alien world were suspect, and the message they brought, unless couched in the most elemental terms, was incomprehensible. In Caulonia, on the Ionic coast of Calabria, the peasants greeted liberation by setting up a village republic. In Senise, in Lucania, an organizer who attempted to establish a party school was welcomed by women who mistakenly thought his purpose was to teach reading.

Later organizers were more thoroughly trained. Many were sent directly by the party office in Rome—the so-called *costruttori*.

4. "Inviato a Sud," *Nord e Sud, 9*, No. 25 (1962 Nuova Serie), 110.

5. Giorgio Amendola, "Per la Rinascita del Mezzogiorno," *Cronache Meridionali, 1*, No. 1 (1954), 33.

They were sent to the South "to instill a spirit of organizational precision" in the southern sections of the party. Their success in electoral campaigns was notable, but those who stayed for longer periods could not easily adjust to local social conditions. Southern leaders today recall their bafflement at the complicated social and political mores of the Mezzogiorno, their "inability to understand the reality in which they operated." [6] Clear signs of their inability to operate successfully were the frequent conflicts that occurred between northern "ambassadors" and southern leadership cadres.

After this early period of organization from the North, local cadres began to direct the PCI. Notable from the beginning was the leadership's middle class intellectual nature, and the absence of peasant and worker cadres. The leader of the party in the South, Giorgio Amendola, who was the son of a famous republican leader, was described by radical enemies as "a liberal intellectual who discovered the working class." When he became a national figure, Amendola's assistants and political heirs were Gerardo Chiaramonte, an engineer by profession, and Mario Alicata, Alfredo Reichlin, and Giorgio Napoletano, three intellectuals of bourgeois background.

The prevalence of middle class social origins among the intermediate and upper level leaders of the PCI in the South is perhaps their most striking characteristic. Like the leaders of mass movements in developing societies in the non-Western world, these leaders have been outraged by the injustices of their society and its historical subjugation to an alien, colonial power (in this case, the North of Italy). They have turned to the disinherited of the society, seeking their transformation into a creative element of modernization.

In Chapter 6, I showed that the leadership of the PCI throughout Italy has a lower social origin and educational level than the leaders of the other Italian parties. Compared to non-Communist leaders who are largely amateurs, PCI leaders are, furthermore, political and organizational technicians who have made party work their career.

These characteristics of the PCI national leadership do not extend to its southern leaders. Very few are of working class back-

6. Interview, March 6, 1964.

ground; most have a high school or college education; and a great
many come from the same liberal professions as the vast majority
of the southern Italian political elite. There is at this time no published account of the social origins and professional careers of PCI
leaders at the parliamentary level that allows us to compare northern and southern leaders. However, the survey cited above, spon-
sored by the Istituto Carlo Cattaneo, compares the national leadership groups of the PCI and the Christian Democrats and analyzes
these dimensions of the party leadership.

TABLE 9.3

Social Status by Family Origin of PCI National Leaders by Region
(in percentages)

	(N)	Lower	Lower Middle	Middle, Upper Middle	Upper	Total
North	(203)	18.2	41.4	26.1	10.8	100.0
Center	(134)	16.8	37.9	28.5	10.2	100.0
South	(107)	13.1	25.2	35.5	23.4	100.0
Islands	(66)	7.6	22.7	42.4	19.7	100.0

Source: Istituto Carlo Cattaneo, unpublished data.

With regard to their social origins, southern Communist leaders
on the national level are mainly an upper middle and upper class
group with a small lower class and lower middle class component.
Among leaders from the North, on the other hand, the largest
component is lower middle class, with substantial minorities coming from both the lower and the upper classes. Table 9.3, which
draws upon the Istituto Carlo Cattaneo data, presents this aspect
of Communist leadership in the North, the Center, the South, and
the southern Italian islands.

Although national southern leaders differ sharply from northern
leaders in their social origins, on the provincial level today's PCI
leaders differ very little in this respect. The data collected by the
author from provincial secretaries show that in both North and
South, slightly more than 50 percent of the federal secretaries are
from lower middle class backgrounds. In the North, however, 28
percent of the remaining respondents reported lower class back-

grounds, and 20 percent reported middle or upper middle class backgrounds. In the South, in contrast, there were fewer lower class leaders (18 percent) and slightly more upper class leaders (30 percent).

Southern Communist leaders on the national level also display a sharp difference from northern leaders in the size of the city of their birth. Almost 40 percent of northern leaders come from cities of more than 100,000 inhabitants, compared to only 20 percent of southern leaders. On the other hand, almost 15 percent of northern leaders come from villages of less than 5,000 inhabitants as compared to 11 percent of the Southerners. The Southerners, in contrast, come mainly from cities of from 5,000 to 20,000 inhabitants (31 percent) or cities of from 20,000 to 100,000 (36 percent). The distribution is interesting, for although it demonstrates that southern leaders do not come from very large cities as do many of the northern leaders, they are certainly not from the smallest villages either. These data are presented in Table 9.4 for the North, the Center, the South, and the southern islands.

TABLE 9.4

Size of Commune of Origin of PCI National Leaders by Region
(in percentages)

	(N)	0–5,000	5,000 to 20,000	20,000 to 100,000	More than 100,000
North	(240)	18.7	22.5	24.2	34.6
Center	(152)	5.3	30.9	25.2	38.1
South	(127)	13.2	25.6	36.4	24.8
Islands	(67)	9.8	36.1	37.7	16.4

Source: Istituto Carlo Cattaneo, unpublished data.

The data for the provincial leaders are more sharply differentiated by region; most northern leaders were either from towns of less than 10,000 inhabitants, (35 percent) or from cities of more than 50,000 inhabitants (42 percent), and only 23 percent were from cities of from 10,000 to 50,000 population. Southern provincial secretaries, in contrast, were largely from this last category of communes (62 percent) with only 5 percent from the small towns and 33 percent from the large cities. In other words, the majority of the southern leaders came from precisely the class of commune in which the party gains its most significant electoral success. Few came from the large cities where we might expect to find working class cadres formed, and *very* few from the peasant villages of less than 10,000 inhabitants. This is another indicator that Communism in southern Italy is most active in medium-sized communes and weak both in the villages and large cities.[7]

We have no detailed educational data on the national level at this time with which to compare the training of northern and southern Communist leaders, but on the provincial level data collected by the author suggest that Communist leaders, much like non-Communist leaders, are more highly educated than their colleagues in the North. Whereas federal PCI secretaries in the North are evenly divided between those with an elementary or junior high school training and those with a secondary school or university background, 62 percent from the South had graduated from high school or college as opposed to 38 percent who attended only elementary or junior high school.

More interesting than their educational background is the geographical mobility of southern Communist provincial leaders, both before and after entering the party. Perhaps reflecting the unstable nature of southern Italian society as well as upward social mobility, 43 percent of the southern provincial secretaries reported having grown up in cities other than those of their birth, whereas only 25 percent of the northern leaders had changed residence during the formative period of their youth.

The localism of leaders in the North, as opposed to the geographical mobility of those from the South, is expressed in the focus of their political activity, too. In the North, 38 percent hold the post of provincial secretary in the city and province of their childhood; 47 percent work in a different city but in the same province; and 15 percent have a position completely outside their home province. In the South, in contrast, half as many (19 percent) hold posts in the city and province in which they grew up; slightly more (52 percent) work in the same province but in different cities; and twice as many as in the North (29 percent) have party positions in an entirely different province.

7. See Chap. 7.

The same regional contrast may be seen in the range of the leadership's political experience in North and South. Contrary to what might be expected in a traditional society, 40 percent of the southern leaders, as opposed to 28 percent of the northern leaders, have held party positions in two or more provinces. In other words, as well as having a generally higher social origin, more educational training, and more geographical mobility in their youth, more southern leaders have had a broad political experience than their northern colleagues.

We might speculate at length about the significance of these data for the problem of the political traditionalism of a so-called backward society. In this context, all that can be done is to present several propositions for analysis later.

First, the greater mobility and experience of the southern provincial leaders is probably linked to the "colonizing" nature of the PCI's campaign in the South. (That is, the South was for many years a political frontier where leaders were shifted about in response to local needs.)

Second, high mobility and experience is definitely linked to the fluid nature of PCI leadership in the South which, like the fluidity of its mass membership, is related to the sporadic nature of politics in a peasant society.

Third, and perhaps most interesting, the social and professional superiority of southern PCI leaders over their northern colleagues suggests the following proposition: there are forces in a "backward society" that favor the formation of a leadership group which, in its social composition, education, and training, is far from backward. In fact, it is precisely the backward nature of the society that is responsible for the weakness of working class and peasant leadership and that turns the attention of middle class intellectuals and professionals to politics partly due to the absence of alternate opportunities. To modify, with apologies to its author, the quotation used to begin this chapter, left-wing political leaders in southern Italy are perhaps doctors *with* patients and lawyers *with* clients.

One might imagine that the preceding discussion would outrage Italian Communist leaders. Yet it is precisely of the bourgeois intellectual character of its southern leadership that PCI national leaders warn the unwary foreigner who expects to find a party led by peasants in a predominantly peasant society. In fact, the party has published statistics that underline the Communist leadership problem in the South. For example, in Table 9.5 the reader will

TABLE 9.5

Professional Distribution of PCI Federal Committee Members by Region, 1954

		North	Center	South	Italy
Urban workers	(N)	951	372	402	1,725
	(%)	46.8	40.8	30.8	40.6
Agricultural	(N)	104	15	92	211
workers	(%)	5.1	1.7	7.1	5.0
Peasants	(N)	142	103	114	359
	(%)	7.0	11.3	8.7	8.5
Artisans	(N)	88	46	78	212
	(%)	4.3	5.1	6.0	5.0
White collar	(N)	298	154	143	595
	(%)	14.7	16.9	11.0	14.0
Professionals,	(N)	337	169	392	898
intellectuals,	(%)	16.6	18.5	30.1	21.1
and technicians					
Housewives	(N)	38	22	52	112
	(%)	1.9	2.4	4.0	2.6
Others	(N)	74	30	30	134
	(%)	3.6	3.3	2.3	3.2
Total	(N)	2,032	911	1,303	4,246
	(%)	100.0	100.0	100.0	100.0

Source: PCI, *Forze ed Attività del Partito Comunista Italiano*, p. 67.

find the professional distribution of members of the PCI provincial federal committees by region. The number of middle class students, technicians, professionals, and intellectuals in the South is very striking indeed.

There is some evidence that the party has made strenuous attempts to combat the middle class intellectual character of the leadership of the party in the South. Interviews with national leaders indicated that the problem places subjective limits upon the party's capacity for expansion. For a start, southern leaders are less professional than their northern colleagues. In the unpublished national data cited above, it was discovered that, whereas 71 percent of northern national leaders listed their occupations as "political," only 54 percent did so in the South.

Second, the commitment to the party of the southern Communist leader is more of an individual matter, as contrasted to the family commitment of the northern leader. Data on the national elite are interesting on this score. Despite the importance of the family in social life in southern Italy, the wives of less than half of the southern leaders are members of the party, as contrasted to 63 percent of leaders' wives in the North. The party membership of other members of the leaders' families is less significant, but, in each case, there is a stronger family identification in the North than in the South. Summary data for the party membership of leaders' wives, siblings, children, and parents are presented in Table 9.6.

TABLE 9.6

Party Membership of Family Members of PCI National Leaders by Region
(in percentages)

	(N)	Spouse	Siblings	Children	Parents
North	(181)	61.3	44.2	32.0	26.0
Center	(126)	64.3	38.1	27.8	23.8
South	(87)	44.8	36.8	26.4	17.2
Islands	(64)	50.0	37.5	23.4	10.9

Source: Istituto Carlo Cattaneo, unpublished data.

Turning once again to the provincial level, Communist leadership in the South is weaker numerically than in the North. For example, according to the questionnaire data collected by the author, only 55 percent of the southern provincial federations are able to employ more than five full-time functionaries, compared to 87 percent in the North. As a result, the southern federations are seldom able to divide their work—organization, youth, women, press, and propaganda—among a sufficient number of individuals. Table 9.7 presents the number of full-time officials found in each provincial federation by region based upon responses to the questionnaire.

The lack of organizational articulation of the movement and the weakness of the secretariat in each province means that provincial secretaries are often called upon to perform the work of propaganda, women's organization, relations with the labor movement, and organizational work as well as the general political direction of the federation. Southern leaders, moreover, are commonly placed first on the local or provincial election lists, with the result that they frequently fill the office of mayor, provincial or city council member, as well as their party office. Sixty-seven percent of the southern leaders have held such posts for over five years, as

TABLE 9.7

Salaried Personnel in PCI Provincial Federations by Region
($N = 80$)

		1–5 Persons	6–10 Persons	Over 10 Persons	Total
North	(N)	6	21	20	47
	(%)	13	45	42	100
South	(N)	15	13	5	33
	(%)	45	40	15	100
Italy	(N)	21	34	25	80
	(%)	26.3	42.4	31.3	100

compared to 56 percent in the North. National leaders complain that "the most qualified part of the southern cadres has been absorbed little by little in the tasks of political direction, public office and union work." [8]

The dominance of middle class intellectuals as leaders and the mass of poorly differentiated peasantry in the rank and file of the party produces a social gap between leaders and followers. Organizers from the North are often surprised and uneasy at the number of lawyers and students they find in the chambers of labor and the federations of the South. The southern leaders, in contrast, are skeptical of the capacity of lower class cadres to organize political activities effectively. Although Italian Communist leaders place a greater value than logic might dictate upon the peasants' battle for the land, attitudes toward the peasants range from skepticism of their political readiness to downright contempt. The peasant is seen in a paternalistic way, much as he is perceived by the traditional Italian political elite. Peasants bow slightly to party leaders, stand while they talk, and come to the federation with problems of the law and land tenure. So wide is the gap between the intellectual

8. Pietro Valenza, no title, *Cronache Meridionali*, 5, No. 5 (1958), 301.

leadership in the provincial capitals and the mass of the peasant membership in the countryside that one union official contended that southern PCI leaders are "antipeasant." [9]

The failure of a permanent peasant cadre to develop in the PCI is possibly linked to these attitudes. Leaders look upon peasant members as unable to think for themselves, and they freely manipulate meetings of party sections and labor organizations. It was maintained at the Ninth Party Congress in 1960 that "the party must advance further to liberate itself courageously from any elements of clientelism and paternalism that still exist here and there." [10] Dealing with the failure of a peasant cadre to emerge in the South, another leader complains, "The development of a new type of cadre of popular extraction is bound to meet, and even to instigate, a certain resistance and danger and distortion from the residues of clientelism in the bosom of the popular movement." [11]

Attitudes toward the opposition are remarkably ambivalent. Few local capitalists are offered as a target; the local bourgeoisie is alternately castigated and approached as potential allies; there remains mainly the North and its "monopolistic industry" as a concrete enemy. This has a certain political force and historical validity, but in the day-to-day struggles of southern politics, the enemy is invisible. He can be bitterly denounced, but he can neither fight back nor be demonstrably defeated. Political discourse, accordingly, takes on an unreal quality.

The political roles of PCI leaders in the South differ markedly from those of the leaders in the North. Among the provincial secretaries who returned questionnaires, there was far less sense of organizational control over the activities of the party's organization, and a stronger perception of autonomous political activity. There appears to be considerably more flexibility, less closure, and more discussion in the southern circles of the party than in

9. Interview, April 15, 1964.

10. PCI, IX° Congresso Nazionale, Atti e Risoluzioni, *1* (Roma, 1960), 231; also see Ruggiero Grieco, "Nuove Tappe della Lotta per la Riforma Agraria," *Rinascita*, 7, No. 1 (1950), 14. In the cooperatives, he notes, "a stratum of opportunistic leaders developed, creating a barrier between mass organizations, party and the masses."

11. Pietro Valenza, "Aspetti del Fanfanismo in Lucania," *Cronache Meridionali*, 5, No. 12 (1958), 865.

the northern federations. Attitudes toward the party's central office, for example, exhibited a surprising degree of candor and sophistication.

Within the federation, there is a very different order of priority assigned to political and organizational work. While the top leadership concerns itself with local government, mass movements, and, increasingly, with relations with other political groups, the more purely organizational work of registration, recruitment, and cell meetings are left to "modest comrades," a practice that has caused agitation in the party's national office.[12]

Southern party leaders attach a great deal of importance to relations with other political groups and to their reputations in the community at large. In personal interviews, provincial leaders stressed such qualities as "prestige," "honesty," and "seriousness" as the factors that recommend them to the admiration of their fellow citizens. In the North, party leaders were more concerned with the impression they make among groups of party members and affiliates than with the opinions of the community at large. Southern leaders were far more conscious of the need to establish a network of ties with political leaders on the local level. Northerners tended to interpret the Leninist policy of alliances as the business of the party on the national level.

The personalistic nature of southern politics affects the leadership of the PCI in the Mezzogiorno and its relations with the rank and file. The federation secretary gains a personal importance in this milieu that he lacks in the party bylaws or in the northern federations. Party secretaries spend much of their time seeking jobs for office seekers and degrees for examination takers, and trying to resolve the legal and land disputes of the peasants. Togliatti writes, "There is a need to overcome the personalism, the tendency to divide into groups around one or another personality. This derives from the type of social organization of the South, a reflection of its social disaggregation in the files of our party." [13]

The personal prestige and power of the federal secretary is linked to another factor: the relative autonomy of the provincial

12. Pietro Valenza, "Lo Stato del Partito nell'Italia Meridionale," *Rinascita, 14,* No. 6 (1957), 32.

13. Quoted by Pietro Valenza, *Cronache Meridionali, 5,* No. 5 (1958), 305.

federation in relation to the party's central office. Federal secretaries were asked their opinion on the role a provincial party federation should play with respect to the national party organization. There were five alternatives representing different degrees of autonomy or central direction, and a scalar value was assigned to each response. The results are represented in Table 9.8. Two-

TABLE 9.8

Perceptions of Party Centralism of PCI Provincial Secretaries by Region
($N = 80$)

		Centralists	Regionalists	Moderates	Total
North	(N)	31	8	8	47
	(%)	66	17	17	100
South	(N)	14	14	5	33
	(%)	42	42	16	100
Italy	(N)	45	22	13	80
	(%)	56	28	16	100

thirds of the Northern leaders were ranged on the side of central direction, with 17 percent perceiving their role autonomously and another 17 percent expressing moderate positions. In the South, in contrast, only two-fifths were centralists, another 42 percent regionalists or autonomists, and 16 percent were moderates.

Personalism, low organizational capacity, and the political sensitivity of southern leaders were prominent features in the opinions expressed of them by national PCI leaders in a series of personal interviews I carried out in Rome in 1964. A sampling of some of these informants' opinions follows.

A high-level union official said:

> The PCI in the South is a party of clienteles. This is true in the sense that they seek power through advancing the interests of their followers on the local level and within the established system. The party in the South partakes of the backwardness of the society.[14]

A leader of the Communist-led cooperative movement said:

> In the North, the activist is a worker who is more talented than the rest. In the South, he is an intellectual. The political

14. Interview, April 15, 1964.

sensitivity of the southern cadres is greater. In the North, where there are workers and progressive peasants, the Marxist-Leninist model applies. In the South, you are guided by the day-to-day facts, and you must be extremely sensitive to them.[15]

A nationally active federation secretary said:

The southern cadre has an ability in making alliances which has brought praise from the rest of the party. They have more political sensitivity than those of the North. They are more alive, more perceptive, more active at the summit than at the base.[16]

A leader in the PCI national Secretariat said:

The cadres in the South are more politically sensitive, more flexible, more sensitive to the political solution of problems. In the South, traditionally, everything is decided politically, for in a disorganized society, it is the relations between individuals that solve problems. In the North, in contrast, we deal more with concrete classes, opposing groups, and less on the basis of contacts on a personal level. In the cadres of the South, political sensitivity and ideological subtleties are more important.[17]

Later he said, with some bitterness:

The northern part of the party is more aware of the need to oppose a strong organization to the strong organizations of the adversary. There is an organizational mentality. In the South, we find better orators. You can see the Greek school of philosophy on any Sunday morning in the piazza of a small southern village.[18]

Another official in the apparatus said:

The characteristic of the southern cadres has always been their fluidity. Yet despite this, they have a very high political level.[19]

15. Interview, April 20, 1964.
16. Interview, March 7, 1964.
17. Interview, April 24, 1964.
18. Ibid.
19. Interview, April 12, 1964.

A third Secretariat official said:

> The differences between northern and southern cadres are the differences in the characteristics of the regions. The Northerner is more of a formalist and the Southerner is more versatile but less organizationally oriented.[20]

In order to tap leaders' personal perceptions of their roles, the question was asked, "In your work as federal party secretary, what are the most important things you do, in the order of their importance?" Responses were not contextually coded, but were classified for broad analytical categories according to their political content, their content of labor orientation, and their organizational content. The results are recorded in Table 9.9. Naturally enough, all the

TABLE 9.9

Individual Role Perceptions of PCI Provincial Secretaries by Region
(N = 80)

		Political Role	Labor Role	Organizational Role	D.K. N.A.	Total
North	(N)	8	4	31	4	47
	(%)	16	9	66	9	100
South	(N)	20	3	5	5	33
	(%)	61	9	15	15	100
Italy	(N)	28	13	36	9	80
	(%)	35	9	45	11	100

responses contained a strong political element, but many incorporated elements that were specifically labor oriented, and many others were based upon organizational tasks such as control of finance, recruitment, and creation of new capillary organizations.

As the table indicates, over two-thirds of the northern respondents perceive their roles in largely organizational terms, whereas three-fifths of the Southerners include mainly political factors in their role perceptions. Although these attitudes do not necessarily represent the actual behavior of the leaders, they do reflect a widely divergent set of role orientations between northern and southern leaders of the Communist Party.

20. Interview, March 20, 1964.

Rather than speculate at this point upon the meaning of these divergences, it will be useful simply to underscore their importance, both for the nature of political leadership in a backward area and for the impact of political dualism upon the PCI. Regarding the first point, it is simply not true, as Banfield assumes, that the organizational incapacity of a backward society automatically leads to political incapacity. All the data that have been assembled suggest that southern Italian Communist leaders are more politically experienced, more politically oriented, and more politically sensitive than their colleagues in the North. In fact, there is a good deal of evidence to suggest that this political capacity is a *correlate* of organizational backwardness rather than a contradiction of it.

The impact of this dualism within the leadership upon the PCI is quite strong. The party's public image, its style of work, and its internal political relationships differ sharply from North to South. National party officials were quite explicit on this point. One official confided that his training as a labor leader in the Po valley leaves him totally unprepared to speak publicly to groups of agricultural workers in Puglia and Sicily, since the style of discourse of the southern leaders who usually address them differs completely from his own.

One can detect distinct differences in rhetoric and style of delivery in the speeches delivered by northern and southern Communist leaders at party congresses and conferences. Even on an impressionistic level, it is clear that the southerner embraces a subject lovingly, whereas the northern orator cuts quickly through to the basic problems.

These differences in rhetoric, however, do not appear to extend to differences in ideology. At least in their responses to questionnaires, southern provincial leaders did not appear to differ significantly from northern leaders on the essentials of the party ideological line. For example, the provincial secretaries were asked to choose the most important task the PCI now faces in southern Italy. The alternatives posed were, (1) to construct socialism, (2) to achieve a working class nucleus, (3) to form a broad popular front, (4) to battle for the rebirth of the region, and (5) to oppose the policies of the government. The general line of the party regarding the South, as will be seen in the following chapter, is the third alternative—to form a broad popular front. At the same time, the PCI has placed increasing emphasis upon the battle for regional autonomy.

The responses of northern and southern provincial leaders differed only in degree on the importance allotted to these various factors. The largest group of positive responses in both regions was the third alternative: the formation of a broad popular front. The second choice in both regions was the "rebirth of the region" alternative, and the third in both cases was the formation of a working class nucleus. These data are presented in Table 9.10. It should be noted that the statistics refer to the number of total responses and to the percentage of total responses by region, since respondents were free to respond affirmatively to more than one choice.

TABLE 9.10

Attitudes of PCI Provincial Secretaries Toward Party Goals
in the South by Region
($N = 80$)

PCI's *basic goal in the South is:*	Number of Total Affirmative Responses		Percentage of Total Affirmative Responses	
	North	*South*	*North*	*South*
To construct socialism	6	3	10.0	6.5
To conquer a working class nucleus	8	7	13.1	15.2
To form a broad popular front	29	15	47.4	32.6
To battle for the rebirth of the region	12	13	19.7	28.4
To oppose the policies of the government	3	6	4.9	13.0
No answer	3	2	4.9	4.4
Total	61	46	100.0	100.0

It is interesting that, although the largest group of positive responses in both regions is in favor of the formation of a broad popular front, fewer Southerners than Northerners chose this alternative, and more Southerners than Northerners chose "the rebirth of the region." Both alternatives are part of the party's ideological line, but the second has been given relatively more emphasis in the South because of the importance of the regional problem in the PCI dialectics. Consequently, the differences between northern and southern responses may simply correspond to a greater emphasis on the region in the South and a greater emphasis on interclass solidarity in the North.

What impresses an observer most is not any particular difference in ideological emphasis between northern and southern leaders, but the absolute weakness of ideology within the southern leadership. Many provincial leaders in the South had no clear idea of dialectics and no firm understanding of Marx's economics. In the previous chapter it was shown that class dialectics play a very small role in Communist electoral campaigns. Leaders who were interviewed in the South did not distinguish clearly between the interests of different classes of the population, particularly the agricultural classes. This subjective weakness is perhaps linked to a very real objective problem. In a fragmented rural society, it is in fact very difficult to distinguish between the interests of different agricultural groups since these groups are not clearly separated from one another.

Ideology does not appear to have been an important issue in many of the defections from the PCI among southern leaders. Defections in Calabria in the 1950s, for example, appear to have been related mainly to the efforts of the Agrarian Reform Agency to co-opt the PCI's most able organizers, rather than for more ideological reasons.[21] In the North, in contrast, there have been a succession of organized defections which have resulted in the formation of left-wing worker and intellectual splinter groups.

However, throughout the 1950s and 1960s there has been a growing undercurrent of *malaise* in southern PCI leaders against what has come to be called *il vecchio meridionalismo*—the old-fashioned brand of regionalism. Younger leaders—particularly those involved in youth groups and in trade union activity—betray a vague consciousness of opportunities lost or squandered, crossroads missed, and issues muddled. It is almost as if the growing electoral success

21. Giovanni Cervigni, "Le Defezioni dal PCI in Calabria," *Nord e Sud*, 2, No. 6 (1955).

of the party against the background of its organizational weakness is a form of political failure in a political setting like the Mezzogiorno.

In several dramatic respects, the Communist Party in the Mezzogiorno resembles a political movement like those in the developing societies of the non-Western world more than it does Communism as we know or imagine it in the West. Its membership is diffuse and discontinuous, its organization is weak and personalized, and its leadership is heavily weighted with middle class intellectuals who are political entrepreneurs rather than organizational technicians. They have turned to the lower classes of city and countryside, but not as revolutionaries, and their programs have failed to stimulate the formation of a solid cadre of working class and peasant militants similar to those we find in northern Italy.

These indicators suggest a series of contradictions within the PCI in the South and between the party's role in the North and its role in the South. There is, first, the contrast between the predominance of peasants in the membership in the South and the middle class intellectual character of the leaders. A second contrast is between the movement's organizational weakness and the apparent political capacity of the leaders. Related to this problem is a factor that, on the surface, does not seem to be a problem at all: the ideological unity of northern and southern leaders exists in a context of radically different political settings. If the Via Italiana al Socialismo was designed for a highly developed North, does this not suggest that southern Communist leaders who depend upon it will find themselves at a disadvantage as political actors in the underdeveloped South?

10. The Ideology of Backwardness

Marxism and backwardness: an explosive combination, or at least so one would think. Lenin certainly thought so. As he told a group of Asian Communists, "It is imperative for you to make a success of applying Communist theory and practice under conditions where the peasant is the primary class of the masses, where the task of struggle pending solution lies in the fight against mediaevalism, and not in the fight against capitalism." And he was convinced that the future revolution in the underdeveloped areas was foreshadowed by the pattern in Russia. He concluded, "The solution to the above tasks . . . can . . . be seen in the overall struggle already started in Russia." [1]

Southern Italy is an underdeveloped area. Is it not, therefore, potentially more volatile, by virtue of its backwardness, than northern Italy, where industrialization has been accompanied by the partial embourgeoisement of the worker? Gramsci certainly thought so, and he shaped his revolutionary program around the anarchic, but potentially powerful, southern peasantry as well as the organized workers of the North.

There were precedents in Marxist theory for Gramsci's formula. Marx and Engels, whom careless bourgeois theorists have accused of ignoring the peasantry, were thoroughly aware of the peasantry's revolutionary potential. In *The Peasant War in Germany,* Engels was positively effusive about the "robust vandalism" of the peasantry.[2] Marx, as usual, was more reflective and more incisive. In *The Eighteenth Brumaire of Louis Bonaparte,* he analyzed the contradictory nature of peasants: they may be the

---

1. From V. I. Lenin, "Report Before the Second All-Russian Representative Congress of the Communist Organization of the Eastern Peoples," *Sochinenya* (Works) *24* (Moscow, 1932), 542–51. Quoted in Lucian Pye, *Guerrilla Communism in Malaya* (Princeton, 1956), p. 26.

2. Friedrich Engels, *The Peasant War in Germany,* p. 33.

mass of maneuver of either the bourgeoisie or the proletariat.[3]

As a sociology of rural politics, *The Eighteenth Brumaire* is unmatched. For example, Marx's metaphor that the "great mass of the French nation is formed by the simple addition of homologous magnitudes, much as potatoes in a sack form a sack of potatoes" suggests the essential *difficulty* in organizing the peasants.[4] But the real value of the book is that Marx points out the *importance* of organizing the peasants as a motor force of the revolution. The treatment is dialectical; the small-holding peasantry is a Napoleonic class in its youth, but an anti-Napoleonic class when the small holding has been outdated. "Hence the peasants find their natural ally and leader in the urban proletariat, whose task is the overthrow of the bourgeois order." [5]

It remained for Lenin to systematize the relationship between peasants and urban proletariat. After studying rural classes in Russia in 1905, he concluded that "the goal of a proletarian revolution, *via* capitalist industrialization, might recede into the dimness of time unless an alliance could be contrived between proletariat and peasantry to speed the revolution forward to a socialist victory." [6] What was most interesting about Lenin's treatment of the peasantry in 1917 was his willingness to leapfrog over "capitalist industrialization" and recruit the peasantry as the insurrectionary army in a socialist revolution.

Lenin divided the peasantry into three groups: rich peasants, agricultural proletarians, and a middle group that was gradually falling into the proletariat. The rich peasants were reactionary enemies, but the growing poor peasantry, oppressed in Eastern Europe by a feudal system, was a natural ally of the working class, and the faltering middle group could be easily neutralized. The idea was to encourage class warfare in the countryside. As Lenin wrote, "To encourage small property, speaking generally, is reactionary, because it is directed against large-scale capitalistic economy and neglects the issue of the class struggle. But in this

3. Karl Marx, *The Eighteenth Brumaire of Louis Bonaparte.*
4. Ibid., p. 124.
5. Ibid., p. 128.
6. V. I. Lenin, "The Agrarian Question in Russia," *Selected Works, 1* (New York, 1951); the quotation is from David Mitrany, *Marx Against the Peasant* (Chapel Hill, 1958), p. 44.

instance we want to support small property not against capitalism but against feudalism." [7] The alliance was posed as a tactical one by a hegemonic working class party and a disorganized and malleable peasantry. Its object was the revolutionary aim of "giving a tremendous spurt to the class struggle." [8]

This is the lesson of Marx's "sack of potatoes" theory. Either the peasant is revolutionized or he remains very conservative; there is no middle ground on which he advances slowly toward socialism. If the lesson was obvious to Lenin, it was dominant for Gramsci, for whom the problem of the peasantry took on special importance because of the peasants' predominance in southern Italy. So negligible was an industrial working class in the South that Gramsci had either to recruit the southern Italian peasantry to the banner of the revolution, or leave the South entirely in the clutches of the bourgeoisie.

But like Lenin, Gramsci had no faith in the loyalty of the peasants in a socialist revolution. In fact, he was as much of a Turinese chauvinist as the bourgeois northern writers of his day. His "city of man" was an Italy that looked like highly industrialized Turin from the Alps to Sicily. But he recognized the essential weakness of the urban proletariat when confronted by the armed force of a threatened bourgeois society. He therefore urged the mobilization of the peasantry as an insurrectionary force which could occupy the army in the countryside while the real revolution took place in the factory. For Gramsci, the southern peasantry was the major guerrilla force in the "war of movement" in the underdeveloped area of the South.

The relations between workers and peasants, North and South, in Gramsci's thought raises the important problem of the nature of Marxist ideology in underdeveloped, agricultural societies. Lenin *and* Gramsci were proponents of a "hard" strategy which expropriated the peasants from their bourgeois masters and set them to work as a precapitalist catalyst for postcapitalist revolution. But the disorganized and spontaneous character of the peasantry made it especially important for both theorists to dis-

7. V. I. Lenin, "The Worker's Party and the Peasantry," *Selected Works, 1,* 312.
8. Ibid., pp. 317–18.

tinguish between the tasks of the peasant and those of the worker in the revolution: made it important, in other words, to super-impose the Marxist consciousness of the party heavily upon the spontaneity of the peasant.

Yet when we turn to Marxist movements in underdeveloped areas today we find a very different situation. In many such movements, the theme of independence has upstaged the theme of revolution, and class dialectics have been obscured by an emphasis on solidarity and nationalism.[9] Parochial loyalties are combatted in the name of national unity, but doctrinal adaptations to tribalism and traditionalism are often justified by the need to appeal to groups that possess these values.[10] Marxism is adapted to these backward societies by the compromise of its postcapitalist ideology with the precapitalist nature of the peasantry.

The distinction is important. Where the vast mass of the population is agricultural, as is true in underdeveloped countries, a Marxist ideology that settles for the bourgeois-democratic revolution has not overcome the "sack of potatoes theory" and has prepared the peasantry only for conservatism. It is problematical, in fact, whether such an ideology may be called Marxist at all.

It is at this point that we return to the problem of Communist ideology in southern Italy. If the lesson of Leninism in Western Europe is that the Russian revolutionary pattern is a failure under highly industrialized conditions, what then is its lesson in southern Italy, where industry is embryonic and the peasantry is the predominant class? What an ideal place for Leninism, or, if we may be so bold, Maoism! Clearly, it would have been logical for the pci to develop an entirely different ideology in northern and southern Italy.

But can political dualism beget ideological dualism within the same Marxist party? We have seen that, in its electoral structure, its membership, organization, and leadership, the pci does indeed reflect the dualistic nature of southern Italian politics.

9. See David E. Apter, ed., *Ideology and Discontent,* pp. 21–28.

10. See, for example, Leopold Senghor, *On African Socialism* (New York, 1964), especially p. 49.

Ideology, however, is something very different. An ideology is not a simple set of formulas, but a symbolic guide to action in a complex modern political arena. Ideology, in the words of one writer, "links particular actions and mundane practices with a wider set of meanings and, by doing so, lends a more honorable and dignified complexion to social conduct." [11] A conscious ideological cleavage between its northern and southern wings would deprive the PCI of precisely the unity it needs to come to power and would pave the way for factional behavior.

Therefore, there is a strategic objection to be made to the otherwise logical adaptation of Communist ideology to its diverse political settings in northern and southern Italy. This is the major strategic problem of Italian Communism: adapting the Via Italiana al Socialismo to two entirely different political settings. How has the party attacked this dilemma? In many ways, it has not been attacked at all, and in others, as I shall try to show, a Marxist ideology *in* a backward area has become an ideology *of* backwardness.

THE CONTENT OF THE IDEOLOGY

The first interesting point about PCI ideology in southern Italy is that the party has tried hard to utilize Gramsci's work as its theoretical basis despite its basic incompatibility with the Via Italiana. In order to understand the evolution of the theory in Togliatti's hands, we should first examine it in detail.

Gramsci's premise was one by now familiar in the ideologies of anticolonial groups in the developing nations: the theme of rape. He viewed the South as the special victim of Italy's conservative pattern of national unification, the Risorgimento. "The bourgeoisie of the North," he wrote, "has subjected the South of Italy and the Islands to the status of colonies for exploitation." [12] The South was controlled through an intricate system of parliamentary transformism and a network of commercial ties. Northern bourgeois groups had as their colonial administrators the reactionary southern landholders and the "liberal" intellectuals,

11. Apter, p. 16.
12. Antonio Gramsci, *Antologia degli Scritti*, 2, 50.

both of whose services were bought through tariff concessions, patronage, and graft.

The southern peasant was trapped. He was "tied to the large landed proprietor through the offices of the intellectuals," who were traditional liberal intellectuals divorced from the productive process. As a result, peasant movements always ended up by being "integrated in the day-to-day functions of the state apparatus . . . through the formation and reformation of parties whose leaders are intellectuals controlled by the great landed proprietors and their henchmen." [13] This agrarian bloc had as "its sole purpose the attempt to conserve the status quo." [14] Feudal contractual relations continued to dominate economic life under the aegis of capitalism, destroying social organization and making of the South a "great social disaggregation" (or a sack of potatoes).[15]

The peasants, the great mass of the population, remained, for Gramsci, bereft of class cohesion. The peasant's mentality was that of the serf, "who reacts violently against the *signori* on particular occasions, but is incapable of thinking of himself as the member of a collectivity." "His psychology is reduced to an infinitesimal sum of primordial sentiments dependent upon the social conditions created by the national state." The class struggle is expressed as brigandage, arson, assault, or other forms of elementary terrorism, without concrete political consequences.[16]

Left to themselves, the massive energies of the peasants of the South would dissolve into a "disorganized mass, a chaotic disorder of exasperated passions." Organized, they could be an element of order and progress.[17] Organized by the industrial proletariat of the North, they became the motor force of the revolution. "The proletariat," Gramsci writes, "will destroy the southern agrarian bloc in the degree that it succeeds, through its party, in organizing ever-larger masses of poor peasants in autonomous and independent organizations." [18]

13. Ibid., p. 70.
14. Ibid., pp. 71–72.
15. Ibid., p. 67.
16. Ibid., p. 51.
17. Ibid., p. 53.
18. Ibid., p. 79.

At this stage, several points become clear about Gramsci's analysis. First, he is not merely taking over Lenin's theory of the worker-peasant alliance en masse; he adds a geographic division to Lenin's distinction between the forces of worker and peasant, and he sees the peasants as a motor force of revolution, rather than as a tactical ally. He writes, "The workers of the factory and the poor peasants are the *two energies* of the proletarian revolution. For them, especially, Communism represents an existential necessity." [19]

Second, Gramsci's worker-peasant alliance, like Lenin's, is essentially revolutionary. "With only the forces of the factory workers, the revolution will not be able to be affirmed widely and stably; it is necessary to solder the city to the countryside." [20] Rather than what he calls the "magical formula" of the division of the latifundia, Gramsci's proposal is for "political alliance between workers of the North and peasants of the South to overthrow the bourgeoisie from the power of the state." [21]

Third, the alliance between workers and peasants appears essentially as a *bilateral* relationship with a special role in Italian conditions. Although Gramsci was also interested in enlisting elements of the middle classes in the revolution, in the Italian setting he saw the policy of alliances in terms of the peasants only.

> The proletariat can become a dominant and ruling class in the measure to which it succeeds in creating a system of class alliances that permit it to mobilize the majority of the working population against capitalism and the bourgeois state. This means, in Italy . . . to the degree it succeeds in obtaining the consent of the broad peasant masses.[22]

He also distinguishes between poor and rich peasants, hoping to stimulate insurrection in the countryside by driving a wedge between them.

To summarize, Gramsci's ideology of alliance between northern industrial workers and southern peasants is an ideology of

19. Ibid., *1*, 52.
20. Ibid., p. 54.
21. Ibid., 2, 51.
22. Ibid., p. 53.

class between two revolutionary partners. Although its language and metaphor are original, it is recognizable as a variant of the revolutionary class ideology successfully employed in Russia by Lenin and the Bolsheviks.

This is no longer true. In their elaboration of an ideology for the South of Italy, Italian Communist leaders have overhauled the Leninist-Gramscian theory, making it akin to socialist ideologies in developing societies, and de-emphasizing the elements of class and revolution which are native to European Marxism. They have emphasized the peculiar structural features of southern Italian society and transformed Marxism's revolutionary message into a paean for social integration and economic development.

First, like Gramsci, the post-World War II leaders of the PCI posed the *Questione Meridionale*—the Problem of the South— as a special question in party ideology, and added a geographic dimension to the Leninist concept of a worker-peasant alliance. "The protagonist of the problem of the South becomes the revolutionary worker of Turin and Milan, who incorporates it with the question of the Italian revolution." [23] But already there are two problems. The particular structural fragmentation of southern Italian society is recognized as the historic barrier to effective peasant organization, and the northern worker is seen as the agent who will overcome it. "The working class," Giorgio Amendola writes, "must join the laboring masses of the South . . . to help them organize and overcome their traditional fragmentation and dispersal of interests." [24]

But, Gramsci's idea of a *revolutionary* alliance of northern workers and southern peasants was radically revised. We learn retrospectively that "Gramsci reaffirmed the real unity between workers and peasants in the common battle for the *structural renewal* of the Italian state." [25] Slogans of insurrection and revolt were replaced by phrases such as "progress and civilization," and

23. Franco Ferri, "Questione Meridionale e Unità Nazionale," in *Rinascita, 9,* No. 1 (1952), p. 9.

24. Giorgio Amendola, "I Partiti e il Mezzogiorno," *Rinascita, 5,* No. 2 (1948), p. 47.

25. Ferri, p. 10. Emphasis added.

"economic, social and cultural renewal." [26] In other words, the PCI grafted Togliatti's formula for a Via Italiana al Socialismo to the revolutionary concept of a worker-peasant alliance.

Third, the alliance between workers and peasants lost its dramatic bilateral character and included wider and wider social groupings. Gramsci had concentrated upon the land-hungry semi-proletariat of the countryside. These groups remain, but others are added to the formula. Whereas Lenin had reasoned that the middle group of peasants should be neutralized by a cautious political and economic program, in Italy, the PCI leaders reasoned, "we do not find ourselves before the task of a socialist revolution, but rather the conquest of a popular, advanced democracy." Therefore, "the middle group of peasants can be attracted into the orbit of policies in defense of their interests." The rich peasants, branded by Lenin as enemies, were entirely admissible to the party, for "sometimes occasional alliances are necessary." [27]

Not only all groups of peasants, but petit bourgeois landholders were fitted into the already crowded Gramscian framework. "The small and medium nonworking proprietors living in the cities do not represent a productive force, but it would be an error to consider them in bloc as an enemy." [28] And, finally, the partnership-turned-coalition was expanded into "a system with the working class at its head . . . and an alliance with the southern peasants, first, with the petit bourgeoisie, the intellectuals and the progressive medium bourgeoisie, isolating the conservative and the upper bourgeoisie." [29]

The expansion of the Gramscian alliance to include large numbers of nonproletarian groups, and its transformation from an ideology of revolution into an ideology of structural reform, required some justification in Leninist terms. This was found in the concept of the two-stage revolution and in the goal of the

26. Giorgio Amendola, "Come si Pone la Questione Meridionale dopo il Voto di 7 Giugno," *Rinascita, 10,* No. 7 (1953), 402.

27. Ruggiero Grieco, *I Comunisti e la Lotta per la Riforma Agraria,* pp. 16–17.

28. Ibid., p. 17.

29. Mauro Scoccimarro, "Dottrina Marxista e Politica Comunista," *Rinascita, 2,* Nos. 5–6 (1945), 138.

destruction of feudal residues. Lenin's analytical distinction between the bourgeois democratic revolution and the socialist revolution was adopted. "The essential part of the resolution of the
problem of the Mezzogiorno is to carry out a bourgeois democratic revolution in the countryside." [30] A metaphorical dialectic
was established between the future achievement of a socialist
revolution and the overdue achievement of a bourgeois democratic revolution in the South. In Togliatti's words, "The struggle
to solve the problem of the South [the democratic revolution]
makes progress for the battle for socialism. The battle for socialism, in turn, carries the problem of the South to a solution." [31]
Thus, a broad range of initiatives that have nothing to do with
the achievement of socialism, *either through revolution or other
means,* are justified as combatting the residues of feudalism.
What Togliatti ignores, however, is that the Russian Revolution
of 1917 represents Lenin's contradiction in action of his distinction in theory between the bourgeois and the socialist revolution.

What is the nature of the initiatives the party has sought in
the South as part of the bourgeois democratic revolution? It began in 1944 with the redistribution of uncultivated land and the
reform of agricultural contracts, seeking the destruction of the
semifeudal latifundia and the establishment of a class of stable,
modern peasant proprietors on the land. Increasingly, from 1944
to 1950, proposals for change were characterized as necessary for
the *rinascita* of the South—its rebirth. The theme of rinascita
began with the idea of destroying feudal residues, but its keynote
became "seeking a policy of public investment capable of breaking down the present imbalance between North and South by a
new popular direction with a spirit of national solidarity." [32] In
other words, rinascita meant economic modernization.

The theme of rebirth of southern Italy found its vehicle in
1948 with the creation of the Movimento per la Rinascita. It

30. Ruggiero Grieco, "Nuove Tappe della Lotta per la Riforma Agraria,"
Rinascita, 7, No. 1 (1950), 12.

31. Palmiro Togliatti, "L'Azione Democratica e Socialista nel Mezzogiorno,"
Cronache Meridionali, 1, No. 6 (1954), 412.

32. Assemblea del Comitato Nazionale per la Rinascita del Mezzogiorno e delle
Isole, "Resoconto dei Lavori," *Cronache Meridionali, 1,* No. 5 (1954), 388.

combined the theme of modernization with the idea of an extended alliance of various social groupings. These two themes were posed dramatically at its first conference.

> The Movement for the Rebirth of Southern Italy calls together all honest and democratic citizens and poses no exclusiveness. There is a place for everyone. Let all actions be turned, all struggles be conducted and all forces be mobilized toward the rebirth of the Mezzogiorno and the progress and civilization of her people.

The keynote of the rinascita theme is the agrarian reform. Its importance is that it lies at the fulcrum of the stratification system embodying all the residues of feudalism that impede the modernization of the South. So attractive has this theme proven that it has been retained long after its economic utility has been shown to be obsolete. The Communist Party still seeks a general agrarian reform at a time when small family farms are no longer economical and large numbers of peasants are emigrating from the land. Similarly, the PCI ignored industrialization as a central theme long after it had become the only possible answer to the South's poverty.

These positions were illustrated by the PCI's reaction to the government's land reform program in the 1950s and its establishment of the Cassa per il Mezzogiorno—an "extraordinary" development agency. The Agrarian Reform was opposed for its failure to divide the large efficient commercial farms, as well as the latifundia. The Cassa was opposed for its embodiment of a "depressed areas" philosophy in a society that needed the destruction of feudal, as well as monopolistic, ties.[33]

During the 1950s, the agrarian reform theme and the idea of destroying feudal residues proved less and less attractive. The party was placed in the embarrassing position of having chosen issues for a popular appeal that were now irrelevant or even conservative. For the peasants were leaving the land for the cities, and government-fostered industrialization had begun to change the complexion of the society. A bourgeois revolution was in fact

---

33. Giorgio Amendola, *La Democrazia nel Mezzogiorno* (Roma, 1957), pp. 265–95.

coming about, but in a pattern of economic development that the PCI was at pains to combat.

In an effort to modernize its appeal, the Communist Party returned again to the theme of colonial exploitation, but this time with a different focus: the monopolies. Where formerly the Mezzogiorno had been portrayed as subject to the exploitation of northern industry through the offices of southern landholders and intellectuals, now the evil was seen as more direct penetration. A recent party document states that "monopolistic expansion has provoked and provokes an anarchic and rapid process of transformation." [34] The party does not reject industrialization in opposing this expansion, but opposes what it sees as a conspiracy by the government to direct popular and peasant pressure toward industry, thereby muting the desire of these masses for a general agrarian reform.[35]

The rinascita idea is muted, but to combat what it sees as a new rape of the South, the PCI returns to programs with a familiar ring: an agrarian reform and a policy of alliances. "To have among its principal goals the solution of the problem of the South, antimonopolistic democratic planning must be based upon structural reforms and, in the first place, upon a general agrarian reform." [36] As a result of the changes afoot in southern Italian society, PCI theoreticians conclude that

> today it is possible to construct a new system of . . . alliances which has at its head the working class of new and old industrial groups, is based upon the peasants and the urban middle class, and finds in the Italian working class and its policies the direction and the fundamental reference point in the battle against the monopolies, for democracy and for socialism.[37]

What explains the PCI's continued adherence to an agrarian reform as a panacea for development and its insistence upon a broad policy of alliances? To some extent, the agrarian reform

34. PCI, *Il PCI e la Battaglia Meridionalistica* (1963), p. 4.
35. Ibid., p. 6.
36. Ibid., p. 15.
37. Ibid., p. 13.

idea must be seen as the attempt to win the votes of the landless peasants. But the policy of alliances is largely the application of the Via Italiana to Socialism in the southern Italian setting.

IDEOLOGY AND SOUTHERN ITALIAN SOCIETY

One function of ideology for a political group is to make a society understandable enough so that coherent, effective action can be taken. Hence it abstracts certain critical elements in the society, enlarges their importance, and suppresses others which may be politically less useful. This is especially important in a party of social change, for party workers must have a model of what is to be transformed. The way that a party's ideology molds its environment intellectually is an index of the adaptations it has made and the limitations placed upon the party by its environment.

The fashioning of an ideological tool in southern Italy began for the Italian Communist Party with Lenin's analysis of the agrarian question and Gramsci's analysis of the society. However, as the basis of the PCI's appeal in the South, it was adapted still further in response to the objective conditions of the milieu.

The social composition of the South is the first important factor influencing the evolution of PCI ideology. As I have shown in Chapter 2, a true industrial working class exists in the South only in isolated enclaves around the coastal areas. Hence, in constructing an ideology, Communist leaders were dealing with a society composed mainly of peasants, agricultural day workers, numerous and ill-defined marginal groups, and a backward middle class. The working class, the protagonist of the Gramscian alliance, is foreign; it is in the North. Its representatives in the South are not workers at all, but peasants and intellectuals. Hence the distortion of the Gramscian theorem to include numerous social groups outside the working class and the poor peasantry has a concrete basis.

A second important influence on Communist ideology in the South is social stratification. As I have shown in Chapter 3, ownership of the land remains a primary sign of social status in the Mezzogiorno. This is true not only among the peasantry and the rural proletariat, but among middle class city dwellers as well. In some regions of the South, every shopkeeper and clerk owns a small piece of land which he either farms himself or rents out to a peasant sharecropper or renter. So important is owner-ship of the land as an index of social evaluation in the South that the PCI quickly made it the center of its program under the general rubric of the "bourgeois democratic revolution." Rather than concentrate upon one rural group to the exclusion of all others, the PCI has sought to generalize support for its programs among many groups with interest in the land.

For example, in its campaign for an agrarian reform, the PCI attempted to support the claims of small family farmers as well as the landless agricultural proletariat or semiproletariat. Its motto became "the land to whoever works it," rather than com-plete expropriation of the land or the establishment of coopera-tives of production. The party, while it had formed cooperatives for the assignment of uncultivated land under a law of 1946 and now organizes cooperatives of distribution, has never supported cooperatives of production in the South because of its conviction that the peasants seek individual ownership. The PCI aims at the diffusion of the small family-sized property and the preservation of the small and medium-sized property. This contrasts markedly with Lenin's program for merely neutralizing the medium-sized peasants and Gramsci's warning against the "magic formula" of division of the latifundia. The PCI seeks the *creation* of a large group of family-sized farms owned by small proprietors.

Perhaps more surprising was the party's attempt to gain a foot-hold among noncultivating urban middle class groups.

> We must protect the rights of the noncultivating landowner, the professional or artisan, the employee who owns a modest plot of land. This group of small and medium-sized bourgeois landowners, who are so much a part of Italian life especially in the Mezzogiorno . . . cannot be confused with the class of the large proprietors, merely because they own a piece of land.[38]

38. Fausto Gullo, "Suggerimenti per una Riforma Agraria," *Rinascita*, 2, No. 12 (1945), 282.

In other words, in its attempt to gain support among land-hungry, land-interested, and landowning groups in the South, the PCI was brought around to a position of supporting some of the most marginal and unprogressive groups in Italian society, many of whom now vote predominantly for the far right!

A third and related area in which southern Italian society has had a dramatic impact on the ideology of the Communist Party regards the social disorganization of the region. In a society characterized by great fragmentation of occupational roles, social groups remain chaotic, and political organization normally resides latently in the clientele ties between landholder and agricultural worker, lawyer and client, and bureaucrat and favor seeker. Local and parochial loyalties suffuse politics. Politics has very little ideological content, and popular imagery recognizes only two basic social groups: peasants and nonpeasants. Yet within each broad grouping there are numerous unstable divisions depending upon ownership or nonownership of the land, personal ties with large landowners, contractual relations, and stability of tenure.

The PCI is hard pressed to put into operation a class politics in such a social milieu. It turns instead, like many ideological movements in developing societies, to a politics of solidarity, distorting the Gramscian theme of a worker-peasant alliance into a frontist theme and suppressing its classist elements in favor of themes that emphasize the need for social "unity" in the face of northern colonialism. A sensitive Italian critic writes,

> Because of the difficulties of revolutionary penetration in a peasant world like the Mezzogiorno, . . . the old scheme of the alliance between the workers of the North and the peasants of the South is no longer enough. We therefore see the transformation of the original class postulate of Gramsci into the frontist formula which today inspires Communist Party action in the South.[39]

The whole concept of the party has changed from the creative socializing agent Gramsci envisioned into an amorphous populist

39. Giuseppe Galasso, "Il Meridionalismo di Complemento," *Nord e Sud, 1*, No. 6 (1954), p. 412.

movement which casts its net through diverse strata of a fragmented society and seeks issues that can unite disparate groups. As Togliatti wrote in a key theoretical article, "Because of the social disorganization of the South, we need an organization of a conspicuously broad, popular nature, more than is necessary in the large industrial centers. The need to work for the construction of alliances is more important there than in the rest of the country." [40]

The whole importance of the agrarian reform in Communist thinking and the determination with which it is still proposed relates to the structural problems of southern Italian society, and the difficulty the party has had in finding stable class support. The agrarian reform has been given such priority, not merely because the South is agricultural, but because it is the single issue that can unite the amorphous peasant masses.

The crystallization of many of these factors is evident, first, in the use of the concept of the bourgeois democratic revolution, second, in the campaign to rid the South of "feudal residues" and, third, in the development of the movement for the rinascita of the South. Whereas in Lenin's thought the bourgeois democratic revolution had a precise set of meanings relating to the achievement of a capitalist economic system in which the workers are ready for revolution, in Italy this meaning breaks down. To southern Italian Communists, the bourgeois democratic revolution comes to mean stripping away all those "feudal residues" that inhibit the formation of broad, stable social classes susceptible of mass organization. Often these "residues" are genuine survivals of feudalism, as are the agrarian contracts common in the South, but often they are not feudal at all, but merely the focuses of parochial loyalties which divide the southern population. For example, articles in the party press criticized Sicilian and Sardinian *banditismo* not merely as morally or socially evil, but as deterrents to political organization and political activity. "Feudal residues" in southern Italian Communist ideology play much the same role as tribalism in new African states: they are evil because they inhibit solidarity.

40. Palmiro Togliatti, "L'Azione Democratica e Socialista nel Mezzogiorno," p. 412.

The theme of rinascita is an attempt to combine the party's dual goals in the South: solidarity and modernization. In analyzing the theme, the first image that arises is the romantic one of a tormented and backward society arising from its toils and flinging off the colonial yoke of the North. However, in analyzing its concrete manifestations, we see that it is far more rhetorical than substantive. Anything that would tend to the destruction of feudal residues and the construction of a broad base of solidarity came to be considered by the PCI as a contribution to the "rebirth" of the South. The Communist Party found itself supporting measures that would establish capitalism in the countryside, and that often broke down into demands for large-scale patronage or interest-group issues of purely local and provincial importance. For example,

> "The party fights to end unemployment and illiteracy . . . to defend southern industry, to aid the struggle of the peasants for a just agrarian reform, to lower the costs of public service and to gain new housing. . . . In a word, to establish working centers for a vast and pluralistic action for the rinascita of the Mezzogiorno." [41]

Sometimes, virtually reactionary positions have resulted. For example, on one occasion Togliatti defended the idea of a general agrarian reform on the basis of its appeal to the bourgeoisie of the South. He said to the bourgeoisie, "When the land . . . is no longer a sterile latifundia . . . then your commerce can flower and even the intellectuals of your cities will have greater possibilities of civility and all of you will have a more progressive role to play in public life." [42]

THE FUNCTIONS OF THE IDEOLOGY

Ideology functions in a political party in three important ways. First, it is a symbolic guide to action; second, it is a source of

41. Giorgio Amendola, "Comuni e Provincia nella Lotta per la Rinascita del Mezzogiorno," *Rinascita, 9,* No. 2 (1952), 69.

42. Palmiro Togliatti, "Discorso su Giolitti," *La Voce del Mezzogiorno, 6,* No. 6 (1953), 14.

solidarity and communication; and, third, it is a means of role definition for party cadres and for the party itself.

As a symbolic guide to action, the ideology of Communism in the South of Italy is dispersive and confused. The party has adumbrated the dramatic Gramscian image of a creative working class impelling a peasant motor force to action. The rinascita theme is an organic, romantic image lacking the fine mechanical metaphors of classical Marxism which depict solid social classes poised against one another in bold relief. In aiming at a disorganized peasant society, the Communist Party has created an ideology that is so permissive it is almost an anti-ideology. Precisely in the backward South, where spontaneity is rampant both among peasants and intellectuals, logic might have indicated an ideology that imposed "consciousness" much more forcefully upon both major groups.

Two specific internal contradictions in the ideology damage its functioning as an effective symbolic guide to action. First, it contains an inherent contradiction between the Gramscian worker-peasant alliance and the theme of rinascita. Gramsci's point was this: so disorganized are the southern peasants that the only way to mobilize them is to convulse the social structure into a revolutionary situation. The rinascita theme and the conversion of the Gramscian partnership into a coalition mean organization on a workmanlike basis. The party has mingled the rhetoric of revolution and the problematics of reform, mottling Gramsci's revolutionary message. This tension is conveyed in the confusion of intraparty dialectics. For example,

> Our line of struggle for structural reform and for a new direction in national politics is nothing more than the translation into timely political terms of the great perspective, delineated by Gramsci, of a revolutionary transformation of Italian society in a democratic and socialist sense, under the direction of the working class and on the basis of the alliance of the workers of the North and the peasants of the South.[43]

43. Giorgio Napoletano, "Continuità e Prospettive della nostra Azione Meridionale," *Rinascita, 14,* No. 4 (1957), 162.

Second, the ideology often breaks down into a proliferation of initiatives among diverse social groups and lends support to a congeries of often unrelated issues. In Amendola's words,

> We must stress the need to be present wherever problems that interest the life of our cities and our regions are debated, and participate in every partial initiative on particular problems, keeping in mind always that the *Movimento per la Rinascita* struggles and gathers all the forces willing to struggle for the democratic, political, economic and social renewal of our regions.[44]

As a result, party policies often are attempts to "resolve some particular problem of the backwardness of the South—as the lack of houses, hospitals or schools—without attacking the primary causes of the backwardness." Tendencies develop to "interpret the idea of the unity of the South as equivocal unanimity, without openly combatting the enemies of the rinascita of the South." [45] Southern party groups often adopt platforms so sweeping that they expropriate the programs of labor and peasant groups, thereby destroying the critical Leninist distinction between the program of the party and that of its mass organizations.[46] At times, the adoption of the concepts and slogans of rinascita have led to actions that are actually reactionary. Such an activity was the short-lived "Milazzo experiment," an attempt of the party to ally with some of the most retrograde elements of the Sicilian Catholic bourgeoisie to form a regional government.

Solidarity is another important function of ideology, and the ideology of Communism in the South of Italy presents serious failures here as well. This may appear paradoxical, since the *content* of the ideology is occupied with the unity and solidarity of a fragmented population. But in the attempt to crowd essentially hostile groups within the framework of the ideology of

44. Assemblea del Comitato Nazionale per la Rinascita del Mezzogiorno e delle Isole, "Resoconto," p. 388.

45. Giorgio Amendola, "Intervento," PCI, VII° Congresso Nazionale, *Resoconto* (Roma, 1951), pp. 66–67.

46. Pietro Secchia, "Intervento," ibid., p. 146.

rinascita, the PCI creates hostilities within the structure of the party.

The most notable internal contradiction is expressed in the conflict between labor leaders and party proponents of the rinascita theme. The latter have wished to organize agricultural proletarians with peasant proprietors and sharecroppers, and the former contend that this attempt to form a coalition damages any meaningful progress toward the agrarian reform.[47] Labor leaders are often accused of "sectarianism and incomprehension" by southern party leaders, but more subtle criticism is reserved for leaders of the party in the North. Virtually every national party congress brings forth complaints from southern party leaders that northern comrades have lost interest in the problem of the Mezzogiorno as an integral part of the problem of the Italian road to socialism. And, simultaneously, there has been a powerful movement of resentment in the North among militant cadres regarding the "petit bourgeois character" of party ideology in the South.

Related to the solidarity function is the problem of communication. Ideology is a symbolic vocabulary which allows members of the same political group to frame specific issues in terms of broader meanings. It has the advantage, first, of a kind of shorthand which allows individuals of even modest intellectual capabilities to talk, think, and act in terms of the movement. Second, the communication function disguises the concrete content of party discourse from the uninitiated.

The Communist Party's ideology in the South of Italy performs the communication function quite poorly. Since rinascita can include virtually any initiative that will battle "feudal residues," encourage solidarity, or contribute to the modernization of the country's economic and social structure, it can mean whatever party leaders mean at a given moment. Like many other facets of Italian Communism, the ideology in the South deceives enemies brilliantly, but fails to enlighten friends. Party congresses and journal articles are full of reports that cadres in particular areas "do not understand the real meaning of the struggle for the rebirth of the South."

47. Interview, April 15, 1964.

Classical Communism is generally considered as a powerful force in organizing the entire psychological life of the militant. This function, which I call role definition, is not salient in the ideology of southern Italian Communism. Because of the ideology's dispersion and internal contradictions, its effect upon personality is likely to be schizophrenic rather than integrating. The anecdote is famous in Italy of the Communist leader who characterized the Sicilian regional committee as "six characters in search of an author."

Italian Communist ideology has responded to southern Italian society in several ways. It has followed Gramsci's example of isolating the Mezzogiorno ideologically from the rest of the country by developing the theme of northern exploitation and by pressing for a program for the economic "rebirth" of the region. It has singled out critical elements of southern Italian social life for special treatment. Particularly important in this regard is the value placed upon landownership by wide strata of the population and the fragmentation of social roles and loyalties. In response to these factors, the PCI has developed an ideology that seeks the solidarity of many groups of the population, rather than a class appeal of great intensity. This pattern has perhaps "overresponded" to the milieu, for it presses an agrarian reform of doubtful utility while its wide-ranging alliance theme has mitigated the force and coherence of the appeal. Paradoxically, an ideology that begins by seeking the creation of new social groups finishes by supporting many parochial interests and issues that appropriate the label of "rebirth."

Gramsci envisioned the Communist Party as a creative integrative and socializing agent which releases the potential energies of the society through the catalyst of its basic elements and the creation of a new class of intellectuals. This characteristic does not emerge in the Communist Party's ideology in the South of Italy. Rather than the "New Prince" Gramsci envisioned, the party at its best is a fine and subtle set of ties among diverse and ill-defined social groups, working in various ways to promote unity and modernization. At its worst, when unity appears in the shape of alliances with backward groups and modernization takes the form of appeals for mass patronage, the Communist Party in the South of Italy appears as a system of well-rationalized in-strumentalism. In other words, the ideology of Communism in the South of Italy does not provide its members with an effective symbolic guide or action, a sensitive basis for communication and solidarity, or a compelling image of what it means to be a member of the Communist Party.

It is interesting that, beginning with the same "objective conditions," Gramsci arrived at an essentially Leninist strategy for the South. The PCI today, in contrast, combines these objective conditions with goals designed for an entirely different setting. As a result, it finishes with an ideology that compromises with the objective conditions rather than utilizing them. In other words, what begins as an ideology of backwardness becomes a backward ideology.

Toward an Interpretation

With imagination and fortitude, the leaders of Italian Communism created a new political edifice in southern Italy. That their creation had a massive impact was demonstrated by the doubling of its vote between 1946 and 1958. That it threatened traditional political forces was proven by the depth of the opposition it evoked. But its character was disturbingly different than had been planned, and it is by no means clear that it constituted the "party of a new type" in southern Italy that Togliatti had envisioned in 1944.

But is there a single pattern discernible in the structure, the leadership, the ideology, and the electorate of the PCI in southern Italy that will allow us to say concretely not only that it differs from other Marxist parties but *how* it differs?

In each aspect discussed in the preceding chapters, common characteristics emerge. In its electoral structure, the PCI in the Mezzogiorno has failed to find solid support either among the new working class of the large industrial centers or the middle class of the provincial cities. As we have seen, its major electoral support comes from small and medium-sized cities of 20,000 to 100,000 population (the peasant dormitories and the mixed urban-rural conglomerations in Puglia and Sicily). In the small towns, where the landowner and the village priest still hold sway, the PCI has had little impact in breaking down traditional electoral preferences.

The most striking characteristic of the Southern Italian Communist vote, however, is that it *reflects*, rather than deflects, the traditional voting behavior of southern Italian voters. Southerners appear to vote for personalities, not for parties, and we have seen the PCI in the South receiving an extraordinary number of votes of individual preference. Southern Italians show strong local allegiances, and we find radical differences in the Communist vote from village to village within homogeneous economic areas. Moreover, the southern voter is capricious, and we find sharp discontinuities in the Communist vote from election to election.

Yet the PCI controls a large and growing portion of the Southern Italian electorate, a factor that seems to compensate for the peculiarities of its voting structure. It has made gains recently among small family farmers, the most stable rural group in the population, and it seems to be gaining the allegiance of at least part of the new industrial labor force. The dilemma is a different one: if the PCI in the Mezzogiorno depends upon the region's unusual political culture, how then does it differ from other political forces? What happens to the appeals of class and ideology in an environment where kinship and personality are dominant?

Classical Marxist parties can offset the compromises necessitated by electoral politics through the discipline of their organization. Indeed, in northern Italy, the PCI's organization provides a solid counterweight to its diffuse electoral appeal. In the South, in contrast, the same formal organization harbors great differences. As we have seen, there are fewer party sections and cells than in the North, and cells in places of employment are virtually nonexistent. The geographic party section is usually the single representative of the PCI in the southern Italian village, and, to all accounts, it functions more as a recreational center than a political action group. The same organizational pattern, seen in North and South, presents a different face in each region, and the southern face has characteristics that resemble the traditional patterns of southern Italian politics.

Similar and more serious problems beset the PCI's mass membership in southern Italy. As we have seen, the proportion of party members to voters is low in the South and high in the North, whereas membership turnover is high in the South and low in the North. Party leaders complain that southern members cluster around dominant personalities and neglect the day-to-day tasks of organization and proselytism. Critics maintain that the evidence points to the PCI's being a typical southern party of clienteles.

The PCI in the Mezzogiorno reflects the culture of its region in its social composition, too. In both North and South, membership rests upon the largest social groups—urban workers in the North and poor peasants in the South. Yet the nature of these categories benefits the party in the North and damages it in the South. The industrial worker has a class conscience, a ready-made organization in the factory, and daily contact with his fellows. The poor peasants of the South, on the other hand, are fragmented by a host of contractual and social differences. Further, their class consciousness is minimal and their participation in party affairs is limited by their dependence upon the changing seasons.

The initial difference in party coherence created by these factors reinforces itself. The North, with a strong tradition of trade union organization, provides the PCI with a base of worker-organizers, whereas the labor movement in the South is of recent origin, a factor that leaves the party the reservoir of the trade unions, rather than vice versa. It follows that the PCI membership group does not provide the party with the cohesive action group typical of successful Marxist parties.

Further, the leadership of the PCI in southern Italy reinforces its dependence upon objective conditions. Although a major factor in the party's success nationally has been the creation of a new group of leaders of lower class origin, in the South, Communist leaders are drawn from the very same social class from which the traditional elite is drawn—the middle class. The party's failure to recruit significant numbers of peasants as leaders is matched by present leaders' diffidence toward the peasants, despite the fact that the PCI claims to represent them. And the chronic organizational difficulties of the party in the South can be linked to its leaders' emphasis on the political aspects of their jobs and their inattention to organizational work, another salient characteristic of southern Italian politicians in general.

Finally, as we have seen, the PCI's ideology in the South underscores these patterns. By segregating the South for separate action and by gearing itself to the region's special problems of backwardness and disorganization, the PCI compromised its ideological position as a revolutionary political force. Its concentration upon the themes of "colonial" exploitation, civil rebirth, and economic development are similar to the ideological appeals of Marxist parties in underdeveloped areas everywhere. But its ideology lacks the coherence, the drama, and the logic to provide an effective communications system and a guide to action for its militants.

It is clear from the evidence presented in the last four chapters that a common theme colors the electoral pattern, the organization, membership, leadership, and ideology of the Communist Party in southern Italy. That theme, simply stated, is dependence upon the objective conditions of its milieu. Leninist doctrine posits that the Marxist party must always adapt to its environment, but only so as to transform that environment in true dialectical fashion. The problem for analysis is the following: is the Communist Party in southern Italy a flourishing version of Marxism in an underdeveloped society, or has the PCI emerged from its dialogue with a backward and disorganized society as a backward and disorganized party? How does the Leninist dialectic operate: to transform the society, the party, or both?

The evidence presented up to now tells only part of the story. How does the PCI's dependence upon the political setting of southern Italy influence its behavior, its programs, and its actions? How does it relate to the government and the governmental parties? And, most important, what has been the long-run impact of Communism upon the southern Italian peasantry and upon the society as a whole?

11. The Mobilization of the Peasants

"There is only one obvious reason for this serious political relapse," said Kautsky in response to a German Socialist agricultural program; "regard for the peasants. We have not yet captured them, but they have already captured us." [1] In the short run, Kautsky had little to fear, for the party soon rejected its moderate peasant program. But over the long run, Kautsky had put his finger on one of the basic theoretical problems in Western Marxism: the problem of the contradiction between advocacy of the peasant cause and socialist revolution.

There has been from the outset a schizoid quality in Marxist thought regarding the peasantry. Marx, who recognized the revolutionary potential of the peasantry, also concluded that the progress of science and capitalism "condemn small-scale peasant farming to gradual extinction, without appeal and without mercy." [2] Engels, who glorified the peasant in his *Peasant Wars in Germany,* proclaimed the peasant's imminent demise in his essay on the agrarian question.[3]

The basis of this dichotomy was, of course, the discrepancy between Marx's economic model and his political methodology. For although Marx saw the peasantry receding before the advance of large-scale industrial production, he also recognized the potential value of a peasant rebellion in a revolution. Yet so basic to Marxism was the economic model that Marx failed to recognize that economic concentration in the countryside might mean something very different from concentration in industry.

This contradiction only became important at the end of the

1. Article in *Die Neue Zeit* (1894), quoted in David Mitrany, *Marx Against the Peasant,* p. 48.
2. Manifesto of the 1869 meeting of the Socialist International; Mitrany, p. 37. See Chap. 10 above, on Marx's analysis of the French peasantry.
3. Friedrich Engels, "La Question Agraire et le Socialisme; Critique du Parti Ouvrier Français," *Le Mouvement Socialiste,* No. 43 (Paris), cited in Mitrany, p. 44.

nineteenth century, when Bernstein collected a great deal of sociological evidence to show, first, that small units of production were not disappearing in either industry or agriculture, and, second, that within agriculture the small peasant property was actually gaining ground.[4] The implications were clear; as long as the peasant and the small producer in industry refused to disappear, the entire Marxian economic equation would fail. It was on the basis of such evidence that Bernstein redefined socialism into a doctrine of social reform through universal suffrage, thereby obfuscating the critical Marxian distinction between the propertyless and the propertied poor.

There was a theoretical problem in Bernstein's analysis. It inferred that the expansion of the small peasant property relegated Marx's thesis of concentration to the ash can. But it assumed, as Marx had done, that concentration in industry and agriculture would follow similar lines, and would be, in both cases, a totally linear process. What Marx and Bernstein both failed to see was that concentration in agriculture might occur *via* the small peasant property. It was entirely consistent with the concentration thesis—and therefore with Marxism—for small farms to increase when they were replacing an older form of semifeudal estate. The small peasant property was in fact simply a stage in the rationalization of enterprise between irrational semifeudal types of tenure and the modern commercial farm. In fact, in much of Europe the growth of small peasant properties did not mean a decrease in the size of the production unit at all, but simply a shift from semifeudal tenancy or rental to small ownership. There was no evidence then (as there is still no evidence now) that the small peasant property would not eventually die out, vindicating Marx and creating a salaried proletariat as the bulk of the rural population.

The distinction is an important one. For if the small peasant property represents only an intermediate stage on the road to concentration, then the tendency to accept it as a finality is a reactionary posture. In other words, by repeating Marx's error of failing to distinguish between industrial concentration and agricultural concentration, the German revisionists made an error

4. Mitrany, p. 38.

Marx would never have made: that of defending the small peasant property against history.

But the revisionists were not the only European Socialists to succumb to this temptation. Orthodox French Marxists like Guesde could declare that "the solution of the social question lies in the partition of the land."[5] The orthodox Marxists dealt with the problem in purely tactical terms, offering the peasant tax relief after telling him he was doomed by the laws of history.[6] It was precisely this tendency that Gramsci criticized in the Italian Socialists, who appealed to the peasantry "with the magic formula of the division of the latifundia" at the same time they accepted the thesis of concentration in its entirety.[7]

The acceptance of the peasant as a full-fledged ally was part of a broader process within European socialism, a process that turned ultimately from the barricades to the ballot boxes. The problem was that while the precapitalist peasant had a spirit of revolt at least equal to that of the industrial worker, the peasant who owned a small commercial farm was simply a conservative. The peasant without land could be organized as a motor force of the revolution, but for what purpose could the small peasant proprietor be organized? He was not a worker but a producer, not a suppliant but a hirer, not a rebel against but a defender of the status quo.

The only way to organize the peasant effectively was in favor of his economic interests. And the instrument created by European socialism to serve these interests was the cooperative.[8] If the peasant was to prosper as well as survive, he needed some way to compete with large commercial firms in an increasingly larger market. He needed help in planting, fertilizing, processing, and distributing his product, and the only organization that could give it to him, short of transforming him into a large commercial farmer, was the cooperative. At the same time, the cooperative might attack the long-term problem of developing a socialist conscience in the petit bourgeois peasant. A distant prospect, to say

5. Ibid., p. 47.
6. Ibid., pp. 40–50.
7. Antonio Gramsci, *Antologia degli Scritti*, 2, 50.
8. Mitrany, pp. 41–44.

the least, but an essential one once the small peasant proprietor had been accepted as an ally of the proletariat.

It is against this historical and theoretical background that we now turn to the Italian Communists' mobilization of the southern peasantry between 1944 and 1952. Had the PCI been a Maoist party in this agricultural, semifeudal society, the story might have ended in a peasant revolution under the leadership of a proletarian party. But the PCI was not such a party. It was inspired by a strategy that had been created for a highly developed industrial society and exported wholesale to the South in 1944. What would happen in southern Italy, given these conditions?

THE POLITICAL SETTING

Nowhere in the Western world has ownership of the land remained in such a confused and embittering tangle of relationships as in the Mezzogiorno. Rural overpopulation, poor soil and resources, and the social value placed upon land ownership by urban and rural groups alike have led to intense pressure on the land. This heritage emerged from the peculiar historical pattern of the formation of social classes and social values in the Mezzogiorno and the circumstances of the society's inclusion in the unified Italian state in 1860. At that time, the greater part of the feudal patrimony of the peasants fell fully legitimized into the hands of the bourgeoisie as the direct result of the reforms of united Italy. In the peasant mind, the identity of interests between the usurping bourgeoisie and the new, liberal state was clearly established and never forgotten.

Simultaneously, the economies of North and South, although at vastly different levels of development, were precipitously merged. Commercialization in the South proceeded rapidly, but industrialization was stillborn. The Mezzogiorno's system of occupational roles remained suspended midway between traditional and modern. Amid a growing population, the aspirations of all social classes were fastened upon the land, and the peasantry remained disorganized.

In terms of the relations between social classes, this process was disastrous. With no outlet in industry or commerce, the southern bourgeoisie fastened its hold upon the land, and the provincial middle class began to gain control of large portions of the latifundia. Every professional and storekeeper held a small piece of land, a factor that was as inimical to agricultural efficiency as it was explosive for class relations. Atomized clientele politics institutionalized these relationships, discouraging the representation of the peasants' interests and the formation of a peasant party.

For the peasants, the memory of bourgeois usurpation and their own political impotence led to a virtual reversal of ideal political roles. The national state, remote and bureaucratic from the first, and identified with the usurpations of the bourgeoisie, was never legitimated. A code of conduct developed which made virtues of those behavior patterns authority condemned and elevated the deviant individual to the status of a hero. The brigand became a Robin Hood, the *Mafioso* a man of honor, *Camorra* an antistate that could advance the aspirations of mobile individuals.

The peasants hungered for the land, embittered by the memory of the bourgeois usurpations but paralyzed by endemic disorganization. The result was periodic insurrection in the countryside. The brigandage of 1861–62, savagely repressed by the Italian army and national guard units of local landowners, was aimed in part at regaining the land lost between 1840 and 1860. The uprisings in Benevento, Foggia, Calabria, and Sicily in the 1870s had a similar aim. The famous *Fasci Siciliani,* at first an urban movement, quickly spread to the countryside and embodied the peasants' hope for the recovery of the lands enclosed in 1861. Peasants returning from the battlefield following World War I reacted to an economic crisis by invading the latifundia, resulting in governmental concessions of over 68,000 acres of uncultivated land.[9]

Between these periodic uprisings a constant stream of oppressed peasants would go to the hills to form bands of brigands. Far from representing mere criminal organizations, these groups were a dramatic expression of the dislocations of the society. They gained the support of the local population and assumed a Robin Hood role with respect to the landowners and the government. Periodi-

9. Alberto Caracciolo, *L'Occupazione delle Terre in Italia* (Roma, n.d.), pp.1–17.

cally, a brigand leader like Fra Diavolo would so capture the imagination of the population that his fame far outstripped that of the more conventional political leaders of the epoch.[10]

For the most part, however, peasant jacqueries and brigandage lacked organization and ideology. The peasants would remain tied to the structure of local clientele politics until a moment of general convulsion of the social structure. Then they would turn on the landowners, burning barns and destroying the tax records of the municipalities. Inhibited from more continual activity by the fragmentation of their social relationships, these peasant agitations took the form of typical peasant anarchism. No political party ever appeared to represent them, since local political formations were clustered around the patronage issues of local clienteles and since the peasants were too socially disorganized to organize themselves.

Beginning in the 1870s, however, a few southern Italian intellectuals, motivated by humanitarian ardor, began to take up the cause of the peasant movement. No greater evidence of the political immaturity of the region can be found than the failure of these groups to understand the message of Marx, or their instant attraction to the teachings of Michael Bakunin. Bakunin, whose stay in Italy followed shortly upon the unification of 1861, found in the Mezzogiorno, "in its disrespect for the law, its fiscal evasions, its rural agitations, its open and militant brigandage, that possibility of dissent and that form of opposition which are natural and native to a prevalently agricultural, backward and culturally impoverished country." [11] Moreover, the southern Italian peasant was an anarchist extraordinary, not only by virtue of his poverty and ignorance, but because of his social instability as well. Bakunin's concept of spontaneous and continual revolution was as appealing in the South of Italy as it was among the anarchic peasant masses of southern Spain.[12]

It was a group of Bakuninists who inspired the uprising of 1877 in Benevento, "proclaiming the revolution and the division of the land, obtaining the support of local village priests, and pro-

10. Eric Hobsbawm, *Social Bandits and Primitive Rebels.*
11. Aldo Romano, *Storia del Movimento Socialista in Italia, 1,* 135.
12. Franz Borkenau, *The Spanish Cockpit* (London, 1937).

voking a rapid and violent insurrection of the peasants." [13] A similar group was later active in the Sicilian *Fasci* movement of the 1890s and in the agitations of 1898 in Puglia, Campania, and Sicily. The first permanent organizations of the peasants, the *società agricole* and the leagues of *braccianti*, were animated by the same spirit of spontaneous uprising. The peasants were united only by hunger for the land, but between agitations their structural fragmentation destroyed whatever organization had been built up in the struggle. The end of the pre-Fascist liberal state saw a peasant movement in the South that was strongly influenced by the ideas of Bakunin, animated by a universal hunger for the land, and characterized by a defiant spirit but a poorly articulated organization.

The twenty-year period of Fascism meant far more to the southern Italian peasantry than Mussolini's banal "Battle of Wheat" and other such programs would suggest. Remittances from Italian immigrants abroad and substantial public investments in reclamation made it possible for many southern peasants to acquire small family farms for the first time. In addition to these factors, the wholesale exodus of large numbers of professionals and petit bourgeois groups from the region to jobs in the Fascist bureaucracy made available a great deal of new land. Some peasants could purchase minor capital goods and educate their children for urban professions, while others fell definitively into the class of hired farm laborers.

When Fascism fell, an enhanced consciousness of the possibilities of landownership characterized the southern peasantry. This difficult period brought about a political crisis greater than any the country had known, with different governments operating in each part of the peninsula. Moreover, the economy was paralyzed, food was scarce, and the immediate need of work was added to the peasants' deep-seated aspirations for the land.

A crude *Pax Americana* was superimposed on the society, abating its turmoil somewhat by the benefits of food allotments and the black market. But as early as 1943, peasant uprisings had begun in Calabria, the heart of the classical Peasant Latifundia. Here, in the notorious Marchesato of Crotone, a few absentee

13. Caracciolo, p. 12.

landowners possessed thousands of acres, much of which was un-cultivated or used as pasture. In 1944, the uncultivated lands of the latifundia were invaded. The peasant leagues which had forcibly occupied the land in 1920–21 were quickly reorganized.[14] The uprising soon spread from Calabria to Lucania, Sicily, and Puglia, differing but little from traditional patterns of peasant uprising.[15]

So sudden was this movement of the southern peasants, and so critical their need of land and work, that the government, under the influence of a Communist Minister of Agriculture, conceded uncultivated land to cooperatives of peasants who were then to divide it among themselves. In effect, the government merely legitimated occupations already made. By the spring of 1945, over 414,000 acres of land had been conceded to the peasants, mostly in the zones of the latifundia in Calabria, Sicily, and Puglia, but with significant acreage in the remainder of the Mezzogiorno.[16] But this temporary measure could not halt for long the growing tide of peasant exasperation.

THE STRUGGLE FOR THE LAND

It was in this setting that the most revolutionary event in post-war Italian history occurred. The struggle for the land from 1949 to 1952 began with many of the classical features of the jacquerie in a backward peasant society. Generations of land hunger and resentment combined with economic and political crisis to catalyze the normally quiescent peasantry to explosive action.

The setting was similar in many essential aspects to other revolutionary agrarian situations in the twentieth century: to China in the 1930s, Andalusia during the Spanish Civil War, and Yugoslavia between 1942 and 1944.[17] In each case, a backward

14. Giuseppe Galasso, "La Riforma Agraria in Sila," p. 9.

15. Emilio Sereni, "La Lotta per la Conquista della Terra nel Mezzogiorno," *Cronache Meridionali, 3* (1956), 15.

16. Fausto Gullo, "Il Latifondo e la Concessione delle Terre Incolte ai Contadini," *Rinascita, 2*, Nos. 7–8 (1945), 175.

17. See, in particular, on China, Mary Wright, "The Chinese Peasant and Com-munism," *Pacific Affairs, 24*, No. 3 (1951), 258–59; on Spain, Edward Malefakis, "Land Tenure, Agrarian Reform and Peasant Revolution in Twentieth Century Spain," unpublished Ph.D. dissertation, Columbia University, 1965; on Yugoslavia, Robert L. Wolff, *The Balkans in Our Time* (Cambridge, 1956).

peasant population overcame its traditional disorganization to support a national revolutionary movement in the name of agrarian reform and national revolution. In each case, traditional disorganization presented no barrier when the land hunger of the peasants could be harnessed to a powerful revolutionary engine.

The outcome of these three revolutionary situations is instructive. In the case of both the Yugoslav and Chinese Communist parties and of the Andalusian Anarchist movement, the number of peasants involved far outweighed the number of workers. In the Spanish case, the almost complete absence of workers led to the dispersion of revolutionary action into inconclusive acts of violence, but in both the Yugoslav and the Chinese revolutions the sheer weight of the peasantry was not an obstacle to revolutionary and military success. The lesson is clear. As Mao said, "the revolution will not fail just because the peasants become more powerful than the workers; it will only fail if the peasants are deprived of the workers' leadership." [18]

When we turn once again to the agrarian ferment in southern Italy, we find the same factors present: an economic and political crisis, a mobilized but backward peasantry, and a national party— the PCI—ready to organize them. Yet in Italy we are dealing with a very different type of Communist party than the Communist parties of China and Yugoslavia. And, if the "struggle for the land" in southern Italy did not develop into a full-scale peasant revolution, the reason does not appear to lie with the peasantry.

To begin with, the patrimony of military organization and nationalist fervor that contributed to the success of both the Yugoslav and the Chinese Communist parties was absent in southern Italy.[19] Although class struggle in northern Italy might grow almost immediately out of the armed Resistance, in the South the Communist Party had to create the conditions for its own success out of native materials.

First, through intellectual missionaries from Naples and the

18. Cited in Stuart R. Schram, ed., *The Political Thought of Mao Tse-Tung* (New York, 1963), p. 189; for a sensitive discussion of Mao's attitude toward the peasantry, see the editor's introduction, pp. 28–42.

19. See the discussion of the role of nationalism in both the Chinese and Yugoslav revolutions in Chalmers A. Johnson, *Peasant Nationalism and Communist Power* (Stanford, 1962).

North, and then through small cadres of local leaders, the PCI began to direct a spontaneous movement already in progress in the countryside. The relationship between party and peasants was almost romantic. The party embodied all those aspirations and resentments regarding the ownership of the land that had characterized the southern peasantry since 1861.

The leadership of the PCI in 1945 had a distinctly libertarian air. Ambitious ex-Fascists and opportunists, seeing the PCI as a party of the provisional government, entered its ranks. Peasants with an anarchist orientation, inactive in politics for twenty years, saw in the party an antistate which might lead to the complete expropriation of the land. Intellectuals and humanitarians, hopeful of a civil renaissance for the entire Mezzogiorno, saw in the PCI the party of national liberation and regeneration.[20] With the arrival of the first official party functionaries in 1946, the party began to lose this heterogeneous character. Opportunists turned to less militant organizations; peasants fell back into the second rank; and the intellectuals emerged at the top.

It is not entirely clear *why* the intellectuals came to direct a home-grown peasant movement, but it is certainly clear *how* it happened: the party sent them from Rome and Naples to take control of the struggle out of the hands of the peasants. The decision was not only fateful, it was ironic; the southern Italian peasants were to be led in the most violent uprising in their history by leaders who came from a class that had always been their worst enemy—the intellectual bourgeoisie. Although there was never any doubt of the party's will to get land for the peasantry, the event raised a fundamental problem. Were the intellectuals sent to constrain the petit bourgeois goals of the peasantry or to brake their revolutionary action?

The party's organization at this point was dictated by the conditions of the moment. Party cells were rare, and organizers were lacking. For its basic units, the party turned to the organizations emerging from the occupations of the land of 1943–45—the cooperatives. These cooperatives, specified by the government as the agencies to receive expropriated land, had an essential economic

20. Giuseppe Ciranna, "La Lotta Politica in Basilicata nel Dopoguerra," *Nord e Sud*, 1 (1958, Nuova Serie), 63.

purpose, thereby giving the party a facile tool for organization. Moreover, they had appeared exactly in those zones of the Mezzogiorno where the need for the land was greatest and the peasants were most militant. Here was an improvised tool for both aiding the peasants' economic life and organizing their further assaults upon the land. But they presented the fundamental difficulty that they were run by the peasants, and were therefore difficult to coordinate in a united action.

The petit bourgeois goals of the peasants soon appeared in these cooperatives in their behavior with regard to the land that had been occupied. The law of 1944 specified that this land could be cultivated by the peasants either in a group, in mixed forms of cultivation, or by single peasants working separate plots of land. Of the 414,000 acres of land that had been temporarily conceded in this way, only 10 percent was cultivated collectively; 7 percent was worked by mixed forms of cultivation and 83 percent was cultivated individually by the peasants. Hence the cooperatives were cooperatives in name only.[21]

Many cooperatives were controlled by non-Communists, and some became the tools of local clientele groups. Often their leaders used them merely as stepping stones into local public office, entering or leaving the Communist Party if opportunity so dictated. Organizationally, this meant chaos for the Communist Party. In some communes, the party controlled the cooperatives and had no other organized presence; in others, powerful party cells existed, and the cooperatives were controlled by non-Communists; in still others the party had no organized presence at all. Conflicts were common between Communist-inspired cooperatives and others. But the cooperatives gave the PCI the opportunity to appear in the South not as an electoral party seeking votes or as a working class party seeking alliances, but as the authentic embodiment of the peasants' aspirations for the land.[22]

The ideological development of the PCI during this period is fascinating. The party suppressed its sophisticated theoretical structure and struck the resonant chord of the occupation of the

21. Giovanni Enrico Marciani, *L'Esperienza di Riforma Agraria in Italia* (Roma, 1966), pp. 24–29.
22. Galasso, "La Riforma Agraria," pp. 15–16.

land that had been taken by the bourgeoisie in the nineteenth century. A propaganda pamphlet of 1945 read, "The problem of the restitution to the people of what was lost over the centuries . . . is a problem that interests millions of poor peasants, and to which the Communist Party looks with much attention." A national leader said in a speech in Calabria in 1946,

> We do not propose the expropriation of all the proprietors without indemnity, but . . . it is the proprietors who must show their right to the ownership of the land. It is well known that many great Calabrian landowners usurped their land from the common lands following the abolition of feudalism at the beginning of the last century and, above all, obtained the legitimation of these usurpations in the first years of the united Italy.[23]

Because of the emphasis upon the lands usurped by the bourgeoisie, the PCI's organizations were strongest in the traditional zones of the classical Peasant Latifundia: in the Sila mountains and the Crotonese in Calabria, in the interior of Sicily, and around the bleak peasant caves of Matera and in the Fucino basin in the Abruzzi. For different reasons, the party grew quickly among the braccianti of the plains of Puglia, where commercialized agriculture and well-defined occupational roles gave it a far more modern reality in which to operate. Here, however, it was the union leagues of the Federterra rather than the party that gained the peasants' primary allegiance.

A rough congruence grew up between the peasants' political memories and the organized strength of the Communist Party. In a society in which the major social group has a historical disrespect for public authority, a political movement that appears to reject this authority completely earns its own legitimacy. To the peasant with an unstable relation to the land, the Communist Party assumed the role of the ultimate brigand, the Robin Hood whose deeds against authority were both legitimate and violent. As a southern PCI leader said, "The Communist Party invented

23. Pietro Grifone, *L'Azione dei Comunisti in Difesa dei Contadini* (Roma, 1945, p. 16); Ruggiero Grieco, "Terra per Tutti: Oggi non Domani," *La Voce del Mezzogiorno*, 2, No. 46 (1948), 1.

nothing in the South. It only picked up the peasant's desire for the land and put it into an organized framework." [24]

Yet this rather primitive ideological appeal was both refined and modified between 1947 and 1950, in line with the whole development of the Via Italiana al Socialismo. An ideology of rebirth, or *rinascita* was developed to appeal to social groups other than the agricultural workers and poor peasants. Increasingly concerned about elections and lacking a modern class structure with which to operate in the Mezzogiorno, the party began to turn to the idea of social solidarity to gain a broader electoral following. Gramsci's revolutionary theorem of the alliance between northern workers and southern poor peasants was toned down into a paean for civil reformation and structural reforms. Small family farmers, artisans, and middle class and professional groups were all courted alongside the poor peasants and agricultural day workers by a set of programs that blurred the differences between them.

The problem of the land remained the focus of the PCI's programs, but it was now phrased in such a way as to attract peasant owners, artisans, and urban groups as well as poor peasants. Giorgio Amendola wrote in 1946, "We must tie together the workers, the agricultural workers, the artisans, the peasants, the petit bourgeoisie and the professionals. This alliance is made possible by the way we pose the problem of the agrarian reform." [25] An ideological link was sought between the land hunger of the poor peasants and the general interest in landowning throughout the Mezzogiorno.[26] This was a fatal step, for it softened the party's support for the most rebellious group: the landless day workers.

Organizationally, the change resulted in the replacement of the cooperatives of poor peasants as the party's basic working units by a network of "Committees for the Land." Begun in 1947, these committees were set up to be "organs of direction and struggle of the movement for the agrarian reform; . . . they do not merely

24. Interview, March 9, 1964.

25. Giorgio Amendola, "Prime Considerazioni sulle Elezioni nel Mezzogiorno," *Rinascita, 3,* Nos. 5–6 (1946), 108.

26. Giorgio Amendola, "La Rinascita nel Mezzorgiorno," *Voce del Mezzogiorno,* 2, No. 10 (1949), 3.

group together the representatives of the peasants, *but of all the population,* because all the population is interested, both directly and indirectly, in the agrarian reform." In other words, the Committees for the Land were front groups with no economic function.

The committees began to add subsidiary issues to that of the land in order to gain the confidence of peasant small owners and middle class groups. "The committees," a party leader wrote, "will resolve the conflicts that can arise between diverse categories of peasants in the general interest of the movement; they also confront all the other questions that are connected with the life of the countryside." [27] Their rather libertarian character allowed individuals to take part whose fear of governmental or church reprisals kept them from actually joining the party. "All progressive citizens," it was announced, "can take part in the Committees for the Land. All the democratic, labor and mass organizations will have their representatives." [28]

The major disadvantage of these groups was that, in seeking a broad, popular appeal, they dissipated the goals of the party's basic revolutionary force, the agricultural workers and poor peasants. The creation of the Committees for the Land inserted the peasants into the party's "Movement for the Rebirth of Southern Italy," a movement whose aims were broad and reformist rather than focused and revolutionary. "Rebirth" might mean distribution of the land, but it might also mean civic rebirth, intellectual rebirth, or an unconnected stream of interest demands. In fact, the party soon held a series of provincial and regional assizes to compile "notebooks" of demands such as those for reform of the educational system, protection for southern industry, and construction of public works. Prominent intellectuals figured noticeably at each of these meetings, a factor intended to increase their appeal to the middle classes.[29]

These forms of organization were instrumental in shifting the party's image from that of the revolutionary vindicator of the poor

27. Ruggiero Grieco, "Prospettive della Riforma Agraria," *Rinascita, 4,* Nos. 11–12 (1947), 327.

28. No author, "La Lotta dei Contadini Meridionali," *La Voce del Mezzogiorno, 1,* No. 2 (1948), 4.

29. See the issues of *La Voce* from March to December 1949.

peasants to the popular representative of many urban or rural groups. What they distinctly did not do was to bring the demands of poor peasants to the state. As a result, state action on the long-needed land reform was delayed, and much poorly cultivated land remained in the hands of the bourgeois owners. This was the most immediate result of the PCI's ideology of solidarity.

At the same time, the peasantry remained at the center of the party's strategy. In 1948, with its failure to gain power in the national elections, it turned to direct tactics. A series of demonstrations, closely linked to meetings of the party's regional assizes, tested the temper of the peasants and the effectiveness of the organizational network that had been created throughout the South. Calabria, where the most bitter heritage of peasant resentment was found, was chosen as the focus of operations. Mario Alicata, a young intellectual born in the region but educated in the North, was made regional secretary.

The two years of agrarian revolt that soon followed were the most dramatic aspect of the Italian postwar scene. The movement's superficial resemblance to past uprisings was quickly noted. It only became clear as it progressed that this movement represented a qualitative leap over all the agitations that had occurred in the history of the Mezzogiorno. As a sensitive non-Communist observer wrote,

> In the post-war period, southern Italian peasant society had one of those uprisings that are chronic in its history, and that derive from a deep-seated aspiration for possession of the land. This time, however, there was a political crisis of proportions unknown to anyone's memory, accompanied by an exceptional scarcity of material goods. In this situation, the active intervention of a political party transformed the peasant uprisings from a jacquerie into a class struggle, directing and instrumentalizing its still amorphous popular aspirations.[30]

In early October 1949, a peasant woman was killed by a policeman in a mountain town in Calabria. As if by signal, organizers

30. Giovanni Cervigni, "Le Defezioni dal PCI in Calabria," Nord e Sud, 2, No. 6 (1955).

were dispatched to all the mountain towns of the Sila. Sixteen towns in the province of Catanzaro and twelve in Cosenza began a series of occupations of the land. Party leaders in Catanzaro province expected six thousand peasants to march on the large estates; when fourteen thousand turned out the next morning, the party was astonished. In most cases, the peasants of entire villages occupied the land in the name of the village; in other areas, villages were banded together to make a more impressive force. Arriving at the borders of the estates, the peasants were divided into squads; they laid claim to predesignated pieces of land and immediately began working. At the appearance of police, they would lock arms, deny that they had any leaders, and refuse to be arrested except en masse.

In many areas, the party's appeal for solidarity paid dividends. Storekeepers, artisans, and clerks joined in the assault upon the land, hoping for a share in the rewards. Often the crucifix and the Italian tricolor accompanied the red flag as the peasants marched. In one village, the parish priest claimed a piece of land for his parish. Supplies were provided by local merchants, and solidarity strikes were called on the part of the industrial workers of Crotone.[31]

On October 30, a group of peasants from the town of Melissa were confronted by a squadron of state police. Smoke bombs were thrown, the demonstrators began to flee, and in the confusion that followed, three peasants were killed and thirteen wounded. The massacre became the object of nationwide strikes and demonstrations of solidarity. The peasants' funerals were marked by speeches from national political leaders, and the occupations of the land soon spread to all the regions of the South. In Calabria, a permanent staff of working class organizers was recruited from the factories of Crotone. A second rank of militants were drawn from the peasant leagues and the cooperatives formed in 1945–46. These peasant leaders each led a squad of ten other peasants, with instructions to direct activity toward the land and to avoid looting and burning.

In Sicily and most of Puglia, the occupations were mainly sym-

31. No author, "Una Forza di Secoli nei Combattenti della Conquista della Terra," *La Voce del Mezzogiorno*, 2, No. 44 (1949), 3.

bolic. The peasants would march out into the country carrying flags and singing, and would seed the land of a large estate. In Puglia, where much of the land had been pasture until 1870, large commercialized operations now dominated, and a single peasant with a plow could not hope to compete on the market. Hence the occupations were limited in scope. However, the thousands of agricultural day workers of the Federbraccianti aided the movement by coordinated work stoppages and demonstrations.

In the Salento peninsula, the very heel of Italy, conditions differed from the rest of Puglia. Much land remained uncultivated, and many of the peasants worked as renters or share tenants. In a forty-five-day period, 2,500 acres were occupied by the peasants. The campaign was organized like a guerrilla war without rifles. Two hundred permanent peasant activists and thirty leaders were divided into five groups, and each group was divided in turn into a mobile work force. They rotated among various plots of land to escape capture by the *carabinieri*. Mushroom pickers on bicycles who knew shortcuts through the fields brought news and provisions. When the police burned the bicycles, code signals were broadcast with firecrackers to inform the peasants that the police were on the way.

In Lucania, the pattern was again different. Many towns participated little in the campaign, but those that had been host to anti-Fascist prisoners during the war were the seats of very powerful peasant movements. Such a town was Ferrandina, the scene of Carlo Levi's *Christ Stopped at Eboli*. The strength of the movement, stimulated mainly by the influence of the left-wing political prisoners, was surprising. The result was a peasant movement at once more anarchic and more atomistic than in Calabria or the rest of the South. Each village was led by a *capopopolo* of peasant background, because working class or intellectual leaders were not often available. Hence violence and disorganization were greater than elsewhere.

In the Fucino basin, in the Abruzzi, the campaign began only in 1950. Here its tremendous success in achieving the division of the Torlonia latifundia was due to a successful alliance between agricultural day workers and small renters. The *braccianti* movement began as a strike in reverse to force the government to create jobs in public works. The renters, organized in the PCI-dominated Autonomous Associations of Renters, went on strike for a reduction of their rentals. An alliance was effected that succeeded in gaining possession of the land for members of both groups. Here, too, while expropriation had been posed unsuccessfully for many years, its proposal brought quick success. Here, too, the forms of organization used were improvised and creative. Women participated in the work strikes for the first time in the Mezzogiorno; their presence confused and demoralized the police.

Nowhere in the South was there any symmetry of organization. The campaign was differently organized according to which units arrived first—the cells, the cooperatives, the committees for the land, the labor leagues—and which groups predominated in leadership. Despite the organizational innovations that had been made, many of the land occupations were anarchic or violent. This was particularly true in Calabria, where a militant group of organizers was willing to let the peasants go beyond party directives. Only in Puglia, where the leagues of braccianti led the militant agricultural proletariat, was the campaign carefully organized and controlled. But the entire movement demonstrated that when the object of organization was the struggle for the land, the peasants were far from disorganized.

The movement was pictured with an extremely romantic flavor. Journalists described the peasant marches in almost religious terms. For example, "They left before dawn in the last darkness, moving with firm, rapid steps toward the conquest of work. The land awaited them. . . . As the sun rose, all the land which lay uncultivated by the large proprietors was occupied by thousands of peasants."[32] In one agitation, pregnant women blocked their men from the police to stop their being arrested. The solidarity aspects were the most surprising. "All the poor classes of the southern population were joined together: the day workers, the unemployed, the artisans, the small shopkeepers. Men and women, old and young, moved toward the conquest of the land in a new and spontaneous unity."[33]

32. No author, "L'Intera Campania in Movimento," *La Voce del Mezzogiorno, 2*, No. 46 (1949), 1.

33. No author, "Un Grande e Continuo Movimento Contadino," *La Voce del Mezzogiorno, 3*, No. 16 (1950), 6.

The importance of age-old land hunger in fueling the movement cannot be underestimated. But the importance of age-old inhibitions was also great. For example, in many places it was verified that the peasants refused to occupy land that was outside the traditional confines of their communes. In other cases, the movement was used as an excuse to settle old vendettas. In other words, the objective conditions—or the traditional social organization of the South—were not only the *cause* of the emergence of the movement; they also influenced its pattern of development.

But the traditional mentality of the peasantry was not the only brake upon the movement. In line with its alliance strategy, the party limited the peasants' violent and extremist tendencies. Wherever possible, their energies were directed only at poorly cultivated big estates, a limitation that protected commercial farms, small owners, and some absentee landlords from attack. In other words, *to project the Via Italiana al Socialismo—a strategy that had been developed for the North—upon the South, the party was sacrificing the Gramscian formula of the revolutionary alliance between workers and peasants for a more inclusive alliance.* The change was not a tactical adaptation; in fact, in terms of tactics, the struggle for the land was a form of jacquerie. The tactical problem only appeared when party leaders realized with whom their northern alliance strategy put them in touch in the South: with small farmers, artisans, middle class landholders, and professionals; in other words, with some of the most traditional forces in Italian society!

But so frightening was the news coming out of the South that the government soon had to act. It had tabled a Christian Democratic land reform bill in April 1949, but in the spring of 1950, moved by fear of a revolutionary situation, over 100,000 acres of land in Calabria were conceded and the Sila Agency for Agrarian Reform was created in that area. Later in the year, similar concessions were made in all the areas of the latifundia, as well as in the Tuscan Maremma and in the Po delta.

In all, almost 1,600,000 acres of land were to be distributed by the various reform agencies before the decade was over. In all, more than 100,000 peasant families were to benefit directly, and more than 700,000 lire per hectare of expropriated land was to be spent. The struggle for the land had succeeded. But we may very well ask, as did many political leaders at the time, "What had it succeeded in doing?"

THE AGRARIAN REFORM

With the passage of an agrarian reform and its rapid implementation in the countryside, an epoch ended in the Mezzogiorno. In an immediate sense, only the acute exasperation of the peasants and their assault upon the latifundia were over. But the impact was, in fact, much deeper, for the Agrarian Reform meant the finish of one structure of landed property and the beginning of another. And with the passage of that antiquated distribution of the land, the entire structure of social and political relations known as *clientelismo* began to change.

To understand the depth of these changes, we must first recall the basic features of land distribution and social relations in the Mezzogiorno at the time of the Riforma. For unlike more highly developed rural societies, southern Italy until 1951 was divided between a few very large landed estates and many minute peasant properties. Both were characterized by an extremely low capital investment, a primitive system of cultivation, and a crop rotation pattern that ravaged the land two or three times a year. Both were found within the very same areas.

The small properties were truly autonomous only in limited areas of intensive agriculture; elsewhere they were usually too small, too infertile, or too high in the mountains to provide an entire family with an adequate income. Moreover, a majority of the small and medium properties were not actually owned by the peasant but were let to him in semifeudal rentals or share tenancies by people "whose only connection with agriculture was to collect the income from their land." [34]

The latifundia, in contrast, were seldom operated as commercial farms using salaried farm workers and modern methods. In an economy with little capital and much available labor, the simplest way of exploiting land was to let small pieces of it to renters or share tenants on short-term contract. It is striking, for example, that of all the *large* property in Italy in 1948, 38.5 percent was

34. Marciani, *L'Esperienza di Riforma Agraria*, p. 17.

cultivated by renters, 24.1 percent was let to share tenants, and only 19.2 percent was run as commercial operations. Table 11.1 below gives the distribution of agricultural land according to the size of the property and the method of its cultivation in 1948–49.

TABLE 11.1

Distribution of Agricultural Land by Size and Method of Cultivation 1948–49
(in percentages)

	Farmer Owner	Commercial Farms	Share Tenancy	Rental	Total
Small	54.0	10.4	16.8	18.8	100.0
Medium	6.9	29.7	26.2	37.2	100.0
Large	3.7	33.7	24.1	38.5	100.0

Source: Istituto Nazionale di Economia Agraria (INEA), I Tipi d'Impresa nell'Agricoltura Italiana (Roma, 1951).

The semifeudal character of the contracts between landowners and peasants on the latifundia, their short-term nature, and the fact that they made no provision for equipment left the peasants on their own. Inevitably, the majority cultivated the only crop that required little human help—wheat—a subsistence crop for which the region was eminently unsuited.

The most basic factor in the economic, social, and political setting of the South was the coexistence in the same areas of the miniscule small property and the sprawling latifundia. The instability of the former, the availability of cheap labor for the latter, the fragmentation of occupational roles, and the political dependence of the peasant upon the landowner were all poised between these two axes. As Giovanni Enrico Marciani writes,

> The major disequilibrium was found in those zones in which the very large property and the miniscule property coexisted. In those areas, the true latifundia were flanked almost without intermediary, by a minute type of peasant property, for the most part localized around the villages. These zones shared all the problems of oversized properties and all the problems of undersized properties.[35]

35. Ibid., pp. 15–16.

The relations between the two were critical:

> The peasants of these zones, who could not realize even the minimal level of subsistence on their own property, were forced to turn to the latifundia, not simply as *braccianti,* but also as small renters and sharecroppers. The *latifundia* were, therefore, cultivated on a multiplicity of small and microscopic plots, although they were owned in a very few large units.[36]

In the occupational instability of the peasant and his dependence upon the landowner is the origin of both the chronic disorganization of the southern peasantry and its political dependence upon a system of *clientelismo.* In the contradiction between the small peasant property and the sprawling latifundia was the source of the endemic bitterness of the southern peasant and his propensity to revolt at the slightest provocation.

The Agrarian Reform changed all that. Its critical role was *not* to create small units out of large ones—for the latifundia were large only in terms of ownership. Its essential role was to redress the tortuous imbalance between the peasant property and the latifundia, enabling the former to maintain itself and ultimately to replace the latter with a more efficient, commercial operation. The Riforma has done exactly that, and in the process it has removed the objective causes for the old system of social relations and the traditional political system in the Mezzogiorno. It has at the same time removed the main cause of the peasants' bitterness and created a clear social distinction between small farm owners and agricultural workers, a distinction formerly clouded by the symbiotic relationship between the unstable small property and the latifundia.

There is little doubt that the Riforma succeeded in destroying the latifundia as the basic agrarian structure of the South. Although the criteria of expropriation differed from area to area, they had the same essential scope throughout. The Sila law in Calabria expropriated land from all estates above 300 hectares (about 700 acres). But lands that had been transformed by intensive cultivation, as well as those unsuited to intensive cultiva-

36. Ibid., p. 16.

tion, were exempted from expropriation. The *Stralcio* law, which governed the expropriation of land in the remaining zones of reform, was based upon the productive capacity of the land as expressed in the taxable income of the property. A scale of expropriation was set so as to fall most heavily upon those lands in extensive cultivation and less heavily upon the intensively cultivated commercial farms.[37]

Both these laws destroyed the power of large landed property in the designated zones of reform. For example, while only 1.1 percent of the properties of 50 to 100 hectares were subject to expropriation, 100 percent of the properties of over 2,500 hectares were subject to expropriation. The number of hectares expropriated from each class of property varied accordingly: from virtually zero for the properties under 100 hectares to 64.8 percent of the land on properties of more than 2,500 hectares. The distribution of the incidence of the reform on various classes of properties is represented in Table 11.2.

TABLE 11.2

Incidence of Expropriated Land on National Agricultural Property
by Class of Hectarage Above 50 Hectares
(in percentages)

Class of Hectares	Percentage of Properties in Each Class	Percentage of Properties Affected by Reform	Percentage of Land Expropriated from Each Class
50–100	55.6	1.1	—
100–150	17.6	7.8	0.3
150–200	8.5	16.8	1.3
200–300	7.9	22.3	3.7
300–500	4.7	32.7	8.4
500–1,000	3.4	39.5	14.3
1,000–2,500	1.1	63.9	27.8
2,500 and over	0.2	100.0	64.8
Total	100.0	9.3	9.9

Source: Giovanni Enrico Marciani, *L'Esperienza di Riforma Agraria in Italia* (Milano, 1966), p. 83.

37. Ibid., pp. 43–48.

The Riforma was particularly hard on properties owned by absentee landlords and operated by peasant renters or share tenants. In a study carried out in the zone of reform in Puglia-Lucania-Molise, it was shown that 60.3 percent of the expropriated hectarage in that zone was taken from proprietors of this type. *Local* landholders who rented or leased their property contributed only 6.6 percent of the expropriated land. Landholders whose land was cultivated intensively, either through commercial techniques or through the *mezzadria*, accounted for 22.9 percent of the expropriated land. A final 10 percent was expropriated from local owners who considered agriculture their secondary economic interest—in other words, middle class landowners.[38]

On the other side of the ledger, the reform benefited not only the landless bracciante, but also the renter, the share tenant, and the marginal small owner. Of the 92,000 peasants who had been assigned land in 1960, 43,000 or 47.1 percent were day workers, 34,000 or 37.1 percent were small renters or share tenants, 8,500 or 9.2 percent were the owners of marginal small farms, and a remaining 6,000 or 6.6 percent came from other categories.[39] In most cases the landless braccianti were given preference, but when the land being expropriated had been cultivated by the same share tenant or renter for a long period of time, that individual was given preference.

Peasants who already owned a piece of land not large enough to sustain their families were to be included in the reform through the device of the *quota*. The typical "allotment" of land was one large enough to sustain a peasant family. The quota was a smaller plot which, added to the land the peasant already owned, was supposed to allow him to make a decent living. The average allotment was 9.7 hectares (24 acres) and the average quota was 2.4 hectares (about 6 acres). A total of 34 percent of the expropriated land was assigned as *quote*, a total of 66 percent was assigned as full-sized allotments.[40]

The allocation of land to small renters, share tenants, and

38. Ibid., p. 143.
39. Ibid., p. 65.
40. Ibid., p. 67.

marginal small owners, as well as to the landless braccianti, broke
the traditional economic and political power of the latifundia.
By creating an independent class of small properties, the Riforma
had eliminated, "on the land it was responsible for expropriating,
all those traditional contracts—the small rentals, share tenancies,
and sharecropping—that had formerly linked the peasants to the
land." Furthermore, the impact soon spread from the land actually
expropriated to surrounding areas. "In demolishing the monopolistic position of large landed property, the reform rapidly led
to a change *even on land that had not been subjected to expropriation.*" [41]

But rather than fragmenting cultivation still further, the Riforma actually led to an increase in the number of average-sized
farms and a decrease in the number of very small farms. For
although the reform was aimed at very large properties, these
properties had usually been cultivated in piecemeal units as rentals and share tenancies. In many areas after the reform, the number of plots of land was much smaller than before. In one town
in Lucania, the number of owners or renters of plots of less than
5 hectares decreased from 122 to 31 as a result of the reform,
and the number of owners of farms of more than 5 hectares increased from 86 to 123.[42] The net result in economic terms was
an increase in the number of stable peasant owners and a growth
in the rationality and efficiency of cultivation.

In social terms, a new distinction was created between independent small farmers and a salaried agricultural proletariat.
And as the results of the reform matured, some peasants began
to pass into the category of small commercial farmers, buying
more land, increasing the intensity of cultivation through capital
investments, and hiring a few agricultural workers either on a
daily or a salaried basis.

Even the economic basis of the small peasant property began
to change. Before the reform, slightly more than half of the land
in the reform areas was planted in seed crops, 2.6 percent was
covered by tree crops, 35.4 percent was pasture, and 8.6 percent
was woods. In 1963, in contrast, aided by agrarian reform credit

41. Ibid., p. 142. Emphasis added.
42. Ibid., p. 153.

and technical assistance, the peasants had increased seed crops to 67.5 percent of the land. They had increased tree crops to 9.4 percent, and had decreased the percentage of the land dedicated to pasture and woods to 16.0 percent and 7.1 percent, respectively. More important, grain had decreased from 52.2 percent of gross product in 1953 to 23.6 percent in 1963. Instead, intensive garden crops, which accounted for 19.4 percent of gross product in 1953, now made up 29.1 percent, while tree crops increased from 5.9 percent to 17.8 percent over the ten-year period.[43]

These statistics are presented, not to give a detailed account of the rural economy in the zones of reform, but to demonstrate precisely what had been accomplished through the Communist-led occupations of the land. The peasant, who had been a marginal economic figure dividing his time between his own pathetic piece of land and the latifundia, and producing mainly subsistence crops, was now an entirely different economic figure. He was now an independent small farmer who possessed the skills and the resources to produce intensive crops for market. And he could produce them well; between 1953 and 1963, gross salable product per hectare increased by 8.5 percent a year on the lands of reform, compared to an annual increase of 3.7 percent in the reform regions as a whole and 2.6 percent a year throughout the country.[44]

But if the peasant was now an independent small farmer who occasionally hired his own farm labor, what were his politics? If, as a marginal economic and social figure, he had been poised between political dependence upon the landowner and an innate propensity to revolt, what were his dependencies and his propensities now?

In attacking this question, it is useful first to recall the problem discussed earlier—the problem of the role of the peasant in Marxist thought and the difficulties it presents. For if Marx had obscured the difference between concentration in industry and concentration in agriculture, Bernstein and the revisionists compounded the error by misinterpreting the growth of small farm property. This phenomenon, which the revisionists interpreted

43. Ibid., pp. 145–47.
44. Ibid., p. 152.

as a refutation of Marx's theory of concentration, was actually a postfeudal rationalization of agrarian structure that would lead eventually to capitalist concentration.

As a result of their two errors, the revisionists accepted the small farm property (and the small farmer) as an economic fixture, thereby helping them survive at the cost of part of the socialists' radical élan. This was no great loss, since European socialism was simultaneously yielding on much more important matters, and it did create a strategic instrument which could someday convert the peasant to socialism while it protected his interests in the market: the farm cooperative. The problem was that by the time the cooperative was fully developed, European socialism had become a thing of the past.

At the same time, the Leninist variant of Marxism had taken a different turn. Flourishing in semifeudal countries in which the small peasant property had not yet gained a foothold, Leninism utilized the *pre*capitalist spirit of revolt of the peasant to arrive at a *post*capitalist solution, thereby leapfrogging over the small peasant property altogether. It was as if Lenin had recognized in the precapitalist peasant the insurrectionary drive that Marx had, perhaps mistakenly, attributed to the industrial worker.

The apotheosis of peasant revolt in a precapitalist society was, of course, the revolution in China, in which the absence of even an excuse for a working class revealed the true revolutionary potential of the precapitalist peasant. The problem in postcapitalist society is that all the contradictions that appear as class conflicts in capitalist society occur as cultural antagonisms in socialist society, antagonisms caused by the sheer numerical importance of a class that has not yet gone through a capitalist stage of development.

But how is all this relevant for the problem of southern Italy? It is relevant as an archetype of what can happen in a precapitalist rural society when the innate revolt of the peasant is converted into revolution by a revolutionary party. It is relevant as an example of what might have happened but did not happen in southern Italy.

The problem is that the only alternative to revolution in an underdeveloped agrarian society is conservatism, for when peasant revolt is not turned into revolution it can only result in the small peasant property—*the most conservative capitalist institution ever developed.* By organizing the peasants of the Mezzogiorno in a struggle for the land that was not aimed at social revolution, the Communists gained the Agrarian Reform, and the Agrarian Reform gained the small peasant property. Nothing could be more direct or more politically barren.

It is in this light that the quotation at the beginning of this chapter takes on new significance, particularly for the kind of transition from an underdeveloped to a modern society that is now beginning in southern Italy. "We have not yet captured the peasants," Kautsky said, "but the peasants have captured us." The only thing left to do was to hope for the ultimate formation of a socialist conscience in the peasants or to turn once again to the proletariat. Or would it be possible to do both at the same time? Kautsky and the German Socialists never had a chance to find out, but the Italian Communists have.

12. The New Structure of Power

Who *had* captured the peasants? The question, while framed in somewhat archaic terms, is a fair statement of what many Italians were asking after the Agrarian Reform of 1951. For if the southern peasants had been traditionally enmeshed in an immobilist clientele system, the destruction of the latifundia had removed that system's lynchpin. Would economic liberation now lead to political independence? Or would the Communist Party, cheered by the success of the struggle for the land, translate that victory into electoral and organizational control of the peasants? It was tempting, for friends and enemies alike, to equate the party's success in mobilizing the peasantry with growing electoral and organizational power.

But such an equation misses the point for several reasons. First, as we have seen, electoral success has been won largely at the price of organizational failure. Second, a peasant with land is a very different political animal from a landless peasant. And third, the equation of peasant mobilization with Communist power leaves out a critical element: the state, and the power exercised over it by the governing Christian Democratic Party.

When the French Revolution helped the peasants gain control of much of the land at the end of the eighteenth century, a peasant with a plow could still hope to compete in European markets. In mid-twentieth-century Italy, this was no longer true. Particularly in southern Italy, new peasant owners would require enormous amounts of technical and financial assistance. What was not provided through the agrarian reform agencies might come from the newly established Cassa per il Mezzogiorno. Peasants who had not received land, as well as many artisans and small tradesmen, might hope to receive employment from the latter agency or from the programs of one of the regular ministries. In one way or another, the hand of the state was stretching over the

South, and where the government sowed, there the government party might reap. Therefore, it is particularly important, in analyzing the political aftermath of the Agrarian Reform, to focus on the political party that has held undisputed power in Italy since 1948—the Christian Democracy.

In the structure of power created by this party in southern Italy, we see much that is old; the techniques of *clientelismo* die hard in any developing society. But we also see a party unwilling to base its power on traditional sources. With a politically creative, if opportunistic, leadership, and with the organizational power of the Catholic Church behind it, the Christian Democrats proceeded in the formation of a new structure of political control in the Mezzogiorno. Had they failed to do so, the PCI would undoubtedly be much more powerful in the South today.

CATHOLIC POLITICS AND THE MEZZOGIORNO

It is ironic that an Italian Catholic party, the Partito Popolare, arose only in 1918, shortly before the formation of the PCI and over fifty years after the birth of the unified state. And, although both parties had a mass base in the North, the leader of each was a Southerner. Don Luigi Sturzo was born in Sicily and received his training in Milan; Antonio Gramsci was Sardinian and was educated in Turin.

Sturzo and Gramsci could not have been more unlike in temperament, but each was, in his own way, a revolutionary, and each placed the problem of the Mezzogiorno at the center of his program. For Gramsci, as we have seen, the problem of the South was a national problem. For Sturzo, too, policy toward the South had to be "a corollary of the general policy of the Italian state, almost a keystone, rather than a particular problem to be confronted with special laws." [1]

The parallel does not end there. Gramsci posed the problem of the Italian revolution in terms of the mobilization of the southern peasantry by the northern workers. Sturzo, too, gave central position to the southern peasants, whom he considered popular Catholicism's major motor force. But long before Gramsci wrote about the peasantry, Sturzo made whistle-stop tours of the

1. Franco Rizzo, *Luigi Sturzo e la Questione Meridionale* (Roma, 1957), p. 34.

South, organizing among the peasants the cooperatives he believed would bring them directly into political life. More than
once he was criticized by ecclesiastical dignitaries as a subversive
and a heretic, but "in reality, . . . he wanted to make Christian
Democracy a spiritual force that would inspire the Sicilian peasant world and from there initiate a process of renovation all over
the South." [2]

Gramsci's rural programs were extremely vague, but the Partito
Popolare's program called for such radical goals as the division
of the common lands and the southern latifundia among the
peasants. This goal was the subject of a bill presented in parliament in 1920, when the advent of Fascism stilled the voice of
Catholic reform.[3]

Counterbalancing Sturzo's concern with the southern peasantry
was his interest in the middle class. The clientele system he saw
throughout southern Italy and the middle class parasitism that
accompanied it led Sturzo to seek to organize a self-conscious
political middle class. A whole series of programs was created
explicitly to attract its attention. "Administrative decentralization,
reform of the bureaucracy, commercial freedom, the battle against
industrial parasitism and customs policies . . . if these ideas of
the Partito Popolare had succeeded, the middle classes of the
Mezzogiorno would have acquired their own power of political
participation." [4] For Sturzo, "Only the politicization of the middle class would have initiated the solution of the problem of the
South." [5]

Proportional representation and regional and local autonomy
were critical points in Sturzo's attack on *clientelismo*. Proportional representation would destroy the power of local notables
through the replacement of single local candidates by party lists,
and decentralization would relieve the poverty-stricken South
from the burdens of a unified finance system, and "break the
vicious circle that runs from the Mafia to the latifundia, and

2. Aldo Moro, *Il Pensiero Politico di Luigi Sturzo* (Naples, 1959), pp. 6–8.
3. Rizzo, p. 70.
4. Gianni Baget Bozzo, "Ceti Medi e Mezzogiorno nella Lotta Politica Italiana,"
Cronache Sociali, 2, Nos. 4–5 (1948), 2.
5. Rizzo, p. 33.

from the corruption of the central bureaucracy to illiteracy." [6]

Sturzo's programs were posited on the independence of the Partito Popolare from the Church. Without this freedom, popular Christianity would degenerate into a political arm of the Vatican. In the North, autonomy from the Vatican could well be conceived, because the doctrines of social Catholicism were widespread, and a network of Catholic lay organizations already existed. But what of the South, where Catholic doctrine was backward and the only important Catholic organizations to be found were the parish churches?

Autonomy from the Vatican, organization of the peasants and middle class, land reform, and constitutional reform; all these problems were soon irrelevant, as Fascism came to power with the Church as its handmaiden. The problems introduced by the Lateran Treaty and the political activity of Catholics under Fascism are outside the scope of this discussion and are extensively treated elsewhere.[7] It suffices to point out that the postwar resurgence of political Catholicism depended largely upon the maintenance of the religious and lay institutions of the Church during Fascism when most other autonomous bodies were suppressed. Hence, the Church emerged from World War II with expanded political opportunities and organizations. This was particularly relevant in the South, where the left-wing parties had never been active and where years of officiating at Fascist public ceremonies had expanded the political importance of the parish priests.

Although it had cast aside its pre-Fascist nomenclature for the more neutral name La Democrazia Cristiana, the Catholic party emerged for a short time after World War II with the same radical program. Under the tutelage of Alcide De Gasperi, the DC until 1948 presented itself to the electorate as a mass party in active competition with the mass parties of the left. As a historian of the party writes:

6. See E. Ragionieri, "Accentramento e Autonominella Storia dell'Italia Unita," in Manin Carabba, ed., *Ruolo degli Enti Locali nella Politica di Sviluppo* (Roma, 1963), p. 34; also see Rizzo, pp. 34, 70.

7. Richard Webster, *The Cross and the Fasces* (Palo Alto, 1960).

The program of De Gasperi and his friends was very near that of the Marxists, so much so that a Communist minister of the third De Gasperi government could write some years later that the DC had presented itself to the Constituent Assembly with a program of structural reforms that responded to the aspirations of Catholic workers and which was substantially identical to that of the Communists and Socialists.[8]

The first party program, which appeared in 1944 during the apocalyptical days of the Resistance, called for "bread, work but also access to property" for all, and "the modification of laws that had until then favored the concentration of the means of production and wealth in a few hands." [9]

In the South, the party's progressive goals verged on the revolutionary, as had Sturzo's twenty years earlier. At the first DC congress in 1946 (in the face of widespread peasant desperation), De Gasperi said,

> Now is the time when the great landowners must make sacrifices, because it is not possible to maintain existing privileges either in the field of agricultural property or in the field of industry. We must move toward a new equilibrium, toward another system of landed property that is based upon social justice.[10]

In 1947, the party established a Permanent Committee for the Mezzogiorno with the ageing Sturzo as president. The South became, in the words of De Gasperi, "the commitment of honor of the Christian Democracy." [11]

More radical still was the approach of Dossetti and his followers. Dossetti, as vice-secretary of the DC, criticized De Gasperi's leadership as an attempt to "first reconstruct and then reform," proposing instead that the DC reform as it reconstructed. It was under pressure from this group that the Permanent Committee

8. Maurice Vassard, *Storia della Democrazia Cristiana* (Bologna, 1959), pp. 329–30.

9. "Idee Ricostruttive della Democrazia Cristiana," in *Atti e Documenti della Democrazia Cristiana, 1943–1959* (Roma, 1960), pp. 1–12.

10. Alcide De Gasperi, "Le Linee programmatiche della DC," in *I Congressi Nazionali della Democrazia Cristiana* (Roma, 1959), p. 23.

11. *Atti e Documenti,* pp. 331–32.

for the Mezzogiorno proposed for the South "a series of public works in transport, roads, irrigation and forests, electrification and reclamation," a proposal that was translated into law in 1950 with the establishment of the Cassa per il Mezzogiorno.[12]

However, the fact that the Cassa was conceived as an "extraordinary" agency brought forth new criticisms from Dossetti and the Catholic left. They maintained that "The political, economic and social problem of the Mezzogiorno does not demand the execution of single projects with an extraordinary character, but demands, for an indefinite time, a systematic initiative and an organic commitment of the state machinery." [13]

These criticisms, it should be noted, were very close to those expressed by the Communists, who held that the problem of the South was a *national* problem which could only be solved by a social transformation.[14] Thus, at least rhetorically, part of the Christian Democratic leadership was as revolutionary as the Communists in its ideas about the South. At the same time, De Gasperi began to move toward the right.

The dispute within the DC regarding its policy toward the South underscored a persistent dilemma: the contradiction between the progressive programs of popular Catholicism and its conservative electoral following in the Mezzogiorno. The party's largest reserve of voters was found among the traditional peasants and middle classes of the South. Between 1946 and 1948, the DC vote in the South rose from 35 percent to 49 percent, largely at the expense of the parties of the right, whose share of the vote decreased from 31 percent to 22 percent.

With the Communists growing on the left, the obvious place to look for votes was on the right. But an appeal to the right meant, first, an explicit contradiction of the party's progressive policies and, second, the utilization of the old clientele system rather than the construction of a modern mass party. As a representative of the Christian Democratic left wrote in 1949,

12. Ibid., p. 362.

13. Giorgio Ceriani Sebregondi, "La Cassa per il Mezzogiorno," *Cronache Sociali*, 4, No. 3 (1950), 12.

14. See Giorgio Amendola, "Contro la Istituzione della Cassa per il Mezzogiorno," in Rosario Villari, ed., *Il Sud nella Storia d'Italia*, pp. 642–45.

At this moment, the battle against local clienteles can only succeed when it is fought by a modern party that instills a national political conscience in its members and overcomes a local vision of the political struggle. . . . Between the two positions there is a difference, not only of method, but of ideological direction.[15]

Mass political party, or conglomeration of clienteles; what was to be the ultimate nature of Christian Democracy in the Mezzogiorno? The issue was complicated by the hybrid nature of the party's leadership. When World War II ended, very few southern Catholic political leaders had not been tainted with Fascist party membership or complicity. The result was that the party was led predominantly by old pre-Fascist liberal notables, many of them landowners and professionals who saw in the Christian Democratic Party a liberal (that is free-enterprise) bastion with progressive outcroppings.

The mass base of the party was composed mainly of peasants and artisans, both of whom have traditionally received a great deal of paternalistic attention from the Church. But the years between 1946 and 1952 saw the active membership of the party growing constantly, at least in part from the ranks of ex-Fascist functionaries and sympathizers. These new activists, attracted mainly by the promise of patronage, were scarcely compatible with the progressive ideological goals the DC continued to proclaim. The new membership deepened the dilemma that "The DC, a party of the center inclined toward the left received almost half of its electoral support from a mass on the right."[16] There was a real danger that the DC would simply re-create the old clientele system under a new rubric.

The paradox was underscored by the Agrarian Reform law passed in 1950. Agrarian reform had been one of the DC's cardinal programs since Sturzo, but if it passed a radical reform law, its conservative agrarian supporters would be alienated. It was for

15. Franco Maria Malfatti, "Analisi del II° Congresso Nazionale della DC," *Cronache Sociali, 3,* No. 11 (1949), 14.

16. Domenico Ravioli, "La Funzione della DC e i suoi Compiti," in *Antologia di Cronache Sociali,* ed. Marcella Glisenti e Leopoldo Elia (Roma, 1961), *1,* 410.

this reason that De Gasperi, growing steadily more conservative, wanted the reform limited to the poorly run latifundia. When, under the desperate pressure of the peasants, three regional laws were passed, the DC immediately felt its political effects. The laws themselves had been opposed by an influential group of southern Christian Democratic deputies, and were passed only when it was made clear that the alternative to a reform was anarchy in the countryside. But it was in the local elections of 1951–52 that the DC felt the double edge of the Agrarian Reform most keenly: its vote fell from 49 percent in 1948 to 32 percent in 1951–52 in the South. A party spokesman wrote,

> The analysis of the electoral returns shows clearly that the political cause of the movement of part of the electorate of the DC in the South to the parties of the right—the Fascists and the Monarchists—was the disaffection of the agrarian class hit by the agrarian reform from the DC.[17]

The Democrazia Cristiana was in a political squeeze between the Communists, who had led the peasants in the assault on the latifundia, and the extreme right, which stood to gain from the disaffection of the possessing classes. As the then-political secretary of the DC, Guido Gonella said: "Every reform gives rise to hostility. Everyone wants to be a reformer, no one wants to be reformed, and the reformed form a coalition against the reformers . . . the beginning of reforms is a season for seeding and not a season for harvest." [18] If the party *did not* appeal to the right, it stood to lose votes on both sides.

The season for reforms was indeed over, as the unsuccessful local elections of 1951–52 and the equally disappointing elections of 1953 showed. But a shift to the right would put the party squarely in the hands of the conservative economic interests of North and South, alienating the Catholic labor movement in the North and playing into the hands of the old clienteles in the South. As in the case of the PCI, Italian political dualism

17. Franco Pecci, "De Gasperi nella Lotta Politica Italiana," in *Civitas*, No. 12 (1954), 69.

18. Guido Gonella, "L'Opera della DC per la Difesa e il Rafforzamento dello Stato Democratico," in *I Congressi Nazionali della Democrazia Cristiana*, p. 353.

threatened to cause an internal contradiction in the Christian Democrats.

The response was to come from another quarter. In 1954, with the illness of De Gasperi, Amintore Fanfani became general secretary of the DC. His response was to sacrifice *neither* the DC's advanced programs *nor* its conservative electorate, but to attempt to reinforce both by making the DC a modern mass party. At the Congress of Naples in 1954, Fanfani said:

> It is necessary to furnish the citizen with the proof that Italy is a republic in which the people are truly sovereign. Broad universal suffrage is not enough. . . . We must improve the competence of our registered members and our activists.[19]

By strengthening the organization of the party, Fanfani hoped to free it from dependence on the outside elements—mainly big business and the Church—which had sustained it at election time, contributing nothing but their demands between elections. As a leading observer writes, Fanfani's initiative was:

> a self-conscious political choice that began with the recognition of the impossibility of conducting an autonomous political program without creating at the same time a true party of active and responsible members, subjected to the discipline of a centralized party and not at the disposition of external pressure groups, foremost among them the Church hierarchy.[20]

In the South, Fanfani's reforms were particularly important. In that region, the Cassa per il Mezzogiorno and the Agrarian Reform were as yet unmatched by a modern, mass party. Fanfani called for the *political*, and not simply the economic, development of the South. "Above all," he said, "we must create active and efficient party sections and organizations in southern Italy, if we want to create a politics of facts and ideas instead of a politics of agitation and macaroni." [21] In the same way as the PCI, Fanfani

19. Amintore Fanfani, "Intervento," V° Congresso della DC, in *I Congressi Nazionali della Democrazia Cristiana*, pp. 556–59.

20. "La Democrazia Cristiana in Italia: Composizione Sociale, Struttura Organizzativa, Distribuzione delle Correnti," *Tempi Moderni, 4* (1961), 12.

21. Fanfani, "Intervento," p. 557.

was attempting to replace the clientele system with a new form of organized politics.

"A politics of agitation and macaroni," terms that epitomized the traditional tools of southern Italian politics: the generic protest, the patronage appointment, the letter of recommendation, the sack of *pasta* on election day—in other words, the clientele system. How did Fanfani propose to replace them with "a politics of facts and ideas"?

In July 1954, the Direction of the party decided "to ask all the members and supporters of the DC to contribute to an office for the Political and Organizational Development of the Depressed Areas." [22] Its scope was "to prepare the people psychologically and spiritually, transforming them from passive recipients of more-or-less appreciated favors into people who self-consciously seek projects that will lift them out of their extraordinary depression." [23]

The Office for the Depressed Areas was to send representatives from Rome to the most isolated villages of the South, stimulating participation and holding meetings at all the DC sections in the region "to illustrate the dynamic action taken by the DC, the decisions made in parliament, the activities of the government and the bureaucracy since 1947 for the true rebirth of the regions of the South." [24] Sending organizers from Rome and using evocative terms like "rebirth" was disconcerting to conservatives; it recalled the organizational drives launched by the Communists in the Mezzogiorno just a few years earlier, and the *Costruttori* they had sent from the Red Belt.

A second aspect of Fanfani's reforms called up the image of the PCI even more strongly. Oppressed by the conservative weight of the old notables upon the party's image, Fanfani sought the formation of a new leadership class within the party organization. He chose to do this by opening the road to parliamentary election to the DC provincial secretaries, individuals who had formerly been regarded as office boys for the notables. The result was two-

22. See *Atti e Documenti,* p. 803.

23. Amintore Fanfani, "Nuovo Imegno DC per il Mezzogiorno," in *Documneti della Democrazia Cristiana* (Roma, 1954), p. 15.

24. Amintore Fanfani, "La Democrazia Cristiana per le Aree Depresse," in *Documenti* (Roma, 1955), p. 15.

fold: it encouraged talented young people to seek political posts via organizational posts, and it gave them the incentive to strengthen the party organization in the process. It was no longer sufficient for an individual to be a prominent landowner or professional in order to run for office under the DC banner; he had to have experience in the party's bureaucracy first.

A third parallel to PCI campaigns in the South was evident in the DC's use of "Popular Assemblies" of representatives from all over the South. The rhetoric of participation and discussion employed recalled the PCI's "Assizes" of 1949–50, and the theme was the same: the people of the South were going to be organized from the top to participate from the bottom. Fanfani said, "From 1955 on, the DC will intensify the participation of the people of the South in the democratic control of the state activity." [25] Christian Democratic mayors were to gather the citizens in the local piazza once a year to explain their party's progress and goals; DC local and provincial councillors were to meet annually to "discuss action already taken and plan action to be taken"; and every year the DC would call a national conference "to discuss and criticize the development of the nation's policies for the development of the South on a national level." [26]

The first Popular Assembly in 1954 complemented the emphasis on organization with a truly popular platform. The order of the day approved by the delegates spoke of stimulating the industrial development of the South, the first time the DC had shifted from its traditional emphasis on agriculture. But it also made a straightforward appeal for the loyalties of the peasants, calling for "the extension of the Agrarian Reform into zones untouched by the laws already passed, and the completion of the reform where it has already begun with the full realization of all its economic and social goals." [27]

But the second Assembly in 1955 signified a shift in emphasis. Whereas the Assembly of Naples had made a strong appeal to workers and peasants, this meeting turned above all to the middle class:

25. Ibid., p. 23.
26. Ibid.
27. *Atti e Documenti*, p. 852.

The Assembly turns its particular attention to the middle class of the South, from whom the hope for justice and the belief in liberty has traditionally been fed, and expresses its faith, that . . . the work of the government will succeed in giving a new sense of dignity and better economic prosperity to the . . . middle class.[28]

On the subject of a general agrarian reform, however, the Assembly was now silent, calling only for the "completion of the reform" on land that had already been expropriated. The organizational theme remained; Fanfani announced the creation of 1,487 new sections, 1,839 new offices for existing sections, and 48,000 new members—all in the South!

Yet Fanfani called for the "acceleration" of the political development of the South through the organization of the southern middle class: "small family farmers, small merchants, white-collar workers, teachers, professionals and journalists."

The DC does not renounce its original solidarity for the poor and the proletarians, solidarity which commits it to continue programs of reform . . . but the DC must not fail to accentuate its self-conscious national inclination to protect as well the *frames and hinges of the social system*.[29]

The DC, Fanfani maintains in closing, must give the middle class of the South "a new force to assume willingly the functions of the *pilot* of southern Italian society."

This was a curious proposal, particularly when one remembers, first, that these so-called "frames and hinges" of the South were the major impediment to the improvement of the peasants' lot; second, that their economic functions were largely unproductive or intermediary; and, third, that many of them currently voted for the Monarchist and Fascist parties! Was Fanfani proposing a disguised return to the traditional clientele system? His language was disconcerting to the DC left. In 1954, he had proposed the following motion to the Congress of Naples:

28. Ibid., pp. 952–53.
29. Amintore Fanfani, "La DC per il Mezzogiorno nel 1955," *IIᵃ Assemblea* DC per il Mezzogiorno, Bari, 18 dicembre 1955, in *Documenti* (Roma, 1956), pp. 8–14.

> To maintain the necessary contact between the party's lead-
> ers and the electoral base, the Congress asks the National
> Council to effect . . . periodic consultations between the
> delegates of the party, on the one hand, and notable per-
> sonalities, on the other, who, because of their administrative
> and cultural experience and their social position, can be use-
> fully consulted regarding the public interest.[30]

These proposals, criticized sharply by the Christian Democratic
left wing,[31] suggest that Fanfani planned to use local middle class
notables to reach the poor and the proletarians who were otherwise indifferent to the party's organizers. But how could the appeal to the notables be reconciled with the organization of a
modern mass party with progressive goals?

Confusion on this question extended to the PCI, whose leaders,
currently making their own Herculean efforts to organize the
South, had watched Fanfani with interest. At first, Communist
reactions were enthusiastic. One leader wrote, "We must not underestimate the importance of the attempt to create a DC with its
autonomous organization in the South, one which will no longer
be based only on the old southern clienteles and on the institutions
of the Church." [32]

But as Fanfani's emphasis shifted from the peasants to the
middle class, and from progressive to moderate programs, southern Communists changed their opinion.

> It is true that one element in Fanfani's organizational cam-
> paign was the attempt to create a new personnel, a new lead-
> ership, more modern politically and organizationally . . .
> but this attempt, if in several cases it led to a battle with the
> old leaders of the party, in other cases was combined with an
> attempt to *absorb* the old political personnel.[33]

30. *Atti e Documenti*, p. 782. Emphasis added.
31. See the speeches of Sullo, Rampa, Oliva, and Zaccagnini in "Il Consiglio
Nazionale DC del 12–14 marzo, 1955," *Documenti* (Roma, 1955).
32. Gerardo Chiaramonte, "I Congressi Democristiani nel Mezzogiorno," *Cronache Meridionali, 6* (novembre 1959), 735.
33. Giorgio Napoletano, "Per un Bilancio del Fanfanismo nel Mezzogiorno,"
Cronache Meridionali, 4, No. 11 (1957), 728–34.

The third and last Popular Assembly for the South in 1957 was directed mainly at the coming elections of 1958, and added nothing to earlier programs except to dilute their progressive origins still more. But the DC's organization had never functioned as well, and while its share of the vote remained stable at 41 percent in the North, it regained its 1953 losses in the South, increasing its percentage of the vote from 38 percent to 44 percent.

But while the public image Fanfani had tried to project was progressive, the party's gains in the South were mainly made at the expense of the far right, which fell from 26.5 percent in 1953 to 19 percent in 1958. The Communist vote continued to rise, increasing from 21.4 percent in 1953 to 22.2 percent in 1958. The DC paradox in the Mezzogiorno was still unresolved; it was still a party of the center, with left-leaning inclinations, which received the bulk of its votes from the right. How had the DC succeeded in gaining many thousands of votes from the far right in 1958 while its programs continued to call for progressive reforms?

The answer began to become clear during the last years of Fanfani's secretaryship of the party. The DC is the party in power. Apart from the Agrarian Reform, the government's program for the South was far from revolutionary. In fact, it was mainly a program of mass patronage, which could gather votes for the party from all groups and shades of opinion in the South. The Cassa per il Mezzogiorno, for example, although formally independent of the ordinary ministries, is paralyzed in its independence, for it is directed by a minister without portfolio and an interministerial committee assisted by a secretariat. The ministerial committee and its secretariat are separate legally and politically from the Cassa.[34] By separating the leadership of the Committee of Ministers from that of the presidency of the Cassa, the government effectively destroys the minister's power to control his own agency. As the present minister, Giulio Pastore, complained in 1965, he was responsible to parliament for the budget of the agency, a budget which, as minister without portfolio, he had no power to influence! [35]

34. See Law of August 10, 1950, No. 646, Article I, *Codice Civile Italiano*.

35. Giulio Pastore, *Politica Nuova per il Mezzogiorno,* Discorso Pronunciato alla Camera dei Deputati il 18 maggio, 1965 (Roma, 1965), p. 28.

Second, the recruitment of Cassa personnel from other Italian ministries and the agency's effective independence from the ministerial committee and its secretariat subjects it easily to the pressures of parliamentarians and local power groups. Hence its expenditures have not always been guided by economic rationality or planning goals, but by the rationality of the ballot box and the goals of local political interests. Thus, the ultramodern soccer stadium in Naples was built with funds appropriated through the Cassa, and much of the money appropriated as subsidies for "industrial training schools" is used to finance courses in dressmaking or needlework given by local churches.

Despite the vast amount of funds spent on the South, the economic imbalance between North and South increased between 1950 and 1965. First, the existence of this extraordinary agency convinced the ordinary ministries to spend less in the South. Second, it was clear that the pattern of spending on visible public works and agriculture was not producing a self-sustaining process of growth in the Mezzogiorno. Accordingly, with the urging of the secretariat of the Committee of Ministers, a new law was passed in 1957 which took the Cassa into a second stage of its life: the stage of direct incentives to industry. Rates of interest were lowered and fiscal exemptions established, the state-run industries of IRI and ENI were required to invest at least 60 percent of their new investments in the region, and loans and grants were advanced to private firms in the industrial sector. Moreover, it was decided to concentrate the efforts of the Cassa in "areas and nuclei of industrial development" throughout the South that were particularly susceptible to industrial investment.[36]

However, the technique for the designation and financing of these areas once again neutralized whatever economic rationality they might have had. While the Committee of Ministers had envisioned "a limited number of industrial areas of development," it was decided that the initiative for their constitution must come from local syndicates that would include the representatives of public and private agencies. These syndicates were to form a de-

36. Comitato dei Ministri per il Mezzogiorno, *Istituzione di Nuclei di Industrializzazione nel Mezzogiorno* (Roma, 1960), pp. 13–14.

velopment plan which would be approved by the Committee, paid for by the Cassa, and executed by the syndicate itself.

This technique led to the approval, not of *ten* areas of development, as had been contemplated, but *thirty-nine,* many of which had little chance of industrialization, but had been created under the combined pressure of the local public and private agencies that made up the syndicates. Hence, despite its shift from public works and agriculture into industry, the Cassa per il Mezzogiorno continues to act as a dispenser of more or less large-scale patronage for the Christian Democrats. This has led to a continual outpouring of funds in some areas that show little sign of economic "take-off" and in others that have developed so rapidly that their major problem is congestion, rather than depression.

As a result of the continual rise in mass patronage administered by the Cassa per il Mezzogiorno, the DC's losses in the elections of 1963 were registered mainly in the North; in the South, the party controlled over 42 percent of the vote, as compared to 38 percent nationally. But with the constitution of a coalition government with the Socialists in 1963, a paradoxical situation faces the DC. The new government has instituted a national economic planning commission whose task will be to plan investment for the entire country. How can the independent existence of the Cassa per il Mezzogiorno be justified in the face of these changes, and, more important, how can it continue as a reservoir of patronage for the DC if the new unified Socialist Party controls the planning agency?

A similar predicament confronts the DC regarding the problem of administrative decentralization. Italian municipalities and provinces have long lacked the resources and powers to solve their crippling financial problems. This is particularly true of the South, where low per capita income limits local governments' revenue from taxation. The Constitution envisages the formation of semifederal governments to confront this problem, but progress in implementing this provision has been blocked by the Christian Democrats. Two reasons underline the party's reluctance; first, regional governments in Tuscany and Emilia would undoubtedly come under the control of the Communists; second, the existence of regional governments in southern Italy would free the region from dependence upon the national bureaucracy (and therefore the DC). Major patronage would shift from the Cassa per il Mezzogiorno and the Ministry of Public Works to the independent *ente regione,* depriving the DC of its most important electoral weapons in the Mezzogiorno.

The entire nature of the center-left coalition re-poses the paradox that has faced the DC since its constitution in 1943, particularly in the South. How can a party that continues to gather the votes of the right move leftward without losing its majority? How can it deal with the contradiction, particularly in the South, "between political leaders oriented toward conservatism, clientelism, against the interests of the South, [and] a policy with an inspiration from the left." [37] The DC in the South has not tried to solve this dilemma, for while such a solution would go far in resolving the persistent problems of the South, it would "prove very unhappy for the circles which have traditionally held power in the South and which still hold it." [38]

ORGANIZATION AND LEADERSHIP

This brief history of the Democrazia Cristiana in southern Italy underscores a point made earlier: that the DC, like the Communists, has had to grapple bodily with the objective conditions of southern Italy. The party has confronted the same contradictions between traditional voters and progressive programs, and the same problems of localism, personalism, and social disorganization. But how has the DC emerged from its campaign for the "political development" of the Mezzogiorno? Has it become a modern mass party, or has it become the servant of the old clientele structures, as Communist and left-wing Catholic critics conclude?

At first glance, the evidence points clearly to the first alternative. Between 1955, the first year for which we possess official statistics, and 1963, the number of DC sections in the South rose from 3,980

37. Francesco Compagna, "Mezzogiorno, Classe Dirigente, Centro-Sinistra," *Nord e Sud, 11,* No. 43 (1964), 6.

38. Ibid., pp. 10–11.

to 4,570, a gain of 14 percent. But even when Fanfani's secretary-ship ended in 1959, the DC organization in the South continued to grow.[39] The number of sections increased 9 percent between 1958 and 1963.

The number of members registered in the DC was 1,606,400 in 1959. However, unlike the Communists, who organize the majority of their members in northern and central Italy, the Christian Democrats find most of their organized membership in the South. According to statistics released at the Congress of Florence and published in the journal *Tempi Moderni,* 51.9 percent of these members are found in the South (excluding Lazio), 30.5 percent are found in the North (including Emilia), and 17.6 percent are found in central Italy.[40]

Moreover, DC membership in southern Italy increased dramatically during the 1950s. According to figures provided by the Istituto Carlo Cattaneo, 25.5 percent of the party's members came from the South in 1946 as compared to 46.4 percent in 1961. At the same time, membership in central Italy remained stable at about 20 percent, while DC registration in the North decreased sharply from 54.3 percent in 1946 to 29.8 percent in 1961. In absolute terms, party membership increased during this period; statistics for the 1940s are not available, but from 1953 to 1963, DC members increased from 1,142,000 to 1,621,600. In other words, the relative gain in the South more than compensated for the relative loss in the North.[41] To this extent, Fanfani's campaign for the "political" development of the South was a great success.

So great is the DC's membership advantage in the South that its ratio of voters to members is twice as favorable in the South as in the North. Table 12.1 shows that the ratio of DC voters to members in the North averages 11.4 to one and ranges from 7.2 to one to 17.9 to one, whereas in the South there are approximately five DC voters for every party member, and a range of from 4.0 to one to 6.0 to one. The strength of organized Catholicism in the South

39. From statistics furnished by DC Office of Organization, July 28, 1966.

40. Membership data are published in "La DC in Italia: Composizione Sociale, Struttura Organizzativa, Distribuzione Geografica delle Correnti," p. 12.

41. Istituto Carlo Cattaneo, *Le Organizzazioni Cattoliche* (Bologna, mimeograph, 1965).

TABLE 12.1

Ratio of Voters to Members of the Christian Democratic Party by Region

Region	Number of Voters (1958)	Number of Members (1959)	Number of Voters For Every Party Member
North			
Lombardy	2,003,267	155,400	12.9
Venice	1,274,257	124,400	10.3
Emilia	734,300	71,300	10.3
Tuscany	760,537	65,400	11.6
Piedmont	1,028,023	57,200	17.9
Marches	370,597	47,600	7.8
Liguria	446,493	30,600	14.6
Trento	199,805	27,800	7.2
Friuli	282,144	23,600	12.0
Umbria	170,237	18,800	9.1
South			
Sicily	1,079,865	207,500	5.2
Campania	1,029,963	183,700	5.6
Lazio	824,485	150,700	5.5
Puglia	794,196	143,900	5.5
Abruzzi	441,845	110,800	4.0
Calabria	483,121	96,800	5.0
Sardinia	337,492	56,200	6.0
Lucania	159,038	34,700	4.6

Source: "La DC in Italia," *Tempi Moderni*, 4 (1961), 14–16.

is remarkable. The DC organizes more people in Avellino than in Como, three times more in Foggia than in Florence, more in Catania than in Milano, and more in Cosenza than in Genoa, Turin and Venice put together.

The ratio of members to voters appears to ignore completely the traditional regions of Catholic strength. For example, in the two most traditionally religious provinces of Italy—Bergamo and Brescia—the DC gained 63 percent and 54.6 percent of the vote in 1963, but has only one member for every 9.8 voters in the former province and one member for every 9.7 voters in the latter. Both provinces are in the North. In Agrigento and Potenza, on the other hand, the party controls only 45.5 percent and 47.4 percent of the vote, but there is one party member for every 4.1 voters and one member for every 4.4 voters respectively.   These provinces are both in the South.[42]

However, although the DC has had immensely more success gaining party members in the South than the Communists, it has been harassed by the same problems of organizing these people into politically active organizations. First, the geographic distribution of party *sections* differs sharply from the distribution of party members. As Table 12.2 shows, only 27.9 percent of the party sec-

TABLE 12.2

Members and Sections of the Christian Democratic Party by Region

	Number and Percentage of Members	Number and Percentage of Sections	Average Number of Members per Section	Members as a Percentage of Adult Population
North	490,300	6,246		
	30.5%	53.0%	78.5	2.8%
Center	282,500	2,252		
	17.6%	19.1%	125.5	3.9%
South	833,600	3,281		
	51.9%	27.9%	254.1	6.4%
Total	1,606,400	11,779		
	100.0%	100.0%	136.4	4.4%

[a] *Note:* Since the Istituto Carlo Cattaneo considers Emilia a northern (and not a central) region, and Lazio a central (and not a southern) region, the entire table has been computed on that basis.

Source: Sections from Istituto Carlo Cattaneo, *Le Organizzazioni Cattoliche* (Bologna, mimeograph, 1965); membership computed from Table 12.1, above.

tions are found in the South, as opposed to 51.9 percent of its members! Thus, the average number of members per party section is 254 in the South, as opposed to 78.5 in the North and 125.5 in the Center. With such a vast number of members in each, it is difficult to conceive of these sections performing the tasks of a modern mass party in the South.

Second, the mass membership in the South is predominantly organized by right-wing Catholic factions, whereas northern members are predominantly left wing. The South, with a disproportionate share of the national membership, is also the heartland

42. "La DC in Italia," p. 16.

of the center-right and the right-wing DC factions. At its 1959
Congress, for example, the DC was divided into seven factions: two
left-wing groups, the *Base* and Rinnovamento, which represent
Catholic progressives and trade unionists; Fanfani's center-left faction; the center-right *Dorotei;* and three right-wing factions
grouped around the personalities of Scelba, Andreotti, and Pella.
The only organized faction with a truly national complexion were
the *Fanfaniani,* who derive their strength from Fanfani's five years
as general secretary. The other groups all have a regional base, with
the left-wing factions concentrated in the North and the *Dorotei*
and the right based largely in the South. In fact, it can be noted in
Table 12.3, that as one moves from left to right through the various
factions, the percentage of southern membership rises steadily from
a low of 31 percent for the left-wing factions to a high of 82 percent for the right.

TABLE 12.3

Factional Strength of the Christian Democratic Party by Region, 1959

| | *Faction* | | | | |
	Left	*Fanfani*	*Dorotei*	*Right*	*Total*
Total Membership	210,000	597,500	496,900	299,100	1,604,200
Number in South	65,200	316,800	328,300	245,100	955,400
Percentage in South	31%	52%	66%	82%	59%

Source: "La DC in Italia," pp. 18–20.

Some factions are present only in a narrow group of provinces.
The extreme case are the *Andreottini,* a right-wing group whose
entire membership is found *only* in the South, except for 6,000
northern members. The provincial breakdown of this faction's
membership is even more instructive; of a total of 218,000 members, 116,000 are registered in Rome and its region of Lazio, where
Andreotti's constituency is found. The rest are scattered throughout the South.

The left-wing factions, on the other hand, find most of their
members in the industrial centers of Lombardy and the Veneto, in
the far North. However, a large bastion of Catholic labor strength

is found in the South in the province of Avellino, where 32,500 trade union faction members live. This is a curious fact, since there are less than 32,500 Catholic trade union *members* in the province. The large number of votes contributed to the trade union faction at the 1959 Congress (and the absence of any other organized faction) can only be attributed to the fact that the local deputy, Fiorentino Sullo, is one of the national leaders of the faction. According to party observers, Sullo and Andreotti, who occupy completely opposed factional positions, collect thousands of Congress votes with exactly the same methods. Andreotti is said to organize summer camps for children of his constituency with secret funds from the Defense Ministry budget, while Sullo has used his position as Minister of Public Works to put thousands of his followers to work on government projects.

The strength of the right-wing DC factions in the South and the overall weakness of the left is puzzling when one recalls that the presidency and the secretariat of the Committee of Ministers for the Mezzogiorno have been in the hands of left-wing Catholics since the creation of the Cassa per il Mezzogiorno. Yet despite their enthusiastic espousal of progressive programs for the South, and the lever they hold on massive state patronage, the base of Catholic membership strength in the South is still essentially right wing.

Third, the image of the DC as a popular mass party is weakened still further by what are, to say the least, spontaneous recruiting practices. From 1954 onward, leaders have complained of strange anomalies in membership lists. Many party membership cards, it appears, have been issued either to people who do not actively use them or have no idea they have been issued. As a leader complained at the Conference of Sorrento, "In some places, the DC has a number of registered members actually higher than the number of voters. . . . We must begin to set up methods of controlling entrance into the ranks of the party."[43] Another delegate was more explicit, "It is not that we lack the number of party members or even the register of their names . . . the problem is that in

43. "Intervento dell'onorevole Pella all'Assemblea Nazionale di Sorrento," in *La Discussione, 13,* Nos. 617–18 (1965), 32.

some cases *we lack the individual, or at least his express desire to be a member.*" [44] The overwhelming number of false membership cards have been found in the South.

What motivates local party leaders to present false membership lists to national DC headquarters? One thinks first of the traditional reason, that politicians want to appear more powerful to the public or the trade unions than they really are. But in this case, the cause is more internal than external; the strength of DC factions at national congresses depends upon the number of registered members enrolled in each faction. The presentation of inflated membership lists increases the weight of the various factions at the national congress. Hence the race for new members, real or imagined, becomes a race for members committed to a particular faction. The logic works both ways; provincial leaders are sometimes unwilling to admit new members to the party when it is plain that they will swell the files of a competing faction. "Mysterious obstructionism exists in many places, where leaders attempt to prevent an influx of new members who will cause changes in the equilibrium of the factions." [45] The power of right-wing factions in the South, therefore, may be taken, not so much as an expression of mass opinion, but as the expression of conservative leaders' control of the membership lists.

But if the DC in the South is conservative and poorly organized, is it also simply a re-creation of the old clientele system? Were Fanfani's organizational reforms merely a cloak for the reconstitution of the old system of transformist cliques, or has a genuine shift in organization and leadership come about? To help answer this question, interviews were carried out with DC party officials and parliamentarians, Catholic trade union leaders and the leaders of other Catholic affiliates, government officials connected with programs in the South, and observers and journalists who have seen the party at close range for many years. Most of the informants were selected from the middle leadership range of their organizations, although a few had held high office in the past.

The results of this inquiry were paradoxical. The informants,

44. "Intervento di Elkan," *La Discussione,* p. 26. Italics added.
45. Ibid.

Catholic and non-Catholic, were almost unanimously agreed that Christian Democracy in the *Mezzogiorno* is dominated by clientelismo. However, almost as many maintained that the party had been transformed during the last ten years, mainly during Fanfani's campaign of "political development"! According to these informants, however, the transformation did not turn a party of notables into a modern mass party, as had been hoped, but *suffused the structures of the mass party with the political techniques that are native to the political culture, a parallel structural evolution to the one described in the case of the* PCI.

To illustrate this phenomenon and to explore some of its ramifications, a sampling of interview responses follows. In response to the question: "How would you characterize the Democrazia Cristiana in the South, in comparison with the DC in the North?" a former DC national youth leader said:

> The southern DC leaders are always hynotized by the conquest or the preservation of local power, demonstrating that they are incapable of coordinated activity and of coherent programs. The South, a stable factor in national politics, is based upon great internal instability—the constant merry-go-round of cliques in which no meaningful ideological tension is to be found.[46]

A leader of another DC affiliate said:

> Very often, it is almost "tribal" factors that influence electoral results; ancient rivalries exist between families and groups, sometimes related to agricultural marketing interests, in which, if one family is Christian Democratic, the rival group will certainly be Communist.[47]

A DC southern deputy made the following comment:

> It is clear that different economic situations and historical vicissitudes have assured that the political nature of all the parties in the South is different from those in the North. Many clientelistic methods widely used in the South do not

46. Interview, May 25, 1966.
47. Interview, July 14, 1966.

exist, or exist only superficially, in the North. . . . In the DC in the South, we unfortunately have not succeeded in forming a real class of professional political leaders.[48]

All of the informants made similar, if less articulate, responses to this question. Only one official denied that there was any essential difference between the DC in North and South, but then went on to describe how he was elected as a local official in the South without campaigning, simply because he was supported by a powerful local group!

However, in response to the question: "Has there been any change in the structure of the Democrazia Cristiana in the South in the last ten years? If so, what change has there been?" over three-fourths of the informants responded that there had indeed been a major structural change. Some of the responses appeared at first to contradict answers to the preceding question. For example, a DC party official said:

Even if the South does have a particular political environment and is riddled with *clientelismo* which could not be transformed in a short time, Fanfani's program was undoubtedly effective. . . . Everyone participated, Congresses and meetings were successful, everyone worked and the ministers followed the directives of the party, even in the South.[49]

Another DC party official emphasizes the "new" factors:

The last ten years have seen a change in political leadership in the South which has replaced the old notables with a younger, more attractive group with new ways of conceiving reality.[50]

And a DC deputy also focused on change:

Given the conditions in the South, Fanfani did what he could to vitalize the party. With reference to the evolution of party leaders, there has been a transfer of power from the old notables to a more expert and energetic political class.[51]

48. Interview, July 7, 1966.
49. Interview, May 26, 1966.
50. Interview, June 20, 1966.
51. Interview, July 10, 1966.

The causes of change are seen as both subjective and objective:

> *Fanfanismo,* by giving more importance to the party organi-
> zation and to new personnel, was deeply involved in this
> process of change. But it could not be attributed so much to
> Fanfani as to a natural process of change in the socioeconomic
> and political system of the South.[52]

The link between "old" and "new" factors in the party is found
in its bureaucratic hierarchy, particularly in the secretaries of the
DC provincial federations. As was pointed out above, Fanfani had
made the federal secretaryship the jumping-off point to a prestigious parliamentary career. He also opened many parliamentary
posts to new contenders by a ruling that made parliamentary
mandate incompatible with many public appointments. Particularly in the South, this ruling had the effect of causing many old
nonprofessional notables to retire from parliamentary life and of
bringing younger, more progressive leaders to power.

What was the reaction of DC informants to these key reforms?
Mainly, it was negative, although all were agreed that they had
heralded a change. A party official said:

> Fanfani created a more efficient party, but he gave too much
> importance to the party bureaucracy, inserting them on elec-
> toral lists to allow them to control other leaders.[53]

A DC women's leader said:

> Unfortunately, the South is still under the control of clien-
> teles, which, in recent years, have become even worse. Once
> the clienteles were affective: for example, you voted for a
> man because your grandfather was his stablehand, and the
> clientele had a personal, even a moral basis. Now only the
> organizations of the party keep a clientele on its feet by
> giving them favors and concessions to take the place of the
> traditional authority they lack.[54]

In other words, as political power shifts from prestigious individuals to party organizations without a corresponding rise in

52. Ibid.
53. Interview, May 26, 1966.
54. Interview, July 14, 1966.

political ideology, patronage must take the place of personal loyalty as a basis of affiliation. Informants were almost unanimous in emphasizing the importance of patronage as the basis of the "new party" in the Mezzogiorno. But it is patronage channeled through an organization, rather than through a chain of individuals. As a former DC youth leader said:

> By giving greater political power to its organizational leaders, the DC transformed clientelismo of the notable into clientelismo of the bureaucracy. The party federation became the source of letters of recommendation, and many new deputies came out of the provincial federations.[55]

Who are the new leaders of the DC in southern Italy, and how does this new clientelismo of the bureaucracy operate? The *Annuario Politico Italiano* shows that the elections of 1958 and 1963 marked a radical change in the career origins of DC candidates. Whereas most successful candidates between 1946 and 1953 had been professionals or landowners, many of the new deputies came from the party's provincial bureaucracy or from three other groups: ex-administrators from the agrarian reform, ex-functionaries of state agencies active in economic development programs, and leaders of the DC youth movement or other affiliate groups.[56]

The professional political origin of the new Christian Democratic deputies means a new tone of political discourse in the South. As a journalist who has covered the DC for many years said in an interview:

> Christian Democratic congresses show that there is a new leadership group in the South, many of whom come from state agencies. They speak a new political language and are better equipped to deal with economic problems than the old leaders.[57]

The new language emphasizes planning and industrialization. Words like "economic take-off," "infrastructure," and "self-sus-

55. Interview, July 8, 1966.
56. Centro Italiano Ricerche e Documentazione, *Annuario Politico Italiano, 1964* (Milano, 1964), pp. 1261–1349.
57. Interview, June 12, 1966.

taining growth" have taken the place of the old personality-oriented polemics of southern Italian politics.

But the governmental origin of many DC leaders means a continual interpenetration between the state bureaucracy and the party and what many informants consider a "privatization of state power for personal political aims." One informant reports that "political leaders in the South are drawn from the new public agencies. . . . In Bari, many of the city councillors come from the Agency of Agrarian Reform in Puglia." [58] Another informant points out that "a confusion exists between political appointments and new officers in recently constituted state agencies. For example, the DC federal secretary of Matera is also president of the Syndicate of Industrial Development in that province." [59] The reform agencies are particularly guilty in this respect. As a government observer pointed out: "The DC in zones of agrarian reform was not very active because it felt itself represented by the reform agency . . . the DC placed some activists in the agency in strategic positions, particularly in the social services where they would be handing out benefits to the peasants." [60]

The frequent interchange of personnel between the DC and the state creates a situation of very close *parentela,* or family relation between the two. As one observer writes:

> It is enough to read any newspaper that sees the light of day in the South. It is never the state or the national community that appropriates sums for this or that project, for the construction of houses or schools, for the realization of public works or industrial programs: it is always thanks to the interest of this or that local deputy or the local secretary of the DC.[61]

The important point is that this is not the old-style patronage of the government job or the letter of recommendation. It is the mass patronage of the modern state and the mass party, distributed

58. Interview, June 11, 1966.
59. Interview, July 15, 1966.
60. Interview, June 9, 1966. Also see Giuseppe Galasso, "La Riforma Agraria in Sila," *Nord e Sud, 4,* No. 32 (1957), 9.
61. Mario Dilio, "Il Notibilato Meridionale," *Nord e Sud, 10,* No. 46 (1963), 48–49.

within the framework of a progressive program of economic development. Thus there is no contradiction between "old" and "new," or between the old political techniques and a modern economic development program. The DC has simply adapted the former to the goals of the latter.

The emphasis on economic development explains the "new language" of political discourse in the South. Deputies and local politicians who deal with problems of patronage must use the language of planning, because it is within the framework of planning that patronage is allocated. As an outside observer of the DC, himself one of the protagonists of the "Questione Meridionale," complained:

> The old world of the South is speaking the new language of planning, the language we introduced ten years ago. . . . We have the ludicrous situation of the most retrograde political figures now speaking the most modern and progressive language.[62]

A second informant, this time from within the government, was more explicit:

> The young leaders of ten years ago now aspire to the seats of the local deputies. . . . They have learned to use the state machinery to this end, employing the language they learned as idealists ten years ago.[63]

The first halting steps toward national economic planning have increased the importance of the "new language" in the South, for provinces can qualify for aid as "areas" or "poles" of development only by presenting economic plans to the Committee of Ministers for the Mezzogiorno. In Sicily, many provinces have called in economic consultants to prepare detailed and advanced development plans. These plans appear to be used mainly to convince national authorities that planning is being carried out. The regional government of Sicily has prepared a plan for agricultural development that is simply an adaptation of an old plan proposed by the Communist-led CGIL. There is no danger of the

62. Interview, June 22, 1966.
63. Interview, July 6, 1966.

plan being carried out, however, as it was mainly drafted to convince national credit agencies that planning was being done.

The prospect of national economic planning under the center-left government has created a paradox for southern Italian politicians. As long as "planning" was under the control of the DC-run Cassa per il Mezzogiorno, it could be quickly converted to patronage. However, under a planning commission that would be strongly influenced by the Socialists, the party would lose its major vote-getting tool in the South. As a result of this threat, the DC has been unwilling to concede any of the powerful perquisites of the Cassa per il Mezzogiorno to the Planning Commission. In the recent parliamentary debates on the renewal of the enabling law of the Cassa, the DC would not agree to discuss the Cassa in relation to national planning in general.[64]

What are the specific techniques of "clientelismo of the bureaucracy"? Certainly, many of the traditional techniques are still in force. One respondent reports that in an inquiry he carried out in Matera, he discovered that the Christian Democratic mayor was the godfather of hundreds of peasant children. Godparenthood is still important for deputies, too, many of whom "attend hundreds of baptisms a year, rather than spending their time on more pressing matters." [65]

Second, the public payroll still operates as an effective means of gathering loyal supporters. In the province of Potenza, for example, there are very few roads, but hundreds of road workers, most of whom carry a DC party card. Of course, this type of recruitment operates efficiently only in the poorest zones of the South, where alternative economic positions are limited. However, a new kind of job-finding operates where ENI or IRI state industry or state-supported big industry has emerged. Since these new industries are required by law to hire local workers, it is inevitable that the criteria of hiring should be political, particularly where thousands of unskilled applicants are competing for relatively few jobs. Local priests, public officials, and labor organizations are all employed by the job seeker for their support.

64. *Atti Parlamentari,* Camera dei Deputati, IVª Legislatura, Discussioni, seduta del 7 maggio, 1965, pp. 14,976–15,203.

65. Interview, July 4, 1966; and Interview, May 25, 1966.

A study of the Edison-Sincat plant near Siracusa concludes that job applicants "base their work chances not on what they know, but on the prestige and authority of 'who' can effectively exert pressure on the firm and testify to their need, their good will, and their integrity." [66]

Third, and most important of the traditional techniques, is the letter of recommendation. Letters to the Prefecture to support a land claim, to the Ministry of Education to bolster a student's application, and to one of the credit institutions connected with the Cassa per il Mezzogiorno to ask for business grants are the most sought-after communications. The major target of recommendation seekers, of course, is the local deputy, but DC provincial federation secretaries and local dignitaries are also employed in this respect. All these people are surrounded by the mystique of the anointed. As one observer writes: "The southern politician, the deputy, the mayor, but also the lawyer and professional, are still surrounded by myths in our towns . . . to reach him you must look for ways to get yourself introduced and wait for hours outside his office." [67]

But there are many indications that the recommendation has lost its effectiveness as a political tool. Admission to state schools has become more routinized than it once was, and government ministries maintain staffs to respond blandly to most requests. As a DC parliamentarian reveals: "Often the positive result of a job application or a ministerial grant is interpreted as the direct effect of a letter of recommendation, when it is really due to the merits of the candidate." [68]

Politics in the modern state is not responsive to the old-style patronage that flourished under clientelismo of the notable. The patent failure of the old system was that it strung out obligation along a thin vertical line of individuals, rather than aggregating interests horizontally. This failure is even more serious in a system in which jobs are created by the hundreds by bureaucratic organi-

66. Confederazione Generale dell'Industria Italiana, *L'Adattamento dei Lavoratori Siciliani in Una Grande Industria della Provincia di Siracusa* (mimeograph, n.d.), p. 19.

67. Dilio, "Il Notibilato Meridionale," pp. 48–49.

68. Interview, July 14, 1966.

zations as part of a program of economic development. The testimony of another highly placed DC observer is fairly convincing. He says:

> The internal structure of the clientele is pyramidal. At the top, there is the politician, at the second level his "great electors," and at the third level is the base, the mass of voters. The second level has direct ties of common interest with the summit, but the third level has no direct connection with the summit, but only with the hierarchy in between, and therefore receives very few direct advantages from its adhesion to this structure.[69]

And a third DC informant sums it up this way:

> Very often, the so-called recommendation is only an act. The politicians write a letter, obtain a response that the candidate will be taken into consideration, and the story finishes there. The real clientele is founded on a closer relationship that the deputy establishes with individuals who control blocs of votes—parish priests, trade union leaders, or other authoritative individuals—and these are the people to obtain the advantages.[70]

Modern politics in the South operates by the judicious manipulation of these blocs of votes through the allocation of economic development projects from the state. The ministerial telegram has become the favored technique for converting development projects into votes. The press is always full of announcements of these political grants. For example, "Because of the lively interest of the Hon. Marcello Chiatante, L.L.B., . . . another difficult problem of our city will be resolved, since he has obtained from his Excellency, Hon. Fiorentino Sullo, Minister of Public Works, sixty billion lire for the completion of a network of aqueducts." And again, "The Minister of Public Works . . . has telephoned to the mayor of Cava dei Tirreni . . . that, following his intervention at the Ministry of Labor, the commune of Cava dei Tirreni has been authorized to open the following public works." A cata-

69. Interview, July 14, 1966.
70. Interview, July 17, 1966.

logue of public works worth several hundred jobs follows.[71] One cannot help recalling the confidence with which Fanfani proclaimed the creation of "a politics of facts and ideas instead of a politics of agitation and macaroni."

Thus, the Christian Democratic Party in southern Italy has indeed replaced the old clientele system with something new, but that something new, as one informant said, is "a *horizontal* clientele system, one that substitutes for the lawyer or notable with great personal prestige the bureaucratic organization that offers economic development, on the strength of which it collects votes for the politician." [72]

THE NEW CLIENTELES

What are the links in these new "horizontal clienteles" that gather votes for the DC in southern Italy? There are, of course, the traditional sources: the mayor, the parish priest, the director of the state employment service. But these individuals have been surpassed in importance by the secondary associations that surround the party. Interviews were held with the leaders of several of these groups, many of whom have now moved on to other jobs in the Catholic political world. These interviews reveal the final stone in the political edifice that has been described in this chapter.

The first factor that emerged from many different interviews is the not surprising fact that the same secondary associations tend to perform different functions in North and South. As in Communist mass organizations, the DC youth movement "has found it hard to get new members to perform a continuous activity in the Mezzogiorno." Similarly, the Catholic Action Youth Movement (GIAC) found it easier to recruit young people in the South than in the North, but the difficulty of integrating their activities with the goals of the organization were immense. One informant said:

> Particularly among young women, recruitment was easier in the South, because Catholic Action was seen as a legitimate way to break free from the toils of the traditional southern

---

71. See "Il Notibilato Meridionale," and Maria R. Boensch, "La Carità Pelosa di Fiorentino Sullo," in *Il Borghese* (27 maggio 1963), p. 177.

72. Interview, June 22, 1966.

family. . . . The renunciation of earthly joys which Catholic Action asked of its members was easier in the South than in the North, because they possessed very few earthly joys to renounce.

The group organized "Weeks in the Villages," a sort of Catholic Peace Corps in which members lived in a village, helping the peasants with their work and demonstrating that the Church has a social conscience. But as economic prosperity began to reach the South,

> renunciation became more and more difficult. Southern Catholic Action youth members would seldom leave the movement as a result, however, preferring to compromise their beliefs with their new affluence. As a result, the personal relationships between the members and the priests became much more complicated, sensitive, and "political." [73]

Similar experiences were reported for the DC Women's Movement in the South where, according to officials, women who participate in DC politics are far more passionate about it than in the North. "In the South, the commitment is to the values of the family and the Church. In the North, political activism costs nothing, but in the South it often means persecution." The same informant pointed out that southern Italian women participate increasingly in political life. Over two hundred women now represent the DC as city councillors, and there are 15 DC women mayors throughout the South. The number is small compared to the 1,200 women in DC city-council posts in the North, but it is a radical innovation in a society like southern Italy. According to the same informant, women are the only DC candidates in the South who can be elected outside the party clienteles, a remarkable break with tradition.[74]

Christian Democratic economic organizations demonstrate the same division between North and South, such as, for example, the National Confederation of Direct Cultivators (Coldiretti), the Catholic group that organizes many of the small family farmers. According to a Coldiretti informant, the organization is stronger

73. Interview, May 25, 1966; Interview, June 26, 1966.
74. Interview, July 8, 1966.

in the North than in the South because it possesses a group of trained agents there who represent the peasants as a trade union. In the South, such functions are performed very poorly. The Coldiretti in the South, according to an outside observer, have a "public assistance mentality," helping peasants with applications to the state, and operating the *Case Mutue,* the public insurance scheme for the peasants. However, unlike other DC (and PCI) organizations in the South, the Coldiretti does not suffer from organizational incapacity, since it has adapted the old Fascist pattern of organizing small farmers as a corporate group of the state. Inevitably, the peasants are represented poorly, but they are organized well.[75]

Another DC organization with great relevance to the South is the Italian Catholic Workers' Association (ACLI), which was organized with the stated goal of "preparing" Italian workers for trade unionism. Whatever that means in the North, where trade unions have been active for over sixty years, its political implications were clear in the South, where both the CISL and the CGIL have to struggle for members. The ACLI has the following official functions: (1) the intellectual formation of workers, (2) social action and education, and (3) social service, such as recreation, tourism, cooperatives, and the processing of applications for pensions or insurance.

It is paradoxical that in the South, precisely where its function in the formation of a working class is most important, the ACLI is organized primarily for the provision of social services and assistance. As one ACLI leader said: "In the South, the ACLI is organized for the provision of services rather than as a social movement. We should really occupy the same political space in the South as Danilo Dolci, but, in reality, our local leaders have been captured by the politicians." According to a second informant, "capture by the politicians" has a very specific meaning in the Mezzogiorno, since local ACLI presidents have complete autonomy. "Because it is hard to implement a general policy for the South, the organization works only as a recreational center and as a means of public assistance, but not for the formation of the working class." [76]

75. Interview, July 14, 1966; Interview, July 6, 1966; Interview, July 9, 1966.
76. Interview, July 2, 1966; Interview, July 11, 1966.

In other words, in the South, where a new working class is emerging, the ACLI, constituted to aid in the formation of a working class conscience, operates mainly as a center of patronage.

The DC's most important affiliate is the Catholic trade union federation, the CISL. As in the case of the Communist-dominated CGIL, the CISL arrived in the South in the train of the political party; it has never quite emerged from an initial sense of dependence. Realizing that CISL local organizers in the South were not motivated by working class ideals, a group of intellectuals at the trade union federation's national office began a campaign of organization and recruitment in the South in 1953. It had become clear, as one CISL official expressed it, that "local CISL officials, who came almost entirely from middle class backgrounds, represented, not the interests of the Catholic trade union movement, but their personal relationships with officials of the state agencies." It was recognized that "the action of the CISL must be planned with the maximum of elasticity to respond to environmental situations," and that because the Confederation in the South "has until now passively accepted the pressures of various groups" it needed most of all "a new type of working class leader" who could "constantly pressure the government and its agencies for a more effective intervention in economic life." [77]

To effect this transformation, two major steps were taken. First, a Permanent Office of Coordination was set up to send representatives to the various southern Provincial Unions to stimulate new trade union activity. These working groups "would locate themselves temporarily at the various Provincial Unions in the South, and interest themselves in projects that were being planned by the government, giving local trade union leaders a sense of the importance of trade union action and forcing the state to satisfy the interests of the workers." [78]

Second, a massive educational effort was launched to train new trade unionists from the South at the CISL school in Florence. Huge sums of money were appropriated "to extract the weak

77. Interview, June 12, 1966, and "La CISL per il Mezzogiorno," in CISL, *Bollettino di Studi e Statistiche*, 2 (agosto–settembre 1954), 27–31.

78. Luigi Macario, "Relazione," I° Convegno Nazionale per l'azione sindacale nel Mezzogiorno, in CISL, *Bollettino di studi e Statistiche, 4* (1956), 12.

structures of the Catholic unions from the pressures and interests of local groups." Seven specialized courses were set up to train organizers from specially chosen "economically homogeneous zones" of the South.[79]

What were the results of these organizational efforts, certainly the most serious made within the Catholic movement? Progress was slow in both organizational and training efforts. The "working groups" of special representatives to CISL provincial unions often met with an awkward reception. They were entering highly politicized political environments in which union officials, who lacked an autonomous power base, were dependent upon the DC and the state agencies for their support. Yet the interests they presumed to represent—those of the poor peasants and workers— were almost inevitably opposed to the politicians and bureaucrats whose support they needed. CISL working groups who tried to stir up disputes with the government were upsetting the entire local political equilibrium. As one CISL informant admitted:

> You felt like a guest who comes to someone's house, makes a racket that wakes the neighbors, and then goes off to leave him to mend his fences. Once you are gone, after having forced him to oppose the government, he has to go around making friends again with all those in the party and in the government whom you have offended.[80]

The CISL was forcing the hand of its local officials, trying to pull them out of the sticky net of local clientele politics and to oppose the policies of the government against their will.

Such a policy could only have limited results. It was only the long-term recruitment and training project in the homogeneous socioeconomic zones that could bear serious fruit. At first, the only possible way to raise the number of working class trade unionists in these zones was simply to import them from the North. In 1955, almost two-thirds of the leaders of the CISL in the Calabria were from the North. But, gradually, a true southern leadership was

79. Luciano Visentini, "I Dirigenti Sindacali nel processo di sviluppo nel Mezzogiorno," p. 28; CISL, "L'Azione Speciale per lo Sviluppo Organizzativo nel Mezzogiorno," in Atti del terzo Congresso Confederale (1959), pp. 103–06.

80. Interview, June 12, 1966.

developed; a survey carried out in 1965 showed that 82 percent of CISL southern leaders are now of southern origin.[81]

The growth in Catholic labor union members that was the goal of all this activity proceeded with mixed success. It is a smaller trade union federation than the Communist-dominated CGIL, with 2,400,000 members nationally as opposed to the CGIL's 3,496,-000.[82] In 1953, before the drive to organize the South began, the CISL had 814,000 of its members in that region, as opposed to the CGIL's 976,000. But as Table 12.4 shows, this figure already constituted 39.9 percent of the Catholic confederation's national membership, perhaps reflecting the DC's electoral supremacy in the South more than the success of Catholic labor organizers.

TABLE 12.4

CGIL and CISL Union Membership for Selected Years by Region[a]

		CGIL		CISL	
		1948	1962	1953	1961
North	(N)	2,824,926	1,360,464	890,628	1,056,674
	(%)	53.2	38.9	43.8	43.9
Center	(N)	1,505,880	1,210,382	331,171	396,846
	(%)	28.4	34.6	16.3	16.5
South	(N)	975,824	925,114	813,713	953,265
	(%)	18.4	26.5	39.9	39.5
Total	(N)	5,310,630	3,495,960	2,035,512	2,406,785
	(%)	100.0	100.0	100.0	100.0

[a] *Note:* The years for which figures are provided do not correspond because both confederations release membership statistics only intermittently.

Source: Istituto Carlo Cattaneo, *Le Organizzazioni di Massa* (Bologna, mimeograph, 1965).

The net result of the organizational campaign described above has been to increase CISL members in the South from 814,000 in 1953 to 953,000 in 1961, during a period in which membership in the Communist-led CGIL decreased to 925,000. But, despite an absolute increase in Catholic union members of over 125,000 in

81. "I Dirigenti Sindacali nel Processo di Sviluppo," p. 28.
82. Istituto Carlo Cattaneo, *Le Organizzazioni di Massa* (Bologna, mimeograph, 1965).

the South, the CISL still organizes 39.5 percent of its members in that region, virtually the same percentage as in 1953.

Although this gain in membership is far from negligible, it should be pointed out that it resulted not so much from the virtues of Catholic unionism as from its obvious advantages to the worker in getting a job with a private firm or public agency. A trade union leader complained that, in many cases, members of the Communist CGIL will enter the Catholic CISL to find a job and then return to the CGIL when they have one. This practice, condoned by CGIL leaders, leaves the Catholic CISL leaders perplexed.

CISL growth in the South has not been accompanied by the healthy withdrawal from dependence upon the government and the DC that its advocates hoped for in 1953. On the contrary, the CISL has successfully opposed the Communist-led CGIL in the South largely because of the patronage of state agencies, the DC, and employers. In line with the entire development in the DC from clientelismo of the notable to clientelismo of the bureaucracy, the CISL has been most heavily dependent upon the industries started by the state holding companies, IRI and ENI, and on big state-supported industry like the Edison-Sincat in Siracusa. It is indicative, for example, that the highest CISL membership gains in the South between 1950 and 1958 were in Puglia (70.3 percent) where the largest state investments have taken place. As a Communist critic of the DC has written, "The attempt to make the organizational strength of the CISL coincide with homogeneous socioeconomic areas has finished as an adaptation of CISL strength to the areas of greatest public spending in this or that locality in the South." An outside observer made the same comment in more extreme form. He said, "The CISL in the South is essentially a clientele system dependent upon state industry." [83]

This weakness, however, may eventually prove an advantage to the CISL. The Communist-led CGIL is still strong mainly among the agricultural workers (*the braccianti*) and the housing construction workers. The first category is diminishing as agriculture is rationalized and emigration increases, and the second group is dependent

83. From data furnished by the CISL, Centro Studi, July 30, 1966; Bruno Trentin, "Il Sindacato nel Mezzogiorno," in *Rassegna Sindacale*, 3 (1957), 228; and Interview, June 20, 1966.

upon a temporary housing boom. CISL strength, on the other hand, is found in flourishing new industries such as natural gas processing, chemicals, and metal-mechanics. Moreover, the CISL has a natural advantage in organizing women, who form an ever larger portion of the Southern Italian work force.

Each of the organizations discussed above—the Christian Democratic youth movement, the women's organization, the Coldiretti, the ACLI, and the CISL—has made its own particular adaptation to the political culture of southern Italy. These adaptations have in some cases been successful—for the CISL and the *Movimento Femminile,* in particular—but they have sometimes been discouraging—particularly in the case of the ACLI. But in each of these cases, the group has emerged from its encounter with southern Italy decidedly different from its counterpart in the North. While the actual adaptation differs from the adaptations to the South made by Communist mass organizations, the parallel processes suggest that political dualism conditions both political movements.

Two common factors appear to dominate the adaptation of the Catholic affiliates to the South: dependence on some aspect of government activity, such as public assistance or state industry, and the greater politicization of the leadership in comparison to the leadership in the North. These common characteristics emerged dramatically in interviews with leaders of these groups. For example:

> The leaders of both the CISL and the CGIL in the South are more highly politicized. Action vis-à-vis the state is more important to them. The CISL nationally has attempted to become less dependent on the DC, and in the North, where most organizers come from the factory, this has been successful. In the South, however, even when the trade unionist received his training outside of politics, he sees politics as his main road to success.[84]

As noted above, an ACLI informant observed that ACLI leaders in the South have been "captured by the politicians." The Coldiretti, which is basically an "organization of category" in the North, is

84. Interview, July 8, 1966; Interview, July 17, 1966; Interview, July 14, 1966.

led by politicians in the South, who present their own slates in elections.

Although the performance of specific economic or trade union functions is sufficient to free most DC secondary groups from direct dependence on the party in the North, in the South they operate as the intermediate links in the "horizontal clienteles" between the party and the voters. As an informant concluded, "It is enough in some places to get the support of some collateral organization of the DC to get yourself elected."

The evidence presented in this chapter, when examined in relation to the discussion of the Communist Party that has preceded it, may lead to a startling conclusion: that Communists and Catholics in southern Italy are exactly alike. No such conclusion is intended. Although the PCI and the DC have experienced similar organizational problems and similar contradictions between ideology and mass following, they remain very different animals. I have spoken of the PCI in the South as a political movement; while leaving further analysis of the Communist Party for the following chapter, it may be useful at this point to classify the DC in southern Italy more definitely than has been done up to now.

In the North, the DC has a mass organization, a broad membership, and a coherent ideology, all of which set it apart from the DC in the South. In the latter region, the mass organization of the DC is based not upon spiritual or ideological adherence, but upon patronage allocated through the party and its secondary organizations and facilitated by the party's control of the government. Its ideology does not fit its followers' goals, but it does mesh smoothly with the provision of mass patronage. The apparent contradiction between progressive ideology and conservative supporters is resolved by this: progressive language is used to symbolize opportunities for patronage.

There is an almost horrifying familiarity about Christian Democracy in southern Italy, in its juxtaposition of modern organization with personalistic allegiance, and of progressive ideology with mass patronage. It is virtually identical in all its essential features to the political machine in the United States in the period when large immigrant populations combined with embryonic economic growth allowed political leaders to make patronage the major weapon of political success. The parallel is instructive: the passage of the DC in the Mezzogiorno from clientelismo of the notable to clientelismo of the bureaucracy, and the change from vertical to horizontal clienteles, essentially follows the evolution of the party machine in America. American parties eventually became bureaucratic parties of patronage rather than the parties of notables they had been or the mass parties they were expected to become.

It is not necessary to celebrate this resemblance in order to appreciate its importance; the American political machine, whatever its failings, was a superb invention for the exercise of political power in a rapidly developing society. Unlike the old party of notables, it was not tied to the interests of a social and economic elite. It could thereby serve as a mobility channel for members of low-status ethnic groups who would then use their control of patronage to expand economic opportunities among their brethren. While the ethnic dimension is lacking in southern Italy, Christian Democratic recruitment has extended far beyond the old elite, and the party's use of patronage has certainly been incremental rather than selective.

Linked to the incremental use of power was the nonideological character of the American machine, for a strong ideological dimension would have wrecked the system's most important feature, its capacity to distribute rewards to all who could vote. As it was, the machine could encompass new ethnic groups without incurring an ideological rift within its membership. While the ethnic dimension is, once again, missing, the Christian Democratic Party in southern Italy demonstrates a similar orientation, for example, in the coexistence of its left-wing trade unionists with conservative local notables.

The ability of the American machine to encompass new groups through broad allocation of resources points to a third parallel with Italian Christian Democracy: its power of discouraging the growth of irreconcilable opposition groups by buying off their potential followers. In every area of politics, the Christian Democracy has created secondary organizations to counter Communist ideological appeals with mass or individual patronage. Nothing is more enervating to an ideological opposition than a government machine that refuses to behave as the narrow protector of ruling class interests. Faced by a choice between seed and ideology, it was not difficult to predict what the peasant would choose.

This is the paradox of Communism in southern Italy. For a variety of reasons, although the Communists began the transformation of the South it was the Catholics who completed it. And they have done so amid the ruins of the old clientele system that the Communists did most to destroy. If the postwar period began with the protest march and the struggle for the land, it has finished in the arena of day-to-day southern politics, where the Christian Democrats, with the resources of the Church and State at their command, have been as inventive as the Communists.

But what of the peasant? Between Communist mobilization and Christian Democratic state patronage, has he succeeded in overcoming his elemental disorganization? Has he ceased to be the displaced person of southern Italian politics, or is he as much a dependent of the new structure of power as he was of the old?

13. The Demobilization of the Peasants

Always the same song with the same chorus. Always. The years passed on and accumulated. The young became old and the old people died. . . . And the planting, the weeding, the spraying, the reaping and the gathering went on. . . . No one at Fontamara had ever thought this way of life could change.

IGNAZIO SILONE

Fifteen years after the passage of an agrarian reform, southern Italy has, in fact, changed. The land has been transformed, the once-denuded mountains are covered with trees, and the peasants' life is better than it was. Some have grown rich, many read, and all watch television at the local bar or party office. If a stranger is still watched with suspicion as he crosses the piazza, that is the nature of a peasant society and may never be any different.

What has been the impact of all this change upon political development? In a certain sense, that has been the subject of this whole book. For if politics was once dominated by landed proprietors, the Agrarian Reform has changed all that. If the government in Rome was remote and uncaring, the number of Cassa per il Mezzogiorno signs along the roads belie that image. And if political discourse dealt in personalities and bleeding words for the peasant, that too is changed, for now left and right both talk the language of economic planning.

But what is puzzling about the Mezzogiorno is the extent to which, as in other developing countries, the old is visible just beyond the shadow of the new. The crime of honor still seems reasonable in a modern legal system. The Mafia has given up running candidates, but it controls real estate. The government clerk will still give you grudging service if you are related to the local deputy—of whatever party.

There is something almost spectral about this kind of modernization. We are all by now familiar with the aphorism that political development does not precisely follow the lines of economic change. If it did, we would have grown to look like one another long before this. But is it possible that a process of economic and social change as deep seated as the one described in the preceding chapters could have occurred without a simultaneous process of political development?

In fact, there has been a very basic political change in the Mezzogiorno: in the transformation of clientelismo of the notable into a system of political power based upon bureaucratic mass patronage and in the creation of an organized opposition party. But despite these changes, the political system is not becoming simply another version of politics in northern Italy. As Schumpeter and Marx both loved to point out, the historical legacies of a society do not simply disappear when that society passes into a new period of its development.[1] Old and new combine in ways that no one could have successfully predicted.

The most telling example of this permeation of the forces of change with the habits of tradition in the Mezzogiorno is in the behavior of both major political parties with respect to the peasantry. In fact, it is in this crucial area that the pattern of political change now under way in the Mezzogiorno is most abundantly clear. The peasant, out of his traditional mixture of lassitude and revolt, was mobilized to conquer the land he had sought for generations. But in a curious way his economic triumph has meant his political failure, a failure so complete that it might well have been the fruit of the collaboration of both political parties.

THE POLITICS OF AGRARIAN REFORM

"Reforms are a season of seeding and not of harvest," said the political secretary of the Democrazia Cristiana just after the

---

1. Joseph A. Schumpeter, *Capitalism, Socialism and Democracy* (New York, 1962), p. 12. Schumpeter writes, "Social structures, types and attitudes are coins that do not readily melt." His statement is intended as a critique of Marxian "determinism," but Schumpeter had probably not seen the following statement of Marx's, which relates to the different *political* pattern in different historical settings; "Thus events strikingly analogous but taking place in different historical surroundings led to totally different political results." See "Russia's Pattern of Development," in Lewis Feuer, ed., *Marx and Engels: Basic Writings on Politics and Philosophy* (New York, 1959), p. 441.

party's substantial electoral losses in the South in 1953.[2] And indeed the Catholics, who had just conceded more than 600,000 hectares of land to the peasants, had been badly burned in most of the areas of reform. The right wing of the party, always powerful in the South, soon reacted violently, calling for the overthrow of De Gasperi's moderate leadership.

The real question was where the DC had lost all the votes: from the injured landowners and their middle class sympathizers, or from the peasants who had received the land at the hands of the party? It was clear that the provincial capitals—inhabited largely by landowning and middle class groups—had voted strongly for the far-right Monarchists and Neo-Fascists. But then, these groups had been nostalgic reactionaries since the election of 1946. The *new* losses, it was reasoned, must therefore come from the peasants in the areas of reform.

Very quickly, a host of studies was prepared by many interested parties, among them the Christian Democrats, the center-left journal *Nord e Sud,* and the American Embassy.[3] All of these studies showed that there had been a rise in Communist voting in towns where the reform had penetrated, despite the concession of the reform. But since a Communist gain was verified *throughout* the South, there was some doubt as to the causal effect of the Riforma.

For example, in the regions of Puglia-Lucania-Molise, one study showed that the Christian Democrats lost an average of 6.1 percent in the reform communes, but lost 10.2 percent in the other communes. The Communists and Socialists had gained 2.7 percent in the reform communes, but gained 7.8 percent in communes where the reform had not penetrated. Similar results were found in other regions of agrarian reform. Moreover, the vote in the reform communes was not always pleasing to the Communists. For example, a PCI internal document was quoted as saying, "In general, we have not succeeded in creating a wide and adequate

2. See Chap. 12 on the Christian Democrats' reaction to its electoral losses in the South.

3. See Achille Ardigò, "Considerazioni sugli Effetti Politico-Sociali della Riforma Fondiaria," in *Dal Latifondo al Podere, Atti del Convegno degli Assegnatari DC delle Terre di Riforma Fondiaria* (Roma, 1955); also see Francesco Compagna e Vittorio De Caprariis, *Geografia delle Elezioni Italiane, 1946–1953* (Bologna, 1954).

spectrum of working class forces to oppose the policies of the reform agencies. Small isolated groups of peasants have not been strongly supported against the agencies, a factor that has resulted in losses here and there." [4]

That the PCI gain had been lower in the areas of reform than in the remainder of the South might have been the result of two very disparate factors: (1) many villages where the reform penetrated had already voted strongly Communist in 1948, and therefore Communist gains in these villages in 1953 were bound to be smaller than in the region as a whole; (2) the villages outside the reform areas might have voted more strongly Communist because the reform had not penetrated to their villages.

The counsels were confused. On the one hand, DC losses in the areas of reform convinced the right wing that the reform should not have been attempted; on the other, the larger losses where there was no reform convinced the left wing that it should have been extended all over the South.[5] Whatever the evidence, the Communists kept their own counsel. The Americans agonized within their palace on Via Veneto and aided a campaign to convince Italo-Americans to write to their erring relatives in the South, pointing out the virtues of capitalism.[6]

In reality, the voting patterns of the reform areas could not be understood as a simple function of who had gotten the land and who had not. By the election of 1958, it was clear that villages within the very same areas of reform showed great voting variations. Some were entirely dominated by the Communists and still are today; others wavered on the edge of left-wing majorities and then fell back to the Christian Democrats; and others have been Christian Democratic right along. In Chapter 7 I showed how this had occurred in the Fucino—one of the most important zones of reform, where virtually every town had participated in the tumultuous struggle for the land, but some are strongly Communist and others are Christian Democratic.

The cause of these peculiar discontinuities in voting behavior

4. Ardigò, pp. 239–40; Compagna and De Caprariis, pp. 52–53.
5. Ardigò, p. 250.
6. The study cited in Chapter 7, by International Research Associates, mentions these letters but does not state that they were solicited from Italo-Americans.

is not to be found in the impact of the Agrarian Reform itself, but in its implementation; not in the norms of the law, but in the behavior of the reform administrators. And in the politics of agrarian reform we are no longer dealing with the "new" in southern Italian politics, but with the very "old."

To begin with, the rapidity with which the land was expropriated threw all the major actors off balance. The law stipulated that plans of expropriation be compiled within six months, and that all the actual distribution be completed within three years.[7] The fact that this was largely accomplished within the stated period astounded all the interested parties; what Italian government had ever promised to distribute the land before and had actually done so? [8]

The initial effect was to dull the edge of the Communist political challenge. The PCI had voted against the reform laws, branding them inadequate ploys to fool the peasants. When the government actually proceeded in the formation of plans for expropriation within one year, the Communists were left unprepared.

But the speed with which the Riforma went into action had negative effects upon the reform agencies, too. Forced to organize rapidly in a hostile environment, the DC's eagerness to set right to work caused it to staff the reform agencies inadequately from the beginning. Early administrators were of two types. First, there were the old notables of the South—the lawyers, professors, and secular Catholic leaders—whose qualification for their position was sometimes having recently lost a seat in parliament. Second, in order to find people with more technical experience, the agencies had to turn to former administrators of the Fascist land reclamation programs.

The political approach of these two groups differed. The notables looked upon their positions as launching pads for future political careers. As one informant said, "When they ran out of money to spend, they lost their interest in acting." [9] The second

7. Giovanni Enrico Marciani, *L'Esperienza di Riforma Agraria in Italia*, p. 30.

8. Except where otherwise noted, the data that follow were provided by officials of the Agrarian Reform, the government, or by the Democrazia Cristiana and its various affiliates.

9. Interview, June 12, 1966.

group was far more competent, but their training in the old reclamation agencies had given them a purely technical approach to their jobs without preparing them to comprehend the broad social and political goals of the Riforma. "They had an ideal vision of the task before them; the only disturbing element was the human one—the peasantry. If they could keep that element outside the door, they would be able to accomplish everything they wanted to do." [10]

While the approach of the first group was highly political and that of the second was, if anything, apolitical, in an important sense they were complementary. For both, the peasant was the object of the Agrarian Reform, rather than its subject. In the assignment of the land and in the technical support the peasant later received from the agencies, the interplay of these two factors was critical for the entire pattern of political development of the South.

There was not much doubt that politics dominated in the allocation of the land. But it was politics with a peculiar double bent; the reform administrators attempted at the same time to favor supporters of the Christian Democratic Party and to co-opt militant Communist groups by including them in the reform. It is interesting in this regard to examine the differences in the land allocation techniques used in the South and those employed in northern Italy in the Po Delta Reform Agency. In the latter, the vast majority of the peasants were Communists and Socialists. "Even if you had wanted to, you couldn't discriminate against the left in that reform area." In the South, in contrast, "political positions were not fixed and stable; while the reform administrators were prepared to base allocations on political grounds, it wasn't always possible to know what a man was politically." [11]

The solution to the problem of assigning land to both DC supporters and PCI activists was found by manipulating the technique of the *quota*. As was explained in Chapter 11, the quota was a piece of land smaller than the allotment, one designed to help marginal farmers whose land was too small to support their

10. Ibid.
11. Interview, June 18, 1966.

families. In reality, the quota was seldom used merely to meet this economic need, but was used almost indiscriminately to distribute land to as many peasants as possible.

Thus, of the 46,000 *quote* distributed as of 1960, almost one-third had been assigned to landless agricultural day workers instead of small farmers.[12] When it is recalled that the average quota measured only 6 acres, it is difficult to conceive that economic criteria dominated the thinking of reform administrators.

In the Po delta, where the Catholics had little local political power, the reform administrators resisted the temptation to divide the land into plots too small to be economical. But in the South, many of the allotments were too small or too infertile to support a family adequately. In Sicily, the average allotment was only 4 hectares in size, and no distinction was made between an allotment and a quota.

The period that followed assignment of the land saw political criteria applied vigorously by the reform agencies in hiring personnel, in distributing seed and fertilizer, and in assisting the new peasant proprietors to make their farms a success. Individuals who had led the struggle for the land were treated with studious contempt; others were hired by the agencies or bribed with extra allotments. Particularly in Calabria, a number of peasant activists left the PCI for positions with either the reform agency or the DC. These defections caused great demoralization within the ranks of Communist voters. Some observers claimed to find a striking coincidence between the distribution of fertilizer and seeds and an increment of the Christian Democratic vote.[13]

The reform agencies soon became massive patronage organizations. In Sicily, it was pointed out that the Sicilian Reform Agency had over 2,500 employees in 1957, although less than 25,000 allotments were to be distributed in all. As a critic commented, "If you had used all the money spent for the running of that agency on the acquisition of land on the open market, it would have been possible to distribute as much land to the peas-

12. Marciani, pp. 90, 65.
13. Giovanni Cervigni, "Le Defezioni dal PCI in Calabria," *Nord e Sud*, 2, No. 6 (1955), 87.

ants for free as they were assigned by the reform." [14] Together with the Cassa per il Mezzogiorno, which began extensive public spending in the South during the same period, the reform agencies constituted an ideal way to pump a large amount of funds into the South in a short time. They employed people to clear the land, to build houses for the new owners, and to provide roads, reclamation, and irrigation. In the four-year period between 1952 and 1956, 155 billion lire ($250,000,000) were spent.[15]

One can scarcely question the need to support the new reform with enough investment to make it a financial success. It is even difficult to quarrel with the obvious political criteria used in the allocation of these funds, for what political party in power would do otherwise? What does, however, overawe the observer is the extent to which the economic stabilization of the peasants was achieved at the price of their political impoverishment. In this respect, the highly political approach of the DC notables and the apolitical approach of the reform agency technicians had the same goal.

The demobilization of the peasantry began after the reform agency acquired the land and decided upon its allocation, but had not yet prepared the farms for cultivation. Many peasants who were to become farm owners were still economically destitute. The reform agencies met this crisis by allowing many peasants to work their own future land in the capacity of dependents of the agencies, which still possessed title to the land! At the same time as the agency was supposed to be creating an independent class of small peasant owners, it was encouraging a mentality of dependence among these individuals. "This stratagem was defended as a means of supporting the peasants until the allotments were ready, but it delayed the direct participation of the peasant in the operation of his land and made it more difficult for him to develop an entrepreneurial spirit later." [16]

The same symptoms of dependence appeared in the cooperatives that the reform agencies created. To make the new peasant prop-

14. Antonio Ramirez, "Risultati e Limiti dell'Attuazione dello Statuto," *Cronache Meridionali, 4* (luglio–agosto 1957), 463–64.

15. Marciani, p. 180.

16. Interview, June 12, 1966.

erties truly stable, it was recognized that cooperatives were necessary for machinery, distribution, processing, and short-term credit. But since the Mezzogiorno had virtually no tradition of cooperation, the agencies (1) made membership in the cooperative obligatory, and (2) used their own officials to direct them.

Both actions had substantially the same result: the peasant looked upon the cooperative as a corporate arm of the reform agency rather than as an autonomous association of peasants. "Membership in the cooperative . . . became a simple act of registration. Nothing was provided in the rules regarding the obligation to actually use the services . . . in this sense, membership in the cooperative did not necessarily lead to results on the practical plane." [17] As a matter of fact, the peasants were not far wrong in seeing these organizations as organs of the reform agencies. They were used to carry out certain administrative needs of the agencies and to control the political life of the peasants.[18] Admittedly, the agencies' concern may be partly traced to their fear that the cooperatives would be Communist-dominated if left on their own, but in part their action resulted from simple paternalism.

The cooperative problem underscores the basic contradiction in the government's entire reform program. On the one hand, agrarian reform leaders called for "the autonomy of the peasant world" and the "formation from the bottom of initiatives of economic solidarity and of new entrepreneurs . . . instead of the agricultural laborer or the welfare recipient." [19] But on the other hand, these officials and their apologists defended the paternalistic nature of the cooperatives on the following basis: "In the formation of organizational cadres . . . for the creation of cooperatives . . . it is a premature hope to depend upon rural elites to accomplish the necessary organizational work." [20]

The result of this contradiction was the suppression of the political autonomy of the peasants. One writer sympathetic to the reform says,

17. Marciani, p. 125.
18. Ibid., pp. 124–32.
19. Tullio Botteri, *Le Cooperative nella Riforma Fondiaria Italiana* (Roma, 1961), pp. 92–93.
20. Ibid., p. 77.

"We must recognize that a certain paternalistic tutelage on
the part of the reform agencies was inevitable in these sectors, even if it sometimes crippled the social formation of the
peasants. . . . The concern with the product of the land as
such, without concern for the maturation of an entrepreneurial conscience in the peasantry, was felt in a highly imperious
way, on occasion verging on corporative solutions.[21]

The contradiction between goals and methodology of reform
was evident in a third, and perhaps most important, stage of the implementation of the reform—in the settlement of the peasants on
the land. The goal of the independent peasant owner, it was felt,
could best be achieved if the peasants lived as close as possible to
their new land. In preceding chapters I have discussed the urban
character of the southern Italian peasantry, and the need for the
peasant to walk miles to his little plot of land, carrying the burden
of his tools or produce on his back.

The government decided to end this pattern by settling the
peasants in isolated houses on their own land, breaking up the
social patterns of generations, much as American urban renewal
experts sometimes break up a community in order to move slum
dwellers to better housing. There was, however, a critical difference. The Agrarian Reform administrators appear to have been
thoroughly aware of the breakdown of community their plans
might cause. For the gregarious southern peasant, nothing was
more inimical to the weak sense of association he already possessed
than being removed from village life.

To replace the amenities of the village, the reform administrators decided to build what they called "service centers" near the
new peasant allotments. Typically, these centers would contain a
church, a few stores, and a police station. There was no planning
for social or community organization and no political entity. Today, the basic problem of the peasants who have received land
from the Agrarian Reform is the absence of a community organization to provide them with entertainment, mutual aid, and, most
important, a political identity. As one observer said, "The Chris-

21. Ibid., p. 111. The author uses the term "collective solutions," but the term
has been translated as "corporative solutions" because he is clearly referring to the
Fascist experience.

tian Democrats failed to create new communities, or even physical entities that could one day become communities. The latifundia were destroyed, but no new social and political organization was provided to prevent the peasants' utter isolation on the land." [22] Many peasants have responded by leaving their perfectly good land either to return to their miserable, but congenial, village life or to emigrate to urban centers in the North.

If the major social malaise of the southern Italian peasantry has always been its "disaggregated" nature, then by settling the peasant on an isolated farm, the government has replaced his old *occupational* fragmentation by a new *geographic* isolation. Similarly, if the traditional political liability of the peasant was his dependence on the landowner, the Christian Democrats, by treating him paternalistically, have transformed him into a dependent of the state. Neither the paternalism of the reform agencies, their cooperatives, or the pattern of settlement have been calculated to prepare the peasantry for an independent political life today.

No one is more aware of his new isolation and dependence than the peasant. At a Christian Democratic conference of peasants who had benefited from the Agrarian Reform, peasant after peasant complained bitterly. The complaints turned on the paternalism of the reform agencies, the purely bureaucratic nature of the relations between their technicians and the peasants, and the failure of the Riforma to stimulate social and political development and to create independent political organizations.[23]

For example, one peasant said, "It should be the peasant owner who seeks the collaboration of the agency and not the agency that acts independently with the peasant owner as its dependent." [24] Another maintained, "The assistance of the agencies of reform must not weigh upon the peasants as paternalistic assistance . . . the agencies should listen to the suggestions of the representative organizations of parties and unions." [25] In much the same vein, an intellectual observer pointed out that the Agrarian Reform cooperatives were too slow in taking on real functions and almost

22. Interview, July 8, 1966.
23. *Dal Latifondo al Podere*, p. 111.
24. Ibid., p. 37.
25. Ibid., p. 45.

totally lacked internal participation by the peasants.[26] It should be underlined that these were Christian Democratic delegates at a Christian Democratic congress; what the Communist and unaffiliated peasants were saying can only be imagined.

It began to become clear that the government had managed to demobilize the peasant. The phenomenon is all the more interesting when compared to the Agrarian Reform agency operating in the North in the Po delta. Here a network of political and economic secondary organizations were flourishing independently around the reform agency. The cooperatives operated independently, and political organization was strong. As one informant said:

> The most important contrast between the agrarian reform in South and North is in the nature of the peasant. In much the same way as the southern peasant used to look to the proprietor, he now sees himself as the dependent of the reform agency. In the Po delta, if the peasant is dependent at all, it is upon the union, the peasant association of the cooperative.[27]

The fact that these northern unions, peasant associations, and cooperatives are affiliated with the Communist Party only makes the dilemma of the South more puzzling. Granted that the reform agencies there may have found it in their interest to demobilize the peasant politically; what of the PCI? Was it unable to consolidate the dramatic gains of the struggle for the land by the permanent mobilization of the peasantry?

THE PEASANT MOVEMENT

"Our party has not always been able to understand the changes that have occurred among the masses of landless peasants and those with little land who have suddenly become proprietors as a result of the struggle for the land." [28] This comment, part of a Communist document that appeared in 1956, synthesizes the entire pattern of PCI reaction to the results of the Agrarian Reform. While

26. Ibid., p. 295.
27. Interview, July 8, 1966.
28. PCI, *Documenti Politici e Direttivi del PCI dalla IV Conferenza al VIII Congresso* (Roma, 1956), p. 221.

there have been successes as well as failures, the underlying theme has been one of confusion, malaise, and self-criticism. An entire tradition of internal self-criticism has grown up within the PCI because of its failure to consolidate an active and well-organized peasant movement in the South.[29]

What is the cause of this deep-seated organizational problem? The party was facing the contradiction outlined at the beginning of the last chapter. As a landless, precapitalist figure, the peasant had been volatile and rebellious. But as a small peasant owner, he was simply a conservative. As an acute non-Communist observer wrote, "for the southern peasant . . . objectives that had seemed possible only by following the red flag were now possible in other ways, through other means."[30]

A series of baffling and contradictory PCI tactics after the Riforma confirmed the peasant's conviction that he could get along outside the party. First, the party voted against the reform, scarcely believing the government capable of implementing it. In Calabria, when the lists of peasants who were to receive land were compiled, the party sought to convince many peasants to refuse the allotments as being too small.[31] When the reform administrators responded by offering this land to other peasants, those who had followed the PCI's advice were left without land. PCI policy soon descended to the level of scandal-mongering against the none-too-honest reform administrators, losing the emotional tone of the apocalyptic struggle for the land.

Communist policy with respect to the reform cooperatives followed a similarly tortuous course. The first response was in favor of the cooperatives, but when it was discovered that the reform administrators planned to direct them, the party called upon all the peasants to refuse to register for membership. When this tactic proved politically indefensible, particularly in the absence of strong PCI cooperatives, it was reversed, to the accompaniment of the slogan "All the peasants into the cooperatives." In the meantime, the cooperatives had been established around nuclei of con-

29. See the issues of *Cronache Meridionali,* in particular, from 1959 to its end in 1965.

30. Giuseppe Galasso, "La Riforma Agraria in Sila," p. 41.

31. Ibid., p. 39.

servative peasants, a factor that made it difficult for the tardy left-wing peasants to exert any influence upon their activity.[32]

At the same time, the traditional problems of organizing a highly disorganized peasant population were far from over. A Central Committee document said, "There is great difficulty in organizing the great masses of the southern peasantry, and, above all, of grouping them in single categories, because of their indeterminate social character." [33] It was in those very zones of the South where the political mobilization of the peasants had been most powerful that the greatest difficulty was now found in organizing them by category. "Exactly in a part of the country where a battle was developed which was an integral and decisive part of the Italian road to socialism, there the strongest barriers are found to the basic political and organizational renewal of the PCI." [34]

The cause of this discrepancy was not difficult to find. The peasants who had participated in the struggle for the land were not really taking part in the Via Italiana al Socialismo. They had sought the land, and if the PCI insisted on calling their search "an integral and decisive part of the Italian road to socialism," that was the party's business.

Once the struggle was over, resulting in only a partial reform which left many peasants without land, the peasants were sharply divided. Where, in the past, the symbiosis between the latifundia and the unstable small property had left occupational lines ambiguous, now the peasants were split into two groups: stable small farmers and the remaining landless poor peasants. The first group was now unalterably petit bourgeois, while the second remained in its chronic state of dissatisfaction and rebellion.

The party was faced with a dilemma; to appeal to the peasants who had gained land, it was necessary to soften its programs, but to continue as the spokesman of the landless would require a renewed assault upon the remaining large estates. The two strategies were mutually incompatible. A sectarian party would have chosen to support the landless in their continuing battle for the land. A

32. Botteri, *La Cooperative*, pp. 135–37.
33. PCI-Comitato Centrale, *Documenti, 1951*, p. 197.
34. Gerardo Chiaramonte, "I Risultati Elettorali e Politica Comunista," *Cronache Meridionali*, 9, No. 6 (1962), 18.

revisionist party, on the other hand, would have left the landless
to their fate, and developed cooperatives for the small peasant
owners. But the PCI was neither sectarian nor revisionist, and its
national strategy called for the organization of a broad popular
electoral support, rather than a narrow, if militant, class support.

The implicit contradiction between the violent struggle for the
land and the pacific Via Italiana al Socialismo was now explicit. As
a Communist leader said, *"The Communist Party in the Mezzogiorno really has two souls—the soul of a movement of the poor
peasants and agricultural day workers and the soul of a national
movement of rebirth."* [35]

Many peasants were anxious to continue the struggle for the land
until all the land was conquered. The party's refusal to do so
seemed to contradict its simultaneous advocacy of a general agrarian reform and its opposition to the reform agencies. Alicata said
at the party's seventh national congress,

> It was difficult to make the peasants understand why we asked
> for the law's immediate and extensive application at the same
> time as we criticized it. The peasants were all saying "If the
> reform agency sets up an office in our village, we will set it
> on fire and throw out the administrators." It was difficult for
> the party to make them understand that this was not the
> proper way to conduct the struggle.[36]

Local and provincial party leaders could not help but sympa-
thize with peasants who were still landless. Many, particularly in
Calabria, feared the dissolution of the peasant movement once it
moved into the traditional sphere of southern politics, and wanted
to conquer more of the land before the peasantry's enthusiasm
could be chilled.

Many of these leaders were disciplined by the party or were
moved to relatively harmless posts in Rome or in less volatile
provinces. The reaction of national leaders to the local and provincial opposition to PCI national strategy was immediate and
violent. Alicata called for "the liquidation of the sectarian group

35. Interview, April 20, 1964.
36. Mario Alicata, "Intervento," *Resoconto del VII° Congresso Nazionale del PCI*
(Roma, 1951), p. 217.

that directed the federation of Catanzaro, who have halted our great possibilities of increasing our influence among diverse strata of the population." [37]

A more serious problem for party leaders was the attitude of the trade unions, and in particular of the Federbraccianti, who insisted on stirring up militant behavior among the agricultural workers just when the party was trying to consolidate its influence among the middle class and the small peasant owners. Federbraccianti leaders were unwilling to sacrifice their class goals to the generic ideals of alliance and solidarity. This policy might work in the North, where employers were more reasonable, but the braccianti in the South had still to win a subsistence wage and an annual contract. Alicata complained, "We have still not succeeded in convincing the unions to adopt the right attitudes toward the South. Until we have convinced the Federbraccianti, for example, of the justice of our strategy, the battle for a general agrarian reform will not be developed in the Mezzogiorno with the necessary thrust and scope." [38]

The contradiction between the party's programs and those of the unions contributed to the paralysis of PCI activism in the South throughout the 1950s. The conflict over the organization of the *coloni*—the share tenants—was only one example. The party maintained that the coloni were producers, and ought therefore to be organized by the Peasant Alliance, while the unions maintained that the coloni were laborers, and ought to be organized by the more militant Federbraccianti.

The contrast is instructive. The party was still attempting to organize the peasants in the same type of amorphous front groups that had succeeded in the struggle for the land. But those groups —the Committees for the Land—had succeeded precisely because the peasants were united by their desire for stable landownership. Now the peasants were divided by the fact of landownership, which meant that they had conflicting occupational interests. The unions were attempting to organize the agricultural workers in response

37. Mario Alicata, "La Conquista dei Contadini nelle Campagne Calabresi," *Rinascita, 11* (maggio 1954), 349.

38. Mario Alicata, "Relazione," Assemblea del Comitato per la Rinascita del Mezzogiorno e delle Isole, *Cronache Meridionali, 3* (1956), 640.

to their economic demands, while the party was still trying to form a broad political front which was in many ways irrelevant to these demands.

It is interesting, in this light, to examine the forms of PCI peasant organization from 1951 to the present. The successful Committees for the Land were transformed into "Committees of Rebirth" in 1951, thereby shifting their image completely from one of peasant mobilization to political alliance. Amendola said,

> Around the party nerve center, around the Committees for the Rebirth of the Mezzogiorno, new popular organizations of the South, from labor to peasants, from cooperatives to women's groups, from youth to cultural organization are being developed. In this way, the democratic movement of the South has found *it possible to mobilize ever larger sectors of the southern population.*[39]

But a broad popular unity was never formed around these new committees, simply because the basis of broad popular unity— the common struggle for possession of the land—no longer existed. Consequently, the party turned to a less inclusive alliance strategy, one that would encompass all categories of peasants except the braccianti. In 1954, the National Alliance of Peasants was formed out of many smaller peasant groups. Its stated goal was "the renewal of Italian agriculture, founded upon the small peasant farm, economically assisted and freely associated." Its leaders called for the "economic and trade union defense of the peasants, both as laborers and as producers who are tied to the market economy but oppressed by those who dominate it."[40]

The conception of the peasants as both laborers and producers reveals the fundamental ambiguity in the strategy of the Peasant Alliance. Either the peasant is a laborer or he is a proprietor; he cannot be both at once. The contradiction has led to a split in the functions of the organization between, first, a "movement" to lead the agitations of the peasants and, second, a contractual organiza-

39. Giorgio Amendola, "Comuni e Provincie nella Lotta per la Rinascita del Mezzogiorno," *Rinascita,* 9, No. 2 (1952), 70. Emphasis added.

40. Alleanza Nazionale dei Contadini, *Primo Congresso Nazionale* (Roma, 1962), pp. 271, 12.

tion to negotiate the sale of their products. Particularly in an underdeveloped area like southern Italy, it is virtually impossible for the Alliance to operate as both at the same time.[41]

Second, against whom were the peasants to be protected? Against the monopolies. But where were these monopolies to be found? Monopolistic industry existed mainly in the North, and its relevance to the economic life of the southern peasant was, at best, indirect. Apart from a few factories owned by northern firms, the closest one could come to finding a monopoly in the South were the distributors, shippers, and processers who handled their products—in other words, the middleman! A Marxist party that attempts to develop an antimonopolistic line where there are few industrial monopolies inevitably sounds like a populist party.

The organizational focus of the Peasant Alliance is populist also, very much like the old Committees for the Land and Committees of Rebirth. A leader states, "We seek the unity of all the small peasant owners—the renters, the share tenants, the sharecroppers, the leasers, the small proprietors—with the mass of the agricultural day laborers . . . and the workers of industry in the common struggle for a democratic and antimonopolistic economy." [42] Once again the theme of solidarity, once again the theme of popular unity.

But the "mass of the agricultural day laborers" were not always willing to ally themselves with the small peasant owners who were, in many ways, their class enemy. "The long isolation of the small peasant owners and their past history of subordination to organizations dominated by large landowners has inevitably led . . . to sectarian and corporative attitudes toward them on the part of certain organizations of agricultural day laborers," a leader said in 1962.[43]

From its inception, the Peasant Alliance has tried to construct an agreement with the leaders of the Federbraccianti union which would help small peasant owners and agricultural workers to build a solid front against the large landowners and agricultural capital-

41. Ibid., pp. 32–33.
42. Ibid., p. 14.
43. Ibid., p. 22.

ists. But agreement between two such hostile groups was difficult to obtain, particularly in the South.

In the North, where agriculture is relatively advanced and specialized, a particular agricultural category dominates each zone. In the far North, most peasants are small owners. In the Lombardy plain and in part of Emilia, salaried farm workers who work on large commercial farms are the dominant occupational group. Finally, in central Italy, the classical *mezzadria* is the typical form of cultivation. In such an advanced setting, it is possible for the party to organize small farmers, salaried agricultural workers, and *mezzadri* simply because each of these groups has little to do with the others.

In the South, this pattern of agricultural specialization is only now beginning to emerge. The large commercial farm is common only in parts of Puglia and Sicily, whereas in many other zones agricultural day workers, share tenants, renters, and small owners are found in uneasy coexistence. Many of the small peasant owners and renters now employ several agricultural workers on a regular or temporary basis.

Under such conditions, it is difficult to carry the national pact between the PCI Peasant Alliance and the PCI-dominated Federbraccianti to the local level. Particularly in Puglia, where the Federbraccianti have the strongest occupational organization, tension between the two groups has been endemic. On several occasions, it has even been impossible to gain the symbolic participation of one group in manifestations organized by the other. As the president of the Peasant Alliance has said, "We know that much remains to be done in order to make this pact operative in every commune, in every village, in every struggle, and in every part of Italy." [44]

Where the leaders of the Federbraccianti and the Peasant Alliance do, in fact, agree upon cooperation, the real difficulties begin. For example, in Campania we find (1) a zone of large commercial farms employing salaried agricultural workers; (2) a zone of peasant rentals and peasant-owned farms employing temporary agri-

44. Ibid., p. 23.

cultural workers; and (3) an interior mountainous zone dominated by small peasant properties and unstable share tenancies.

The PCI bases its policies in this varied agricultural zone upon "an ever stronger unity between stable, semistable and temporary agricultural workers, between agricultural workers and renters, and more advanced forms of common struggle between dependent farm workers and peasant owners." [45] This policy line has met with some success, for example, in the support that agricultural day laborers have given to the attempt of the renters to get their rental fees reduced.

However, the implicit contradictions of the unity line were soon evident. In the commercial zones, the unions have a relatively easy time organizing the salaried agricultural workers against the large commercial farms. But when it comes to organizing the temporary farm workers in the second zone, conflicts immediately come to the surface between these individuals and the peasant renters who employ them. Thus, a Federbraccianti document reads,

> We are faced by the problem of unity [of the agricultural workers] with the small renters, who—in order to raise salaries—must solve their own problems in the battle against large landed property and monopolistic centers of power. *In this respect, it is necessary to repeat with great force that these renters cannot hope to raise their incomes at the cost of the agricultural workers.*" [46]

The obvious difficulty of finding a basis of unity among agricultural workers, renters, and peasants leads to a very basic problem: "that of the organisms which will have the dual task of leading the battle for the land and defending the trade union rights of the diverse social forces that make up the front for the agrarian reform." [47] To coordinate the policies of these various groups on the local level, the party has developed what it calls "communal agrarian conferences" between the representatives of the Peasant Alliances and the agricultural workers. The reaction of the Federbrac-

45. Federbraccianti, *Documento di Discussione per la Conferenza Regionale delle Federbraccianti della Campania* (mimeograph, n.d.), p. 12.
46. Ibid., p. 4. Emphasis added.
47. Ibid., p. 14.

cianti is instructive: "While the role of the communal agrarian conferences should be confirmed, it should also be pointed out that they must direct the struggle permanently with direct reference to the trade union problems of the different categories and social forces" [48]—in other words, to the Federbraccianti unions.

The weakness of the Peasant Alliances, and the conflicts between peasants, renters, and share tenants on the one hand, and agricultural workers on the other, is related to the basic organizational problem of the entire Communist peasant movement in the South: the weakness of its cadres. Both industrial and steady agricultural workers are occupational groups with a "natural" form of organization. They work in large groups on specialized tasks that increase their propensity for association as they deepen their resentment against their employer. The salaried agricultural workers of Puglia are the best-organized category in the Mezzogiorno simply because they work in the conditions of a highly developed agricultural economy.

But where the peasants either own their own land or work as renters, sharecroppers, or tenants, the peasant movement has been hard pressed to find an adequate number of organizers. Since its inception, the Peasant Alliance has been dependent for its cadres upon the party. "The working class has given to the creation of our organizations a contribution of cadres and materials for which we are profoundly grateful. But a mass organization cannot live without its own means." [49]

The situation was ironic; on the one hand, the Peasant Alliance was calling for the "autonomous organization of the small peasant owner," but on the other hand, it was dependent for most of its cadres on the working class. "From its inception, in effect, *whatever has been the personal social origin or the personal ideological orientation of its cadres,* the Alliance has justly posed the problem of ending the long isolation of the small peasants." [50]

As recently as 1962, it was clear that the Peasant Alliance had still not found leaders of peasant origin, "cadres who work the land in that village, who are known in that village as honest, intelligent,

48. Ibid.
49. Alleanza Nazionale, *Primo Congresso,* p. 260.
50. Ibid., p. 20. Emphasis added.

courageous, wise people." [51] How was the organization to meet this grave deficiency? The response of its president, Emilio Sereni, was startling. He said:

> Many of you have probably fought in the partisan war or seen it from close up. . . . How did we fight the partisan war? Who gave us our arms. . . . Our arms were taken from the Germans.

What did this have to do with the problem of peasant cadres in the Mezzogiorno?

> In the organizations of the Catholic Confederation of Direct Cultivators [*Coldiretti*], there are thousands of good, intelligent, honest, capable peasant cadres. We must make them our cadres. We can make them our cadres in the struggle, because they essentially agree with us.[52]

In other words, the cadres of peasant derivation who ought to be leading the Communist peasant movement can be stolen from the Catholics. But the Catholic Confederation of Direct Cultivators is really a corporate arm of the government which dispenses patronage to the peasants through a complicated system of interlocking directorates with the provincial agricultural syndicates.[53] The chain of causation is revealing. In leading the struggle for the land, the Communists forced the Agrarian Reform; but in the achievement of the Reform, many peasants became dependents of the Christian Democrats and of the state. And the PCI, which led the struggle for the land, has no way of forming peasant leaders of its own.

The problem of peasant cadres is also critical in the Communist Cooperative League, an organization that has actually lost ground in the South since 1951. In contrast to the flourishing PCI cooperative movement in the North, cooperatives in the South have always had hard sailing, precisely because of the manner in which the party has outlined its strategy. It is interesting, in this

51. Ibid., p. 259.

52. Ibid., pp. 259–60.

53. See Joseph LaPalombara, *Interest Groups in Italian Politics*, p. 236, on the role of these organizations.

respect, that in the debate that preceded the Agrarian Reform, the PCI had supported the formation of small peasant properties, while the Christian Democratic left had sought the distribution of the land in the form of cooperatives. The PCI based its opposition to cooperatives on the example of the abortive cooperatives of 1944–46, maintaining that "in reality, the peasants only want the individual ownership of the land." [54]

After the reform, no real attempt was made to use cooperatives as the basic economic and political organization of the peasantry. Although such a strategy was in fact proposed by some leaders of the cooperative movement, no support was received from other circles of the party. Even in recent years, although the government will now subsidize cooperatives through the Cassa per il Mezzogiorno, the PCI cooperative movement in the South continues to languish.

The failure of the PCI in the South to develop a class of peasant leaders is directly linked to this puzzling lacuna, for where else can peasant farm owners be led to socialism through policies in their economic interests other than in cooperatives? As a government official said, "The creation of a new political class in the South would have had to come from cooperation, but no major political group, government or opposition, has ever taken the problem of cooperation in the South seriously." [55]

"The creation of a new political class" is a phrase with a strangely familiar ring. It was Gramsci who first called for the creation of a class of "organic intellectuals" coming from the mass of the people. Without such a leadership group, he felt, the party could never hope to transform the society through education and organization. The failure of the PCI in the South to develop a leadership of peasant origin means, very simply, the weakness of "organic intellectuals" in the leadership of the party and its domination by middle class intellectuals—in other words, the traditional political class of the Mezzogiorno.

But the absence of a peasant leadership is not an isolated phenomenon. It is linked to the entire organizational weakness of the

54. Marciani, *L'Esperienza di Riforma Agraria*, p. 24.
55. Interview, June 12, 1966.

PCI in the South and to the party's failure to develop a program that could revive the mobilization of the peasantry. It is not simply the organizational incapacity of the South that is responsible; as the struggle for the land demonstrated, when the peasants are united by a common goal their capacity for organized action is very great.

The real responsibility for the failure of a Communist peasant movement to take hold in the South lies with the party's strategy. In imposing a strategy developed by Togliatti for the advanced, industrial North upon the backward, agricultural South, the party was simply falling prey to the objective conditions it had hoped to demolish. What emerges as a sound strategy of structural reform and mass organization in the North becomes a vague strategy of populist rebirth and mass solidarity in the South.

There is no *causal* mechanism between the backward conditions of southern Italy and the disorganization of the peasant movement, or, for that matter, between the intellectual character of the leadership and the weakness of peasant cadres. The entire complex of forces is almost embarrassingly *dialectical*. As a party leader said in 1964,

> The Movement of Rebirth in the Mezzogiorno [that is, the Via Italiana al Socialismo] halted what the party really needed in the South—the consolidation of the peasant movement begun in the struggle for the land. When the strategy of the Movement of Rebirth began, the peasant movement was somehow crippled. We still find ourselves in this perplexing situation in the Mezzogiorno today.[56]

The peasant movement, which began as the vanguard of Communism, has ended as its rearguard. While the PCI doubled its portion of the vote in southern Italy between 1946 and 1963, the absence of an organizational "network" in the countryside may preclude further gains there.[57] Moreover, the party's attempt to

56. Interview, April 4, 1964.

57. I am indebted for this phrase to Giovanni Sartori. See his "European Political Parties: The Case of Polarized Pluralism," in LaPalombara and Weiner, eds., *Political Parties and Political Development*, p. 147.

put together an ill-assorted electoral alliance damages its ability to agitate in favor of the economic demands of particular categories of peasants.

In recent years, the party has recognized the failure of its peasant movement with consistent attempts at self-criticism and reform. But so closely attached to the Via Italiana al Socialismo was PCI strategy in the South that all attempts at reform were bound to fall short of the mark. More recently, a tendency may be detected among some leaders to scrap the "old" approach to the South altogether. The problem of the South, they feel, is a secondary contradiction in Italian society, and has consequently become less important as Italian capitalism has matured. They want to focus instead on the primary contradiction between capital and labor, a focus that would neglect the peasant movement and concentrate upon the emerging urban proletariat. While such a shift has the virtue of realism, it would leave the peasantry once and for all the hunting ground of the Christian Democrats.

This is the irony of peasant Communism in southern Italy. While the Communist Party designed an ideological and organizational structure to combat the "old" factors in southern Italian society, its Catholic opponents were successfully designing a *new* structure of power based on the resources of the state. Time, politics, and economic change have conspired to make the peasant dependent on this new machine, while the Communist Party, precisely because its appeal was so well geared to the old, has become that much more irrelevant to the new. The land has been transformed, the mountains are covered with trees, and the peasants' life is better than it was. But in the piazza, as election day nears, there is always the same song with the same chorus.

Bibliography

Books and Articles in English

Adams, John Clarke and Paolo Barile, *The Government of Republican Italy*, Boston, Houghton Mifflin, 1961.

Albrecht-Carrie, Rene, *Italy from Napoleon to Mussolini*, New York, Columbia University Press, 1950.

Almond, Gabriel, *The Appeals of Communism*, Princeton, Princeton University Press, 1954.

——— and Sidney Verba, *The Civic Culture*, Boston, Little, Brown, 1965.

Apter, David E., "A Comparative Method for the Study of Politics," *American Journal of Sociology, 64* (1958), No. 4.

———, "Political Religion in the New States," in Clifford Geertz, ed., *Old Societies and New States*, Glencoe, The Free Press, 1963.

———, Introduction, to David E. Apter, ed., *Ideology and Discontent*, Glencoe, The Free Press, 1963.

———, *The Politics of Modernization*, Chicago, University of Chicago Press, 1965.

Banfield, Edward, *The Moral Basis of a Backward Society*, Glencoe, The Free Press, 1958.

Barber, Bernard, *Social Stratification*, New York, Harcourt, Brace, 1957.

Barzini, Luigi, *The Italians*, New York, Atheneum, 1964.

Blackmer, Donald L. M., *Italian Communism and the International Communist Movement*, Cambridge, Mass., Massachusetts Institute of Technology, Center for International Studies (mimeo), 1966.

Bloch, Marc, *Feudal Society*, trans. from the French by L. S. Manyon, Chicago, University of Chicago Press, 1961.

Clough, Shepard B., and Carlo Livi, "Economic Growth in Italy: An Analysis of the Uneven Development of North and South," *Journal of Economic History, 16* (1956), No. 3.

Dickinson, Robert, *The Population Problem of Southern Italy*, Syracuse, Syracuse University Press, 1955.

Duverger, Maurice, *Political Parties*, 2nd rev. ed., New York, Praeger, 1965.

Edelman, Murray, "Sources of Fluctuations in Popular Support for the Italian Communist Party since 1946," *Journal of Politics, 20* (1958), No. 3.

Einaudi, Mario, Jean-Marie Domenach, and Aldo Garosci, *Communism in Western Europe,* Ithaca, Cornell University Press, 1953.

Engels, Friedrich, *The Peasant War in Germany,* New York, International Publishers, 1926.

Gerschenkron, Alexander, "Notes on the Rate of Industrial Growth in Italy: 1881–1913," *Journal of Economic History, 15* (1955), No. 4.

Greenfield, Kent R., *Economics and Liberalism in the Risorgimento,* Baltimore, Johns Hopkins University Press, 1934.

Hobsbawm, Eric, *Social Bandits and Primitive Rebels,* Glencoe, The Free Press, 1959.

Hughes, H. Stuart, *The United States and Italy,* Cambridge, Mass., Harvard University Press, 1953.

Johnson, Chalmers A., *Peasant Nationalism and Communist Power,* Stanford, Stanford University Press, 1962.

Kogan, Norman, *The Government of Italy,* New York, Crowell, 1962.

———, *Italy and the Allies,* Cambridge, Mass., Harvard University Press, 1956.

———, *A Political History of Italy,* New York, Praeger, 1966.

LaPalombara, Joseph, *Interest Groups in Italian Politics,* Princeton, Princeton University Press, 1964.

———, *The Italian Labor Movement: Problems and Prospects,* Ithaca, Cornell University Press, 1957.

———, *Italy: The Politics of Planning,* Syracuse, Syracuse University Press, 1966.

———, "Italy: Fragmentation, Isolation, Alienation," in Lucian W. Pye and Sidney Verba, eds., *Political Culture and Political Development,* Princeton, Princeton University Press, 1965.

Lenin, V. I., *Selected Works,* 3 vols., New York, International Publishers, 1951.

Lichtheim, George, *Marxism: An Historical and Critical Analysis,* New York, Praeger, 1963.

Linz, Juan, and de Miguel, Amando, "Eight Spains," in Richard Merritt and Stein Rokkan, eds., *Comparing Nations,* New Haven, Yale University Press, 1966.

LoPreato, Joseph, "Class and Achievement in a Developing Society: Causes and Effects of Emigration," unpublished MS, 1966.

————, "Interpersonal Relations in Peasant Society: The Peasant's View," *Human Organization*, *21* (1962), No. 1.

————, "The Role of Emigration," *Human Organization*, *21* (1962), No. 3.

————, "Social Stratification and Mobility in a South Italian Town," *American Sociological Review*, *26* (1961), No. 4.

Lutz, Vera, *Italy: A Study in Economic Development*, London, Oxford University Press, 1962.

Marx, Karl, *The Eighteenth Brumaire of Louis Bonaparte*, New York, International Publishers, 1963.

Mitrany, David, *Marx Against the Peasant*, Chapel Hill, University of North Carolina Press, 1958.

Moss, Leonard W., and Stephen C. Cappannari, "Estate and Class in a South Italian Hill Village," *American Anthropologist*, *64* (1962).

Neufeld, Maurice, *Italy: School for Awakening Countries*, Ithaca, Cornell University Press, 1961.

Pitt-Rivers, Julian, *The People of the Sierra*, Chicago, University of Chicago Press, 1961.

Pye, Lucian, *Guerrilla Communism in Malaya*, Princeton, Princeton University Press, 1956.

Sartori, Giovanni, "European Political Parties: The Case of Polarized Pluralism," in Joseph LaPalombara and Myron Weiner, eds., *Political Parties and Political Development*, Princeton, Princeton University Press, 1966.

Schram, Stuart R., ed., *The Political Thought of Mao Tse-Tung*, New York, Praeger, 1963.

Selznick, Philip, *The Organizational Weapon*, Glencoe, The Free Press, 1960.

Smith, Denis Mack, *Cavour and Garibaldi: 1860*, Cambridge, Mass., Harvard University Press, 1954.

————, *Italy: A Modern History*, Ann Arbor, University of Michigan Press, 1959.

Surace, Samuel, *Ideology, Economic Change and the Working Class: The Case of Italy*, Berkeley and Los Angeles, University of California Press, 1966.

Vöchting, Friedrich, "Considerations on the Industrialization of the Mezzogiorno," *Banca Nazionale Quarterly Review* (Sept. 1958), No. 46.

Wylie, Lawrence, *Village in the Vaucluse*, Cambridge, Mass., Harvard University Press, 1957.

Documents, Statistics, and Government Sources

Alleanza Nazionale dei Contadini, *Atti del Primo Congresso*, Roma, 1962.

Associazione dei Contadini del Mezzogiorno, *II° Congresso*, Roma, 1958.

Confederazione Generale Italiana di Lavoro (CGIL), *Per il Rinnovamento Economico e Sociale del Mezzogiorno*, Napoli, 1961.

Confederazione Italiana Sindacati Lavoratori, *L'Azione Sindacale nel Mezzogiorno*, Roma, 1962.

Democrazia Cristiana, *Atti e Documenti della Democrazia Cristiana, 1943–1959*, Roma, 1960.

———, *I Congressi Nazionali della Democrazia Cristiana*, Roma, 1959.

(Governo Italiano), *La Cassa per il Mezzogiorno*, Roma, Istituto Poligrafico dello Stato, 1960.

———, Comitato dei Ministri per il Mezzogiorno, *Relazione sulla Attività di Coordinamento*, Vol. 1, *Premessa Generale*, Roma, Istituto Poligrafico dello Stato, 1963.

———, Istituto Centrale di Statistica (ISTAT). *I° Censimento Generale dell'Agricultura*, 1961, Vol. 2, Dati Provinciali su Alcuni Principali delle Aziende, Appendice, Dati Riassuntivi Nazionali, Roma, Soc. ABETE, 1963.

———, ISTAT, *IX° Censimento Generale della Popolazione*, 1951, Vol. 1, Dati Sommari per Comune, Appendice A, Dati Riassuntivi Provinciali, Roma, Soc. ABETE, 1956.

———, ISTAT, *X° Censimento Generale della Popolazione*, 1961, Vol. 1, Dati Riassuntivi Comunali e Provinciali sulla Popolazione e sulle Abitazioni, Roma, Soc. ABETE, 1963.

———, ISTAT, *La Struttura della Popolazione Rurale Italiana e le Nuove Figure Agricole Rilevate nell'VIII° Censimento*, Roma, Istituto Poligrafico dello Stato, 1937.

———, Ministero dell'Interno, *Compendio dei Risultati delle Consultazioni Popolari dal 1848 al 1954*, Roma, Istituto Poligrafico dello Stato, 1955.

———, Ministero dell'Interno-ISTAT, *Elezioni della Camera dei Deputati*, 25 maggio 1958, Vol. 1, *Risultati desunti dai Verbali Elettorali di Sezione*, Roma, Istituto Poligrafico dello Stato, 1950, 1955.

———, Ministero dell'Interno-ISTAT, *Elezioni della Camera dei Deputati del 28 Aprile 1963*, Dati per Comune, Roma, Istituto Poligrafico dello Stato, 1964.

Istituto Nazionale di Economia Agraria (INEA), *Carta dei Tipi d'Im-*

presa nell'Agricoltura Italiana, Giuseppe Medici, ed., Roma, Garzanti, 1958.

————, *La Distribuzione della Proprietà Fondiaria in Italia,* 2 vols., Giuseppe Medici, ed., Roma, INEA, 1956.

————, *I Tipi d'Impresa nell'Agricoltura Italiana,* Giuseppe Medici, ed., Roma, INEA, 1951.

Partito Comunista Italiano (PCI), Commissione Centrale d'Organizzazione, *L'Attività del Partito in Cifre,* VI° Congresso Nazionale, Roma, 1948.

————, Comitato Centrale, *Documenti, 1951,* "Risoluzioni della Direzione," Roma, 1951.

————, Comitato Centrale, *Documenti Politici del Comitato Centrale, della Direzione, e della Secretaria,* Roma, 1954.

————, Comitato Centrale, "Report on the Debate of the Central Committee of the Italian Communist Party on the Twenty-second Congress of the CPSU" (translated), *New Left Review* (April–June 1962), Nos. 13–14.

————, Comitato Centrale. *Adeguare l'Organizzazione del PCI ai Problemi e ai Compiti Attuali,* Roma, 1964.

————, IVᵃ Conferenza Nazionale d'Organizzazione, *Forza ed Attività del Partito,* Roma, 1954.

————, IVᵃ Conferenza Nazionale d'Organizzazione, *Rapporto di Pietro Secchia,* "Il Partito della Rinascita," Firenze, 1947.

————, IVᵃ Conferenza Nazionale d'Organizzazione, *Risoluzioni e Mozioni,* Roma, Centro di Diffusione del PCI, 1947.

————, VII° Congresso, *Resoconto,* Roma, Edizioni di Cultura Sociale, 1951.

————, VIII° Congresso, *Atti e Risoluzioni,* Roma, 1957.

————, IX° Congresso, *Atti e Risoluzioni,* Vol. 1, Roma, Editori Riuniti, 1960.

————, X° Congresso, *Atti e Risoluzioni,* Roma, 1963.

————, X° Congresso, *Il PCI e la Battaglia Meridionalistica,* Roma, 1963.

————, Sezione Centrale d'Organizzazione, *Dati sull'Organizzazione del PCI,* Roma, 1964.

————, Sezione Centrale d'Organizzazione, *Forza ed Attività del Partito,* Roma, 1954.

————, Sezione Centrale d'Organizzazione, *Organizzazione del PCI,* Roma, 1961.

————, Sezione Centrale d'Organizzazione, *Organizzazione del PCI,* Roma, 1962.

SVIMEZ (Associazione per lo Sviluppo dell'Industria nel Mezzogiorno), *Un Secolo di Statistiche Italiane: Nord e Sud 1861–1961,* Roma, SVIMEZ, 1961.

————, *Statistiche sul Mezzogiorno d'Italia: 1861–1963,* Roma, 1954.

BOOKS IN ITALIAN

Amendola, Giorgio, ed., *Il Comunismo Italiano nella Seconda Guerra Mondiale,* Roma, Editori Riuniti, 1963.

————, *La Democrazia nel Mezzogiorno,* Roma, Editori Riuniti, 1957.

Barbero, Giuseppe, *La Riforma Agraria Italiana,* Milano, Feltrinelli, 1960.

Braga, Giorgio, *Il Comunismo fra gli Italiani,* Milano, Comunità, 1956.

Cafiero, Salvatore, ed., *Le Migrazioni Interne,* Napoli, SVIMEZ, 1963.

Caizzi, Bruno, ed., *Antologia della Questione Meridionale,* Milano, Comunità, 1955.

Caracciolo, Alberto, ed., *La Formazione dell'Italia Industriale,* Bari, Laterza, 1963.

————, *Il Movimento Contadino nel Lazio,* Roma, Editori Riuniti, 1952.

————, *L'Occupazione delle Terre in Italia,* Roma, Edizione di Cultura Sociali, n.d.

Castagnola, Alberto, *Le Iniziative Industriali nel Mezzogiorno,* Napoli, SVIMEZ, 1963.

Centro Permanente dei Problemi del Mezzogiorno, *Dati Storici e Prospettivi Attuali della Questione Meridonale: Atti del Convegno di Studi Meridionali,* Bari, 1946.

Colajanni, Napoleono, *La Sicilia dai Borboni ai Sabaudi,* Milano, Universale Economica, n.d.

Compagna, Franceso, *Il Labirinto Meridionale,* Venezia, Nari Pozza, 1955.

————, *La Lotta Politica Italiana nel Secondo Dopoguerra e il Mezzogiorno,* Bari, Laterza, 1950.

————, ed., *Il Mezzogiorno davanti agli Anni Sessanta,* Milano, Comunità, 1961.

————, *La Questione Meridionale,* Garzanti, Milano, 1963.

————, e Vittorio de Caprariis, *Studi di Geografia Elettorale, 1946–1958,* Napoli, Centro Studi Nord e Sud, 1959.

Croce, Benedetto, *Storia del Regno di Napoli,* Bari, Laterza, 1958.

Fortunato, Giustino, *Il Mezzogiorno e lo Stato Italiano,* Bari, Laterza, 1911.

Galli, Giorgio, *Il Bipartismo Imperfetto*, Bologna, Il Mulino, 1966.

———, *La Sinistra Italiana nel Dopoguerra*, Bologna, Il Mulino, 1958.

———, *Storia del Partito Comunista Italiano*, Milano, Schwartz, 1958.

———, e Paolo Facchi, *La Sinistra Democristiana: Storia e Ideologia*, Milano, Feltrinelli, 1962.

Gerschenkron, A., e R. Romeo, *Lo Sviluppo Industriale Italiano*, Roma, SVIMEZ, 1962.

Girelli, Ugo, ed., *Radici Storiche della Depressione Meridionale*, Roma, SVIMEZ, 1963.

Glisenti, Marcella, e Leopoldo Elia, *Antologia di Cronache Sociali*, 2 vols., Roma, 1961.

Gramsci, Antonio, *Antologia degli Scritti*, Carlo Salinari e Mario Spinella, eds., 2 vols., Roma, Editori Riuniti, 1963.

———, *Gli Intellettuali e l'Organizzazione della Cultura*, Torino, Einaudi, 1955.

———, *L'Ordine Nuovo, 1919–1921*, Torino, Einaudi, 1955.

———, *Note sul Machiavelli, sulla Politica e sullo Stato Moderno*, Torino, Einaudi, 1955.

———, *Il Risorgimento*, Torino, Einaudi, 1955.

Grieco, Ruggiero, *Battaglie per la Terra e per la Libertà*, Roma, Editori Riuniti, 1956.

———, *I Comunisti e la Lotta per la Riforma Agraria*, Roma, Centro di Documentazione Sociale, 1949.

———, *La Crisi Agraria e i Monopoli*, Roma, Editori Riuniti, 1955.

———, *La Lotta per la Terra*, Roma, Edizione di Cultura Sociale, 1951.

Grifone, Pietro, *L'Azione dei Comunisti in Difesa dei Contadini*, Roma, Edizione di Cultura Sociale, 1945.

Istituto Carlo Cattaneo, *La Partecipazione Politica in Italia*, 4 vols., Bologna (mimeo) 1965.

La Malfa, Ugo, *Verso la Politica di Piano*, Napoli, Edizioni Scientifiche Italiane, 1962.

Marciani, Giovanni Enrico, *L'Esperienza di Riforma Agraria in Italia*, Roma, Giuffrè, 1966.

Molfese, Franco, *Storia del Brigantaggio dopo L'Unità*, Milano, Feltrinelli, 1964.

Moro, Aldo, *Il Pensiero Politico di Luigi Sturzo*, Napoli, Edizioni Politica Popolare, 1959.

Nitti, Francesco Saverio, *Scritti sulla Questione Meridionale*, 2 vols., Bari, Laterza, 1958.

Onofri, Fabrizio, *Classe Operaia e Partito*, Bari, Laterza, 1957.

———, *Socialismo e Potere*, Milano, Comunità, 1963.

Pantaleone, Michele, *Mafia e Politica, 1943–1962*, Torino, Einaudi, 1962.

Racioppi, Giacomo, *Storia dei Moti in Basilicata nel 1860*, Napoli, 1868.

Rizzo, Franco, *Luigi Sturzo e la Questione Meridionale*, Roma, Edizioni Cinque Lune, 1957.

Rodanò, Carlo, *Mezzogiorno e Sviluppo Economico*, Bari, Laterza, 1954.

Romano, Aldo, *Storia del Movimento Socialista in Italia*, 3 vols., Milano-Roma, Fratelli Bocca, 1954.

Romano, Salvatore Francesco, *Storia della Mafia*, Milano, Sugar, 1963.

Romeo, Rosario, *Breve Storia della Grande Industria in Italia*, Rocca San Casciano, Cappelli, 1961.

——, *Mezzogiorno e Sicilia nel Risorgimento*, Napoli, Edizioni Scientifiche Italiane, 1963.

——, *Risorgimento e Capitalismo*, Bari, Laterza, 1963.

——, *Il Risorgimento in Sicilia*, Bari, Laterza, 1950.

Rossi-Doria, Manlio, *Dieci Anni di Politica Agraria nel Mezzogiorno*, Bari, Laterza, 1958.

——, *Riforma Agraria e Azione Meridionale*, Bologna, Edizioni Agricole, 1948.

Salandra, Antonio, *Politica e Legislazione*, Bari, Laterza, 1915.

Salvemini, Gaetano, *Scritti sulla Questione Meridionale, 1896–1955*, 4 vols., Torino, Einaudi, 1955.

Saraceno, Pasquale, *L'Italia verso la Piana Occupazione*, Milano, Feltrinelli, 1963.

——, *La Mancata Unificazione Economica Italiana a Cento Anni dall'Unificazione Politica*, Roma, Giuffrè, 1961.

——, *I Termini del Problema del Mezzogiorno a Un Decennio dall'Inizio dell'Intervento*, Roma, SVIMEZ, 1961.

Sartori, Giovanni, et al., *Il Parlamento Italiano*, Napoli, ESI, 1963.

Sereni, Emilio, *Il Capitalismo nelle Campagne*, Bari, Laterza, 1946.

——, *Mezzogiorno all'Opposizione*, Torino, Einaudi, 1948.

——, *Vecchio e Nuovo nelle Campagne Italiane*, Roma, Editori Riuniti, 1956.

Sonnino, Sidney, e Leopoldo Franchetti, *La Sicilia nel 1876*, Firenze, V. Barbera, 1877.

Spreafico, Alberto, e Joseph LaPalombara, *Elezioni e Comportamento Politico in Italia*, Milano, Comunità, 1963.

SVIMEZ, *Sviluppo Industriale e Imprenditori Locali*, Roma, Giuffrè, 1962.

Togliatti, Palmiro, *Sul Movimento Operaio Internazionale*, Roma, Editori Riuniti, 1964.

———, *Il Partito*, Roma, Editori Riuniti, 1964.

———, *Il Partito Comunista Italiano*, Roma, Editori Riuniti, 1961.

———, *La Via Italiana al Socialismo*, Roma, Editori Riuniti, 1964.

Vassard, Maurice, *Storia della Democrazia Cristiana*, Bologna, Cappelli, 1959.

Villani, Pasquale, *Mezzogiorno tra Riforma e Rivoluzione*, Bari, Laterza, 1962.

Villari, Pasquale, *Scritti sulla Questione Sociale in Italia*, Firenze, Sansoni, 1902.

Villari, Rosario, *Mezzogiorno e Contadini nell'Età Moderna*, Bari, Laterza, 1961.

———, ed., *Il Sud nella Storia d'Italia*, Bari, Laterza, 1961.

Vöchting, Friedrich, *La Questione Meridionale*, Napoli, Centro Studi della Cassa per il Mezzogiorno, 1955.

Zangheri, Renato, ed., *Lotte Agrarie in Italia: La Federazione Nazionale dei Lavoratori della Terra, 1901–1926*, Milano, Feltrinelli, 1960.

Selected Articles in Italian

Ajello, Nello, e Giovanni Cervigni, "Giornali di Provincia," *Nord e Sud*, 2 (1955), No. 7.

Alicata, Mario, "La Conquista dei Contadini nelle Campagne Calabresi," *Rinascita, 11* (1954), No. 5.

———, "La Riforma Fondiaria in Calabria," *Rinascita, 8* (1951), No. 2.

Alinovi, Abdon, "Problemi della Politica Comunista nel Mezzogiorno," *Cronache Meridionali, 8* (1961), No. 1.

Amendola, Giorgio, "Comuni e Provincie nella Lotta per la Rinascita del Mezzogiorno," *Rinascita, 9* (1952), No. 2.

———, "Per la Rinascita del Mezzogiorno," *Cronache Meridionali, 1* (1954), No. 1.

Cervigni, Giovanni, "Le Defezioni dal PCI in Calabria," *Nord e Sud, 2* (1955), No. 6.

Chiaramonte, Gerardo, "Relazione Introduttiva, Assemblea Generale del Comitato Nazionale per la Rinascita del Mezzogiorno," *Cronache Meridionali, 2* (1956), No. 10.

———, "Il Movimento Operaio Italiano e L'Industrializzazione del Mezzogiorno," *Cronache Meridionali, 9* (1962), No. 2.

———, "I Risultati Elettorali e Politica Comunista," *Cronache Meridionali, 9* (1962), No. 6.

Ferri, Franco, "L'Alleanza tra Operai e Contadini," *Rinascita, 8* (1950), No. 3.

———, "Questione Meridionale e Unità Nazionale," *Rinascita, 9* (1952), No. 1.

Galasso, Giuseppe, "La Crisi del Meridionalismo Comunista," *Nord e Sud, 9* (1962, Nuova Serie), No. 34.

———, "Il Meridionalismo di Complemento," *Nord e Sud, 1* (1954), No. 6.

———, "La Riforma Agraria in Sila," *Nord e Sud, 4* (1957, Nuova Serie), No. 32.

Ghino, Celso, "Aspetti della Struttura della Organizzazione," *Rinascita, 7* (1950), No. 3.

———, "La Composizione Sociale del Partito," *Rinascita, 6* (1949), No. 3.

Gullo, Fausto, "Il Latifondo e la Concessione delle Terre Incolte ai Contadini," *Rinascita, 2* (1945), Nos. 7–8.

———, "Suggerimenti per una Riforma Agraria," *Rinascita, 2* (1945), No. 12.

Napoletano, Giorgio, "Continuità e Prospettive della Nostra Azione Meridionalista," *Rinascita, 14* (1957), No. 4.

No author, "Una Forza di Secoli nei Combattenti della Conquista della Terra," *La Voce del Mezzogiorno, 2* (1949), No. 44.

———, "La Lotta dei Contadini Meridionali," *La Voce del Mezzogiorno, 1* (1948), No. 2.

Procacci, G., "Geografia e Struttura del Movimento Contadino della Valle Padana," *Studi Storici, 5* (1964), No. 1.

Rossi-Doria, Manlio, "Contadini e Agricoltura nell'Avvenire del Mezzogiorno," *Nord e Sud, 2* (1955), No. 6.

Scoccimarro, Mauro, "Dottrina Marxista e Politica Comunista," *Rinascita, 2* (1945), Nos. 5–6.

Secchia, Pietro, "L'Arte dell'Organizzazione," *Rinascita, 2* (1945), No. 12.

Sforza, Marco Cesarini, "Inviato a Sud," *Nord e Sud, 9* (1962, Nuova Serie), No. 25.

Togliatti, Palmiro, "L'Azione Democratica e Socialista nel Mezzogiorno," *Cronache Meridionali, 1* (1954), No. 6.

———, "Che Cos'è Il Partito Nuovo," *Rinascita, 1* (1944), No. 4.

———, "I Compiti Nuovi nella Lotta per la Rinascita del PCI," *Cronache Meridionali, 4* (1957), Nos. 7–8.

———, "Il Mezzogiorno all'Opposizione," *La Voce del Mezzogiorno, 4* (1951), No. 14.

Valenza, Pietro, "Aspetti del Fanfanismo in Lucania," *Cronache Meridionali*, 5 (1958), No. 12.

——, "Lo Stato del Partito nell'Italia Meridionale," *Rinascita*, 14 (1957), No. 6.

Visentini, Luciano, "I Dirigenti Sindacali nel Processo di Sviluppo del Mezzogiorno," *Tempi Moderni*, 8 (1965), No. 23.

Vitale, Giuseppe, "Cooperazione e Battaglia Antimonopolistica," *Cronache Meridionali*, 8 (1961), No. 4.

——, "Il Movimento Democratico e la Riforma Agraria," *Cronache Meridionali*, 3 (1956), No. 11.

Viviani, Luciana, "Il Lavoro Femminile nella Società Meridionale," *Cronache Meridionali*, 2 (1955), No. 6.

Index

Abruzzi, 56, 65, 166, 283, 318
ACLI (Italian Catholic Workers' Association), 334–35, 339
Action Party, 107
Adams, John Clarke, 12 n., 153 n., 175 n.
Affitti. See Renters
Agrarian Reform: and absentee landlords, 295; administration of, 347–48; allotment under 295, 348–49; and *braccianti,* 295–96; and changing clientele relations, 291–93; and cooperatives, 350–51; implementation of in South, 347; and increase in productivity, 296–97; land allocation, 348–49; land expropriation, 293–96; and the latifundia, 291–95; and mass patronage, 349–50; quota under, 295, 348–49; results of, 296–99; and share tenants, 296–96; Sila Agency, 290; and small farmer, 295–96; Stralcio law, 294
Agricultural day workers (*braccianti*), 33; and agricultural reform, 295–96, 349, 358
Agricultural structure (South), 30–35; definition of zones, 31–32; productivity by zones, 32
Agrigento, 318
Ajello, Nello, 86 n.
Alicata, Mario, 230, 357 n., 358 n.
Alleanza dei Contadini. *See* Peasant Alliance
Almond, Gabriel, 72 n., 76, 79, 80 n., 96, 99 n., 100, 160, 161 n.
Amendola, Giorgio, 105 n., 117 n., 229, 230, 254, 255 n., 257 n., 263, 265 n., 284 n., 305 n., 359 n.
Andreotti, Giulio, 320 f.
Anti-system party, 99–101
Apolitical dissent, 91–94
Apter, David, 4, 6 n., 13 n., 59 n., 73 n., 224 n., 250 n., 251 n.

Ardigó, Achille, 177 n., 345 n., 346 n.
Avellino, 203, 318, 320

Badoglio, Pietro, 106
Bakunin, Michael, 101, 226, 277
Banfield, Edward, 3, 5, 6 n., 7, 55, 58, 59 n., 62 n., 67 n., 72, 73, 80, 199 n., 226
Barber, Bernard, 73 n.
Bari, 207, 327
Barile, Paolo, 12 n., 153 n., 175 n.
Barzini, Luigi, 21 n., 36, 88 n.
Basilicata, 18, 42, 53, 166, 174
"Battle of the Wheat," 26
Beloch, K. J., 41 n.
Benevento, 203, 276, 277
Bergamo, 318
Berlinguer, Enrico, 142 n.
Bernstein, Eduard, 124, 273, 297
Blackmer, Donald L. M., 109 n., 110 n., 118 n.
Bloch, Marc, 69 n.
Boensch, Maria R., 332 n.
Bonazzi, G., 191 n.
Bordiga, Amedeo, 102, 103, 104
Borkenau, Franz, 277 n.
Botteri, Tullio, 351 n.
Bourbon Monarchy, 21, 46–48, 50
Bourgeoisie: development of in South, 49–50; land ownership of, 51, 60–61; occupational roles, 51; and Risorgimento, 50–51
Bozzo, Gianni Baget, 302 n.
Braccianti. See Agricultural day workers
Brea, p. 191 n.
Brescia, 318
Brigandage, 91–93, 276–77. *See also* Peasant uprisings
Brindisi, 207

Caizzi, Bruno, 45 n., 66 n., 83 n.

Calabria, 18, 166, 193 f., 200, 203, 229, 245, 276, 278, 279, 283, 286 ff., 293, 318, 336, 349, 355, 357

Campania, 42, 53, 166, 278, 318, 361

Cappannari, Stephen C., 56 n., 65 n.

Carabba, Manin, 303 n.

Caracciolo, Alberto, 27 n., 276 n., 278 n.

Casa del Popolo, 216

Cassa per il Mezzogiorno (Fund for the Development of Southern Italy; Cassa), 6, 37 f.; and mass patronage, 89, 313–15; and PCI in South, 257; and weakness of entrepreneurship in South, 57–58

Catania, 203

Catanzaro, 287, 358

Catholic Action Youth Movement (GIAC), 332–33

Catholic Church: and Fascism, 170–71; and Partito Popolare, 303; and the PCI, 156; political role in South, 170–71; recruitment of political elite, 82

Cavour, Camillo, 22, 126

Cervigni, Giovanni, 86 n., 245 n., 286 n., 349 n.

CGIL. See General Confederation of Italian Labor

Chalmers, Douglas A., 101 n.

Chiaramonte, Gerardo, 230, 312 n., 356 n.

Chiatante, Marcello, 331

Christian Democratic Party (DC), 81, 91, 93, 107 f.; and ACLI, 334–35; and Agrarian Reform, 306–07, 311; and Aventine Secession, 104; and the Cassa, 304–05, 313–15, 329; and center-left coalition, 316; and clientelismo in South, 323–24; and Coldiretti, 333–34; compared to American political machine, 340–41; and ENI, 329; factions in, 319–22; false membership cards, 321–33; geographic polarization of vote, 180–83; and industrial development in South, 314–15; and IRI, 329; leadership characteristics, 145–48; leadership recruitment, 309–10; mass organizations, 154; membership, 317–22; member to voter ratio, 317–19; and "new clientelismo" 326–28, 329–32; origins of, 301–03; party sections, 319;

policy toward South, 308–09, 310–15 passim; Popular Assemblies, 310–13; postwar programs of, 303–04; problems of administrative decentralization, 315–16; recruitment, 321; role of De Gasperi in, 303–07 passim; role of Dossetti in, 304–05; role of Fanfani in, 308–13; secondary associations in South, 332–40; and structural change in South, 324–26; vote, 131–37 passim, 176, 313, 315, 345–46; vote and PCI vote, 180–83; Women's Movement, 333, 339

Cilento, 18

Ciranna, Giuseppe, 281 n.

CISL (Italian Confederation of Workers' Unions), 154, 219, 335–39; and CGIL in South, 220; membership, 337–38; and state industry, 339–40

Clientelismo. See Clientele system

Clientele system, 68–69; and the Agrarian Reform, 291–93; and cooperatives, 282; definition of, 74–76; and Fascism, 170–71; and local government, 88; "new," of the DC, 326–28, 329–32; and participation, 77; and political parties in South, 81; and preference vote, 77–78

CLN. See Committee of National Liberation

Clough, Shepard, 14 n., 20 n.

Coldiretti. See National Confederation of Direct Cultivators

Colletta, Pietro, 45 n., 46 n., 47 n., 49 n., 50 n.

Coloni. See Share tenants

Coltivatori Diretti. See National Confederation of Direct Cultivators

Combat Party, 98–99

Commercialization without industrialization, 13–14; effects on economy and occupational roles, 39

Committee of National Liberation (CLN), 106–07

Committees for the Land, 294–95, 358–59

Communist Cooperative League (Lega delle Cooperativi), 222–23; and peasant cadres, 364–65

Communist parties: Chinese, 280; theories of, 97–101; types of, 97–101; Yugoslav, 280

Compagna, Francesco, 37, 175, 316 n., 345 n.

Compartecipanti. See Sharecroppers

Consigli di Fabbrica. See Factory councils

Cooperatives: and clientele groups, 282; and demobilization of the peasant, 350–52; Lega delle Cooperativi, 222–23; and PCI policy, 355–56; and peasant cadres, 364–65; and peasant movement, 271–82

Cosenza, 287

Costruttori (PCI organizers), 229–30, 309

Crispi, Francesco, 87, 93, 169

Croce, Benedetto, 6, 24 n., 45 n., 46 n., 47 n., 83, 174

Cultural dualism, of Southern Italy, 55–59

Cultural values in the South: cynicism, 59; entrepreneurship, 56–59; and family structure, 55–59 passim; formation of, 55–59; "traditional" nature of, 55

DC. *See* Christian Democratic Party

De Caprariis Vittorio, 175, 345 n.

De Cesare, Raffaele, 47 n.

De Gasperi, Alcide, 303, 304 n., 305, 307 f., 345

Dell'Angelo, G. G., 16 n.

De Marco, Domenico, 47 n.

De Miguel, Armando, 10

Democratic National Union, 174, 175

De Pasquale, P., 218 n.

Devotee party, 97–98

Dialectic, 4, 162–63, 256, 281

Diavolo, Fra, 277

Dickinson, Robert, 18, 42

Dilio, Mario, 327 n., 330 n.

Di Renzo, Gordon, 157 n.

Dogan, Mattei, 131, 132, 133, 176

Dolci, Danilo, 334

Domenach, Jean Marie, 102 n.

Dossetti, Giuseppe, 304–05

Durkheim, Emile, 59

Duverger, Maurice, 97 ff., 149 n.

Eckaus, Richard, 27, 28

Economic change in South, 27, 73–39, 296–97

Economic dualism: consumption patterns, 15; national income, 15; national unification as cause of, 21–24; natural causes of, 17–21; policies of national state as cause of, 24–28; sector distribution, 16–17; unemployment, 16; wage rates, 15–16;

Economic growth, disparity between North and South, 26–27

Education: of DC leadership, 145; of PCI leadership, 133, 144–45; of PSI leadership, 145; and social status, 62–63

Einaudi, Mario, 102 n., 103 n., 105 n., 106 n., 107 n.

Elia, Leopoldo, 306 n.

Emigrants' remittances and land purchase, 38, 53, 65

Emilia, 155 f., 166, 177, 180, 201, 315, 318, 361

Engels, Friedrich, 10, 247 n., 272

ENI. *See* Ente Nazionale Idrocarburi

Ente Nazionale Idrocarburi (ENI), 20, 37, 314, 329, 338

Factory councils, 103, 118, 128, 217

Family structure in South; amoral familism, 55; nuclear family, 55 ff., 67, 73; role of in political organization, 72–73

Fanfani, Amintore, 308–13, 317, 320, 324

Faraglia, N. F., 47 n.

Fasci Siciliani, 93, 276, 278

Fascism: and Catholic Church, 170–71; and clientele structure, 170–71; effect of on South, 170–71; and the Mafia, 91; and the PCI, 104–06; and the peasantry, 278; policy toward South, 26; political allocation under, 88; and political dualism, 171; and political elite, 83

Fascist Party, 168

Federation of Young Communists (FGCI), 110, 154, 208 f., 214–15

Federbraccianti (Agricultural Workers Union): and PCI strategy in South, 358; and peasant alliance, 360–63

Federterra (National Federation of Workers of the Land), 101, 283
Ferdinand II, 21
Ferrarotti, Franco, 30 n.
Ferri, Franco, 254 n.
Feudalism in South, 45–48, 262–63; compared to clientele system, 69; and the peasantry, 52
Feuer, Lewis S., 9 n., 344 n.
FGCI. See Federation of Young Communists
Filangieri, G., 47 n.
Foggia, 207, 276
Fortunato, Giustino, 24 n., 83 n.
Franchetti, Leopoldo, 24 n., 91
Friuli, 318
Fucino Basin, 18, 283, 288, 346

Galanti, Gian Maria, 49 n.
Galasso, Giuseppe, 261 n., 279 n., 282 n., 327 n., 355 n.
Galli, Giorgio, 102 n., 103 n., 105 n., 106 n.
Garibaldi, Giuseppe, 22, 48, 71, 92, 126
Garosci, Aldo, 102 n.
General Confederation of Italian Labor (CGIL), 123, 153 f., 328, 335, 338; and CISL in South, 220; membership, 218–19, 337; organizational weakness in South, 219–21
Geographic mobility in South: among high-status groups, 64; among peasants, 63–64
Ghino, Celso, 150 n., 215 n.
GIAC. See Catholic Action Youth Movement
Giannini, Guglielmo, 175
Giolitti, Giovanni, 87, 88, 169
Giuliano, Salvatore, 93, 174
Glisenti, Marcella, 306 n.
Gonella, Guido, 307
Gramsci, Antonio, 199, 225, 247, 251, 259 ff., 267 f., 274, 284; and Bordiga and the extremists, 104; compared to Sturzo, 301–02; compared to Togliatti, 112–29; expansion of theme of alliances, 255; and factory councils, 103, 118, 128; and Fascism, 104; and Leninism, 103, 120, 124, 128, 161; and organic intellectuals, 120–21, 137, 140 f., 365; and party organization, 119–21; and the peasantry, 115–16, 117, 249, 252; and strategy for conquest of power, 118–21; as theorist, 112–28; and theses of Lyon Congress, 103; and traditional intellectuals, 120–21; and war of movement, 126–29, 130; and war of position, 126–29, 130; and worker-peasant alliance, 252–54, 264, 284; and working class, 115–18
Greenfield, Kent R., 21 n.
Grieco, Ruggerio, 117, 214 n., 238 n., 255 n., 283 n., 285 n.
Grifone, Pietro, 283 n.
Guesde, Jules, 274
Gullo, Fausto, 260 n., 279 n.

Historical Left, 25 f.
Hobsbawm, Eric, 91, 92 n., 277 n.
Hughes, H. Stewart, 107 n.

Iannuzzi, Lino, 196 n.
Industrial structure: North and South, 28–30; personnel distribution, 30; size of units, 29
Intellectuals: and direction of peasant movement, 280–81; organic, 120–21, 129; traditional, 120–21, 129
IRI. See Istituto per la Ricostruzione Industriale
Istituto Magestrale, 63
Istituto per la Ricostruzione Industriale (IRI), 26, 37, 314, 329, 338
Italian Catholic Workers' Association (ACLI), 334–35, 339
Italian Communist Party (PCI); character of in South, 268–71; and "Chinese question," 153; and the Church, 156; in CLN, 106–07; Congress of 1956, 110; and direction of peasant movement, 280; factions in, 161; and foreign activity under Fascism, 105; historical development of, 101–02; as innovation in world Communism, 111–12; and lack of peasant leaders, 365–66; as mass party, 149; "new left" in, 109–10, 161; and peasant movement, 366–67; politi-

cal attitudes of supporters, 157–61; as popular movement in South, 214; reaction to the Agrarian Reform, 354–55; and reformists, 161; and the Resistance, 105; response to objective conditions, 8–9; response to reform cooperatives, 355–56; war of movement, 161; war of position, 161

ideology: adaptation to South, 267–68; and the Agrarian Reform, 257–59; bourgeoisie democratic revolution, 256, 262; and Cassa, 257; and defections, 245; and feudal residues, 262–63; functions of in South, 264–67; Gramsci's contribution to, 249, 251–54; impact on policy, 155; influence of social composition on, 259; influence of social disorganization on, 261; patterns of, 112–28; of peasant movement, 282–85; and peasantry, 252–55; and peasant-worker alliance, 252–55; relevance of Lenin to, 247–50; relevance of Marx to, 247–50; *rinascita*, 256–57, 263, 284; and southern society, 259–63; theme of alliances in South, 257 f.

leadership: attitudes toward opposition in South, 238; breadth of experience, 146–47; commune of origin, 232–33; early organization from North, 228–30; educational level, 144–45, 233; evolution of by region, 228; family members in party, 236; geographic mobility of, 233; ideology of, 243–45; length of experience, 146–47; middle-class intellectual character of in South, 235, 237–38; militants, 140–42; and party centralism, 240; and personalism in South, 239; political behavior of, 156–57; political experience of, 234; political role of in South, 238–39; professionalism of, 148, 235–36; recruitment route, 228; and the Resistance, 227–29; secretaries in, 142–43; social origins of, 143–45, 230–32; southern leadership as seen by national leadership, 240–41

membership: agricultural workers, 206, 207–08; discontinuity of in South, 202–03; evolution of by region, 200–01;

fluctuation of, 138–39; intellectuals, 206, 208; member to voter ratio, 138, 203–04; middle class groups, 206, 208–09; poor peasants, 205–07; regional distribution, 201–03; sharecroppers and tenants, 206, 208; social composition, 139–40, 205–10; students, 206, 208; turnover, 205; women, 206, 208–09, 210, 212; youth, 206, 209, 210

organization: Central Committee, 153; Direction, 153; fragmentation of social roles, 212–13; intermediate party organs, 151–53; party cells, 150, 152, 214, 215; party sections, 150, 152, 214, 215; provincial federations, 150–51, 216; recruitment methods, 211; role of Togliatti in, 213–14; Secretariat, 153

organizations: Alleanza dei Contadini, 221–22; CGIL, 153 f., 218–20, 328, 335, 337, 338; Committees for the Land, 284–85; cooperatives, 155–56, 222–23, 364–65; *Federbraccianti*, 222; FGCI, 154, 208 f., 214–15; origins of in South, 199

vote: age composition of, 137; and agrarian reform, 196–97; and campaigning in South, 195–98; and DC vote, 180–83; educational level of, 137; effects of political dualism on, 163–76 passim; and far right vote, 183; geographic polarization of, 180–83; growth of, *1946–63*, 130–31; inconsistency of, 177, 180; and industrialization, 190–91; internal migration, 131, 191; in local and provincial elections, 194–96; and localism, 194–98; in medium-sized cities, 187–89; occupational distribution of, 133–34; and personalism, 194–98; in provincial capitals, 185–86, 189; regional imbalance of, 135–36; social composition of, 131–35; and Socialist vote, 183–85; socioeconomic status, 136; structure of in South, 192–98; and urbanization, 191

Italian Monarchist Party (PDIUM), 81, 131, 134, 137, 345

Italian Republican Party (PRI), 134, 168

Italian Socialist Party (PSI), 101–02, 107 f.; and Aventine Secession, 104; leader-

ship characteristics, 143–48; vote, 131, 132, 134, 167, 175, 345
Italian Social Movement (MSI; neo-Fascist), 81, 134, 345

Jacini, Stefano, 24 n.
Jacquerie, 277, 279, 290. *See also* Peasant uprisings
Johnson, Chalmers A., 280 n.
Johnston, R. H., 50 n.

Kautsky, Karl, 124 n., 272, 299
Key, V. O., 164 n.
Kingdom of Two Sicilies, 22, 24. *See also* Bourbon Monarchy
Kogan, Norman, 107 n.
Khrushchev, Nikita K., 110, 138

Labor force distribution: by industrial sector, 27–28; by "traditional" and "modern" sectors, 28–29
Labor unions in South, 217–20
Lampedusa, Giuseppe, 71
Land tenure systems in South, 31–34, 60–61
LaPalombara, Joseph, 12 n., 23 n., 25, 27 n., 54, 57 n., 58 n., 62 n., 66, 77 n., 78 n., 80 n., 81 n., 89, 96, 97 n., 99 n., 132, 154, 169 n., 176 n., 177 n., 195, 364 n., 366 n.
Lateran Treaty, 156, 303
Latifundia, 31–34; and the Agrarian Reform, 293–95; before the Agrarian Reform, 291–93
Lauro, Achille, 81
Lazio, 165, 166, 201, 318, 320
Lecce, 207
Lega delle Cooperativi. *See* Communist Cooperative League
Legitimacy: and authority roles, 89; vacuum in South, 93
Lenin, V. I., 4, 8, 99, 102, 103 n., 120, 124, 126, 155, 162, 205, 253 ff., 260, 262; and the peasants, 10, 247–49
Levi, Carlo, 288
Liberal Party (PLI), 133, 134, 174, 175
Liberals, 168, 171–72
Liceo Classico, 63
Liceo Scientifico, 63

Lichtheim, George, 162 n.
Liguria, 166, 318
Linz, Juan, 10
Lipson, Leon, 227 n.
Livi, Carlo, 14 n., 20 n., 191 n.
Local government in South, 86–87; and clientelismo, 88–89
Lombardy, 20, 53, 135, 166, 185, 318, 320, 361
Longo, Luigi, 111
LoPreato, Joseph, 56, 65 n., 78, 79
Lucania, 139, 203, 229, 279, 318, 345
Lutz, Vera, 14, 15, 16 n., 17 n., 21 n., 28, 29, 34 n., 35, 36, 37 n.
Luxemberg, Rosa L., 126
Lyon Congress of *1926*, 103

Macario, Luigi, 335 n.
Mafia, 69; as clientele system, 91; political role of, 90–91
Malefakis, Edward, 279 n.
Malfatti, Franco Maria, 306 n.
Mao Tse-tung, 8, 10, 247 ff., 280 n.
Marches, the, 166, 318
Marciani, Giovanni E., 137 n., 138 n., 282 n., 291 n., 292, 294, 347 n., 349 n., 350 n., 351 n., 365 n.
Marsica, the (Fucino), 192 f.
Marsilio, S., 93 n.
Marx, Karl, 9 n., 116, 162, 245, 247 n., 248 n., 249, 277, 297, 298, 344; and Italian Socialists, 226; and the peasants, 10, 272–73
Mass party, 97–98
Matera, 219, 220, 283, 327, 329
Mazzini, Giuseppe, 126
Mazzochi-Alemani, Nello, 33 n.
Merli-Brandini, Pietro, 161 n.
Merritt, Richard, 10
Messina, 203
Mezzadri. *See* Share tenants
Middle class professionals, development of, 65–66
Migration: internal, 44; permanent, 44; seasonal, 44
Mitrany, David, 272 n., 274 n.
Molfese, Franco, 52 n., 92 n.
Molise, 345
Monti, Gennaro, 45 n.

Moro, Aldo, 302 n.
Moss, Leonard W., 56 n., 65 n.
Movimento per la Rinascita, 256–57
MSI. *See* Italian Social Movement
Mussolini, Benito, 26, 101, 104, 168, 170, 278

Napoletano, Giorgio, 230, 264 n., 312 n.
National Alliance of Peasants. *See* Peasant Alliance
National Confederation of Direct Cultivators (Coltivatori Diretti; Coldiretti), 154, 333–34, 339; and Peasant Alliance, 364
National Unification: and bourgeoisie, 50–51; as cause of economic dualism, 21–24; as cause of legitimacy vacuum in South, 89; government policy toward South, 24–26; support for, 22–23
Neufeld, Maurice, 20, 21 n., 24, 53 n.
New Left, 109–10, 161
Niceforo, Alfredo, 12 n.
Nitti, Francesco, 6, 24 n., 169, 174
Nobility in South, 48–49
Novella, Agostino, 220

Occupational roles: fragmentation of in South, 14, 34; in industry, 28–29, 53–54
Oliva, Giorgio, 312 n.
Onofri, Fabrizio, 109 n.
Osborne, James Van Wyck, 45 n.

Pantaleone, Michele, 69 n., 91 n.
Parentela, 67 ff.
Partito Comunista d'Italia. *See* Italian Communist Party
Partito Populare, 168; and the Church, 303; and clientelismo, 302–03; and Fascism, 303
Partito Socialista Italiano. *See* Italian Socialist Party
Party of notables, 97
Pastore, Giulio, 313
Patronage. *See* Clientele system
PCI. *See* Italian Communist Party
PDIUM. *See* Italian Monarchist Party
Peasant Alliance (Alleanza dei Contadini): and Coldiretti cadres, 364; and

Federbraccianti, 222, 359–63; and party cadres, 363–64; and PCI, 221–22
Peasant movement, 354–67; and PCI strategy, 366–37
Peasant uprisings, 92–93, 276–79, 290; and intellectuals, 277–78
Peasantry: demobilization of, 350–54; development of in South, 51–52; and Fascism, 278; and feudalism, 52; geographic isolation following reform, 353–54; geographic mobility of, 63–64; as object of the Agrarian Reform, 348; occupational roles of, 52–53; political setting for mobilization of in South, 275–79; and settlement on the land, 352–53; structural fragmentation of, 51
Pecci, Franco, 307 n.
Pella, Giuseppe, 320
Pepe, Gabrielle, 45 n.
Pescatore, Gabriele, 58 n.
Piedmont, 23 ff., 51, 88, 126, 135, 165, 166, 318
Pitt-Rivers, Julian, 5, 6 n., 68 n., 75
PLI. *See* Liberal Party
Pochettino, Giuseppe, 45 n.
Poggi, Gianfranco, 220 n., 227 n.
Political allocation: under Fascism, 88; and local government, 86–88; and patronage, 87; patterns of in South, 86–89; and prefecture, 87 f.
Political capacity, 7–8; of PCI leaders in the South, 243; in South, 71
Political consciousness, 79–80
Political culture, North and South compared, 76–80
Political dualism, 94–95; and Fascism, 171; and PCI strategy, 164; and the vote, 164–76
Political elite: education of, 83, 85–86; and Fascism, 83; ideology of, 83, 85–86; occupational distribution of, 85; recruitment of and the Church, 82; recruitment of and clientelism, 83
Political leaders. *See* Political elite
Political parties, development of in South, 80–81
Population structure: birth rate, 41–42; death rate, 42; emigration, 42–43;

internal migration, 44; seasonal migration, 44; urbanization, 43–44
Potenza, 203, 318, 329
Po Valley, 20, 51, 101, 176, 201, 217, 243
Prefecture, 87 f.
Preference vote, 77–78, 194–98
Preferenza. See Preference vote
PRI. *See* Italian Republican Party
Procacci, G., 101 n., 168 n.
PSDI. *See* Social Democratic Party
PSI. *See* Italian Socialist Party
Puglia, 18, 43, 68, 166, 187, 203, 207, 208, 243, 268, 276, 283, 287 ff., 327, 338, 345, 361
Pye, Lucian W., 96 n., 247 n.

Questione Meridionale, 254

Racioppi, G., 47 n., 50 n., 92 n.
Ragionieri, E., 303 n.
Ramirez, Antonio, 350 n.
Rampa, Leandro, 312 n.
Ravioli, Domenico, 306 n.
Red Belt, 132, 177, 180, 201
Reichlin, Alfredo, 230
Renters (*affitti*), 33, 53–54; and the Agrarian Reform, 295
Resistance movement, and PCI, 105, 227–29
Riforma Agraria. See Agrarian Reform
Risorgimento. *See* National Unification
Rizzo, Franco, 301 n., 302 n.
Rokkan, Stein, 10
Romano, Aldo, 101 n., 226 n., 277 n.
Romano, Salvatore Francesco, 90, 91 n., 93 n.
Romeo, Rosario, 23, 45 n., 47, 48 n.
Rossi-Doria, Manlio, 31, 32, 34, 51, 52 n., 60 n.

Sacca, Leonardo, 220 n., 224 n.
Salandra, Antonio, 169, 174
Salinari, Carlo, 3, 83 n.
Salvatorelli, Luigi, 45 n.
Salvemini, Gaetano, 6, 23, 24 n., 66 n., 82, 83, 86, 170
Saraceno, Pasquale, 24 n., 26
Sardinia, 18, 41 f., 166, 185, 200, 262, 318
Sartori, Giovanni, 84 f., 97, 99, 100 n.,

143, 144, 145, 147, 148, 156 n., 366 n.
Scelba, Mario, 320
Scheler, Max, 59
Schepis, Giovanni, 78 n., 195
Schram, Stuart R., 280 n.
Schumpeter, Joseph A., 94, 344
Scoccimarro, Mauro, 255 n.
Scurti, Sebastiano Cammarari, 90 n.
Sebregondi, Giorgio Ceriani, 305 n.
Secchia, Pietro, 150 n., 211 n., 217 n., 265 n.
Secondary associations: DC in South, 332–40; underdevelopment of in South, 69–70, 80
Selznick, Philip, 98 ff.
Senghor, Leopold, 250 n.
Sereni, Emilio, 49, 279 n.
Service sector in South, 35–36
Sforza, Marco Cesarini, 229
Sharecroppers (*compartecipanti*), 33
Share tenants (*mezzadri* and *coloni*), 33, 52–53; and the Agrarian Reform, 295–96
Sicilian Independence Movement, 174
Sicilian separatism, 93
Sicily, 18, 20, 41, 43, 46, 53 f., 71, 90, 165, 166, 169, 187, 200, 203, 212, 243, 262, 268, 276, 278 f., 283, 287, 318, 328, 349, 361
Sila, the, 18, 193, 287
Sila Agency, 290
Sila Law, 293
Silone, Ignazio, 192, 343
Siracusa, 203
Smith, Denis Mack, 22, 48, 52 n., 93 n.
Social class, development of in South: bourgeoisie, 49–50; middle class professionals, 65–66; nobility, 48–49; peasantry, 51–52
Social Democratic Party (PSDI), 131, 132, 134, 175
Social mobility: of middle class, 65–66; of peasants, 64–65
Social stratification of the South, 59–63
Sonnino, Sidney, 24 n., 91
Spano, Velio, 213 n.
Spinella, Mario, 3, 83 n.
Spreafico, Alberto, 78 n., 132, 176 n., 177 n., 195

Stralcio Law, 294
Struggle for the land, *1949–52:* in the Abruzzi, 289–90; in Calabria, 286–87, 289; in Catanzaro, 287; and cooperatives, 281–82; in Cosenza, 287; in Lucania, 288; and PCI ideology, 282–85; in Puglia, 287–88; and *rinascita*, 284; role of PCI in, 281–91; in Sicily, 287–88; in the Sila, 287; and the Via Italiana, 284, 290
Sturzo, Don Luigi, 104, 301–04
Sullo, Fiorentino, 312 n., 321, 331
Swabian Monarchy, 45

Taradel, Alessandro, 51 n.
Taranto, 207
Tasca, Angelo, 102
Terracini, Umberto, 102
Tingsten, Herbert, 189
Togliatti, Palmiro, 155 f., 163, 176, 199, 212 f., 215 n., 239, 251, 262, 366; and bourgeoisie, 116, 263; compared to Gramsci, 112–29; and concept of mass party, 121–23; leadership of party, 106; and the new left, 109 f.; and parliamentary democracy, 114–15; and party organization, 121–24; and the peasantry, 117; as revisionist, 124, 161; and strategy for conquest of power, 121–24; theme of alliance of, 116–18, 130, 133; as theorist, 114–28; and working class, 115–18
Trento, 318
Trevelyan, Janet, 45 n., 50 n.
Trotsky, Leon, 126 f.
Turati, Filippo, 101
Tuscany, 156, 177, 180, 201, 315, 318

UIL (Unione Italiano di Lavoro), 154, 219
Umbria, 165, 166, 318
Uomo Qualunque Party, 175

Vailland, Roger, 40

Valenza, Pietro, 216 n., 217 n., 237 n., 238 n., 239 n.
Vassard, Maurice, 304 n.
Veneto, 166, 201, 318, 320
Verba, Sidney, 72 n., 76, 79, 80 n., 96 n., 160, 161 n.
Veterans' Party (Combattenti), 168
Via Italiana al Socialismo (Italian Road to Socialism), 108 ff., 204–05, 213, 251, 360; and southern PCI leadership attitudes, 244–45; and struggle for the land, 284, 290
Victor Emmanuel, King, 22
Villani, Pasquale, 46 n., 52 n., 49 n.
Villari, Rosario, 45 n., 46, 47 n., 50 n., 52 n., 170 n., 305 n.
Visentini, Luciano, 219 n., 336 n.
Vitale, Giuseppe, 222 n., 224 n.
Viviani, Luciana, 213 n.
Vöchting, Friedrich, 18 n., 19, 23 n., 31 n., 46 n., 48 n., 64 n., 86 n.
Voting: campaign techniques, 169–70; and the Church, 176; and clientelismo, 168–69; for monarchy or republic, 173–74; and political dualism, 164–76; regional distribution, 171; size of franchise, 164–69; turnout, 165–66; and women, 176

Waters, Jerry B., 57 n., 66
Webster, Richard, 303 n.
Weiner, Myron, 97 n., 99 n., 366 n.
Wolff, Robert L., 279 n.
Working class, development of in South, 53–54
Wright, Mary, 279 n.
Wylie, Lawrence, 5, 6 n.

Zaccagnini, Benigno, 312 n.
Zangheri, Renato, 101 n.
Zappa, Goffredo, 64 n.
Zurlo, Giuseppe, 50 n.

Yale Studies in Political Science

1. Robert E. Lane, THE REGULATION OF BUSINESSMEN
2. Charles Blitzer, AN IMMORTAL COMMONWEALTH: THE POLITICAL THOUGHT OF JAMES HARRINGTON
3. Aaron Wildavsky, DIXON-YATES: A STUDY IN POWER POLITICS
4. Robert A. Dahl, WHO GOVERNS? DEMOCRACY AND POWER IN AN AMERICAN CITY
5. Herbert Jacob, GERMAN ADMINISTRATION SINCE BISMARCK: CENTRAL AUTHORITY VERSUS LOCAL AUTONOMY
6. Robert C. Fried, THE ITALIAN PREFECTS: A STUDY IN ADMINISTRATIVE POLITICS
7. Nelson W. Polsby, COMMUNITY POWER AND POLITICAL THEORY
8. Joseph Hamburger, JAMES MILL AND THE ART OF REVOLUTION
9. Takehiko Yoshihashi, CONSPIRACY AT MUKDEN: THE RISE OF THE JAPANESE MILITARY
10. Douglas A. Chalmers, THE SOCIAL DEMOCRATIC PARTY OF GERMANY: FROM WORKING-CLASS MOVEMENT TO MODERN POLITICAL PARTY
11. James D. Barber, THE LAWMAKERS: RECRUITMENT AND ADAPTATION TO LEGISLATIVE LIFE
12. William J. Foltz, FROM FRENCH WEST AFRICA TO THE MALI FEDERATION
13. Fred I. Greenstein, CHILDREN AND POLITICS
14. Joseph Hamburger, INTELLECTUALS IN POLITICS: JOHN STUART MILL AND THE PHILOSOPHIC RADICALS
15. Hayward R. Alker, Jr., and Bruce M. Russett, WORLD POLITICS IN THE GENERAL ASSEMBLY
16. Richard L. Merritt, SYMBOLS OF AMERICAN COMMUNITY, 1735–1775
17. Arend Lijphart, THE TRAUMA OF DECOLONIZATION: THE DUTCH AND WEST NEW GUINEA

18. David P. Calleo, COLERIDGE AND THE IDEA OF THE MODERN STATE

19. Ronald C. Nairn, INTERNATIONAL AID TO THAILAND: THE NEW COLONIALISM?

20. Robert H. Dix, COLOMBIA: THE POLITICAL DIMENSIONS OF CHANGE